*The* NEW ENCYCLOPEDIA *of* SOUTHERN CULTURE

VOLUME 8 : ENVIRONMENT

Volumes to appear in

*The New Encyclopedia of Southern Culture*

are:

*The* NEW

ENCYCLOPEDIA *of* SOUTHERN CULTURE

CHARLES REAGAN WILSON  General Editor

JAMES G. THOMAS JR.  Managing Editor

ANN J. ABADIE  Associate Editor

## VOLUME 8

# Environment

MARTIN MELOSI

Volume Editor

Sponsored by

THE CENTER FOR THE STUDY OF SOUTHERN CULTURE

at the University of Mississippi

THE UNIVERSITY OF NORTH CAROLINA PRESS

Chapel Hill

© 2007 The University of North Carolina Press

All rights reserved

This book was published with the assistance of the Anniversary
Endowment Fund of the University of North Carolina Press.

Designed by Richard Hendel

Set in Minion types by Tseng Information Systems, Inc.

Manufactured in the United States of America

Library of Congress Cataloging-in-Publication Data

The new encyclopedia of Southern culture / Charles Reagan
Wilson, general editor ; James G. Thomas Jr., managing editor ;
Ann J. Abadie, associate editor,

p. cm.

Rev. ed. of: Encyclopedia of Southern culture. 1991.

"Sponsored by The Center for the Study of Southern Culture
at the University of Mississippi."

Includes bibliographical references and index.

Contents: — v. 8. Environment

ISBN 978-0-8078-3170-0 (cloth: v. 8 : alk. paper)

ISBN 978-0-8078-5856-1 (pbk.: v. 8 : alk. paper)

1. Southern States—Civilization—Encyclopedias. 2. Southern
States—Encyclopedias. I. Wilson, Charles Reagan. II. Thomas,
James G. III. Abadie, Ann J. IV. University of Mississippi.
Center for the Study of Southern Culture.
V. Encyclopedia of Southern culture.

F209.N47 2006

975.003—dc22

2005024807

The *Encyclopedia of Southern Culture*, sponsored by the Center for
the Study of Southern Culture at the University of Mississippi, was
published by the University of North Carolina Press in 1989.

cloth   11 10 09 08 07   5 4 3 2 1

paper   11 10 09 08 07   5 4 3 2 1

*Tell about the South. What's it like there.*

*What do they do there. Why do they live there.*

*Why do they live at all.*

WILLIAM FAULKNER

Absalom, Absalom!

# CONTENTS

In 1989 years of planning and hard work came to fruition when the University of North Carolina Press joined the Center for the Study of Southern Culture at the University of Mississippi to publish the *Encyclopedia of Southern Culture.* While all those involved in writing, reviewing, editing, and producing the volume believed it would be received as a vital contribution to our understanding of the American South, no one could have anticipated fully the widespread acclaim it would receive from reviewers and other commentators. But the *Encyclopedia* was indeed celebrated, not only by scholars but also by popular audiences with a deep, abiding interest in the region. At a time when some people talked of the "vanishing South," the book helped remind a national audience that the region was alive and well, and it has continued to shape national perceptions of the South through the work of its many users—journalists, scholars, teachers, students, and general readers.

As the introduction to the *Encyclopedia* noted, its conceptualization and organization reflected a cultural approach to the South. It highlighted such issues as the core zones and margins of southern culture, the boundaries where "the South" overlapped with other cultures, the role of history in contemporary culture, and the centrality of regional consciousness, symbolism, and mythology. By 1989 scholars had moved beyond the idea of cultures as real, tangible entities, viewing them instead as abstractions. The *Encyclopedia*'s editors and contributors thus included a full range of social indicators, trait groupings, literary concepts, and historical evidence typically used in regional studies, carefully working to address the distinctive and characteristic traits that made the American South a particular place. The introduction to the *Encyclopedia* concluded that the fundamental uniqueness of southern culture was reflected in the volume's composite portrait of the South. We asked contributors to consider aspects that were unique to the region but also those that suggested its internal diversity. The volume was not a reference book of southern history, which explained something of the design of entries. There were fewer essays on colonial and antebellum history than on the postbellum and modern periods, befitting our conception of the volume as one trying not only to chart the cultural landscape of the South but also to illuminate the contemporary era.

When C. Vann Woodward reviewed the *Encyclopedia* in the *New York Review of Books*, he concluded his review by noting "the continued liveliness of interest in the South and its seeming inexhaustibility as a field of study." Research on the South, he wrote, furnishes "proof of the value of the *Encyclopedia* as a scholarly undertaking as well as suggesting future needs for revision or supplement to keep up with ongoing scholarship." The decade and a half since the publication of the *Encyclopedia of Southern Culture* have certainly suggested that Woodward was correct. The American South has undergone significant changes that make for a different context for the study of the region. The South has undergone social, economic, political, intellectual, and literary transformations, creating the need for a new edition of the *Encyclopedia* that will remain relevant to a changing region. Globalization has become a major issue, seen in the South through the appearance of Japanese automobile factories, Hispanic workers who have immigrated from Latin America or Cuba, and a new prominence for Asian and Middle Eastern religions that were hardly present in the 1980s South. The African American return migration to the South, which started in the 1970s, dramatically increased in the 1990s, as countless books simultaneously appeared asserting powerfully the claims of African Americans as formative influences on southern culture. Politically, southerners from both parties have played crucial leadership roles in national politics, and the Republican Party has dominated a near-solid South in national elections. Meanwhile, new forms of music, like hip-hop, have emerged with distinct southern expressions, and the term "dirty South" has taken on new musical meanings not thought of in 1989. New genres of writing by creative southerners, such as gay and lesbian literature and "white trash" writing, extend the southern literary tradition.

Meanwhile, as Woodward foresaw, scholars have continued their engagement with the history and culture of the South since the publication of the *Encyclopedia*, raising new scholarly issues and opening new areas of study. Historians have moved beyond their earlier preoccupation with social history to write new cultural history as well. They have used the categories of race, social class, and gender to illuminate the diversity of the South, rather than a unified "mind of the South." Previously underexplored areas within the field of southern historical studies, such as the colonial era, are now seen as formative periods of the region's character, with the South's positioning within a larger Atlantic world a productive new area of study. Cultural memory has become a major topic in the exploration of how the social construction of "the South" benefited some social groups and exploited others. Scholars in many disciplines have made the southern identity a major topic, and they have used a variety of methodologies to suggest what that identity has meant to different social groups. Literary critics have adapted cultural theories to the South and have raised the issue of postsouthern literature to a major category of concern as well as exploring the links between the literature of the American South and that of the Caribbean. Anthropologists have used different theoretical formulations from literary critics, providing models for their fieldwork in southern communities. In the past 30 years anthropologists have set increasing numbers of their ethnographic studies in the South, with many of them now exploring topics specifically linked to southern cultural issues. Scholars now place the Native American story, from prehistory to the contemporary era, as a central part of southern history. Comparative and interdisciplinary approaches to the South have encouraged scholars to look at such issues as the borders and boundaries of the South, specific places and spaces with distinct identities within the American South, and the global and transnational Souths, linking the American South with many formerly colonial societies around the world.

The first edition of the *Encyclopedia of Southern Culture* anticipated many of these approaches and indeed stimulated the growth of Southern Studies as a distinct interdisciplinary field. The Center for the Study of Southern Culture has worked for more than a quarter century to encourage research and teaching about the American South. Its academic programs have produced graduates who have gone on to write interdisciplinary studies of the South, while others have staffed the cultural institutions of the region and in turn encouraged those institutions to document and present the South's culture to broad public audiences. The center's conferences and publications have continued its long tradition of promoting understanding of the history, literature, and music of the South, with new initiatives focused on southern foodways, the future of the South, and the global Souths, expressing the center's mission to bring the best current scholarship to broad public audiences. Its documentary studies projects build oral and visual archives, and the New Directions in Southern Studies book series, published by the University of North Carolina Press, offers an important venue for innovative scholarship.

Since the *Encyclopedia of Southern Culture* appeared, the field of Southern Studies has dramatically developed, with an extensive network now of academic and research institutions whose projects focus specifically on the interdisciplinary study of the South. The Center for the Study of the American South at the University of North Carolina at Chapel Hill, led by Director Harry Watson and Associate Director and *Encyclopedia* coeditor William Ferris, publishes the lively journal *Southern Cultures* and is now at the organizational center of many other Southern Studies projects. The Institute for Southern Studies at the University of South Carolina, the Southern Intellectual History Circle, the Society for the Study of Southern Literature, the Southern Studies Forum of the European American Studies Association, Emory University's SouthernSpaces.org, and the South Atlantic Humanities Center (at the Virginia Foundation for the Humanities, the University of Virginia, and Virginia Polytechnic Institute and State University) express the recent expansion of interest in regional study.

Observers of the American South have had much to absorb, given the rapid pace of recent change. The institutional framework for studying the South is broader and deeper than ever, yet the relationship between the older verities of regional study and new realities remains unclear. Given the extent of changes in the American South and in Southern Studies since the publication of the *Encyclopedia of Southern Culture*, the need for a new edition of that work is clear. Therefore, the Center for the Study of Southern Culture has once again joined the University of North Carolina Press to produce *The New Encyclopedia of Southern Culture*. As readers of the original edition will quickly see, *The New Encyclopedia* follows many of the scholarly principles and editorial conventions established in the original, but with one key difference; rather than being published in a single hardback volume, *The New Encyclopedia* is presented in a series of shorter individual volumes that build on the 24 original subject categories used in the *Encyclopedia* and adapt them to new scholarly developments. Some earlier *Encyclopedia* categories have been reconceptualized in light of new academic interests. For example, the subject section originally titled "Women's Life" is reconceived as a new volume, *Gender*, and the original "Black Life" section is more broadly interpreted as a volume on race. These changes reflect new analytical concerns that place the study of women and blacks in broader cultural systems, reflecting the emergence of, among other topics, the study of male culture and of whiteness. Both volumes draw as well from the rich recent scholarship on women's life and black life. In addition, topics with some thematic coherence are combined in a volume, such as *Law and Politics* and *Agriculture and Industry*. One new topic, *Foodways*, is the basis of a separate volume, reflecting its new prominence in the interdisciplinary study of southern culture.

Numerous individual topical volumes together make up *The New Encyclopedia of Southern Culture* and extend the reach of the reference work to wider audiences. This approach should enhance the use of the *Encyclopedia* in academic courses and is intended to be convenient for readers with more focused interests within the larger context of southern culture. Readers will have handy access to one-volume, authoritative, and comprehensive scholarly treatments of the major areas of southern culture.

We have been fortunate that, in nearly all cases, subject consultants who offered crucial direction in shaping the topical sections for the original edition have agreed to join us in this new endeavor as volume editors. When new volume editors have been added, we have again looked for respected figures who can provide not only their own expertise but also strong networks of scholars to help develop relevant lists of topics and to serve as contributors in their areas. The reputations of all our volume editors as leading scholars in their areas encouraged the contributions of other scholars and added to *The New Encyclopedia*'s authority as a reference work.

*The New Encyclopedia of Southern Culture* builds on the strengths of articles in the original edition in several ways. For many existing articles, original authors agreed to update their contributions with new interpretations and theoretical perspectives, current statistics, new bibliographies, or simple factual developments that needed to be included. If the original contributor was unable to update an article, the editorial staff added new material or sent it to another scholar for assessment. In some cases, the general editor and volume editors selected a new contributor if an article seemed particularly dated and new work indicated the need for a fresh perspective. And importantly, where new developments have warranted treatment of topics not addressed in the original edition, volume editors have commissioned entirely new essays and articles that are published here for the first time.

The American South embodies a powerful historical and mythical presence, both a complex environmental and geographic landscape and a place of the imagination. Changes in the region's contemporary socioeconomic realities and new developments in scholarship have been incorporated in the conceptualization and approach of *The New Encyclopedia of Southern Culture*. Anthropologist Clifford Geertz has spoken of culture as context, and this encyclopedia looks at the American South as a complex place that has served as the context for cultural expression. This volume provides information and perspective on the diversity of cultures in a geographic and imaginative place with a long history and distinctive character.

The *Encyclopedia of Southern Culture* was produced through major grants from the Program for Research Tools and Reference Works of the National Endowment for the Humanities, the Ford Foundation, the Atlantic-Richfield Foundation, and the Mary Doyle Trust. We are grateful as well to the College of Liberal Arts at the University of Mississippi for support and to the individual donors to the Center for the Study of Southern Culture who have directly or indirectly supported work on *The New Encyclopedia of Southern Culture*. We thank the volume editors for their ideas in reimagining their subjects and the contributors of articles for their work in extending the usefulness of the book in new ways. We acknowledge the support and contributions of the faculty and staff at the Center for the Study of Southern Culture. Finally, we want especially to honor the work of William Ferris and Mary Hart on the *Encyclopedia of Southern Culture*. Bill, the founding director of the Center for the Study of Southern Culture, was coeditor, and his good work recruiting authors, editing text, selecting images, and publicizing the volume among a wide network of people was, of course, invaluable. Despite the many changes in the new encyclopedia, Bill's influence remains. Mary "Sue" Hart was also an invaluable member of the original encyclopedia team, bringing the careful and precise eye of the librarian, and an iconoclastic spirit, to our work.

The environment was an under-studied subject in 1989 when the *Encyclopedia of Southern Culture* made it one of the defining categories for the study of the American South. Much new work has appeared since then, reflecting the growth in American environmental history in general and the now-recognized importance of the topic to understanding the region's experience.

The environment, to be sure, has long been seen as one of the factors that made the South different from other parts of the United States. Agricultural historians especially had an early appreciation of the role of climate, soil, and other factors that created a long growing season and particular types of agricultural organization. Images of lush tropical conditions in the South often framed discussions attempting to lure colonial settlers to a new Garden of Eden or, later, into new phases of the frontier. Proslavery advocates fell back on the hot and humid climate as an easy justification for using enslaved Africans who came from similar climates. The social construction of the environment included appealing scenes of Spanish moss–draped trees and lazy, hazy days in the South. The environment has given us many cultural icons, from the mockingbird to kudzu to the firefly of summer nights. An editor famously told Eudora Welty to remember in mentioning the moon in a story to make sure she had it in the right position in the sky—good advice to show she understood the environmental context for storytelling and for the experience of life in the region.

The environment now engages historians, geographers, biologists, sociologists, and other scholars who attempt to analyze the natural world not just as a stage setting for southern history but as an active force in its making. The extraordinary devastation of Hurricane Katrina in 2005 underlined the potentially violent power of nature in the region, but natural resources, weather and climate, and soil types have been less dramatic but essential factors in establishing conditions for the creation of wealth, the economic disparities among people in the region, and the ever-changing basis of interaction between humans and nature.

This volume explores the environmental complexity of the regions within the South, from semitropical coastal areas to high mountain peaks, from swampy lowlands to modern cities. Among the new topics in this volume of *The New Encyclopedia of Southern Culture* are birds and birding, coastal marshes, environmental justice, and invasive and alien species of flora and fauna, as well as some two dozen shorter entries on specific environmental sites within the South. Martin Melosi's overview essay introduces key concepts within a historical narrative that moves from the diverse physiography of the region to the establishment of ways of living and the environmental changes that have accompanied modernization and now globalization. Melosi emphasizes that constant change has been a key theme of southern environmental history and remains so today. From new attention on the environmental impact of the destructive fighting of Civil War armies on southern soil to the injustices of environmental exploitation of some of the South's people in the contemporary period, this volume offers a timely view of the fundamental importance of the environment to shaping the character of the American South.

*The* NEW ENCYCLOPEDIA *of* SOUTHERN CULTURE

**VOLUME 8 : ENVIRONMENT**

# ENVIRONMENT

In *The Colonial Search for a Southern Eden* (1953), historian Louis B. Wright noted, "The notion that the earthly paradise, similar to if not the veritable site of the Scriptural Eden, might be found in some southern region of the New World was widely held in the seventeenth and early eighteenth centuries." Some explorers claimed that God had placed Eden on the 35th parallel of north latitude, along a line from New Bern, N.C., to Memphis, Tenn. In more recent times the idea of a southern Eden has faded, but the post–World War II New South helped restore a little piece of the myth and raised the esteem of the South as a land of opportunity.

Although the South may not represent a scriptural or a temporal Eden, its history has been influenced nonetheless by environmental factors. A long-standing dispute over the relative importance of environment and culture permeates the study of the region. Some viewed geography as the key variable in its development. Others cited ideology and social and cultural factors. The issue of environment versus culture also has found its way into the debate over whether the South is best viewed as a "region" or as a "section." As a section, the South can be perceived as a cultural entity, a state of mind, an idea. This perspective is most useful for understanding the social, cultural, and political currents that run through southern history. Viewing the South as a region or a geographic area directs attention to the physical characteristics of the South and especially to its relationship to the rest of the nation.

**Climate and the Sectional South.** Environmental factors traditionally have been used in a deterministic way to reinforce cultural stereotypes about the South as a region—particularly to reinforce the notion of a southern distinctiveness. The most significant presumption is how climate became a justification for the South's agricultural monoculture—the "plantation legend"—dependent on commodities such as tobacco, rice, and cotton, and for the inevitability of slavery-driven plantations. While the South's long growing season, substantial rainfall, and generally warm weather shaped its economic life, climate is not a static physical force with predictable impacts. Perceptions and attitudes about the southern climate, however, pervade countless treatments of southern culture and thus provide insights about the region's self-image.

Clarence Cason's *90° in the Shade* (1935) fused climate and culture into formulaic clichés: "If snow falls infrequently on the southern land, the sun displays no such niggardly tendencies. In Mississippi there is justification for the old saying that only mules and black men can face the sun in July. Summer heat along the middle Atlantic coast and on the middle western plains causes more human prostrations than it does in the South. The difference lies partially in the regularity of high summer temperatures in the South but mainly in the way the southerner takes the heat."

Much of the South surely suffers through oppressively hot and humid summers and enjoys mild winters, but to what degree has the climate actually influenced southern history? Writing about the colonial period in the South, Karen Ordahl Kupperman suggested that English settlers had expectations about weather patterns in North America "based on the common-sense assumption that climate is constant in any latitude around the globe." Yet despite their practical experience in confronting the vagaries of climate, the colonists' adjustment to the realities of their situation was "both slow and costly in money as well as lives." Later generations apparently learned not to depend so heavily on static views of weather and nature. Mart Stewart suggested that southern farmers and planters did not take the weather predictions from the almanac as gospel but engaged in "an intuitive dialogue with the weather to attempt to forestall disaster in the fields." Likewise, southern medical practitioners gave greater attention to "the unique qualities of climate in each locale than to larger patterns." Carl N. Degler suggested that climate has had "a passive, if not active, influence" in shaping the region's past. The commitment to agriculture, especially the opportunity to grow commercial crops such as cotton and tobacco, was made possible by a favorable climate. Cotton, for instance, requires a growing season of 200 frost-free days, a condition that can be duplicated in few regions outside the South. Rice and sugarcane also require long growing seasons. Degler asserts, "That the climate permitted the growth of these peculiarly southern crops goes a long way to explaining why the South is the only region of the United States that developed plantation agriculture. Certainly the plantation did not spread in the South because of the climate; but without a climate favorable to tobacco, cotton, sugar, and rice southern agriculture would probably have been like that of the North in both crops and organization."

While climate has been a controlling influence in the development of the southern economy, it is a specious rationalization for traits such as laziness, emotionalism, and volatility. At its least appealing, climate has been used as a justification for slavery and the persistence of a social order associated with plantation life. Edgar T. Thompson, a critic of the climatic theory of the plantation, asserted that "a theory which makes the plantation depend upon something outside the processes of human interaction, that is, a theory which makes the plantation depend upon a fixed and static something like climate, is a theory which operates to justify an existing social order and the vested interests connected with that order."

Relying on only one variable to evaluate the history of the South serves environmental history badly. However, discounting the importance of environment in understanding the regional and sectional Souths is equally limiting. To fully comprehend the impact of the physical environment on southerners—and vice versa—requires an appreciation of the common physical characteristics, as well as the diversity, of the southern states and a comprehensive view of southern physiography, ecology, and modifications through human action.

**Physiography.** In popular usage, the Old South is often divided into a "Lower" South—the land of cotton and slavery, the heart of the Confederacy—and an "Upper" South, an area dominated by slaveless farmers with more ambiguous allegiances. Not only has there been an Old South, but a Deep South and several New Souths as well. All these designations, despite the imagery they evoke, are rather imprecise renderings of the physical South, because the region has never been a clearly defined geographical unit. This is a key to the difficulty of specifying the precise nature of the South along its borders—Delaware and Maryland to the east, West Virginia, Kentucky, and Missouri to the north, Oklahoma and Texas to the west. However, two features dominate the physical South, whether the boundaries are drawn along the Coastal Plain or the Appalachian Mountains. These landscape features are also competing influences, which have divided rather than unified the region.

The South's coast is its most dominant physical feature. Stretching more than 3,000 miles, it falls within the Atlantic and Gulf coastal plains. Most of the harbors are drowned river mouths that are shallow and subject to silting. The shore is composed of sandy beaches abutted in some cases by swamps, such as Dismal Swamp in Virginia and North Carolina. Along the Mississippi River run several muddy flats. The Coastal Plain, from the Potomac River to the Rio Grande, is an elevated sea bottom with low topographic relief and many marshy tracts. Coastal altitudes are mostly below 500 feet, and more than half are below 100 feet. The Coastal Plain is widest at Texas—about 300 miles—and narrows to 100 miles as it winds eastward. It comprises about one-third of the South.

A major feature of the Coastal Plain is the Mississippi River Valley, which originates in the Central Lowlands of the United States and meanders to the sea. The Mississippi and Missouri rivers drain two-thirds of the continental United States and together comprise the longest waterway in the world. Tra-

*Flavius J. Fisher,* Dismal Swamp *(1858) (Virginia Museum of Fine Arts, Richmond)*

ditionally the South's greatest "artery of commerce," the Mississippi continually changes the landscape along its route. Wide and marshy, with muddy and sandy banks, the Mississippi has long been an economic lifeline in the South, but it has also been a physical barrier and an environmental threat because of flooding (such as the great flood of 1927), steamboat and other traffic, and the expansion of agriculture and urbanization along its banks.

Before reaching the higher elevation of the mountains, the Coastal Plain connects with the Piedmont Plateau. Extending from central Alabama northward, the Piedmont Plateau is really a plain of denudation with only a few hills rising about the gently rolling landscape. The western border of the Piedmont Plateau is formed by the Blue Ridge Mountains.

West and north of the Coastal Plain lies the Appalachian system (named for the Apalachee Indians), which begins in Newfoundland and extends to central Alabama. The southern section of the system is formed by two parallel belts and includes the Appalachian Mountains themselves. Historically, this range was the major barrier to east-west movement in what became the United States. The Cumberland Gap was one of very few routes through the mountains. The

Appalachians gave the impression of a single geological system because of their formidable nature. In truth, the landscape varies considerably. For example, the southern Appalachians in western North Carolina and northern Georgia are various short ridges and isolated peaks separated by basins and valleys. In or near the Great Smoky Mountains and the Blue Ridge are the highest peaks of the system, including Mount Mitchell (6,684 feet), Cattail Peak (6,609 feet), Mount Guyot (6,621 feet), Mount Le Conte (6,593 feet), and Clingman's Dome (6,643 feet). Unlike the rugged and jagged Rockies, the Appalachians are rounder and substantially lower. Due in part to high humidity, weathering and erosion have shaped the Appalachian skyline. Winters are milder in the Appalachians than in the Rockies.

The northwestern and western reaches of the South—part of the Upper South and east Texas—fall within the Central Lowlands. The Central Lowlands are essentially a vast plain between the Appalachian Plateau and the Rockies. At the eastern edge, where the Lowlands join the Appalachians, the elevation is about 1,000 feet, sloping westward to an altitude of about 500 feet along the Mississippi, then rising again westward. The most distinctive feature of the Lowlands within the South is the Ozark-Ouachita section. Sometimes referred to as the Interior Highlands, this group of low mountains interrupts the monotony of the Lowland landscape. The Ozark Mountains have a drainage pattern and landscape similar to that of the Appalachian Plateau. South of the Ozarks, beyond the Arkansas River, lie the Ouachita Mountains. The Ouachitas' highest point is 2,700 feet, whereas the Ozarks' peak is about 2,000 feet.

An examination of the physiography of the South suggests the region's diversity and uniqueness. The contrast between the Coastal Plain and the Appalachian system helps explain many of the historical differences between the Upper and Lower Souths. And although three-fourths of the South has an elevation of less than 1,000 feet above sea level, barriers to east-west movement in the form of the Appalachians and the Mississippi have played an important role in determining regional settlement patterns. The South's geography also demonstrates the important physical connection of the region to the rest of the nation. The Coastal Plain links the South with the Atlantic seaboard; the Appalachians, with the Northeast; and the Lowlands, with the Midwest and Southwest. In no way has the South been geographically isolated from the other regions of the nation.

**Ecology of the South.** The great majority of the South lies within the Temperate Deciduous Forest Biome (natural community), which extends from the Great Lakes to the Gulf of Mexico. It also covers a large portion of the Florida peninsula and extends west to the Ozarks. Broadleaf trees dominate the biome, but evergreens are plentiful to the extreme southern reaches. The shedding of leaves by the deciduous trees in the autumn produces dramatic changes in light conditions and provides shelter for animals. The annual rainfall in the biome ranges from 28 to 60 inches, with the greatest amount near the Gulf.

The Temperate Deciduous Biome is composed of the oak-hickory region and the magnolia-maritime region. The oak-hickory region extends along a line from New Jersey to Alabama, westward into Arkansas and Texas, and then northward to central Illinois. The magnolia-maritime region begins in the southeastern corner of Virginia and extends southward to the magnolia forest near Charleston and then continues along the coast to Houston. A southeastern pine forest runs along the Coastal Plain from North Carolina to Texas. By contrast, the low, wet outer portion of the Coastal Plain is dominated by savannas, everglades, and flatwoods. Indeed, the geography of south Florida has been defined by the Everglades, or what Marjorie Stoneman Douglas labeled as a "river of grass." Despite human modification of the southern forests over the years, forest cover is an important endowment of the South. The region has approximately 40 percent of the nation's commercial forests, including the largest portion of its hardwood reserves.

Within or adjacent to the Temperate Deciduous Forest are several other natural communities in the regional South. The Mississippi River floodplain sports light-colored cottonwoods along the riverbank. To the extreme west, desert or mesquite grassland of a temperate grassland biome extends into the lowlands of west Texas. The southern boundary of the warm temperate magnolia forest is near Palm Beach on the Florida east coast. The vegetation of Florida is transitional between the tropics and the temperate regions with palms, mangroves, tall grass, sedge, rubber trees, hammocks, banyans, pine, and Spanish moss.

Southern soils reflect the significance of the forest cover. The region is blanketed largely by forest soils (podzols). Lime-rich brown soils are found in the bluegrass areas and the Great Valley of Virginia. In most other areas red and yellow soils are common. Along the coast are water podzols and marsh soils, and along the river valleys dark, fertile soils brought by floods are typical. Because the South escaped the last glaciations, southern soils lack the minerals ground by the ice. Heavy rains have leached the soil of its nutrients as well, leaving large deposits of clay throughout the South. Organic material is often vaporized by the heat, and the absence of sustained ground freezing traps nutrients above the ice. In large measure the South has medium- or low-grade soils, subject to erosion because of the considerable slope of the land. It is unlikely that most of the South ever had deep, fertile, heavy soils like those in the Midwest.

Despite its mediocre soils, the region possesses other important resources. Large quantities of bauxite are to be found in Arkansas; hematite iron ore, near Birmingham; phosphate, south of Nashville; titanium, in Virginia; manganese, copper, and chromites, in the mountains of eastern Tennessee and in the Carolinas. By far the most significant mineral resources are found along the fringes of the South: coal in the Appalachians and oil and natural gas in Texas, Oklahoma, and Louisiana. Sources of water have been crucial to the region. Blessed with several good waterways for inland navigation, fine ports from Houston-Galveston to the Chesapeake, and many lakes and streams, the South in recent times has faced diminishing surface water supplies because of increased use, rapid economic growth, and pollution. The major rivers, especially the Mississippi and the Tennessee, are among the most significant natural forces for ongoing physical change in the region.

Although the climate and weather of the South vary more than popular lore would suggest, distinctive climatic features do exist. In general, the climate is rainy (except in the Southwest), the summers are hot, and the winters are mild. Compared with the rest of the nation, tornadoes, hurricanes, and fog are frequent.

East of the Rockies the climate of North America is the product of the interaction of two air masses: the continental air mass in the northern portions of Canada and the tropical maritime air mass in the Atlantic/Gulf of Mexico area. In the summer the latter is associated with high temperatures and especially high humidity. In the winter the tropical maritime air mass produces mild spells with rain and fog. Because of the interaction of these air masses, two of the three parts of North America with the most precipitation lie in the South: the southern Appalachians and the southeastern states. In the Southeast and as far west as central Texas, humid subtropical or warm temperate weather is typical. Rainfall tends to be evenly distributed among the seasons. The South does not necessarily produce "hotter" highs than other portions of the nation, but the hot spells are of greater length. About three-fourths of the South has more than 30 inches of rainfall in an average year. The hottest section in the summer is the northern half of the Gulf Coast states. Although considerable variance occurs in the climate, especially between the Coastal Plain and the Appalachian system, no part of the South is subject to prolonged cold. That fact has been vital to its emergence in recent years as an important focus of human migration.

**Southerners and Their Environment.** Native Americans were the "original southerners." And like later immigrants from Europe and Africa, they were important modifiers of their physical world and agents of change. Little is known about the earliest people in the South. For many generations, aborigines there were hunters and gatherers. By the 16th century they had become more deeply involved in agriculture, part of the maize culture that arrived from Mesoamerica. Particularly in the Virginia and Carolina Tidewater, a mix of a northern hunting culture and a southern agrarian tradition can be seen. In contrast with the Plains Indians to the west, many Native Americans in the South lived in villages and towns when they first encountered white settlers. To romanticize southern Native Americans as the "first ecologists" in the region is to discount their roles in influencing fishing and hunting practices, the use of the forests, agriculture, and even town building. However, equally important is to recognize that European settlers in particular intensified and sped up change because of their numbers and their own interest in utilizing and exploiting the natural environment.

Southerners—especially in the postcolonial era—have long exhibited a fierce pride in their section and its heritage. Indeed, this pride has some environmental roots. As writer James Seay noted, "The traditional concept of the southerner as one possessing a strong attachment to the land—and, by extension, a predilection for outdoor sports, especially hunting and fishing—has not diminished appreciably." The South's agrarian tradition (at least in days past) accounted for much of the southern affinity for the outdoors. At the same time, the hostility of environmental conditions in the form of disease or violent weather conditions could threaten humans as much as uplift them. In turn, human modification—as much as the natural heritage—has shaped the sectional and regional South. The exploitation of forests and wildlife, the impact of the agricultural system, the Civil War, urbanization, and industrialization all have had major roles in transforming the South.

**Health and Disease.** As Margaret Humphreys has stated, "From the colonial era to the 1960s the American South held the unfortunate distinction as the most diseased region of the United States." This is not to say, however, that all disease and unhealthiness was environmentally determined. Living conditions, diet, and human action often contributed to the problem, as did the genetic heritage of the wide variety of people living in or moving to the South. The earliest European settlers, for example, transmitted various diseases to the native populations with catastrophic results.

The first years of the Jamestown settlement were marred by mortality rates of as much as 50 percent per year among white settlers. In the initial period of South Carolina's Lowcountry, early death was widespread and malaria ravaged the colony. In 1732 yellow fever overtook Charleston. During the height of the epidemic, 8 to 12 whites died daily along with many black slaves. Virginia experienced yellow fever outbreaks in 1737 and 1741, as did Charleston again in 1745. Yellow fever had first attacked the Atlantic Coast in the 1690s, peaking around 1745 and then subsiding for much of the remainder of the century. It reappeared in the port cities of Boston and New Orleans. While the disease virtually disappeared in the northern states by the 1820s, however, it remained a chronic problem from Florida to Texas. Not until 1905 did it dissipate with a final outbreak in New Orleans. Epidemics of all types had struck southern cities with particular ferocity, but health planning was not taken up with much direction until the 19th century.

Throughout the antebellum period, the South developed a reputation for poor health. Besides the yellow fever scourges, malaria was extensive. Malaria's debilitating effects clearly contributed to the image of the "lazy southerner"—a convenient stereotype that failed to take into account the impact on health of insect vectors, climatic conditions, the frontier lifestyle of many areas, and the crippling effect of slavery. The devastation of the Civil War and its aftermath only made health conditions worse in the South. To the ravages of yellow fever, malaria, and typhoid were added pellagra and hookworm—diseases regarded as primarily southern in occurrence—resulting from the region's poverty and "backwardness." Not until after World War II, as the South modernized and became less distinctive from other regions of the country, in the eyes of many, did the correlation between the South and bad health subside.

Throughout much of the 19th century it was common—not only in the South but elsewhere—to blame the poor, the infirm, or members of nonwhite races for the scourge of epidemic disease. In southern cities, for example, cholera was considered a class disease, but most especially a race disease. Cholera indeed lurked in the back alleys and poor dwellings of the cities where poor blacks lived, and not surprisingly in cities such as Richmond, Nashville, and Atlanta, cholera appeared first in black sections of town. Unlike cholera, however, yellow fever spared more black lives than white. People of West African extraction suffered least. In the great yellow fever epidemic of 1878, only 183 of 4,046 victims in New Orleans were black. In Memphis—where at least 14,000 of the 20,000 souls who remained in the city through the epidemic were black—only 946 of the more than 5,000 yellow fever deaths in the city came from the "colored population." Of course, as with settlers from Europe, populations brought to America involuntarily from Africa contributed to the disease environment. But in some respects, other than as objects of criticism, nonwhites and the poor remained "invisible" when the need for effective public health measures or medical care became public issues.

**Exploitation of Forests and Wildlife.** As late as 1600 the forests of the south Atlantic and Gulf states were probably less modified than those of the Northeast, with the exception of Virginia, where the Native American population was large. In the Lowland region they burned forests to facilitate hunting or to favor certain game. The burning produced savanna-type vegetation in the valleys.

Settlers in the southern colonies adopted Native American burning practices. Especially in the piney woods, in remote hills, and in areas of sandy soils, where hunting and herding persisted, wood-burning practices endured for many years. Wood burning was first carried out not for purposes of forestry but for hunting, grazing, and the eradication of pests. According to Stephen J. Pyne, "Fire practices were incorporated into the fabric of frontier existence. What made the South special, however, was the confluence of economic, social, and historical events that worked to sustain this pattern of frontier economy long after it disappeared elsewhere in the United States, a pattern that created a socioeconomic environment for the continuance of woodburning." Given the persistence of using fire for pasturage and game, efforts to stop or reduce burning were slow to develop in the South.

Firing of land was also extremely important in the development of southern agriculture. Here, too, Native American methods were adopted. Agricultural fires were used to prepare sites, to manage fallow fields, to eradicate pests, and to dispose of debris. And because plantation owners acquired the best agricultural lands, smaller farmers found themselves cultivating inferior sites, including piney woods, sandy barrens, and worn-out cotton fields, where annual firing kept the pines from overtaking them. An important result of firing for agricultural purposes was the replacement of many hardwood stands with pines.

Commercial logging did not spread through the South much before the 1880s. Some harvesting of pines and hardwoods had occurred in the antebellum South, but the Appalachian hardwood region generally remained inaccessible until railroad lines were extended into the region. Forests also were spared early commercial development because of the extensive cutting taking place elsewhere, but after 1880 commercial logging grew by leaps and bounds. The national timber industry moved to the South from the mid-Atlantic and midwestern region, and logging in the southern Appalachians reached its peak. By 1920 the virgin pine forests were gone and little regeneration had occurred;

Mississippi timber worker, Warren County, Miss., 1968 (William R. Ferris Collection, Southern Folklife Collection, Wilson Library, University of North Carolina at Chapel Hill)

the resulting environmental degradation caused flooding, pollution of streams, and serious erosion. Quite significantly, Appalachia was changed from an agricultural society that depended on virgin forests to, as Ronald L. Lewis suggested, "a twentieth-century society denuded of the forest and fully enmeshed in capitalism and the markets." Land abandoned because of logging—as well as cotton fields ravaged by boll weevil infestations—deeply hurt the South.

Forest fires became more plentiful as industry moved in. Not until after 1930 did most southern states give any real attention to preserving the remaining virgin forests. As professional foresters entered the region to encourage the development of new crops of timber, they met resistance from the owners of rangelands. Southern forests were too intricately woven into the fabric of the southern economy to be easily protected by modern conservation laws and practices. Clear-cutting forestry methods have, since World War II, in fact, decimated the southern hardwood population, introducing a new southern monoculture: pine farms. Into the 21st century, debates still raged over how to utilize the woodlands and how to manage them, with competing demands for wood and wood fiber, foraging, recreation, and preservation.

Wildlife was often a casualty of the use and abuse of southern forests in the past (also as a result of agricultural development, industrialization, and urbanization). In the colonial South, deer were hunted heavily as an essential source of meat. Numbers increased again after the several Indian expulsions and when cattle replaced deer in the leather trade. Hunting game for sale, however, persisted. White settlement also led to the extermination of bison east of the Mississippi. Among birds, turkey and quail were plentiful, but passenger pigeons were hunted eventually to extinction and parakeets were killed by farmers as pests or turned into pets. Predators such as wolves and black bear had bounties placed on them for threatening humans, livestock, or corn crops. Although the destruction of wildlife was not systematic, by the late 19th century many species, namely the eastern elk, cougar, timber wolf, red wolf, bison, Labrador duck, Carolina parakeet, whooping crane, and ivory-billed woodpecker, were either declining rapidly or nearing extinction. As Albert E. Cowdrey noted, "The destruction was much more than a regional phenomenon. These were, after all, the times when New Yorkers ate game shot in Minnesota, and when processing centers in Kansas City and Chicago received every week trainloads of 'ducks, geese, cranes, plovers, and prairie chickens'—a continental spoil." A revival of interest in wildlife conservation spread to the South in the 1870s but was slow in developing over the years. When economic interests were threatened, as in the case of commercial fishing, state governments were quicker to act.

**Agricultural System.** Southern agriculture is generally thought of as a combination of monocultures. Although this is an overly simplistic view of a region that also practiced stock raising and mixed farming, the environmental implications of southern agriculture were most significant with respect to the staple-crop economies that emerged over the centuries. The long, hot summers in most of the South have made the growing of shallow-root crops difficult. Fodder crops, especially, have been hard to grow, limiting the effective combination of livestock and food crops that encouraged the profitability of small farms.

The notion that several staple crops—especially tobacco, sugar, rice, indigo, and cotton—were "ideal" for the southern clime ignores the pervasive problems, such as soil exhaustion and erosion (and deforestation, which made soil replenishment difficult), that resulted from the widespread development of these monocultures. Even when land rotation was employed as early as the 18th century, the pressure of population growth hurt farming because land ran short and the fallow season was shortened. Commercial dependence on these crops meant that immediate profit rather than long-term planning dominated the rise of the plantation system and its consequent dependence on slave labor. Commercial production of tobacco led to wasteful clearing of forests. Acreage of Tidewater plantations was increased in an attempt to counteract the low productivity of the poor soil. Exacerbating the problem of widespread and incessant planting was the draining of nitrogen and potassium. Planters were often ignorant of the repercussions of their planting activity. They were unaware that the typical wooden plows did not cut deep enough to bring the necessary nutrients to the surface, or, at least, they exhibited little concern for their impact on the land, since new lands farther inland were obtainable.

The use of fertilizers—when available—and the switch to other crops, such as corn or wheat, eventually improved farming in Tidewater Virginia. But in the Atlantic Piedmont, erosion was more likely in the weathered soil. Soil exhaustion was a chronic problem beyond the Piedmont—and not just from the planting of tobacco but also from the cultivation of corn. Overall, the South had the ignominious honor of sustaining the first large-scale soil erosion in the country, centered in the tobacco-growing regions of Virginia, Maryland, and North Carolina. The pattern continued as settlers moved west.

The cultivation of cotton and the emergence of the great cotton belt from the Carolinas to east Texas did little to reverse the pattern of soil erosion and soil exhaustion throughout the South. Over the years the cotton belt shifted, spreading westward in the 19th century as areas in the Southeast were infested with boll weevils or the soil was worn out by years of monoculture. After spreading into Texas, the belt contracted again, and the western portion of cotton country was revitalized. The early cultivation of cotton in the Piedmont regions resulted in tens of thousands of gullies. Some of the gullies in Georgia were more than 150 feet deep. The long process of erosion in the Piedmont climaxed in 1920. In the years since the Civil War, massive quantities of topsoil had disappeared, some estimates reaching as high as six cubic miles or more.

Both large and small landholders abused their soils, although smaller farmers may have done more damage because they had less land in reserve for rotation or for lying fallow. (However, some small farmers, especially in Georgia and the Carolinas, practiced more diversified forms of agriculture focused on family use rather than commercial purposes. In these cases, soil exhaustion may not have been as severe.) Land policy was largely nonexistent. Nonetheless, until about 1945 cotton was still the agricultural byword in the South, and soil conservation was an unappreciated idea. Eventually extension workers, soil conservationists, and some private individuals began a slow process of educating southern farmers to terracing, contour plowing, and other techniques to avoid soil exhaustion and to improve yields.

In more recent times southern agriculture has changed dramatically. Cotton and corn areas contracted as new and localized special crops, such as soybeans and peanuts, appeared. The total area under cultivation declined as grazing returned to the South. Those staple crops that remained were grown under rotation systems as mechanization increased. Agricultural productivity returned to the South but often in new guises, such as in the fruit and truck belt of the Atlantic Coast and in the subtropical crop belt of the Gulf of Mexico.

**Civil War.** The environmental impact of war is often overlooked by scholars and other observers. It was difficult to forget that between 600,000 and 1 million people lost their lives in the Civil War, but bullet wounds and other battlefield perils were not the only reason why that number was so high. Many soldiers had never suffered from many common childhood diseases or been exposed to such a wide range of viruses and bacteria now present in the huge human populations brought together by war. They sometimes faced mosquito-borne parasites that caused malaria; contracted dysentery, diarrhea, typhus, typhoid, and paratyphoid in unsanitary campsites; and faced virulent infections in field hospitals. At least two-thirds of the soldiers died from disease and infection rather than battlefield wounds during the war.

The thousands of animals, especially horses and mules, that accompanied the troops into battle also experienced high casualties from the fighting and from highly infectious diseases such as glanders. The thousands of carcasses littering the battlefield also presented a major health hazard.

Life on the home front was neither secure nor safe, especially in the South, which was the primary battleground for much of the war. As Timothy Silver aptly noted, the war's most immediate and visible effect "was to empty the land of a sizeable portion of its human male population." This placed extraordinary pressure on women—and the few hired male laborers that remained— to maintain farms and family lands. To make things worse, dry summers between 1862 and 1864—particularly in Appalachia—ruined much of the crops, and cold weather arriving in autumn proved to be a finishing touch. In Mississippi, flooding combined with drought in 1862 devastated arable lands. Along with local deprivation and hunger, the loss of crops meant much less food and fodder for the troops and their horses away from home fighting the war. This also was true for Yankee troops, who were also fighting a war away from home and were barely able to feed themselves or their horses on many occasions, often turning to foraging.

The physical devastation of the South caused by war also was staggering. As John Brinckerhoff Jackson noted in his historical tour through the United States during its centennial years, the post–Civil War Reconstruction era required "the almost total reorganization of the Southern landscape—an undertaking scarcely less arduous than the creating of a brand-new landscape in the West." The Civil War left southern cities in ruins, railroad lines ripped from the ground, plantations burned, and factories and mills gutted, and it made itinerants of many southerners. Visitors were struck by the absence of fences, which had been burned as firewood by raiding Yankees or trampled by Confederates searching for food. Other signs of human construction—bridges, trestles, and even roads—were destroyed, creating an eerie sense of stillness and emptiness. Woodlands appeared in the deserted countryside where they had not existed for years; other forested areas were barren in the aftermath of battle. The urban South presented an equally depressing picture, be it the smoldering remains in Atlanta, Columbia, and Richmond; the bombarded Vicksburg; or the deserted wharves of Charleston.

Recovery came more quickly in the major cities than in the countryside in the postwar South. In time, the physical scars of the war would disappear, but the ravages were a constant reminder that devastation need not come in the form of a hurricane, flood, or tornado. Of all human modifications on the physical environment, war was one of the most frightening.

**Industrialization and Urbanization.** The slow transformation of the agrarian South into a region with a mixed economy and thriving cities may very well represent the most dramatic environmental change in the South. Until the 1870s southern industrialism, playing a supportive role to agriculture, was largely restricted to tobacco processing, textiles, and iron production. As late as World War I many southern cities had little more than regional influence. The "Sunbelt" phenomenon of the post–World War II era, however, dramatically points to the transformation made in the last 100 years.

Before the Civil War a large percentage of industry in the South involved processing raw materials and agricultural products: lumbering, flour and corn milling, tobacco processing, and cotton milling. However, iron producing was important, especially in places like the Richmond foundry. Not so much the lack of investment opportunities but the preference of planters and slaveholders for agriculture and their fear of competition weakened the growth of manufacturing in this period. In the 1860s industrial growth showed signs of change. The number of manufacturing enterprises increased 80 percent; the number of workers, 30 percent; and the value of products, 28 percent. Unfortunately, capital investment (an increase of 3 percent) and wages (up 8 percent) did not keep pace with this growth, but after the disruptions of Reconstruction had subsided, manufacturing again made an upturn. Between 1880 and 1930 a transition to industrialization was under way in southern Appalachia—an area that had been relatively untouched by earlier phases of the Industrial Revolution.

In the New South era, industrial growth was more extensive, especially after 1880, but it was not similar in kind or scale to what was taking place in the Northeast. Antebellum activities such as the processing of agricultural goods, extractive enterprises, and the labor-intensive manufacture of furniture and textiles continued. Only in the production of iron and steel and in the extracting of minerals did the South truly emulate northern industrial practices. By the turn of the century, despite the gains, the economy of the urban South remained primarily commercial. Rapid urbanization was limited because southern industry tended to locate outside cities. "Plantation industries" in the rural South, as James Cobb suggested, helped keep "the plantation at the center of the New South's political and economic order." Industry was becoming more important in the South than it had been in the mid-19th century, but the economy still depended heavily on agriculture.

Although this industrial growth was not impressive by the national standards of the time—in 1904 the South had about 15 percent of the nation's manufacturing establishments and 11 percent of capital invested in manufacturing—the activity could not help but provide a bridge between the monoculture activity of the past and the economic diversity of the present. In the Southeast as early as the 1960s, nonagricultural employment increased 45 percent, from 8.6 million to 12.5 million jobs. A good portion of this growth did not come in manufacturing but in the professions, technical fields, and the clerical area, suggesting the emergence of a vital white-collar sector in the economy. Also characteristic of nonagricultural economic growth was the dispersal rather than heavy concentration of industry. Few southern areas physically resembled the Northeast even after the infusion of an industrial capacity. However, the South's favorable business climate in the latter 20th century—low taxes, open shops, cheap land, lax pollution laws, and the absence of harsh winters—made the way for a significant migration of businesses away from the old "Rustbelt" to the South.

This is not to say that the physical South was little influenced by industrialization. The desire to improve inland navigation led to the transformation of the Mississippi River. The U.S. Army Corps of Engineers constructed the Tennessee-Tombigbee Waterway, a 234-mile-long navigational channel flowing through Mississippi and Alabama, as an alternative commercial waterway to the Mississippi. To connect the two rivers, a 27-mile cut was made. As John Opie noted, it was "the biggest earthmoving cut since the Panama Canal." The Tennessee Valley Authority (TVA) virtually remade a gigantic portion of the Upper South by providing navigation, flood control, power generation, economic development, and reforestation to an area overlapping seven states. By 1970 the TVA was the single largest electric utility in the nation, increasingly depending on coal-fired steam plants and nuclear power plants. Greater exploitation of natural resources led to strip-mining, squandering of oil and gas resources, and all manner of pollution. Oil spills, waste matter in major waterways, smoke, and smog were reminders of a newly emerging South. The creeks and rivers of much of the South were already polluted by cotton mill effluent in the 1920s and 1930s, well before anyone talked of a Sunbelt or a new New South. Not until the rise of the modern ecology movement in the 1970s did southern political leaders hear raised voices about protecting the environment. But a choice between jobs and profits or environmental protection often fell on the side of the former. In this respect, the South may not have been much different from the rest of the country. Nevertheless, the South often ranked very low in curbing industrial emissions of toxic chemicals, in limiting the volume of hazardous wastes, and in controlling other forms of pollution. Federal legislation on air, water, and land pollution recently nudged several southern states toward a more balanced approach in some instances.

The emergence of the environmental justice movement in the 1980s also drew attention to environmental pollution. Activists—especially among people of color—combined concern for environmental reform, social justice, and civil rights to assert that race and class have played a major role in exposure to environmental threats. Indeed, the first lawsuit using the violation of civil rights in an environmental lawsuit was filed in Houston, and many of the battlegrounds for protest—from the siting of a toxic landfill in Warren County, N.C., to identifying a "Cancer Alley" along the Louisiana coast—have taken place in the South.

Urbanization of the South was probably the most dramatic aspect of the modernization and physical transformation of the region. Urban growth in most southern states outstripped the section's increase in general population between 1840 and 1860. Yet by 1900 southern states averaged only about 15 to 19 percent urban population. Prior to 1940 cities and towns with fewer than 10,000 people grew faster than the big cities and represented the largest share of such urban places in the country. In striking contrast, by the 1970s the urban portion of the southern states averaged from 54 to 72 percent. The continuation of World War II prosperity into the postwar years played a large part in the emergence of the Sunbelt South as a vital economic, but also urban, force similar to the New West. The location of important southern cities also changed, from the dominant coastal and river-bound cities of New Orleans, Charleston, Savannah, Mobile, Norfolk, and Memphis to Atlanta, Charlotte, Dallas, and Houston. As David Goldfield noted, the South underwent three great building booms in the 20th century: the 1920s when "urban prosperity contrasted with rural poverty," after World War II with the rise of the Sunbelt, and during the 1980s.

The environmental implications of southern urbanization are many. Certainly, technological innovations such as air-conditioning encouraged the development of large cities and industries in a part of the country annually racked with long spells of heat and humidity. The rise of the automobile paralleled the emergence of many southern cities. Urban sprawl, suburbanization, congestion, exploitation of available resources, and pollution are characteristic of both southern and northern cities. Competition for water resources has increased among cities and between rural and urban populations. Stream pollution, saltwater intrusion on the coast, and the reduction of water tables threaten a once-abundant resource.

Industrialization and urbanization in the South in recent times point to a characteristic not associated with its antebellum past: constant change. The diversity of the southern environment embedded in the contrast between the Coastal Plain and the Appalachian system has been magnified by the various forms of human modification over the years. In many ways these modifications have produced changes that link the South to the rest of the nation, undermining some of its unique physical characteristics. At the same time, the emergence of a "modern" South suggests a region still in flux and likely to undergo additional environmental change.

Human modification of the environment, in the South as elsewhere, also suggests a constantly changing relationship with the natural world. Make no mistake about it, the impact of "natural disasters" in environmental history has been anything but "natural"—as southerners dramatically discovered in the summer of 2005. Hurricane Katrina may be the best example. As noted on the dust jacket of Douglas Brinkley's *The Great Deluge* (2006), "In the span of five violent hours on August 29, 2005, Hurricane Katrina destroyed major Gulf Coast cities and flattened 150 miles of coastline. Yet those wind-torn hours represented only the first stage of the relentless triple tragedy that Katrina brought to the entire Gulf Coast, from Louisiana to Mississippi to Alabama." The hurricane, one of the three strongest to make landfall in the United States, was first. The storm surge flooding, which placed about 80 percent of New Orleans under water, was second. And third was "the human tragedy of government mismanagement, which proved as cruel as the natural disaster itself." But Katrina and disasters like it feed on human decisions. People construct houses and businesses in unpredictable floodplains, build high-rise casinos along a capricious coast, and—as is the case of New Orleans—depend on an immense but vulnerable levee system to keep cities dry. These decisions can and often do have future impacts.

Hurricane Rita, the fourth most intense Atlantic hurricane ever recorded, slammed into the Texas-Louisiana coast in September 2005, causing extensive damage and forcing thousands of Houstonians to flee their city in fear for life and property. Houston was spared the assault, but the storm was an acute reminder of not only an active hurricane season but the choices people make in placing themselves in harm's way.

The southern environment, therefore, is at once natural and human made or human altered. It is distinctive in many ways but also subject to the same forces as any place on earth. The better we understand its history, the better we will be able to appreciate it, protect it, and learn from it.

MARTIN V. MELOSI
*University of Houston*

John M. Barry, *Rising Tide: The Great Mississippi Flood of 1927 and How It Changed America* (1997); Ralph H. Brown, *Historical Geography of the United States* (1948); Douglas Brinkley, *The Great Deluge: Hurricane Katrina, New Orleans, and the Mississippi Gulf Coast* (2006); Robert D. Bullard, *Dumping in Dixie: Race, Class, and Environmental Quality* (1990); Thomas D. Clark, *The Greening of the South: The Recovery of Land and Forest* (1984); James C. Cobb, *Industrialization and Southern Society, 1877–1984* (1984); Craig E. Colten, ed., *Transforming New Orleans and Its Environs* (2000); Albert E. Cowdrey, *This Land, This South: An Environmental History* (1996); Donald Edward Davis, *Where There Are Mountains: An Environmental History of the Southern Appalachians* (2000); Wilma A. Dunaway, *The First American Frontier* (1996); John H. Ellis, *Yellow Fever and Public Health in the New South* (1992); Gilbert C. Fite, *Cotton Fields No More: Southern Agriculture, 1865–1980* (1984); David R. Goldfield, *Region, Race, and Cities* (1997); Terry G. Jordan and Matti Kaups, *The American Backwoods Frontier* (1989); Jack Temple Kirby, *Mockingbird Song: Ecological Landscapes of the South* (2006), *Poquosin: A Study of Rural Landscape and Society* (1995); Ronald L. Lewis, *Transforming the Appalachian Countryside* (1998); David McCally, *The Everglades* (1999); Howard W. Odum, *Southern Regions of the United States* (1936); Stephen J. Pyne, *Fire in America: A Cultural History of Wildland and Rural Fire* (1982); Timothy Silver, *A New Face on the Countryside: Indians, Colonists, and Slaves in South Atlantic Forests, 1500–1800* (1990); Mart Stewart, *"What Nature Suffers to Groe": Life, Labor, and Landscape on the Georgia Coast, 1680–1920* (1996); Rupert B. Vance, *Human Geography of the South* (1932); Lawrence C. Walker, *The Southern Forest* (1991).

# Animals

The woods and waters of the American South provide a rich habitat for the fauna of its lands, and this varied animal life has nourished the needs of peoples who have lived there. With its large populations of birds, mammals, fish, reptiles, and amphibians, the South was a bountiful wilderness of mixed forests, pine barrens, swamps, grasslands, and fish-bearing streams in the era before settlement. Its extensive coastline provided access to the marine wealth of the Atlantic Ocean and the Gulf of Mexico. The growing presence of humans in the South altered the biotic capabilities of the area to support wildlife. With Indians and white settlers utilizing the fauna of the region as a major source of food, the populations of specific animal species were subsequently reduced. In the South, as in the rest of the nation, the flora and fauna of an area were a larder of nondomestic foods upon which Indians and white settlers depended.

As white settlement increased its pace in southern states, the face of the land was noticeably altered. The development of agriculture in the South and the consequent clearing of land reduced the habitat for some animals and created new microhabitats for others. Civilization's incessant campaign against coyotes, wolves, bears, and cougars reduced their numbers and permitted the animals upon which they preyed to increase their populations. Deer, rabbit, and quail were frequently helped by the noncontiguous patterns of land clearing and the second-growth vegetation that developed. While bears, wolves, and cougars found the presence of humans detrimental, deer found increased food, rabbits dined on a variety of new crops, and quail increased their numbers as they fed on domestic grains. These animals, and others, learned to live with civilization and to be nourished by the fruits of newly planted fields.

Although the buffalo, the American bison, lived in historic times in all the southern states except Florida, by the early 18th century it was becoming rare in the southeastern states and was increasingly confined primarily to western lands. The buffalo did not play the crucial role in the evolution of the South that it played in the development of the trans-Mississippi West. The whitetail deer assumed the role of the buffalo in the South and became an antlered commissary for Indians and settlers. It provided them with meat for food; hides for shirts, moccasins, and gloves; and horns for implements and knife handles. In America from the 16th century to the present the whitetail deer has ranked only below cattle and sheep as an animal useful to humans. Deer milk contains three times the protein and butterfat of dairy cow milk, and vain attempts were made to domesticate deer for milk production. During World War II the nation consumed millions of pounds of deer meat as America stretched its limited meat rations.

Remarkably adept at increasing its numbers, the whitetail has been esti-mated to have once reached a population of 40 million throughout its natural ranges on the North American continent. When tobacco prices declined in the late 17th and early 18th centuries, the trade in deerskins increased, providing substantial economic activity for the developing region.

Trappers and traders in deerskins entered the Mississippi Valley and the lands along the Gulf Coast. From 1765 to 1773 Georgia exported 200,000 pounds of deerskins annually. As with the buffalo in the latter half of the 19th century, deer were slain primarily for their hides, and most of their meat was left rotting on the ground. Confronted by the reality of a declining resource, Virginia, North Carolina, and South Carolina in the 18th century passed legislation that limited unrestrained hunting. Seasons were closed, dog packs were not permitted, fire and night hunting were forbidden, and the meat of a deer could not be left on the ground. By the 1770s every southern colony had passed laws protecting game, with deer receiving special attention. Writing of deer, John James Audubon remarked that the "tender, juicy, savoury, and above all digestible qualities of its flesh are well known and venison is held in highest esteem from the camp of the backwoodman to the luxurious tables of the opulent." In the South, the population of whitetail deer was probably more than 6 million in the years immediately prior to the Civil War. With its capacity to adapt itself to a variety of habitats and to increase its num-bers through its remarkable fertility, the whitetail will maintain itself in the South as long as states preserve a balanced hunting season for this graceful species.

The capacity of deer populations to exceed the resources of their immediate habitat is well known. The mountain lion, or cougar or puma, provided an ideal check on deer populations in the South until hunting reduced the numbers of this beautiful animal. Playful and secretive, it once was found in all the south-ern states. Today it is confined primarily to Florida. In spite of popular belief that it frequently preyed upon humans, its principal food has been deer. When settlers began to introduce pigs, sheep, calves, and horses into the South, these animals fell prey to the mountain lion. Presently an endangered species, the mountain lion has an unsure future in the South.

Still common in the forests, swamps, and mountainous areas of all southern states, the black bear has been hunted since the colonial period. Omnivorous in its diet, it is a vegetarian throughout much of the year, although it is always willing to dine on carrion or any animal it can catch. While agile, it does not usually possess the speed necessary to bring down a deer. Indians and settlers hunted the bear for its meat, oil, and hide. Its lengthy two-year breeding cycle usually produces two cubs, but its low reproductive rate makes it susceptible to overhunting.

Squirrels and rabbits have historically augmented the diets of Indians, blacks, and whites in the South, and in the 18th and 19th centuries they were important additions to southern meals. The gray squirrel with its characteristic white-bordered tail is a favorite target for southern hunters. Among the most agile of the tree squirrels, it prefers a habitat of hardwood forests, where it feeds on acorns and hickory nuts, usually foraging within 200 yards of its den or nest. Audubon observed that the gray squirrel's occasional nocturnal activities made it easy prey to the great horned owl.

The fox squirrel is also common in the South and often shares the same range as the gray squirrel. It is larger than the gray squirrel and varies in color from a reddish, yellowish rust to a gray shade. In the darker phases, it has a white nose the gray squirrel lacks. It is also characterized by its large head and is less graceful than other tree squirrels. Its preferred habitat is old-growth forests of oak or longleaf pine or the fringes of cypress swamps.

The most graceful squirrel of the southern states is the southern flying squirrel. Although it is the smallest and most carnivorous of the tree squirrels, these are not its only distinguishing characteristics. It is nocturnal and sometimes sleeps and eats while hanging by its claws upside down. Stretching the loose skin of its white stomach by extending its four feet, it can glide up to 150 feet. Intrigued by this small, gentle animal, southerners have often kept them as pets.

Equally gentle in its habits is the cottontail rabbit. The most common rabbit in America, the Eastern Cottontail played a substantial role in the dietary history of the South. It is the most numerous of all southern game mammals. In the 19th century it was frequently trapped by slaves and became an important addition to their diet. Adapting well to a habitat altered by humans, the cottontail continues to prosper in the South, although most die before they are a year old.

The opossum, the only marsupial in North America, is an interesting and significant member of the fauna of the South. Living easily in the presence of civilization, it has an omnivorous diet that often includes dead animals and that allows it to maintain itself in various habitats. Seldom exceeding 12 pounds in weight, this nocturnal, gray, coarse-furred animal has a long, scaly, prehensile tail and is easily "treed" by hunters with dogs. When frightened, it feigns death, becomes rigid, and "plays possum." In the 19th and early 20th centuries, opossums were a favorite southern food. Easily captured, they were then caged and fed bread, sweet potatoes, or vegetables to improve their taste before they themselves became the meal.

Birds play an important role in the fauna of the South, gracing the region with the beauty of their songs, color, and activity. More species of birds can be found here than in any other region of the nation, and the South is privileged to bear witness yearly to the pageantry of migration. Numerous species, including wrens, warblers, sparrows, vultures, hawks, owls, woodpeckers, tanagers, vireos, doves, turkeys, and quail, breed regularly in southern states. The mockingbird is closely identified with the human culture of the South. Some birds once common in the South, such as the passenger pigeon and Carolina parakeet, have become extinct. Other southern birds—the ivory-billed woodpecker, whooping crane, brown pelican, bald eagle, and Everglade kite—are endangered or threatened species.

The passenger pigeon once filled the skies of some southern states with numbers that defy description. The dedicated Scottish naturalist Alexander Wilson calculated that he saw a flock of passenger pigeons a mile in breadth and 240 miles in length. It took four hours for this great flock to pass before him. While passenger pigeons contributed significantly to the diet of the rural poor in the 18th and 19th centuries, their numbers were somewhat reduced in the Deep South. Pigeons were cooked in a variety of fashions and preserved in fat and by pickling and drying. Their fat was used for cooking and as a base for soap, and their feathers were used for mattress ticking. Some pigeons were used as feed for hogs. This 16-inch bird, which flew gracefully through the skies, gained for itself the title of "blue meteor." Despite its speed and grace, it was easy prey for hunters. In 1914 the last of the species died. The cattle egret is a species that recently migrated to the South from Africa by way of South America. Each summer their flocks migrate north from Central America and nest in the Deep South. They are frequently seen devouring insects on the backs of cattle, and at times the white-plumed birds fill trees like blossoms.

Wild turkeys and quail are still important southern game birds. The turkey has been pursued for almost three centuries. Reaching a height of up to 40 inches, these gregarious birds roost in trees but nest and feed upon the ground. Early travelers commented on the indifference these birds showed to human presence, but once they began to be hunted, they became among the most wary animals of the South. Their eggs, flesh, and feathers were used by Indians and early settlers. By 1900 the turkey's numbers were quite small, but game management practices, which emphasized seasonal protection and maintenance of habitat, have allowed their numbers to increase in southern states.

Considerably more diminutive is the bobwhite quail. Less than 10 inches in height, it is the smallest of the nation's quail. It often congregates in coveys of up to 30 birds, which explode with a characteristic burst of energy and frenetic fluttering when flushed. In the early 1930s, it has been estimated, 10 million bobwhites were taken each year. Today, they flourish in southern farmlands and scrub areas.

The lakes, rivers, bayous, and coastal waters nourish an abundance of marine and aquatic life. In freshwaters, bass, catfish, sunfish, and crappie are important sport fish; in the coastal waters, pompano, tarpon, snook, bonefish, snappers, bluefish, mackerel, shark, and sailfish attract anglers. Commercially, shrimp, oysters, and crabs are still significant products of the Gulf of Mexico, although Hurricane Katrina in 2005 disrupted their harvesting.

Mark Twain's Huckleberry Finn caught a catfish that was as big as a man and "weighed over two hundred pounds," but no documented southern catfish has yet attained this size. A blue cat caught at St. Louis weighed 150 pounds. Although 26 species of catfish may be found in the waters of the South, few reach the size of the blue catfish. Channel cats, bullheads, flatheads, and yellow cats are still pursued eagerly by southern anglers, and both commercially and as sport fish, catfish are important inhabitants of southern waters.

The largemouth bass is the most popular freshwater game fish in the nation. Found in lakes, bayous, and ponds across the South, specimens weighing more than 20 pounds are occasionally caught. Largemouth bass energetically strike artificial lures and are pursued diligently by southern anglers. Many bass tournaments are organized yearly to catch this exciting fish.

In the tropical saltwaters of the Gulf of Mexico, sport and commercial fish appear in large numbers. Great variety exists in the species that can be caught, and each year millions of anglers seek to harvest the products of this marine realm. The most exciting game fish of the world's waters is the tarpon. Reaching lengths of up to eight feet and weights of more than 300 pounds, this fish has long been praised for its strength, skill, agility, and fighting ability. From the west coast of Florida to the waters off south Texas, the explosive leaps of the silver king when hooked have captured the imagination of anglers.

The southern environment has sustained a variety of reptiles and amphibians. The American alligator is found exclusively within the South. It once was common along the Atlantic and Gulf coasts, from North Carolina south to Florida and west to Texas, but hunting for sport and commercial use of its hides have greatly reduced the alligator population. From early frontier days, gator killing was a popular sport. The alligator's large size and menacing shape seemed to make it fair game. The American crocodile has had a more limited range, mainly in south Florida, and was never large in numbers in the South. The Carolina anole is a slender, bright green lizard known as the American chameleon because its coloring changes in different situations.

No family of North American salamanders is distinctively southern, yet many species can be found limited to specific regions of the South—the ringed salamander of the Ozark and Ouachita mountains, the flatwoods salamander of the Atlantic and Gulf coasts, and the hellbender of southern rivers. The largest toad in the South (*B. marinus*) is not native to the region but was introduced from South America to help control insects. Frogs found in the South include the leopard frog, the green frog, the eastern spadefoot frog, the carpenter frog, the pig frog, and the river frog. The best-known frog in the South may be the bullfrog, whose distinctive call of the male punctuates the southern night. His legs have been a prized food delicacy and led to attempts at setting up frog farms. Turtles found in the South include the pond slider (the familiar dime-store turtle), the river cooter, and the common snapping turtle. The alligator snapping turtle is the largest freshwater turtle in the world; its languid movements allow green algae to grow on its shell. The gopher tortoise burrows underground along the southern coasts when temperatures become too high.

Four venomous snakes reside in the South: rattlesnakes, copperheads, coral snakes, and cottonmouths. Among rattlers, the eastern diamondback, which can reach a length of eight feet, and the canebreak rattler are found only in the South. The copperhead feeds on small animals and is rarely seen by humans, whom it avoids. The cottonmouth is also called the water moccasin. It is an aggressive reptile, found near swamps, rice fields, lakes, and rivers. Its bite is particularly dangerous, and it is fond of climbing trees and then dropping from the limbs when frightened. The eastern coral snake is found in the woods and grasses from the East Coast to Texas. It is among the most colorful of reptiles because of its ringed markings. Most southern snakes are nonvenomous and have been looked upon kindly by humans for keeping down the numbers of animal predators. The eastern indigo snake grows to eight feet in length and is the largest snake in North America. It is frequently seen at roadside snake farms in the Deep South, sometimes advertised as a cobra. The rainbow snake is found in swamps along the coast. Other reptiles found in the South include the redbellied mud snake, the scarlet coral snake, racers, eastern worm snakes, rat snakes, king snakes, water snakes, milk snakes, and hognose snakes.

Since the time of early American Indian societies, animals have profoundly influenced human culture in the South. Animals, especially birds and reptiles, have long been dominant design motifs in Native American pottery in the South, reflecting the importance of serpent and bird symbolism in the Indians' belief system. Pottery effigies of the opossum, snake, deer, cougar, and assorted birds appeared in prehistoric Indian cultures in south Georgia, and examples have often been found at burial sites in the Gulf Coast area. Indian shell art in

*Child and animal friend, Vicksburg, Miss., 1977 (William R. Ferris Collection, Southern Folklife Collection, Wilson Library, University of North Carolina at Chapel Hill)*

the Southeast included iconographic representations of such animals as rattle-snakes, woodpeckers, and spiders. Animals were central symbols of Indian religion, and objects such as eagle feathers and swan wings had ritual importance. Indian folklore included stories illustrating the personalities of various animals, such as the Choctaw tale "Why the Possum Grins."

Blacks and whites have similarly used animals in the culture they built in the South. Blacks brought to the New World an African tradition of animal tales about lions, elephants, and monkeys, who appeared in folktales, as did animals encountered by the slaves in the New World. African omens and signs were altered to fit American fauna. Animals played a role in black folk medicine. The plantation conjurer might wear a snakeskin around his or her neck or carry a petrified frog in one pocket and a dead lizard in the other. A large body of black folklore related the stories of humanized animals such as Brer Rabbit and Brer Fox. African and American Indian prototypes for these trickster tales have been discovered, but, whatever their origins, most of these animal folktales suggested how clever slaves outsmarted their masters.

There is also a rich tradition among southern blacks, whites, and Indians of folk sayings and beliefs about animals. In Louisiana, for example, if a dog howls with his nose in the earth, some people believe a fire will occur; if a rooster crows at the back door, it means death; if animals in the woods and swamps are unusually noisy, then it will rain soon. Black children have even incorporated the snake into a children's game ("Black snake, black snake, where are you hiding?").

In the folk arts and crafts of the whites of southern Appalachia animals emerge, as in Indian and black art, as a major design motif in wood carving, quilting, pottery, basket making, and toy making. Animals are the central figures of Anglo-American folk songs such as "Froggie Went a Courtin'," "Raccoon," "Groundhog," "Little Sparrow," and "Bear Went over the Mountain." Again, as with Indians and blacks, animals fulfilled for mountain and rural whites in the South a variety of practical and symbolic functions. They served as a direct source of food and clothing, as an economic resource from trading in animal products, as an ingredient in the prevention and treatment of disease and illness, and as figures in folk art and lore. One group of Appalachian whites even made serpents the ritual center of a snake handler's religion.

Animals have figured in the musical and literary traditions of the modern South. Blues singers, for example, apply animal comparisons to themselves through lyrics such as "the rattlesnakin' daddy who wants to rattle all the time," the "black wolf that hollers," or the "rootin' ground hog who roots both night and day." Southern writers generally see animals the same way rural people have over the years, as simply part of the land, beings encountered as part of normal living. Their portrayal of animals is rooted in familiarity. Marjorie Kinnan Rawlings raises her hat when she sees the water moccasin, which once refrained from biting her nervous horse. William Faulkner used an animal for what critics regard as one of his most profound tales, "The Bear." He conveyed an almost mystical awareness of the relationship between human and animal in the southern woods, an attitude rooted in American Indian belief. For Faulkner's southern hunters, there is great respect for the animals hunted, because hunters discover an identity between themselves and their prey. Harry Crews captures the drama of the rattlesnake roundup, a southern subcultural ritual, in his novel *A Feast of Snakes*.

PHILLIP DRENNON THOMAS
*Wichita State University*

Henry Hill Collins, *Complete Field Guide to American Wildlife* (1959); Albert E. Cowdrey, *This Land, This South: An Environmental History* (1983); Gilbert C. Fite, *Cotton Fields No More: Southern Agriculture, 1865–1980* (1984); Sam B. Hilliard, *Hog Meat and Hoecake: Food Supply in the Old South, 1840–1860* (1972); David Starr Jordan and Barton Warren Everman, *American Food and Game Fishes* (1902); Edward T. LaRoe, *Our Living Resources: A Report to the Nation on the Distribution, Abundance, and Health of U.S. Plants, Animals, and Ecosystems* (1995); Howard W. Odum, *Southern Regions of the United States* (1936); Olin Sewall Pettingill Jr., *A Guide to Bird Finding East of the Mississippi* (1977); A. W. Schorger, *The Passenger Pigeon: Its Natural History and Extinction* (1955), *The Wild Turkey: Its History and Domestication* (1966); Theodore Steinberg, *Down to Earth: Nature's Role in American History* (2002); Walter P. Taylor, ed., *The Deer of North America: The White-Tailed Mule and Black-Tailed Deer, Genus "Odocoileus," Their History and Management* (1956); John M. Thompson, *Wildlands of the Upper South* (2004); Frank Bedingfield Vinson, *Conservation and the South, 1890–1920* (1971).

## Aquatic Life, Freshwater

The South has diverse aquatic ecosystems that harbor an astonishing variety of aquatic, or semiaquatic, organisms, many of which occur nowhere else in the world. Aquatic ecosystems of the South include running water systems, such as small, clear, rocky streams and large, muddy, meandering rivers. Standing water systems include lakes, bogs, swamps, and seasonally flooded systems such as bottomland hardwood forests. There are about 20,000 caves with unusual species living in underground springs and streams.

Glaciation was not responsible for formation of lakes in the South, as it was in the northern United States. Instead, natural lakes in the South were formed mainly by cutoff river meanders (oxbow lakes) or, as in Florida, dissolution of soluble, carbonate-rich rock (solution lakes). Other, less common mechanisms of lake formation include coastal ponds formed by sand deposition across streams; landslides blocking streams (Mountain Lake, Va.); local subsidence of the land surface (Reelfoot Lake, Tenn., resulting from the 1819 Madrid earthquake); and impoundment of streams by beavers. Lake Okeechobee in south

Florida is the largest lake in the South (730 square miles) and is a seafloor depression left behind after sea levels dropped and the Florida peninsula emerged. Besides the exceptions mentioned above, large natural lakes are uncommon in the South, but there are at least 144 major man-made reservoirs. Constructed ponds, including farm ponds built to catch sediment and for catfish aquaculture, dot the landscape across the region.

In the South, 30 major river systems drain to the Gulf of Mexico or the Atlantic Ocean. Notable examples include the lower Mississippi River and its major tributaries; the Mobile River Basin, the largest Gulf Coast drainage east of the Mississippi; the Pascagoula River in southern Mississippi, the largest river in the continental United States without a dam on the main channel; and the Rio Grande of southwest Texas.

The South contains about 36 percent of all wetlands and 65 percent of forested wetlands in the continental United States today. Vast wetland areas include the Okefenokee Swamp in Georgia and north Florida; the Dismal Swamp in Virginia and North Carolina; the Atchafalaya Swamp in Louisiana, which is the largest river overflow swamp in North America; and the Everglades of southern Florida. The "river of grass" that Marjorie Stoneman Douglas described as the Everglades is actually a river of saw grass (*Cladium jamaicense*), which is not in the grass family but is a sedge with narrow, grasslike leaves.

Along the Atlantic Coastal Plain, extending from Delaware to Florida, are the numerous (more than 10,000) Carolina Bays. These shallow, often marshy, oval-shaped depressions depend mostly on rainwater for hydrology, but their origin is uncertain. The Carolina Bays are important habitat for many rare plants and, depending on location, are inhabited by a diverse fauna that can tolerate fluctuating water levels, including alligators, amphibians, turtles, and mollusks. Bogs, a type of wetland dominated by peat moss (*Sphagnum* sp.), and pocosins, which are wetlands dominated by broad-leaved, evergreen shrubs and small trees, once covered more than a million acres along the Atlantic Coastal Plain and Gulf Coastal Plain. Characteristic vascular plants (plants unlike mosses) of the acidic, nutrient-poor bogs and pocosins are holly, bay, loblolly pine, and a multitude of carnivorous plants including the Venus flytrap (*Dionaea muscipula*) and pitcher plants. Carnivorous plants obtain their nutrients from the capture and digestion of animals, mostly insects. The South contains the highest diversity of carnivorous plants in the world, with 54 species in five genera, some of which are endangered. Bogs and pocosins, and wetlands in general, have in the last century been dramatically reduced in area by conversion to agriculture, development, or timber production.

When it comes to variety of freshwater life, the South cannot be beat, with a greater diversity of aquatic organisms than anyplace else in the nation. This is partly a consequence of the lack of glaciers in what is now the South. It is also a consequence of alternating changes in sea level, changing climates, and meandering rivers and streams that result in long-term isolation of many organisms in restricted locations. Prolonged isolation of a population (individuals of the same species in a particular area) can lead to genetic changes and evolutionary divergence of the population from the parent species. This phenomenon is most striking for biota of rivers and streams, and particularly for organisms with low dispersal abilities, such as mussels and snails. Indeed, the running waters of this region have been described as an "evolutionary laboratory" with extraordinary species richness and local endemism (species native to the region and found nowhere else). According to a recent U.S. Geological Survey report, continental high points of biological diversity occur in the South in fishes (535 species), salamanders (51 species in 19 genera), aquatic insects, crayfishes (300 species in 11 genera), and mollusks (especially mussels, family *Unionoida*). Approximately 90 percent of the mussel fauna of all of North America occurs in the South, with 270 species in 49 genera of mussels. Fish diversity in the South is greater than any comparable area in the temperate regions of the world, with as much as 48 percent of the native fish species found nowhere else in the country.

The Mobile Basin, in particular, is an epicenter of biological diversity, home to 40 percent of North American turtles, third among the nation's river basins in fish diversity (160 species), and one of the richest areas in the world for mussels and aquatic snails. As of the year 2000, endemic fauna in the Mobile Basin alone included 40 species of fishes, 33 species of mussels, 110 species of aquatic snails, and 3 species of turtles. Including endemic and nonendemic species, snail and freshwater turtle diversity is comparable to no place else in the world except Asia.

Among invertebrate benthic organisms (organisms without backbones living in or at the surface of the sediments at the bottom of aquatic ecosystems), you will find worms, insects, freshwater prawns, mussels, snails, and crayfish. Crayfish, lobsterlike crustaceans more often called crawfish or crawdads by southerners, occur throughout the world but are most diverse in species in the freshwaters of the South. They are particularly abundant in waters of the lower Mississippi basin, where they are an important source of food and income, particularly in Louisiana, considered by some the "crawfish capital of the world."

Vertebrates (animals with backbones) common in southern aquatic ecosystems include fish, snakes, frogs and toads, mammals, wading birds, and migratory waterfowl (ducks and geese). High diversity of fishes is particularly striking among the minnows (family *Cyprinidae*) and the darters (family *Percidae*),

*The common channel catfish thrives in small rivers, large rivers, reservoirs, natural lakes, and ponds. (Eric Engbretson, photographer, U.S. Fish and Wildlife Service)*

which can be found in swift-moving streams flowing over coarse gravel. Popular game fish in southern reservoirs, lakes, and swamps include the largemouth bass (*Micropterus salmoides salmoides*), buffalo fish (*Ictiobus* sp.), black and white crappie (*Pomoxis* sp.), various sunfishes (bluegills, redear, and pickerel), and blue and channel catfish (*Ictalurus* sp.).

In the lower Mississippi and Atchafalaya rivers, there are an estimated 150 fish species. Fishes in the main stem of larger rivers like the Mississippi must be adapted to a fast, strong current, and fishes requiring a slower current exist in backwater environments. Fishes characteristic of large southern rivers include all of the reservoir fishes mentioned above, plus paddlefish (*Polyodon spathula*), various kinds of carp (common, grass, and the recently invasive silver and bighead carp), several species of gar (*Lepisosteus* sp. and *Atractosteus* sp.), and sturgeon (*Scaphirhynchus* sp.), including the endangered pallid sturgeon (*S. platorynchus*). The alligator gar, *Atractosteus spatula*, is the largest exclusively freshwater fish in North America, achieving lengths of up to 10 feet. Sturgeon and gars, sometimes referred to as "living fossils," have existed since before the dinosaurs.

Around ponds and wetlands in the Southeast, it is easy to find many species of salamanders, frogs, toads, and snakes. Snakes common to the region, and always occurring around water, include the venomous and somewhat territorial cottonmouth snake (or water moccasin, *Agkistrodon piscivorus*) and nonvenomous water snakes (genus *Nerodia*). A rare, rather astonishing reptile, found mostly in lakes, swamps, and slow-moving streams, is the alligator snapping turtle (*Macrochelys temminckii*), perhaps the largest freshwater turtle in the world. Turtles on the endangered species list include the ringed sawback, the yellow-blotched sawback, and the black-knobbed sawback, which occur in rivers of Mississippi, Alabama, and Louisiana. The largest, and probably most fearsome, freshwater reptile in southern aquatic ecosystems is the American alligator (*Alligator mississippiensis*). The alligator occurs from the Carolinas to Florida and along the Gulf Coast but is most abundant in ponds, marshes, rivers, and swamps of southern Florida and Louisiana. In marshes it creates pools that serve as habitat for many other species.

Amphibious mammals, fairly common but not restricted to the South, include beavers, muskrats, and river otters. The beaver (*Castor canadensis*), a semiaquatic rodent, was historically important in building dams and creating ponds on stream basins, but the southern subspecies was hunted to extinction around 1900. Today's southern beavers are descendants of the northern subspecies, which was introduced in 1930. In the absence of natural predators (coyotes, wolves, bears), beavers and beaver lodges are once again a common sight in southern ponds and wetlands. River otters (*Lutra canadensis*) occur in ponds, marshes, bayous, and brackish inlets along the Gulf Coast. Their playful nature and impressive swimming and fishing skills make river otters great fun to watch. The future status of the river otter is linked directly to the availability of wetlands, where they fish and mate.

As we have seen for other animal groups, the South has the continent's highest number of species of wading birds, most of which occur in coastal wetlands. Large wading birds common in southern freshwater ecosystems include various species of herons, egrets, the endangered Mississippi sandhill crane, the roseate spoonbill (*Platalea ajaja*), and the wood stork (*Mycteria americana*). These birds feed primarily in shallow water on small fish, insects, crustaceans, and frogs. Herons and egrets (family *Ardeidae*) can be found throughout the United States but are common around wetlands and lakes of the South. The sandhill crane occurs in wet pine savanna, such as along the lower coastal plain of Mississippi. The wood stork can be found near the coast from Mississippi to Florida.

In Everglades National Park, the wood stork is considered a good "indicator species" of environmental conditions. The wood stork feeds on small fish, crayfish, reptiles, and amphibians by sweeping its long bill across the bottom of shallow ponds. Due to man-made alteration in the natural hydrology of the Everglades, opportunities for feeding have been disrupted, the number of storks has declined precipitously, and the species is now considered endangered. Overall, populations of wading birds in Everglades National Park have decreased by about 10 to 20 percent with decrease in wetland foraging habitat. The wood stork is federally listed as endangered.

Floodplains, bottomland hardwood forests, often occur along rivers and lake edges. These systems are so important to the function of adjacent aquatic ecosystems that they can be considered an occasionally dry portion of a river . or lake, rather than an occasionally flooded forest. During flooding, these forests are important habitat for young fish, insects, crayfish, and worms. Plants in this ecosystem are adapted to regular flooding, and many bottomland trees depend on occasional floodwaters for seed dispersal. Seeds may be dispersed with movement of the water or after passing through the gut of a seed-eating animal. A characteristic tree of these forests is the majestic bald cypress (*Taxodium* sp.), a deciduous conifer that can survive, but is not restricted to, permanent standing water. In natural water-filled depressions, these trees may form dense clusters called cypress domes. The floodplain, a bottomland hardwood ecosystem that once covered vast areas of the South, has largely been converted to agricultural land.

Because of human-induced disturbances such as degradation in water quality, river impoundment and channelization, mining, dredging, draining of wetlands, and excessive harvesting, many freshwater organisms in the South are endangered or have gone extinct. The vulnerability of the region's species is compounded by the fact that so many species exist only in narrowly restricted places, such as headwater streams, and because very good water quality is essential to their survival. Snails and mussels are particularly susceptible to disturbance; for example, in the Mobile Basin at least 17 species of mussels and 37 species of aquatic snails are presumed extinct, most within the last few decades. Because these animals have limited mobility, they cannot leave when their environment is no longer suitable. Another problem faced by mussels is that they reproduce and disperse by attaching their larvae to the gills of stream fish. Many of these parasitic interactions are species-specific, so if a particular fish species declines in number or is extirpated, the associated mussel species will decline or be lost as well. Freshwater mussels currently at risk (federally listed as either threatened or endangered) include species in the genera *Pleuro-*

*bema* (clubshells and pigtoes) and *Epioblasma* (pearlymussels, combshells, acornshells, and riffleshells).

Invasive species are another problem faced by native aquatic biota. The federal government considers an invasive to be any species, including its seeds, eggs, spores, or other propagating material, that is not native to an ecosystem and likely to cause harm. The U.S. Department of Agriculture's National Invasive Species Information Center currently tracks 10 plants and three animals that are invading freshwater habitats in the South. This does not include all invasive species in the South, but only the ones where there is enough verifiable information for public notice. For instance, the Asian carp (bighead carp and silver carp), which are currently moving down the Mississippi River watershed in large numbers, are not included.

Two well-known invasive animal species affecting freshwater ecosystems of the South are the nutria and the zebra mussel. Nutria (*Myocastor coypus*) are large, semiaquatic rodents originally from South America. In the 1930s nutria (called *coypu* in other countries) were introduced to the United States for their fur. Voracious herbivores, these rodents can consume up to 25 percent of their body weight daily and have damaged tens of thousands of wetlands in Louisiana alone. Nutria also cause damage to croplands, particularly sugar and rice fields, and their burrowing can cause agricultural levees to fail. The Louisiana Department of Wildlife and Fisheries has an active control program.

Another example of a destructive invasive aquatic species is the zebra mussel (*Dreissena polymorpha*), which invaded the United States in 1988 and has quickly spread from the Great Lakes down the Mississippi River to the South. Zebra mussels grow so thick that they can restrict pipe flow and increase boat drag. As filter feeders, zebra mussels alter the biological communities in which they live by consuming large amounts of phytoplankton (microscopic algae). Phytoplankton are the base of the food web in many aquatic systems, so although the water may look clearer after a zebra mussel invasion, species farther up the food web (other mussels, fish) may be directly or indirectly harmed by large numbers of zebra mussels.

Despite the loss of vast areas of presettlement aquatic habitat, the disturbance to remaining habitat, and the resulting difficulties in survival of many native aquatic organisms, the South still contains some of the most extensive, biologically diverse aquatic ecosystems in the United States. Besides being home to an astounding diversity of organisms, including many found nowhere else in the world, these ecosystems are important as sources of drinking water, for water storage, for natural water purification, and for recreational activities such as fishing, hunting, boating, and simply relaxing and enjoying nature. The beauty and wildness of these aquatic ecosystems, and the uniqueness of so many of the organisms that live there, help explain the strong lure and fascination the outdoors has for so many southerners. There is no question, however, that greater dedication to preservation and restoration of these systems is necessary to prevent them from degrading further and to halt the extinction of the remarkable southern aquatic biota.

CLIFFORD A. OCHS AND HEATH E. CAPELLO
*University of Mississippi*

Albert E. Cowdrey, *This Land, This South: An Environmental History* (1996); C. T. Hackney, S. M. Adams, and W. H. Marin, eds., *Biodiversity of the Southeastern United States: Aquatic Communities* (1992); U.S. Fish and Wildlife Service, *Mobile River Basin Aquatic Recovery Plan* (2000); P. S. White, S. P. Wilds, and G. A. Thornhorst, in *Status and Trends of the Nation's Biological Resources*, vol. 1, ed. M. J. Mac, P. A. Opler, C. E. Puckett Haecker, and P. D. Doran (1998).

## Birds and Birding

A wide variety of birds reside in or migrate through the South. While Native Americans were intimately familiar with the diversity of species that lived on or migrated through their land, the British naturalist Mark Catesby assembled the first authoritative catalog of southern avifauna. His two-volume *Natural History of Carolina, Florida, and the Bahama Islands* (1731–43) included 109 hand-colored bird illustrations. Fifty years later, William Bartram incorporated a list of 215 southern birds into his widely acclaimed book *Travels through North and South Carolina, Georgia, East and West Florida* (1791). In the first half of the 19th century, the artist-naturalists Alexander Wilson and John James Audubon made numerous other additions to the inventory of birds known to inhabit the region.

Ironically, increasing knowledge about southern birds was accompanied by increasing threats to their well-being. By the end of the 19th century, deforestation, the introduction of exotic species, large-scale market hunting for food and the millinery trade, and predator control campaigns were decimating bird populations across North America, resulting in mounting calls for their protection. Of particular concern in the South were the herons, egrets, and other colonial nesting species that proved both economically valuable and especially vulnerable to hunters; two increasingly rare species that inhabited the region's bottomlands hardwood forests (the ivory-billed woodpecker and the Carolina parakeet); and the passenger pigeon, which congregated in massive winter roosts in southern forests. By the early 20th century, the passenger pigeon and the Carolina parakeet were both lost to extinction.

Bird protection societies organized in response to the decline of these and other birds. The first Audubon Society, created by George Bird Grinnell in New York in 1886, proved short-lived, but most of the state Audubon societies that began forming a decade later survive to this day. By 1904 all southern states except Mississippi, Alabama, and Arkansas boasted such institutions. These reform-minded organizations lobbied for uniform state laws protecting non-game birds, helped enforce existing state and federal legislation, established private bird sanctuaries, pressured officials to create public wildlife refuges, promoted bird study in schools, and encouraged the activity of bird-watching (also known as birding).

With promotion from Audubon societies, increases in leisure time, a rise in discretionary income, a growing general interest in outdoor recreation, the publication of easy-to-use field guides, and the development of lightweight binoculars, birding has evolved into one of the most popular recreational activities in post–World War II America. By 2001 more than 70 million Americans reported that they had gone outdoors to watch birds one or more times per year, an impressive figure that represents more than 33 percent of the entire population over age 16.

The region with the largest growth in birding at the end of the 20th century was the South, which boasts numerous sites renowned for the variety and abundance of their bird life. South Florida, which includes the Everglades National Park, is one of the region's most prized areas for birding. Some of the uncommon birds most often sought there include not only native species like the smooth-billed ani, limpkin, snail kite, and burrowing owl but also such exotics as the spot-breasted oriole, red-whiskered bulbul, white-winged parakeet, and purple swamphen. Most of Florida is within the Atlantic Flyway, a migratory route that follows the North American east coast and Appalachian Mountains from the Canadian maritimes to the Gulf of Mexico and beyond. During spring migration, well over 200 species of birds travel through the Dry Tortugas National Park, and many of the same birds make annual stops in Everglades, Biscayne, and Big Cypress national parks in Florida, the Great Smoky Mountains of North Carolina and Tennessee, and Shenandoah National Park in Virginia.

Also along the Atlantic Flyway lies the Pea Island National Wildlife Refuge on Hatteras Island, N.C., one of the top birding sites on the south Atlantic coast. Pelagic birds like black-capped petrels, several species of shearwaters and storm petrels, pomarine jaegers, sooty terns, herald petrels, white-tailed tropicbirds, masked boobies, south polar skuas, and parasitic and long-tailed jaegers can sometimes be spotted here following hurricanes. During November, thousands of waterfowl winter in North Carolina's Mattamuskeet National Wildlife Refuge. Migratory birds such as the tundra swan and snow and Canada geese provide highlights for birders, as do the year-round wader and shorebird populations.

The Lower Rio Grande Valley in Texas and the upper Texas Gulf Coast are two other prized areas for southern birding. Species of special interest in both areas are the whooping crane, least grebe, fulvous whistling duck, Muscovy duck, white-tailed hawk, crested caracara, plain chachalaca, red-crowned parrot, groove-billed ani, buff-bellied hummingbird, Chihuahuan raven, and Audubon's oriole. Southern and eastern Texas are part of the Central Flyway, which follows the Great Plains from Canada to Mexico, and the spring migration brings numerous passerines, raptors, and shorebirds to the Lower Rio Grande Valley, an area that is the year-round home to more than 300 species of birds. Along the Texas Gulf Coast, in places such as Sea Rim State Park and High Island, least bitterns and gallinules are plentiful.

Many species of birds are common across the South and can be enjoyed by the adventure birder and neighborhood stroller alike. The ruby-throated hummingbird, northern mockingbird, blue jay, American robin, Carolina wren, red-tailed hawk, red-shouldered hawk, mourning dove, eastern bluebird, and northern cardinal are all birds that children across the South learn to identify at early ages. Most of these species can be spotted outside southern windows year-round.

Increasingly, communities across the South are establishing birding trails and bird festivals, such as the annual Space Coast Birding and Wildlife Festival in Titusville, Fla.; the Wings over Water Birding Festival on the Outer Banks of North Carolina; and the Brownsville (Tex.) International Birding Festival, designed to lure bird enthusiasts (and their dollars) to their area.

MARK V. BARROW JR.
*Virginia Polytechnic Institute and State University*

JAMES G. THOMAS JR.
*University of Mississippi*

Mark V. Barrow Jr., *A Passion for Birds: American Ornithology after Audubon* (1998); Ken Cordell and Nancy G. Herbert, in *Birding* (2002); Alan Feduccia, ed., *Catesby's Birds of Colonial America* (1985); Frank Graham, *The Audubon Ark: A History of the National Audubon Society* (1990).

# Climate and Weather

Scholars and other observers have long seen the region's climate and weather as the key to understanding its people. James McBride Dabbs saw in the violence of southern thunderstorms a parallel for the violence of the region's people, nurturing the tension that demanded release. He called the weather a "demigod." Wilbur J. Cash portrayed the southern climate creating "a cosmic conspiracy against reality in favor of romance." Clarence Cason, in *90° in the Shade* (1935), used the weather to explain the southerner's slow talk and movement. Sociologist Rupert Vance blamed the prevalence of hookworm in the South partly on the warm climate, which encouraged people to go shoeless and thus expose themselves to infection through the feet. He also argued that barns in the South were not as tightly constructed as those in New England because southerners did not have the incentive of the harsh northern winters. Certainly, the architecture of the South—with its high ceilings and tall windows and its porches, galleries, verandas, and dogtrot breezeways, all of which promote summer cooling—has testified to the southerner's awareness of the weather's importance in terms of daily living.

The warm, humid climate, long growing season, and abundant moisture of most of the South have indeed had a far-reaching impact on the region's economy and culture. Much of the South's early history involved the raising of agricultural products for export. Even in Texas, where the climate of the northern and western two-thirds of the state differs dramatically from the rest of the South, conditions proved ideal for large livestock operations. The southern climate has helped to make agricultural pursuits profitable. Southerners also have had to work to overcome the disadvantages imposed upon them by their climate. The hot and humid weather that produced unhealthy conditions took many an early southerner's life. Advances in medicine, architecture, and technology have curbed the outbreak of disease, permitted the construction of artificially cooled environments, and helped to create a healthy environment in which to live.

The South is divided into three large climate regions: the southern Plains and Lowlands, the Middle Atlantic Lowlands, and the Appalachian Mountains. The largest of these three is the southern Plains and Lowlands, a vast area including the states of Texas, Georgia, Florida, and South Carolina. The area inland from the Gulf and Atlantic coastlines has a continental climate featuring cold winters, warm to hot summers, and great extremes of temperature. Coastal regions are modified by the warm waters of the Gulf of Mexico and the Atlantic. Winters there are relatively humid and mild; summers, very humid and warm. The southern portion of Florida has a special subtropical climate marked by dominating northwest trade winds that differentiate it from the rest of the South.

As a whole the climate of the southern Plains and Lowlands is influenced by the interaction between strong, cold, and dry polar air masses from the interior and warm, moist maritime air masses from the Atlantic and, especially, from the Gulf. In winter the cold inland air is heavier and is drawn toward the warmer, lighter air over the water. This situation allows cold winter storms to penetrate, at times, as far as the coastal regions. When this occurs, there can be freezes as far south as central Florida. In summer the inland air mass is warmer than the air over the ocean, and a reverse flow occurs that carries moist maritime air northward and provides a major source of precipitation for the interior. Along the Atlantic Coast precipitation is carried by southerly and easterly winds off the ocean. The intense summer heat of inland areas helps produce violent tornadoes and thunderstorms. Coastal areas are exposed to hurricanes with strong tides, considerable rain, and high winds. Four hurricanes made landfall in Florida in 2004, and Hurricane Katrina devastated New Orleans and the Mississippi coast in August 2005.

With the exception of extreme southern Texas and Florida, temperatures in January range from a mean maximum of 70°F to a mean minimum of 20°F (in north Texas). In general there can be 0 to 30 days along the coast when temperatures fall below 32°F and as many as 90 days in more northerly and westerly areas. In southern Texas and Florida temperatures range on average in January from 50°F to 80°F, and days below 32°F are very rare. July temperatures for this region range from 70°F to 100°F inland and from 70°F to 90°F on the immediate coast. The number of days with temperatures above 90°F ranges from 60 to 120. Growing seasons for the most southerly parts of the region have a mean length of 330 days, though the most northern portions of Texas and Arkansas have growing seasons as short as 200 days.

Yearly snowfall accumulations decrease from north to south. In far northern regions three feet of snow is a normal yearly total, while it rarely falls in coastal areas. With the exception of Atlantic coastal areas and Texas, yearly precipitation accumulations range from 48 to 64 inches and in scattered locations along the Gulf Coast may reach as high as 100 inches. Along the Atlantic Coast there is less precipitation, with yearly means of 32 to 48 inches. In Texas the amount of yearly precipitation decreases from east to west with a high in eastern coastal areas of 56 inches and a low of 8 inches at El Paso.

Humidity levels are high for this entire region except in western Texas. Winter levels range from 60 to 85 percent, and summer readings average over 90 percent. In more northern and western regions, humidity levels are somewhat decreased, with El Paso having summer levels of only 60 to 70 percent.

The remaining two climate regions of the South are climatically connected to each other. The Middle Atlantic Lowlands comprise an approximately 200-mile-wide strip along the coastlines of North Carolina and Virginia. The Appalachian Mountain region is an upland area that extends northeastward from Georgia and includes eastern Tennessee and western North Carolina and Virginia. The mountain peaks, averaging from 2,000 to 4,000 feet above sea level, act as a partial barrier to air masses moving in from the west. Although some fronts cross the mountains and head to the coast, others are forced north and east away from the Middle Atlantic Lowlands. Other fronts are pushed south into South Carolina, Georgia, and Florida. When the latter occurs in winter, Atlantic coastal areas in the southern Plains and Lowlands climate region may be colder than coastal Virginia or North Carolina. As air masses approach the mountains from the west, they are forced to rise and often lose their moisture, producing considerable rain and snow for the western slopes. The Atlantic coastal region and the eastern slopes of the Appalachian chain receive their moisture from maritime air masses moving ashore from the Atlantic. Occasionally snow reaches these areas from air masses that pass over the mountain barrier.

Temperatures in these two regions range from annual mean minimums of 20°F in winter to summer highs in the 90s. Along the coast there are from 30 to 90 days with temperatures below 32°F, whereas in the mountains there may be as many as 150 days with temperatures below freezing. On the coast more humidity is typical (around 90 percent in summer). Humidity levels are relatively low in mountainous areas. Great extremes of both temperature and humidity occur as one moves from mountain valleys to higher elevations. Annual precipitation amounts range from 32 to 48 inches in coastal areas to as much as 64 inches in some mountain locations.

Although numerous old weather records are available for the South, no climate reconstructions have been made. However, from studies conducted on other regions of North America, one can deduce the climatic changes that have taken place in the South. Considerable evidence suggests that a period of increased cold weather and variable temperatures and precipitation greeted the first Europeans to reach the American coast. Called the Little Ice Age, it lasted until the last third of the 19th century. In the South this period was probably marked by more outbreaks of cold, freezing weather in Gulf coastal regions and somewhat cooler temperatures in northern, western, and mountain areas.

A thermometer and a cola — southern icons, Reganton, Miss., 1975 (William R. Ferris Collection, Southern Folklife Collection, Wilson Library, University of North Carolina at Chapel Hill)

In the 20th century there was a gradual warming trend and a relative decrease in variable weather until the late 1940s. Since then, climatic conditions have remained fairly stable.

Talking about the weather has always been a favorite southern pastime. The region's folklore tradition contains a body of sayings geared toward predicting the weather. The wider the stripes on a caterpillar's back, the colder the winter. A row of dark spots on a goose bone also means a harsh winter. Some of these sayings originated in Africa, some in Europe, and others with American Indians. The thicker an onion skin, the colder the winter is a Deep South regional saying found in Georgia, Mississippi, and Alabama, and similar proverbs about the weather can be found in other subregions of the South.

Southern writers have absorbed this interest in climate. Critic Malcolm Cowley has noted of William Faulkner that "no other American writer takes such delight in the weather," but Faulkner was merely typical of southern writers in this regard. "That's the one trouble with this country," says Dr. Peabody in *As I Lay Dying* (1930), "everything, weather, all hangs on too long." But not only southern writers noted the weather's importance. Henry Adams wrote in *The Education of Henry Adams* (1907) of his visit to the South, whose people he portrayed negatively but whose climate left him enthralled. He viscerally recalled "the May sunshine and shadow," "the thickness of foliage and the heavy smells," "the sense of atmosphere," and "the brooding indolence of a warm climate and a negro population."

The changing South can be seen in the modern southern attitude toward weather. Historian Francis Butler Simkins once noted that a key change in the South had been "the disappearance of the fear of the hot climate inherited from European ancestors." Technology had much to do with this through the invention of artificial ice and refrigeration; air-conditioning has had a profound role in freeing southerners of the climate's debilitating effects. Climate-related diseases such as malaria, yellow fever, and hookworm have been all but eliminated. Southerners, even more than other Americans, wear light and loose garments. "The South has learned to regard the sun as a beneficient god instead of a cruel tyrant," concluded Simkins. The southern attitude toward beauty and health now emphasizes that a brown skin is more attractive than a fair one. This is a true aesthetic revolution for a people as racially conscious as southern whites, but it also reflects a different attitude toward climate and weather than earlier in southern history.

WILLIAM R. BARON
*Northern Arizona University*

John L. Baldwin, *Climates of the United States* (1973); Lorin Blodget, *Climatology of the United States* (1857); James C. Bonner, in *Writing Southern History: Essays in Historiography in Honor of Fletcher M. Green*, ed. Arthur S. Link and Rembert W. Patrick (1965); David Hackett Fischer, *Journal of Interdisciplinary History* (Spring 1980); James R. Fleming, *Meteorology in America, 1800–1870* (1990); Hubert H. Lamb, *Climate, History, and the Modern World* (1982); David M. Ludlam, *Early American Winters II, 1821–1870* (1968); W. J. Maunder, *The Value of the Weather* (1970); Cary J. Mock, in *Hurricanes and Typhoons: Past, Present, and Future*, ed. Richard J. Murnane and Kam-biu Liu (2004); Edgar T. Thompson, *Agricultural History* (January 1941); U.S. Department of Agriculture, *Climate and Man* (1941).

## Coastal Marshes

Coastal marshes are much more prominent in the South than elsewhere in the United States. Indeed, if we ignore Alaska, Hawaii, and coastal marshes along inland lakes in the United States, 58 percent of the nation's coastal marshes border the Gulf of Mexico, and another 26 percent can be found along the south Atlantic coastline from North Carolina to the southern tip of the Florida peninsula. Only 14 percent of such wetlands are found along the Atlantic Coast north of North Carolina (much of this is in Chesapeake Bay), and just under 2 percent of the U.S. total can be found along the Pacific Coast from California to Washington. This lopsided distribution exists because there are a couple of critical physical geographic characteristics necessary for coastal wetland development.

To begin with, most coastal wetlands are found along gently sloping portions of the continental shelf because this is where there is the greatest potential for sediment accumulation, and much of the Atlantic and especially Gulf coasts are indeed gently sloping. Moreover, coastal wetland vegetation must have protection from significant, daily wave energy. Accordingly, the ideal settings for the development of coastal wetlands in the United States are as follows: low-energy coastlines created by gently sloping coastlines (especially along the Gulf of Mexico), the back or mainland-facing sides of barrier islands (which line much of the southeast coast of the United States), and protected areas of bays and estuaries (prevalent along the north Atlantic Coast).

Coastal marshes share the basic attributes of virtually all other wetlands, such as the periodic presence of water at or near the surface, a prevalence of hydrophytic vegetation (plants adapted to wet conditions), and hydric soils (dirt that develops certain characteristics because of the relatively frequent presence of water). Yet there are some important differences between coastal marshes and inland wetlands. Perhaps the most significant difference is that most coastal marshes have a much higher salinity than most other swamps and marshes. Roughly 70 percent of coastal wetlands are regularly bathed by ocean water, and portions of these wetlands that experience high rates of evaporation or are not regularly flushed of seawater may develop salt levels much higher than ocean water. Another critical difference between many coastal marshes and most inland and riverine systems is that many coastal zones are inundated daily rather than seasonally. In coastal wetlands, the stress of high salinity and daily flooding (and drying) reduces the number of species of plants and animals that can permanently reside here (even if there are large numbers of individuals present). And even though relatively few species of mammals, reptiles, or amphibians live in coastal marshes, 95 percent of commercially valuable species of fish and shellfish spend at least part of their life cycle in coastal wetlands, seeking protection from larger predators by hiding in shallow water among marsh grasses.

Finally, although it is almost a cliché to refer to many ecosystems (including wetlands) as "fragile," many coastal marshes are relatively resilient. Unless they are completely obliterated by dredging, filling, draining, or sea level rise, coastal wetlands can occasionally overcome physical abuse by people. Daily inputs of energy from the rising tide bring sediments and flush waste products that might otherwise accumulate and reach toxic levels. Furthermore, since most plant and animal species find the coastal zone a forbidding environment, coastal wetlands usually experience relative stability in terms of species composition. As an example of the resiliency of coastal wetlands, consider the coastal marshes of

South Carolina: many of these marshes were converted to rice fields during the early 19th century, yet many have reverted back into functioning wetlands after plantations were abandoned in the aftermath of the Civil War. Of course, this generalization has its limits, because many coastal wetlands in southern Louisiana are quickly disappearing beneath the Gulf of Mexico as a result of several natural and anthropogenic processes. Many of Louisiana's coastal marshes are turning into open water because deeply buried deltaic silts are slowly compacting, sea level is rising (independent of land subsidence), several dams along the Mississippi River have reduced the region's sediment supply, and the petroleum and natural gas industry has cut many miles of canals through the coastal marshes—and these canals encourage further saltwater penetration that kills freshwater plants. It has been estimated that between 1956 and 2000, nearly 4,000 square kilometers of coastal marshes in Louisiana disappeared beneath the Gulf, and this was before Hurricane Katrina, which some observers claim did even further damage to Louisiana's remaining coastal marshes.

CHRISTOPHER F. MEINDL
*University of South Florida at St. Petersburg*

Robert A. Chabreck, *Coastal Marshes: Ecology and Wildlife Management* (1988); William J. Mitsch and James G. Gosselink, *Wetlands* (2000); Mike Tidwell, *Bayou Farewell: The Rich Life and Tragic Death of Louisiana's Cajun Coast* (2003).

## Dams

In the context of southern history, the Tennessee Valley Authority (TVA) is usually perceived as the central and essential locus of dam construction and operation in the region. Authorized in May 1933 (at the beginning of Franklin D. Roosevelt's first term as president) the federally sponsored TVA oversaw the construction of numerous dams in the Tennessee River Valley and attained worldwide fame as a regional agency devoted to multiple-purpose water resources development. Focused around the recently built Wilson Dam (originally authorized by Congress in 1916 to help power nitrate/explosives plants vital to national defense), the TVA soon undertook construction of other prominent dams designed to provide for electric power production, flood control, and river navigation. These included the 262-foot-high Norris Dam (completed 1936) across the Clinch River in northeastern Tennessee (originally called Cove Creek Dam and renamed in honor of Senator George Norris of Nebraska, a long-standing supporter of publicly financed electric power systems); the 72-foot-high Wheeler Dam (completed 1936) in northern Alabama, upstream from Wilson Dam; and the 480-foot-high Fontana Dam (completed

1945) across the Little Tennessee River in southwestern North Carolina. The latter dam was designed and constructed by the TVA engineering staff, but, in fact, the site had originally been surveyed for a hydroelectric power project by the Aluminum Company of America (ALCOA) and later subsumed into the TVA system. With roots extending back to a privately financed electric power initiative, Fontana Dam did not represent an anomaly in TVA history; in 1930 ALCOA had built the 232-foot-high Calderwood Dam on the Little Tennessee River, and this was later taken over by the TVA. Similarly, 135-foot-high Ocoee Dam No. 1 across the Ocoee River in southeastern Tennessee was built by the Eastern Tennessee Power Company in 1911 and, more than 20 years later, was incorporated into the TVA. The multifaceted origins of the TVA system do not detract from the importance of the agency in terms of regional development, but they do point to a more complex relationship between dam building and southern history than might generally be understood.

The earliest southern dams were small diversion structures built to supply water to gristmills and sawmills that played important roles in rural agriculture. Prior to the Civil War the South did not develop a major industrial economy, and, with exceptions such as the Harpers Ferry Armory in Virginia's upper Potomac River Valley, few large, water-powered factories were built in the region. After the Civil War the growth of a southern-based textile industry took advantage of the region's waterpower, and mill complexes in communities such as Danville, Va.; Columbia, S.C.; and Augusta and Columbus, Ga., sprang to life in the late 19th century. With the development of long-distance, high-voltage, alternating current power transmission in the 1890s, the development of southern waterpower sites soon entered a new era. During the first three decades of the 20th century privately financed hydroelectric power projects flourished throughout much of the South. These included the major dams built by the Eastern Tennessee Power Company (Ocoee No. 1, 1911), the Alabama Power Company (Lay Dam across the Coosa River, 1914, and Martin Dam across the Tallapoosa River, 1926), Stone & Webster Company (Goat Rock Dam across the Chattahoochee River upstream from Columbus, Ga., 1911), the Georgia Railway and Power Company (Tallulah Dam across the Tallulah River, 1913), and the Lexington Water Power Company in South Carolina (Saluda Dam, 1930). Aluminum companies also built major dams during this era, and, along with major structures built by ALCOA in the upper Tennessee River watershed, capital from French investors (L'Aluminum Français) was used to help build the Badin Dam across the Yadkin River in central North Carolina in 1914–16. In the early 20th century, municipalities also undertook the construction of large dams to ensure a steady supply of water for domestic use. For example, in 1904 the city of Lynchburg, Va., significantly expanded its water supply system by building the Pedlar Dam across the Pedlar River and connecting it to the city via a 12-mile-long aqueduct. And in the mid-1920s the city of Birmingham, Ala., built the Lake Purdy Dam across the Little Cahuba River for municipal water supply.

With the coming of the Great Depression and the New Deal–inspired TVA, the role of private finance in building southern dams faded. In the post–World War II era, federal financing for flood control and water supply projects flourished, and in the latter half of the 20th century the U.S. Army Corps of Engineers became the key dam building agency in the region that extended beyond the Tennessee Valley. Some of the major dams built by the corps include Sardis Dam (1940) in western Mississippi across the Tallahatchie River, Kerr Dam (1953) across the Roanoke River in Virginia, and Hartwell Dam (1961) across the upper Savannah River on the Georgia/South Carolina border. Today, dams in the South are used for hydroelectric power, municipal water supply, flood control, navigation, and recreation.

D. C. JACKSON
*Lafayette College*

Harvey H. Jackson, *Putting "Loafing Streams" to Work: The Building of the Lay, Mitchell, Martin, and Jordan Dams, 1910–1929* (1997); David E. Lilienthal, *TVA: Democracy on the March* (1944); Arthur E. Morgan, *The Making of the TVA* (1974).


## Endangered Species

Through millions of millennia, the actions of climate, rainfall, and other agents of geological change have sculpted in the American South a rich and diverse topography. From the unique coral islands that form the Florida Keys to the expansive delta of the Mississippi River with its wilderness of bayous to the great pine forests with their mixed stands of hardwoods, this area's distinctive habitat has nourished a rich and diverse flora and fauna. White settlement in the region led to a gradual but sustained alteration of the natural setting in which southern wildlife maintained itself. The rapid pace of urbanization and industrialization in the South in the 19th, 20th, and early 21st centuries has altered the region's habitat. The greatest decline in wildlife occurred in the latter half of the 19th century, while the greatest decline in the region's flora occurred in the 20th century. The reduction of virgin forests, alteration of waterways, introduction of domestic prey species, and consumption of land through urban development have encroached decade after decade upon the habitat of the South's wildlife. All of these developments have biologically impoverished the natural environment for every species but humans and have demonstrated the fragility of ecosystems. The future biodiversity of the South is a paramount conservation issue.

In every southern state most of the native flora and fauna are under pressure, with some species threatened, some endangered, and some on the verge of becoming extinct. The larger the species, the more likely it is under pressure by habitat encroachment. "Endangered species" are those species in danger of becoming extinct in wild, natural environments. "Threatened species" are those species that will become endangered if present conditions are not altered. In the South, as in other regions of the nation, animal species became extinct or endangered through the alteration and destruction of habitat, competition with introduced species, predation, disease, or the more direct pressure of unrestrained hunting. In the early decades of the 21st century, the southern states averaged more than 65 plants and animals that were endangered, with Florida, Alabama, Tennessee, and Texas having more than 90 plants and animals endangered. For all of the southern states, the future of more than 130 terrestrial vertebrates is uncertain. In all of these states more animals than plants were in the endangered category. The primary factor in the endangerment of these species is habitat alteration and destruction. Pressure on species is particularly high in the southern Appalachians, the Atlantic and eastern Gulf coasts, the Gulf Coast marsh and prairie region, and the Florida peninsula. Although few animals in America have become extinct through the pressures of hunting alone, the demise of the passenger pigeon and the Carolina parakeet were substantially, if not decisively, aided by such activities, and the American alligator's future was threatened.

Passenger pigeons once ranged throughout most of the lands east of the Rocky Mountains and wintered in the southern states. Among the most numerous of all the world's birds, they were the greatest population of birds in North America. The noted early American naturalist Alexander Wilson recorded that in 1810 he had seen a flock of migrating passenger pigeons whose numbers he estimated at 2,230,272,000. In spite of such numbers, a century later the species was at the threshold of extinction because of a century of unrestricted hunting. In 1914 at the Cincinnati Zoological Garden, Martha, the last known passenger pigeon, died.

In the same year, the Carolina parakeet experienced a similar fate. North America's only parrot and a bird once numerous in the southern states, this aggressive yellow, green, and orange bird frequently devoured the fruits and nuts of orchards; consequently it had been hunted since colonial times. The bird's bright plumage attracted milliners, and it subsequently fell subject to commercial utilization. Its pattern of behavior made it easy prey for bird catchers and market hunters. Since the death of a captive Carolina parakeet in 1914, no verified sightings of this colorful and active bird have been recorded. For the passenger pigeon and the Carolina parakeet, the pressures of hunting, habitat destruction, and behavior patterns that limited their dispersal in times of danger led to their extinction.

Other birds have experienced the threat of extinction in the South, and the whooping crane, Mississippi sandhill crane, brown pelican, bald eagle, and Everglade kite are endangered or threatened in all southern states. The whooping crane is North America's tallest extant bird and a survivor from the Pleistocene era. Rare in historic times, it was by the end of the 19th century confined primarily to the region west of the Mississippi River. Hunted for sport, meat, and eggs and experiencing changes in its habitat as the result of agriculture, its numbers declined dramatically. Restricted to a population that numbers fewer than 75 today, this magnificent bird makes a 2,300-mile migration each spring from its wintering site at the Aransas Refuge in Texas to nesting sites in the Wood Buffalo Park in Canada. The whooping crane is protected by the governments of both the United States and Canada and the energetic advocacy of conservation groups who have made its plight well known. Attempts to improve its breeding cycle have met with some success, and determined efforts have been initiated to maintain this graceful but endangered species. Perhaps even more endangered than the whooping crane is its relative, the Mississippi sandhill crane, which has an even smaller population. This endangered species is now protected at the Mississippi Sandhill Crane Refuge.

Endangered in all southern states but Florida, where it is threatened, the brown pelican is an excellent example of an animal that can become suddenly devastated by the actions of pesticides on an avian species. Until the 1960s the brown pelican existed in abundant numbers, but the increased use of endrin to control the boll weevil, the bollworm, and the sugarcane borer in the Mississippi Delta led to the demise of brown pelicans by directly killing them, destroying their food supplies, and altering their physiological processes. Endrin was responsible for massive fish kills in the Mississippi River in the late 1950s and early 1960s. Brown pelicans have been transplanted from Florida, where the population is stable, to Louisiana to reestablish colonies of this once-plentiful bird. In Texas, colonies are still limited, with the population not yet considered viable.

Overspecialization in a species introduces an element of rigidity in the ability of that species to adapt to changing environmental circumstances. America's largest woodpecker, the ivory-billed woodpecker, confronted a limited future

*An endangered whooping crane in the Chassahowitzka National Wildlife Refuge, Florida (Ryan Hagerty, U.S. Fish and Wildlife Service)*

because of its dependence on the South's virgin, old-growth forests with their characteristic dead and dying trees. Logging has so reduced its habitat that sightings have become limited and often unverified, and the species may be extinct.

Specialization has also limited the future of the Everglade kite. Until the second decade of the 20th century, this strikingly beautiful hawk was frequently observed soaring above the freshwater marshes of Florida. Its principal food source was the large freshwater apple snail. Dependent upon this one snail, which in turn depended on the standing water of a marsh for habitat, it had a fragile ecosystem. The progressive draining of wetlands in Florida for agriculture and urban development destroyed the populations of the apple snail and reduced the food supply of the Everglade kite. Today, its severely limited population is confined primarily to the southwestern reaches of Lake Okeechobee, with a few small nesting sites at the Loxahatchee National Wildlife Refuge. This graceful and noble bird's future is now tied to the preservation of the apple snail's environment.

The federal government declared the piping plover, a once-common Atlantic and Gulf coastal shorebird, an endangered and threatened species in 1985. Scientists launched a major effort in the 1980s to save another bird, the dusky seaside sparrow, from extinction. The last known example of the species survives in a protected environment in Florida, as scientists continue crossbreeding experiments hoping to save the species.

Because of the habitat alteration and hunting pressures, the American alligator has long been an endangered species in Alabama, Arkansas, Georgia, Mississippi, North Carolina, South Carolina, and Texas. John Bartram could observe in the mid-18th century that alligators were so thick in Florida's St. Johns River that one could have walked across the river on their heads if they had been harmless; by the middle years of the 20th century, hide hunters had severely reduced their numbers. Legislation that reduced the market for their skins and protected their habitat has permitted their numbers to increase in Florida and Louisiana, and they are no longer endangered in those states. Their situation is more precarious in other southern states.

A more timid and more nocturnal relative of the American alligator, the American crocodile, is also an endangered species in the South. Because of its limited range and specialized habitat, its prospects are less bright than those of the alligator. Confined primarily to the mangrove estuaries of southern Florida, the American crocodile is the only representative of this genera in North America, although its range includes the coastal littoral of Columbia and eastern Venezuela, the Caribbean and West Indies, the Pacific coasts of Ecuador and Columbia, and most of the Pacific coast of Central America and Mexico. Protected today and watched carefully in the Everglades National Park and the lower Keys, it is no longer subjected to hide hunters, and habitat encroachment has now been restricted. There is hope that the declining numbers of this fierce-countenanced reptile have been stabilized and that a species that has existed for 140 million years will be able to maintain itself.

The crocodile's relatives, the sea turtles, are also endangered in the southern states. All five genera of sea turtles may be found in the Gulf of Mexico, and all once nested on the sun-caressed beaches of the southern states. Sea turtles are particularly vulnerable to predation and habitat alteration. After spending years at sea, they return to nest on the limited expanse of shore on which they were hatched. Once laid, their eggs are desired by humans both as a source of protein and as an aphrodisiac that renews sexual vigor. Sea turtles are easily caught and drowned in trawlers' nets. The green turtle is among the most valuable of all reptiles and was once common to the majority of the world's oceans where temperatures did not drop below 68°F. Classified as an endangered species in the United States, it is still harvested outside this nation because of the quality of its meat for soup, the skin of its forequarters for shoes, and its oil for cosmetics and soap. The Atlantic hawksbill turtle also serves the needs of fashion by providing a source for tortoiseshell. It is also harvested for its calipee, a cartilaginous material removed from the bones of the bottom shell, which is used in clear green turtle soup and for leather. Immature hawksbill turtles are often mounted for sale to tourists in Latin American countries.

In the warm waters of Florida and perhaps as far west as Texas in the Gulf of Mexico and as far north as southern Georgia, the docile, slow-breeding, marine herbivore the manatee is attempting to maintain its population against increasing habitat destruction and human intrusion into its domain. This imperfectly studied, large marine mammal, whose nearest relative is the elephant, can reach a length of 12 feet and a weight of 1,200 pounds. During the course of a day, it may consume up to 150 pounds of aquatic plants. It has no natural enemies, unless humans are placed in this category, but it is among the most endangered of all marine mammals. Until the end of the 19th century, it was hunted by the Seminole Indians and early settlers because of the veal-like quality of its meat. Its hide made a strong, durable leather; its bones, with their ivory appearance, were often carved into small objects; and its fat was used for lubrication and light. Declining populations of this tranquil animal encouraged the Florida legislature to pass in 1893 a bill to protect the manatee. In 1907 additional legislation imposed a $600 fine and a six-month prison term for killing a manatee. Part of a population that is probably fewer than 1,000, the manatee does not have a secure future. Even in protected waters, manatees are often injured by the propellers of motorboats. Development has restricted their access to warm springs. Highly susceptible to cold weather, they frequently become victims of harsh winters. Protected by state and federal legislature, their future depends on the stability of their habitat.

Although the manatee is an elusive animal to investigate, even more secretive in its habits is the Florida panther, or eastern cougar. Historically, the cougar, or mountain lion or panther, had the greatest natural range of any terrestrial mammal in the New World, ranging from Tierra del Fuego at the tip of South America to southeastern Alaska in the north. The eastern cougar still maintains a limited presence in Florida and other southeastern states. While its present population is difficult to determine, its future is dependent on the preservation of a protected habitat where it may range widely in pursuit of food. The Everglades National Park and other such large southern preserves may be ultimately the Florida panther's last refuge.

Florida is also the home for the endangered key deer, a small subspecies of the Virginia whitetail deer. With bucks ranging in weight from 60 to 110 pounds, with the does smaller, this dwarf deer of the Florida Keys was constantly hunted by the inhabitants of the area. Reduced in numbers during the 20th century, key deer were protected from hunters by a ban passed by the

Florida legislature in 1939. Poaching and the devastations of fire and hurricane continued to reduce their numbers, and by 1949 their population was estimated to be down to 30. After much political debate, conservationists secured the establishment in 1957 of the Key Deer National Wildlife Refuge. This 7,000-acre refuge, which embraces 16 Keys, provides a sanctuary not only for the key deer but also for 11 other endangered or threatened species. The population of the key deer has increased and presently numbers more than 400.

One of the tragedies of a species approaching the brink of extinction is that their population reaches such low numbers that it becomes very difficult to study the natural history of the animal. The southern red wolf faces such a predicament, and the study of the animal is confronted by countless difficulties. Early colonists in the South frequently confronted a distinctive native wolf population. Although called the red wolf, most members of this species had gray-brown, black, or tawny coats, with only a few of them having the distinctive red coat. They were generally larger than a coyote but smaller than their relatives, the gray wolves. The red wolf was perhaps slightly less predatory than the gray wolf, but its natural history was quite similar. Civilization's constant war on carnivores and increased patterns of settlement reduced the red wolves' range and numbers. By the 1920s the red wolf had been eliminated from most regions east of the Mississippi River. Populations of red wolves still existed in the Coastal Prairie of Louisiana and Texas, in eastern Oklahoma, and in the Ozark-Ouachita Highlands of Arkansas. Among these animals, there was interbreeding with coyotes, and consequently the gene pool has been degraded by hybridization. In the mid-1960s the red wolf was placed on the rare and endangered species list. The future for this species lies in the protection of the limited number of nonhybridized members of this gene pool, which still reside in the upper Gulf Coast region of Texas.

The federal government, seeking to address the problems of habitat destruction and alteration as significant factors in the decline of the nation's flora and fauna, has enacted a variety of legislation to help confront these national problems, including the Duck Stamp Act of 1934, the Pittman-Robertson Act, the Dingle-Johnson Act, the Wilderness Act, the Endangered Species Act, the National Environmental Policy Act, and the National Forest Management Act. In the 21st century the flora and fauna of the South will continue to confront human population growth, coastal development, modification of waterways, wetland degradation, ground and water contamination of waterways, and competition with introduced and exotic species.

PHILLIP DRENNON THOMAS
*Wichita State University*

Douglas H. Chadwick and Joel Sartore, *The Company We Keep: America's Endangered Species* (1996); Albert E. Cowdrey, *This Land, This South: An Environmental History* (1983); Robin W. Doughty, *Wildlife and Man in Texas: Environmental Change and Conservation* (1983); David Lowe, John R. Matthews, Charles J. Moseley, and Walton Becham, *The Official World Wildlife Fund Guide to Endangered Species of North America* (1990); Peter Matthiessen, *Wildlife in America* (1959); Arlie W. Schorger, *The Passenger Pigeon: Its Natural History and Extinction* (1973); Bruce A. Stein, Lynn S. Kutner, and Jonathan S Adams, *Precious Heritage: The Status of Biodiversity in the United States* (2000); Stanley A. Temple, ed., *Endangered Birds: Management Techniques for Preserving Threatened Species* (1978); James A. Tober, *Who Owns the Wildlife? The Political Economy of Conservation in Nineteenth-Century America* (1981).

## Energy Use and Development

The energy sources of the South have contributed to the region's and the nation's economic development, but because of the prolific natural resources of the area, it has dominated the domestic energy market for much of U.S. history. Residents and industrialists exploited the region's many rivers and stands of timber, but the vast sources of coal, oil, and natural gas in the South have left an indelible mark on its economy and culture.

Industrialization in the United States through the 19th and early 20th centuries saw waterpower and wood as fuels for the industrial engine. Although individuals and businesses used coal to a limited extent, wood remained important for home use and as an industrial fuel to produce steam power. Before the Civil War, steamboats had gobbled up millions of cords of wood, much of which came from the southern United States. Charcoal also was an important fuel for the coke-making ovens of the early iron industry. Although many parts of the industrialized world had already adopted coal, the United States continued to rely on wood because supplies of timber, especially in the South, were so vast. The country did not begin to use coal more readily until after the Civil War, as the forests dwindled in the East and coal's superiority for industry began to be realized.

Vast coalfields in western Pennsylvania and throughout Appalachia helped make coal a dominant energy source. Even so, coal did not overtake wood as the prime fuel of production until after 1890. The anthracite regions of Pennsylvania could not satisfy the coal appetite of the country. Large bituminous fields running through the Appalachians into Alabama provided energy for the growing industrial economy. The coalfields of the South have huge deposits in West Virginia, eastern Kentucky, middle Tennessee, and Alabama. In the late 19th century mining companies began to exploit those coal resources. An extremely large field near Birmingham, Ala., produced nearly 90,000 tons of coal in 1890 and nearly 150,000 tons in 1900. Such a prolific field helped make Birmingham the leading industrial city of the South. Iron making first utilized anthracite coal, but manufacturers found that the softer bituminous variety of the Appalachians was better for the process. Even with its seemingly unlimited potential as an energy source, king coal found its dominance threatened by competing energy sources, internal competition, and labor unrest. The pressures of the Great Depression combined with labor unrest to almost destroy the Appalachian coal industry.

Oil and natural gas effectively made coal no longer dominant by 1940. However, even with the drop in importance as a natural resource, coal still controlled half of the U.S. energy market. Mining companies increasingly turned to strip-mining techniques through the mid-20th century in order to stay competitive with other sources of energy. By the late 1950s two of every three tons of coal came from strip mines. The environmental damage from underground coal mines is dramatic, but the strip mines have the potential to literally remove the tops of mountains, forever changing the landscape of Appalachia. Southern coal remains an important energy source for the United States.

Oil is currently the most important source of energy in the world, and the historically fertile supplies of petroleum in the South have made the region important on an international scale. The southern oil-producing regions did not experience the same exploitive circumstances as coal-rich Appalachia. In fact, Texas, through the Texas Railroad Commission, experienced dominance in the world market during the mid-20th century that rivaled the present-day Organization of Petroleum Exporting Countries. Continued production in the region has led to offshore petroleum development, vast refining regions, and a productive chemical corridor.

Although small fields had been found in Texas at the trailing edge of the 19th century, the discovery of oil at Spindletop near Beaumont, Tex., in 1901 marked the dramatic entry of the South into the oil business. The boom was on as major oil companies, independent producers, and fevered investors sought to exploit the new fields of east Texas. By 1909 Texas boasted two major oil companies that attempted to compete with Standard Oil. However, the South experienced an even bigger boom in 1930 near Kilgore, Tex. The gusher at Kilgore was one of the largest ever to occur in the world. Even though there was a glut in the oil market, large refiners moved into the area.

East Texas became the major refining region of the United States. By 1939 the navy fueled most of its warships with oil rather than coal. Texas produced most of the oil in the United States and half of the global supply by 1940. World War II saw continued reliance on oil for the country, and the government constructed two major pipelines, Big Inch and Little Inch, running from the East Texas fields to the northeastern United States. Between 1940 and 1970 the Texas Gulf Coast grew to the point where chemical facilities produced 40 percent of the nation's chemical stock. Texas was not alone in the dramatic growth of the refining region. Louisiana developed its petrochemical industry along the Mississippi River, and by the 1950s almost one-quarter of all state tax revenue came from energy producers.

The dramatic growth of the oil industry on the Gulf Coast eventually extended offshore. The Mississippi River throughout the millennia laid a foundation of hydrocarbons underneath the waters of much of the Gulf of Mexico. Aside from the possibility of dramatic petroleum deposits, the waters of the Gulf are relatively calm and shallow. These conditions made the development of offshore technology a reality. The 1930s saw the first forays into the Gulf offshore environment with marginal success. By the late 1940s U.S. consumption of petroleum caused the country to be a net importer of oil. This condition made attempts at oil production in deeper water more economical. Drilling offshore had and still does generally cost several times the amount of money that similar wells cost on land. However, by 1956 the oil industry saw significant returns from offshore adventures and boasted 777 wells with 530 producing oil or natural gas. The energy crises of the 1970s encouraged further developments in deeper Gulf waters. These offshore wells require an incredible support system that makes offshore oil production exponentially important to the southern economy.

A close cousin of oil is natural gas, and with the discoveries of petroleum in the South, natural gas developed as an important energy source for the region. In the early years, oil-field developers often disposed of natural gas through flaring, a method of controlled burning, because many did not understand the product's value. This hindered the recognition of the commodity as an energy source. Another problem with utilizing natural gas was that it was only usable in areas immediately near oil fields. There was no large transportation network to move the product to market. West Virginia attempted to sell natural gas from local fields to some of the more industrial areas of the northeast with mixed success. Energy users were not equipped to deal with natural gas as a fuel to the extent that they were able to handle other sources. New discoveries farther south helped make the commodity more marketable to the country. Southern refineries had used natural gas to fuel part of their processes throughout much of the petroleum bonanza. By the 1940s natural gas from Texas fueled the majority of refineries in the state. Those refineries in turn produced 80 percent of the nation's gasoline.

By the mid-20th century natural gas had become a crucial energy player. Gas transmission companies formed and were able to purchase and convert the World War II pipelines that had carried crude oil during the war and make them natural gas lines. As a result the industry grew rapidly as the country adopted the now more widely available energy source. It had many benefits over coal or oil, specifically for power generation. Natural gas created less pollution and was easier to move and burn than coal. By 1969 power generators used natural gas to generate one-fourth of the nation's electricity. Much of that natural gas came from the hydrocarbon regions of the south, including offshore platforms.

Energy from coal, oil, and natural gas did not fuel all development in the South. As the region became more settled, southern cities began to have the same energy demands as northern cities. Private companies were often not willing to put forth the capital to supply electricity to many areas of the South, even with the region's prolific sources of energy. This resulted in government intervention. One of the most well-known programs was the Tennessee Valley Authority (TVA). The Franklin D. Roosevelt administration started the ambitious TVA in 1933 to accomplish a wide variety of goals, one of which was to generate cheap electricity. The TVA constructed dams on southern rivers to generate power for the growing region. As a caveat to this, the government encouraged southerners within reach of the TVA power grid to use more electricity. Their encouragement eventually caused the power generators to rely on sources of energy other than hydropower, including nuclear energy.

The South grew to utilize dramatic amounts of energy and continues to exercise tremendous control over the energy market. The discovery of energy sources in the region brought more people south, and they in turn consumed more energy. The TVA of 1933 and the Rural Electrification Act of 1936 dramatically affected the lives of many small communities. The 1936 act literally brought many southern farmers into the 20th century. As the region grew, it demanded more energy, and new technologies increased the load. The adoption of air-conditioning throughout much of the South made the area more attractive to the country while increasing the region's energy needs. The automobile, although adopted throughout the country, had a special impact on many cities in the South. Many southern cities experienced their most dramatic growth as the automobile became the dominant mode of transportation. As a result, the region uses much of the petroleum it refines. The region's continued growth requires that more of its resources are reserved for local use.

The South's wealth of natural resources has enabled the region to attract industry and population. However, industrialization combined with the harshness of natural resource exploitation made areas of the South a sacrifice zone in terms of the environment. How the region manages its natural resources in the future will determine the overall health of the economy, the people, and the land.

JOSEPH STROMBERG
*University of Houston*

Edwin L. Brown and Colin J. Davis, eds., *It Is Union and Liberty: Alabama Coal Miners and the UMW* (1999); Christopher J. Castaneda and Joseph A. Pratt, *From Texas to the East: A Strategic History of Texas Eastern Corporation* (1993); William R. Childs, *The Texas Railroad Commission: Understanding Regulation in America to the Mid-Twentieth Century* (2005); Walter L. Creese, *TVA's Public Planning: The Vision, the Reality* (1990); Gerald Markowitz and David Rosner, *Deceit and Denial: The Deadly Politics of Industrial Pollution* (2002); Martin V. Melosi, *Coping with Abundance: Energy and Environment in Industrial America* (1985); Chad Montrie, *To Save the Land and Its People: A History of Opposition to Surface Coal Mining in Appalachia* (2003); Diana Davids Olien and Roger M. Olien, *Oil in Texas: The Gusher Age, 1895–1945* (2002); Joseph A. Pratt, *The Growth of a Refining Region* (1980); Joseph A. Pratt, Tyler Priest, and Christopher J. Castaneda, *Brown and Root and the History of Offshore Oil and Gas* (1997).

## Environmental Justice

Environmental justice activists claim that poor, minority neighborhoods suffer disproportionate burdens of environmental pollution. The reality of environmental injustice has existed throughout American history. Elite white neighborhoods and residents have had access to modern conveniences, higher standards of sanitation, and city services denied to poor blacks both at home and at work. The earliest legal case involving this concept, however, erupted in 1979 through the activism of the African American women in a Houston neighborhood known as Northwood Manor. During the summer of 1977, Southwestern Waste Management Corporation purchased property in northwest Houston and applied for a landfill permit in the area. Part of the resistance by the neighborhood involved filing a lawsuit, *Bean v. Southwestern Waste Management*, which alleged that the landfill violated the African American commu-

*African American church quarantined as a result of hazardous contamination
(David Wharton, photographer)*

nity's civil rights. Residents fervently believed that the corporation had located the landfill in their area because they were black. To substantiate the charge of "environmental racism," the neighborhood hired Robert Bullard, a sociologist at Texas Southern University and husband of the neighborhood's attorney. Bullard and the residents completed substantial research on Houston's history of siting landfills, finding that minority neighborhoods were far more likely to host a landfill, or other waste site, than white neighborhoods. The courts, however, failed to agree with Bullard's assessment, finding numerous holes in his methodology and conclusions. Although the Northwood Manor case failed to stop the landfill, it began Bullard's interest in the issue of environmental racism, a pivotal event since he would become a key player in the movement.

Three years after Northwood Manor, the environmental justice movement began to coalesce from the more local level, characterized by the *Bean* case, to the national front with opposition to a proposed hazardous waste site in Warren County, N.C. Residents of Warren County, a predominantly African American area with several waste disposal sites, protested the location of another such facility in their county. During one of the protests in October 1982, police arrested more than 500 people, including notable politicians and activists. The protest brought substantial national media attention to the issue of environmental racism but failed to stop construction of the site.

The environmental justice movement gained currency through numerous official studies and academic conferences during the 1980s and early 1990s. Two prominent studies that verified many activists' claims included the U.S. General Accounting Office's *The Siting of Hazardous Waste Landfills* (1983), prompted by the Warren County incident, and the United Church of Christ Commission on Racial Justice's *Toxic Waste and Race in the United States* (1987). Both studies concluded that minority neighborhoods saw greater amounts of pollution and more health hazards than white areas. In 1991, in response to growing concern, activists held the First National People of Color Environmental Leadership Summit in Washington, D.C. More than 500 people from across the country adopted the "Principles of Environmental Justice" at the summit. Among other things, these principles "affirm[ed] the sacredness of Mother Earth, ecological unity and the interdependence of all species, and the right to be free from eco-logical destruction . . . and demand[ed] that public policy be based on mutual respect and justice for all peoples, free from any form of discrimination or bias." Activists built on the accomplishments of the 1991 conference with a second in October 2002.

Across the nation, grassroots activism continued after Warren County, often independent of the raging scholastic and official debates. Women of all races and classes have played a pivotal role in many of these struggles. Because of the health threats to children from pollution, women often see their activism as a part of their role in protecting their children and communities. The Mothers of East Los Angeles, for example, a group of Hispanic women in a poverty-stricken area, successfully opposed the construction of several toxic waste sites during the 1980s. Women also form a large part of the opposition to the chemi-cal pollution in Cancer Alley, an area dominated by poor African American communities between Baton Rouge and New Orleans. In addition to these fights for a healthier home and neighborhood, the grassroots environmental justice movement has also focused on workplace pollution and hazards. Poor, minority workers, relegated to the lowest-level and most menial jobs, come into contact with hazardous waste and other pollution far more frequently than elite white workers.

Several national-level groups exist to assist these beleaguered communi-ties in their struggles. One of the most prominent of these is the Center for Health, Environment, and Justice, founded in 1981 by Lois Gibbs. Famous for her activism in relocating her Love Canal community in the early 1980s, Gibbs's organization helps neighborhoods understand the often highly scientific issues they face, develop responses, and empower local leadership. Other organizations, including Bullard's Ejnet.org, also provide information and assistance to activists.

As studies and activism continued, the very definition of the problem grassroots groups faced expanded and developed over time, becoming more inclusive and global. Initially, as seen in the *Bean* case, "environmental justice" existed as "environmental racism." Credited with coining the term, Benjamin Muhammad (formerly Rev. Benjamin Chavis Jr.) defines environmental racism as racial discrimination in environmental policy making. It is racial discrimination in the enforcement of regulations and laws. It is racial discrimination in the deliberate targeting of communities of color for toxic waste disposal and the siting of polluting industries. And it is racial discrimination in the history of excluding people of color from the mainstream environmental groups, decision-making boards, commissions, and regulatory bodies.

The term "environmental racism" underwent significant criticism from other scholars, who debated the primacy of race in environmental hazards. Many scholars felt that poverty played an equal, or perhaps more significant, role in pollution exposure than race. Several academic studies emerged to indicate that the issue of environmental racism was far more complicated than previously thought. Scholar and activist Robert Bullard later adopted a more inclusive definition of environmental racism, specifically to include global and class issues brought to the forefront of the discussion. "Environmental racism," he notes, "refers to any policy, practice or directive that differentially affects or disadvantages (whether intended or unintended) individuals, groups, or communities based on race or color. . . . Environmental racism is not just a domestic practice. It is global. Environmental racism extends to the export of hazardous waste, risky technologies, and pesticides and the application of nonsustainable and exploited development models to the Third World just as it has been targeted toward people of color, working class people, and poor people in this country."

The Environmental Protection Agency later decided to use the more inclusive term "environmental justice," rather than the limited "environmental racism." Environmental justice, the agency stated, was "the fair treatment for people of all races, cultures, and incomes, regarding the development of environmental laws, regulations, and policies." Overall, environmental justice began as a very narrowly defined "environmental racism," specifically aimed at African Americans, and later grew to incorporate hazards borne by all minorities and poverty-stricken populations.

With the increased level of national attention to the issues of environmental justice, President William J. Clinton issued Executive Order 12898 in February 1994. The order, seen as a substantial achievement by the environmental justice movement, demanded that federal agencies "make achieving environmental justice part of [their] mission by identifying and addressing, as appropriate, disproportionately high and adverse human health or environmental effects of its programs, policies, and activities on minority populations and low-income populations in the United States." Activists seeing the order as only a first step continue to work for environmental justice and enforcement of environmental laws at the local, grassroots level by removing polluting industries, landfills, and hazardous waste sites from their communities or preventing their siting in the first place.

ELIZABETH BLUM
*Troy University*

Bunyan Bryant and Paul Mohai, *Race and the Incidence of Environmental Hazards: A Time for Discourse* (1992); Robert D. Bullard, *Dumping in Dixie: Race, Class, and Environmental Quality* (1994), *Unequal Protection: Environmental Justice and Communities of Color* (1994); Melissa Checker, *Polluted Promises: Environmental Racism and the Search for Justice in a Southern Town* (2005); Christopher Foreman, *The Promise and Peril of Environmental Justice* (1998); Andrew Hurley, *Environmental Inequalities: Class, Race, and Industrial Pollution in Gary, Indiana, 1945–1980* (1995).

## Environmental Movements

The South followed, although sometimes tardily, the rest of the nation in its evolution from natural resource conservation to the environmentalism of the 1960s. Cooperative efforts often developed between federal and state governments, but at times various state governments followed federal guidelines only reluctantly. While the South faced conservation problems similar to those throughout the country, its geography, history, and economic and social conditions gave southern conservation activities their own regional characteristics. Just as the environmental movements began to develop in the 1960s, the southern economy lagged. The southern legacy of individualism and resentment of outside authority also affected southern attitudes toward conservation and environmental policy.

Although the Indians were not necessarily the natural ecologists they are often portrayed as being, they were the first humans to begin to change the environment of the South and to learn to live with its characteristics. Early European settlers, less inclined to adapt to the natural environment than the Indian, generally wanted to transform the landscape. England expected its American colonies to produce certain products. In addition to the native tobacco, Europeans introduced other crops such as wheat, silk, indigo, and rice, thus contributing new flora and fauna as well as new diseases to the southern environment.

Even before the American Revolution soil exhaustion caused southern planters to become concerned with soil conservation. Both George Washington and Thomas Jefferson evidenced a concern for soil depletion and its consequences in the Tidewater region. While he advocated soil conservation methods, Jefferson realized that most people would solve their soil fertility problem by simply moving to cheaper lands farther west. In all probability the Moravians represented the first group to treat natural resources in a conservationist manner.

Colonials viewed forests ambivalently, as a nuisance to agriculture to be removed as soon as possible and as a useful product for sale or building use. The English crown made some attempts to regulate cutting of the American forests through the Broad Arrow Policy, but most colonists resented such laws and contended that their freedom to cut forests was a right. In fact, it was a practical reality that conditioned future American attitudes toward use of forest resources. Much of the cut timber was wasted, often burned for clearing; thus by the time of the Revolution southern forests had been much modified.

Early European settlers found an abundance of wildlife in the South. Indians had already depleted some forms of wildlife by indiscriminate killing. The colonials killed either for food or to eliminate predators that interfered with agriculture. While they did not eliminate any species, the colonials' actions often created an ecological imbalance. In England hunting rights had been considered a privilege of the upper class, and attempts to impose restrictions on the colonials created resentment as much as the Corn Laws did in England. As with the cutting of trees, the settlers generally believed they had a right to hunt. Such attitudes have persisted, making the contemporary hunting laws in states such as Texas a patchwork of state and local control.

European settlers and travelers took an early interest in the exotic flora and fauna they found in the southern colonies. Planters like Jefferson and William Byrd II as well as other lesser-known settlers provided important accounts of colonial wildlife, laying the groundwork for further study. William Bartram, a Philadelphia botanist, and the English traveler Mark Catesby provided significant information concerning southern wildlife, although Catesby's writings provided misinformation as well.

Prior to the American Revolution both the crown and the colonial legislatures passed conservation laws. Some colonial laws restricted the slaughter of deer, while others controlled fishing activities. In practice colonials generally ignored conservation laws, but they established the principle, persisting into modern times, that the sovereign had the authority to control game resources.

Between the American Revolution and the Civil War, movement of population across the Appalachian Mountains and into the Mississippi River Valley had a tremendous impact on southern soils, forests, rivers, and wildlife. Rapid expansion of cotton agriculture between 1790 and 1835 exhausted the soil in the more easterly parts of the South. By the 1830s much of the older South needed considerable fertilizer to maintain production, setting in motion a cycle that continues to characterize American agriculture. The use of fertilizer to maintain or increase production resulted in the demand for more, and increasingly expensive, fertilizers. Cutting timber and the destruction of natural ground cover combined with the clean field and row crop cultivation of cotton, corn, and tobacco to accelerate soil erosion. A few advocates of agricultural reform, such as Edmund Ruffin, urged the use of contour plowing and cheaper natural fertilizers. With a seemingly endless abundance of cheap land farther west, few southern farmers heeded the advice of these prophets.

Both national and state governments attempted to control destruction of forests before 1860. The national government reserved certain trees for naval use, like the Live Oak preserves of Grover Island, Ga., and the Santa Rosa Peninsula in Florida, while most southern states prohibited burning of trees because of the danger to other property. Only the settlers' capacity to use and sell wood limited the continued exploitation of southern forest resources in the antebellum period.

In the postrevolutionary era, naturalists, particularly John James Audubon, focused attention on the South. Ignoring the development of conservation for aesthetic reasons, and often taking abundance for granted, they were extremely important in providing scientific understanding of southern flora and fauna. Also important to the use of southern resources in the postrevolutionary period was concern for improving navigation and controlling floods on the rivers of the South. Because most southern rivers provided an unreliable means of transportation, local, state, and national governments attempted to transform rivers to make them more navigable. The South's greatest river, the Mississippi, proved both a blessing and a threat. While providing fertile land and an avenue for much southern commerce, it often brought devastating floods. Settlers attempted to hold back the river's rampages with levees. Constriction of the river forced its floodwaters to rise higher, requiring further heightening of the levees. Both federal and state governments attempted to improve navigation and to control floods on the Mississippi. Studies and recommendations made prior to the Civil War long influenced government policy toward the Mississippi and its tributaries.

So far as wetlands were concerned, neither antebellum southerners nor other Americans had any understanding of their ecological value, generally regarding them as a nuisance. In 1849 and 1850 the national government turned much of the wetlands over to state control for reclamation through drainage. Although exploitation characterized the general southern (and American) approach to resource use, a small population and limited industrial development moderated the degree of this exploitation prior to the Civil War.

After the Civil War the development of technology created an opportunity for almost unlimited exploitation of southern natural resources. Northern industrialists, Europeans, and some southerners saw in these resources opportunities for quick wealth. Both federal and state governments encouraged railroad construction through land grants. Much of the most valuable publicly owned timber and mineral lands in the South passed to private ownership between 1865 and 1900.

Although southerners played some role in calling for wiser use of natural resources, the impetus for conservation, like much of the force for exploitation, came from outside the South. In particular, government scientists occupied a prominent position in the early conservation movement. They helped establish national parks, forest reserves, and other important programs for natural resource management. Outside leadership focused on conservation of southern resources as part of a larger movement throughout the nation. While contributing some leaders in the struggle, the South more often provided the battleground for conservation controversies.

Agriculture and the extractive industries took the greatest toll on southern resources, ravaging soil, timber, and wildlife. Increased cotton production, fostered by the tenant system, encouraged a single crop economy greater in extent than prior to the Civil War. The use of fertilizers, promoted by agricultural reformers, helped maintain production in the face of a decline in natural soil fertility. A midwesterner who moved to Louisiana in the 1870s made one of the most significant contributions to southern agricultural reform. In 1903, at Terrell, Tex., Seaman A. Knapp introduced the demonstration farm as a means of agricultural education, a concept that became federal law with establishment of the Agricultural Extension Program. The spread of the boll weevil across the South demonstrated problems associated with a cotton monoculture, although little was effectively done about the threat prior to 1900.

The exploitation and conservation of southern forests during the Gilded Age followed an erratic course. Reconstruction government had restricted sale of public lands in the South. With Redemption, southern Democrats supported laws promoting the sale of such land, which included much forested land, although by 1889 southern members of Congress led a campaign to keep the few remaining areas under governmental control. During the period of sale large tracts of southern timber passed to speculators and lumbermen, especially nonsoutherners, most of whom considered timber a commodity and little understood its relationship to the rest of the environment. Although lumbermen attempted reforestation, in 1873 a committee established by the American Association for the Advancement of Science encouraged federal and state governments to pass laws protecting forests and promoting timber cultivation. Gradually, support grew for development of national and state forest reserves.

The development of scientific forestry began at Yale University, but the first practical demonstration of its principles occurred, serendipitously, in North Carolina. George W. Vanderbilt hired the young forester Gifford Pinchot to manage the forest reserves of his Biltmore estate. In 1898 the Biltmore Forest School opened. The South's oldest forestry school in continuous existence was established at the University of Georgia in 1906. Although Pinchot's activities at Biltmore influenced other areas of the South, he was not alone in his concern for southern forest resources. The Mississippi politician L. Q. C. Lamar, in his position as secretary of the interior, supported President Grover Cleveland's call for forest reserves. All these attempts to protect and manage southern forests, however, clashed with the strong American traditions of quick profits and individualism as well as the southern suspicion of outside interference.

The commercial development of agriculture and forestry along with the fashion trade's desire for fur and feathers sped depletion of southern wildlife. The passenger pigeon and the Carolina parakeet disappeared completely, while other species experienced rapid decline. State laws designed to protect favored species such as fish were partially enforced, if at all. One historian claimed that the imposition of game and hunting laws in the South stemmed partially from the determination of southern whites to maintain control of blacks after Reconstruction. Many blacks had supplied some of the food for their families by hunting on unfenced public and private land, so hunting restrictions made the blacks more dependent on white landowners for their employment. Throughout the Gilded Age the American Ornithologists Union joined with the Audubon Society to promote passage of model laws listing game birds and protecting nongame species. Although these attempts were often ineffective, their proposal represented a changing attitude among scientists and some sportsmen concerning feathered wildlife. Passage by Congress of the Lacey Act in 1900 spurred more effective state regulation of commercial hunting.

Water projects, both reclamation and flood control, became prominent during the Gilded Age. Southern interest in water projects centered generally on attempts to control floods on the Mississippi River or to improve navigation on southern streams. Responding to a proposal by Louisiana congressman Randall L. Gibson, President Rutherford B. Hayes signed a bill establishing the Mississippi River Commission (MRC) in 1879—the first time the federal government had agreed to help control floods on an American river. Throughout the Gilded Age both the MRC and government policy makers debated the best technology for controlling floods on the mighty river, as well as the constitutionality of federal aid for flood control. Southern support helped establish the precedent for active federal participation in flood control activities. Ironically, by adopting a "levees only" approach the MRC actually aggravated flooding on the river. Levees constricted the river, forcing floods to rise higher and bringing extensive damage to property in the floodplain.

The period from 1900 to 1930 saw the development of embryonic conservation movements in the South that promised to halt the exploitation of southern resources. Many factors, ranging from the boll weevil pestilence to the influence of agricultural experiment stations, moved southern farmers toward more scientific and modern agricultural methods. Even southern youth were recruited into the movement through the creation of corn clubs, which eventually became the 4-H Club. In many ways the South responded positively to the Progressive conservation movement. Rational development of natural resources coincided with the New South emphasis on economic development, whether it be forest cultivation, river basin planning, or wildlife management. The passage of the Weeks Act in 1911 and the Clarke-McNary Act in 1924 laid the foundation for the establishment of national forests and scientific forestry in the South on "the lands nobody wanted." Following the lead of Theodore Roosevelt, many southern governments began to focus more attention on conservation matters, yet there was still much resistance to centralized control over resources, whether from the state or national government. Forest conservation was most often embraced by larger corporations concerned with sustained yield. By the 1920s support for scientific forestry had become widespread throughout the South with establishment of several forestry programs in regional colleges and universities and the famous Yale forestry camp at Crossett, Ark. Concern for wildlife conservation and management grew among certain groups in the South, often with guidance from the Audubon Society. Although more southern states passed game control laws after 1900, enforcement still proved difficult.

Economic developments of the 1920s both challenged and encouraged the southern conservation movements. Settlement in Florida during the 1920s led to attempts to drain swamps, including the Everglades and the Okefenokee Swamp. Looked upon as progressive, such drainage often created long-range problems similar to those associated with use of levees for flood control. Discovery of oil in Texas in 1901 ushered in a new era of opportunity and conservation problems; prior to World War II most efforts to conserve oil were prompted by wise use, rather than pollution concerns. Perhaps no idea so attracted those concerned with southern economic development as did river basin planning. By 1925 the principle of comprehensive river basin development had been embodied in federal law, as demands for new approaches to flood control on the Mississippi gained support. Senator George Norris attracted increased southern support for his plans to transform the Tennessee Valley through scientific planning.

The New Deal had a profound effect on southern conservation and development policy. This effect was nowhere more evident than in the implementation of water projects in the Mississippi and Tennessee valleys. The Corps of Engineers began the impressive Atchafalaya Floodway project to help relieve floods on the lower Mississippi. Engineers were soon to learn that nature had ways of pursuing its goals despite human activities. Some scientists predicted that despite money and human effort the Mississippi would eventually change its main channel to the Atchafalaya, leaving New Orleans on a backwater tributary. In no way, however, did the New Deal touch southern resources and influence conservation ideas as it did with establishment of the Tennessee Valley Authority.

New Deal policies influenced southern policies concerning forest and wildlife conservation as well. Most noted of these influences were the reforestation programs carried out by the Civilian Conservation Corps. The federal practice of purchasing cutover and eroded land for development of parks and national forests was emulated by many states. The New Deal also focused attention on the need for soil conservation, important to a region that had some of the most exhausted and eroded soil in the nation. Above all, conservation activities during the New Deal created a greater understanding of the interrelated nature of natural resource use and preservation. The experiences of World War II altered the attitude of many southerners toward conservation. Private organizations, universities, and public bureaus cooperated to provide more effective development of southern resources. Tree farming combined with improved fire prevention methods laid the basis for a sustained yield of southern timber. Critics questioned the wisdom of a timber monoculture, and while cotton remained a significant part of farm production, a revolution occurred in southern agriculture. New crops such as soybeans, improved fertilizers and farming techniques, and the use of insecticides all profoundly affected the nature of southern farming. As with the changes in timber cultivation certain groups began to question whether these changes were environmentally beneficial.

From 1960 to 1970 Roosevelt-Pinchot concepts of utilitarian conservation gave way to ideas stressing environmental quality. Again the South followed the national trends, not always enthusiastically. The National Environmental Protection Act (1969) was most important in promoting environmental activity at the state level both through its general philosophy and through its direct application in the South. Most southern states began to develop plans to protect public lands and supervise the use of natural resources, often consciously to avoid federal intervention. In addition, some of the first federal actions to enforce environmental protection laws were taken in the South. In 1971, under the Clean Air Act, the federal government obtained its first restraining order for environmental enforcement to control air pollution in Birmingham, Ala. Bringing about a complete, if temporary, stoppage of steel manufacturing in Birmingham, the national government demonstrated the potential power it could exercise to achieve environmental improvement.

Since 1960 local environmental groups in the South have independently or in cooperation with national organizations attempted to influence environmental policy within the southern states. Efforts were made to protect the biologically unique Big Thicket of Texas and to prevent development of expensive and environmentally questionable water projects.

While most southerners continue to consider economic growth more important than environmental protection, some groups increasingly insist that the South's water supply, air quality, coastal areas, and general environment have to be considered as part of the Sunbelt movement. Given the South's advantages for economic growth, such as labor and land costs, taxes, and climate, southerners need no longer fear that industry could be attracted only at the cost of a livable environment.

J. B. SMALLWOOD
*North Texas State University*

ROBERT L. IZLAR
*Warnell School of Forest Resources*
*University of Georgia*

Nelson M. Blake, *Land into Water—Water into Land: A History of Water Management in Florida* (1980); Thomas D. Clark, *Mississippi Quarterly* (Spring 1972); Albert E. Cowdrey, *This Land, This South: An Environmental History* (1983); Samuel T. Dana and Sally K. Fairfax, *Forest and Range Policy: Its Development in the United States*

(1980); Robert L. Dorman, *A Word for Nature: Four Pioneering Environmental Advocates, 1845–1913* (1998); Gilbert C. Fite, *Agricultural History* (January 1979); Paul W. Gates, *Agricultural History* (January 1979); Jack Temple Kirby, *Mockingbird Song: Ecological Landscapes of the South* (2006); Martin Reuss, *Louisiana History* (Spring 1982); Stanley W. Trimble, *Man-Induced Soil Erosion on the Southern Piedmont, 1700–1970* (1974).

## Flood Control and Drainage

Although most sections of the United States have had to cope with floods, these problems have assumed extraordinary magnitude in two regions of the South: the lower Mississippi River Valley and the Florida peninsula.

The Mississippi River both blesses and curses lower valley residents. Bearing its tremendous burden of water, the river has built up a delta of rich alluvial soil ideal for agriculture, but at times it has also overflowed its banks and taken a tragic toll in lives, homes, and property. Recognizing its threat, the founders of New Orleans ordered a protective embankment to be built. As early as 1727 Governor Étienne de Perier reported construction of an earthen wall a mile long and 18 feet wide. Thus began the type of flood control on which valley residents would have to depend for the next 200 years. Appropriately, *levée*, the French word for such an earthen embankment, passed into the American language.

From 1718 to 1850 most of the burden of flood control was carried by individual owners of riverfront property. The French government required each owner to build and maintain a levee as a condition of his grant; the government intervened only to enforce the requirement and occasionally to inspect the levees. The system established by the French continued after the United States purchased the territory. This early policy resulted in the extension of levees along both banks of the Mississippi as far as they were settled. But the levees provided a frail defense. With one man's levees poorly joined to the next and differing in size and condition, the raging river would frequently break through.

A great flood in 1844 strengthened a growing demand for federal help. Arguing that the destructive waters originated in remote parts of the Union, proponents urged Congress to appropriate funds for building levees just as it provided aid for oceanic commerce. Although strict constructionists opposed any such expenditure, Congress did find a way to provide indirect assistance. In 1849 it transferred to the state of Louisiana all unsold public swampland within its borders; in 1850 it made a similar grant to Arkansas on condition that the state apply the proceeds to reclaiming the land by means of levees and drains.

The provisions of the 1850 act were extended to each state where swamp and overflowed land might be situated. Fifteen states received grants totaling almost 64 million acres. The South acquired almost two-thirds of this land: Florida, 20.2 million acres; Louisiana, 9.3 million acres; Arkansas, 7.6 million acres; Mississippi, 2.2 million acres; and Alabama, 0.4 million acres.

The swampland grants resulted in much state and local governmental activity, representing a second period of flood control efforts. Florida's huge share encouraged schemes for draining the Everglades, but reversals of policy, diversions of land to the railroads, and the disruption caused by the Civil War delayed any effective reclamation. The lower Mississippi Valley states made a stronger effort to use the swamplands for the specified purpose. State and local agencies initiated works to prevent floods and provide drainage, but poor management, unsound projects, local jealousies, and fiscal chicanery handicapped the movement. Most of the new structures were swept away by floods in 1858 and 1859, and the whole levee system was devastated by military action and neglect during the Civil War.

A third period marked by renewed state activity and a cautious infusion of federal aid began in 1879 when Congress established the Mississippi River Commission to supervise all federal public works on the river. At first these projects were intended for the benefit of navigation, but the Army Corps of Engineers found indirect ways to help with the flood problem. As early as 1861 Captain Andrew Humphreys and Lieutenant Henry Abbot published an influential report, *Physics and Hydraulics of the Mississippi River*, which analyzed the inadequacies of existing levees. In planning later works for improving navigation, the Army Corps began to design levees that would also protect against floods. Local levee districts still bore the major burden, but the commission served a vital coordinating function. By 1912 the combined efforts of state, local, and federal agencies had extended the levees along the Mississippi and its tributaries for 1,500 miles—the length of the Great Wall of China.

In Florida the ancient dream of draining the Everglades was revived by Hamilton Disston, heir to a Philadelphia toolmaker's fortune, who in 1881 contracted with the state to reclaim a vast area overflowed by Lake Okeechobee and nearby lakes and rivers. Disston was to receive half of the drained land. Despite a major effort, the enterprise failed. In 1906 the state itself began to build a system of canals to lower the level of Lake Okeechobee and reclaim Everglades land. Modestly successful in opening new regions for agriculture and residence, the program put the state so deeply in debt that it had to be halted during the Great Depression.

The latest period of flood control began about 1928, with the federal government accepting major responsibility. Great floods in 1912, 1922, and 1927 demonstrated the inadequacy of the Mississippi levees. The 1927 flood, the most catastrophic of all, inundated 26,000 square miles of land, took 214 lives, drove 637,000 people from their homes, and ruined $236 million worth of property. Poet William Alexander Percy chronicled it in *Lanterns on the Levee* (1941). Events elsewhere emphasized that the problem had become a national one. In 1926 and 1928 hurricanes drove the waters of Lake Okeechobee through frail local levees and took more than 2,000 lives. California and New England both suffered serious floods, strengthening the call for federal government assistance.

At the request of Congress the Army Corps of Engineers began to study the flood problem on a national basis. In 1928 Lieutenant General Edgar Jadwin, Chief of the Corps, laid out a $300 million program for the Mississippi and its tributaries. In addition to stronger levees, Jadwin advised deepening river channels, establishing floodways, and studying the feasibility of storage reservoirs. In the so-called 308 reports the corps provided studies of more than 200 other rivers, showing how they might be managed to serve multiple purposes—flood control, navigation, irrigation, and power generation.

Congress accepted the federal responsibility in a series of laws. The Reid-Jones Act of 1928 authorized the corps to proceed with the Jadwin Plan. A 1930 law provided for the construction of Hoover Dike, an 85-mile-long levee around Lake Okeechobee. In 1933 the Tennessee Valley Authority was established with a mandate to build multipurpose dams. The movement culminated in the Flood Control Act of 1936, affirming that flood control was "a proper activity of the Federal Government" and "in the interest of the general welfare." Some 2,111 projects spread over 31 states were approved.

These historic laws, extended by later ones, have resulted in a huge federal flood control program. The Mississippi levees have been strengthened with revetments of cement and steel. To speed the passage of the water, the channel has been deepened and made 152 miles shorter by cutoffs across the bends. Floodways have been provided to release surplus water in times of emergency. Dams across the Yazoo River and other tributaries provide storage reservoirs and "green tree" reservoirs for wildlife management. While these improvements have helped, catastrophic events show remaining vulnerabilities, as when Hurricane Katrina in 2005 caused the levees around New Orleans to fail. The federal government has also spent large sums in Florida. In 1948 Congress authorized the Central and Southern Florida Flood Control Project, a complex system of water management to benefit a large area both north and south of

Lake Okeechobee. The idea of a Cross-Florida Barge Canal connecting the Gulf of Mexico and the Atlantic Ocean surfaced around 1935 and was again actively promoted in the late 1960s.

Despite general acceptance of the value of flood control, this interference with nature often involved environmental damage. For example, canalizing the Kissimmee River, the principal source of Lake Okeechobee, has helped to create a serious pollution problem in the lake itself. In other places, regulating development on the floodplain might have been wiser than building dams or altering river courses, as evidenced by the tragic 1980 Pearl River Easter flood in Jackson, Miss., or the 1994 floods in Georgia. Federal budgetary problems may compel a more careful scrutiny of future proposals.

Pare Lorentz's 1937 film *The River*, which was made for the Farm Security Administration, was a striking visual portrait of the Mississippi River, its valleys and tributaries, and its exploitation and pollution, and of flood control by levee building along its banks and through reforestation efforts. The vivid memory of southern flooding survives in music through blues songs such as Blind Lemon Jefferson's "Risin' High Water Blues" (1927), Sippie Wallace's "The Flood Blues" (1927), Joe Pullum's "Mississippi Heavy Water Blues" (1935), and Alabama Sam's "Red Cross Blues" (1933). "How high's the water, man?" sang Johnny Cash. "Six feet high and risin.'"

NELSON M. BLAKE
*Syracuse University*

ROBERT L. IZLAR
*Warnell School of Forest Resources*
*University of Georgia*

John M. Barry, *Rising Tide: The Great Mississippi Flood of 1927 and How It Changed America* (1997); Nelson M. Blake, *Land into Water—Water into Land: A History of Water Management in Florida* (1980); Chris Bolgiano, *The Appalachian Forest: A Search for Roots and Renewal* (1998); Hodding Carter, *Man and the River: The Mississippi* (1970); Craig E. Colten, *An Unnatural Metropolis: Wresting New Orleans from Nature* (2004); Pete Daniel, *Deep'n as It Come: The 1927 Mississippi River Flood* (1977); Robert W. Harrison, *Alluvial Empire: A Study of State and Local Efforts toward Land Development in the Alluvial Valley of the Lower Mississippi River* (1961); William G. Hoyt and Walter B. Langbein, *Floods* (1955); Luna B. Leopold and Thomas Maddock Jr., *The Flood Control Controversy: Big Dams, Little Dams, and Land Management* (1954); Gary B. Mills, *Of Men and Rivers: The Story of the Vicksburg District* (1978).

## Forests

The history of the South's forests is one of decline, destruction, and recovery. Though human manipulation of the forests had begun centuries before European settlers arrived, the forest's destruction since the mid-1800s has had a far greater impact on the land than the activity of the preceding 10,000 years. When the lumber industry moved into the region in the 1880s, the large-scale harvesting of trees radically altered entire ecosystems, bringing some to the edge of obliteration. By 1938 the combination of logging and timber removal for homes, crops, and pasture eliminated one-third of the South's estimated original forested area of 354 million acres. Since then, management practices and changing societal attitudes have aided in forest recovery.

The Forest Inventory and Analysis, a U.S. Department of Agriculture Forest Service research program that periodically conducts a forest inventory for each state, recognizes five broad categories of forest types in the South: upland hardwoods (including oak-hickory and beech-birch-maple), lowland hardwoods (including oak-gum-cypress), natural pines (including longleaf, slash, shortleaf, and loblolly not established by planting), planted pines (all species), and mixed oak-pine. The hardwoods, used in furniture manufacture and for charcoal, occupy much of the southern Appalachians, bottomlands and floodplains, and riverine environments throughout the Piedmont. Longleaf and slash pine are found along the Coastal Plain, and loblolly and shortleaf across the Piedmont and within interior highlands. Longleaf, the backbone of the southern lumber industry, was the primary sawtimber species; slash, along with the longleaf, was the source for naval stores; and loblolly and shortleaf were secondary sawtimber sources and, since the 1930s, used for pulp.

With more than 5 million private owners controlling 89 percent of southern forests, diverse landowner interests and objectives have long influenced forest area and conditions. Upland hardwoods increased somewhat between 1953 and 1999. Lowland hardwood areas declined somewhat between 1962 and 1970 but have been essentially stable since the 1970s. Pine forest types, though, have experienced the most change. The area of natural pine declined from about 72 million acres in 1953 to about 33 million acres in 1999. Planted pine increased from about 2 million acres in 1953 to more than 30 million acres in 1999.

Native Americans first cleared the land for cultivation and then maintained it as a prairie or a savanna by burning. Natural events, such as storms, insects, and diseases, also altered the southern forests. When Europeans arrived, the landscape of the Southeast was an assortment of open pine and hardwood woodlands, prairies, meadows, and oak or pine savannas in a variety of successional forest stages. As Native American populations were driven from the land, the

5773 I Pine for Thee at Gulfport, Miss.

*This looks as lonely as I sometimes feel.—*

Pine trees, Mississippi coast, postcard, date unknown (Ann Rayburn Paper Americana
Collection, Archives and Special Collections University of Mississippi Library, Oxford)

open spaces they left behind reverted to the dense forests later mythologized by European and American writers. Early settlers viewed forests as impediments to be removed, and they quickly accelerated Indian practices of slash-and-burn agriculture. They planted tobacco, corn, and cotton; but those crops soon depleted the soil of nutrients, and settlers pushed westward in search of more fertile land. Agricultural land clearing across the Piedmont was completed by the time of the Civil War, although pockets of forest remained in undesirable areas.

The Reconstruction era was as much about rebuilding the nation politically as it was about building the nation's infrastructure. That infrastructure was made predominantly of wood. Having exhausted timber supplies in the Northeast and Great Lake states during Reconstruction, industrial logging moved into the South. Southern timber made possible the expansion of the railroads, telegraph lines, and plank roads and the rapid growth of new midwestern cities, along with the rebuilding of southern cities. By the 1880s, sawmills had become the dominant industry in the southern economy.

Yet the greatest impact on southern forests was yet to come. Between 1890 and 1920 production of lumber in the South rose from 1.6 billion board feet in 1880 to 15.4 billion board feet in 1920, peaking in 1909. The South was producing 37 percent of all the lumber of the United States. The original woodland area had dropped by nearly 50 percent, from nearly 354 million acres to 178 million acres by 1919, leaving only 39 million acres of virgin, or "first," forest. A mere ten years later, the first forest had been nearly exhausted.

Despite the destructive method of clear-cutting the land, the southern forest should have regenerated. Instead, the forests failed to do so for several reasons: overharvesting of timber; lack of reforestation effort; destruction of naturally regenerated and standing timber through wildfire and then, later, oversuppression of fire; losses to agriculture and development; and erosion. Wildlife populations dropped precipitously for many of the same reasons.

But industrial logging in the South coincided with the conservation reforms of the Progressive era. The introduction of forest conservation and professional forestry led to the formation of the second forest. Foresters at the Biltmore Estate in North Carolina scientifically managed its vast holdings and established the nation's first forestry school in 1898. The Weeks Act (1911) allowed for the acquisition of land for national forests. The U.S. Forest Service immediately had an impact and greatly expanded its influence through cooperative programs with state forestry bureaus, which largely sprang into existence after passage of the Clarke-McNary Act (1924). During the 1930s, as tax-delinquent land accumulated and the Franklin D. Roosevelt administration pushed major conservation programs, the federal government quadrupled its holdings. The Forest Service also created forestry research and demonstration sites throughout the South and reintroduced fire via the technique of prescribed burning—one of the South's great contributions to land management in the United States.

Prior to the 1930s, private landowners and the timber industry had little monetary incentive to undertake forest renewal and management. The development of a pulp industry based on the southern pines during the 1930s changed all that. Eventually, the South would produce half the pulp and a third of the paper in the United States. The migration of wood-based industries to the region and the increasing value for southern wood led many private landholders and the forest industry to embrace forest renewal and management practices on a widespread basis. Pine plantations for pulp production became big business and brought much-desired industry to the region by the outbreak of World War II. In 1941 the Forest Farmers Association was created as a southern counterpart to the Tree Farm movement founded in the Northwest.

The unprecedented demands for lumber during the war and immediate post-war construction boom periods; mechanization of fire control, tree planting, and timber harvesting; rising values for timber; and favorable tax treatment spurred further economic growth and development in the region and within the southern forest products industry. Consequently, the mid-20th century saw the demise of much of the second forest and the emergence of the third forest.

The third forest quickly became a mosaic of forest types, ages, and management objectives. Significant progress in wildlife conservation and a growing interest in outdoor recreation and the environment in general led to new and different demands on both private and public land. At the same time, technological improvements throughout the forest industry meant that wood was being used more efficiently and reduced pressure on land use. Cooperative forestry assistance given to private, nonindustrial landowners since 1951 helped perpetuate and enhance not only timber but also wildlife, soil, water, air, recreation, urban forests, and threatened and endangered species. The environmental movement of the 1960s and the societal demands for environmental protection resulted in the adoption of a broad range of new management objectives on federal as well as state and private lands.

Emulating the U.S. Forest Service model, land managers altered their objectives from that of forest rehabilitation to sustained yield, multiple-use management in the 1960s and 1970s, and to ecosystem management in the 1980s. Federal forest resource programs that had been based on the need for a future timber supply, in particular pine, now had to take into account all activity in and users of the forest. The Endangered Species Act, Water Quality Act, National Environmental Policy Act, and concern for global warming further influenced management policies and objectives.

Much of the long-term decline in natural pine and lowland hardwood stands can be attributed to diversions to agriculture and urbanization. Along with pine plantations, reforestation efforts in the 1970s and 1980s began to include more hardwood in the stand composition. New markets for hardwoods encouraged further efforts. The Conservation Reserve Program, established in the 1980s to alleviate strains on the federal farm price support system, has been used to retire marginally and highly erodible farmland into forestland and/or wildlife habitat, helping to offset land being lost to agriculture and urbanization. These new pine and hardwood stands mark the beginning of the fourth forest.

The fourth forest faces unique challenges. Urban uses, though currently a small share of land in the South, are expanding rapidly. Forecast models predict that about 12 million acres of southern forests will be urbanized between 1992 and 2020. Between 2020 and 2040, forecasters predict 19 million acres of forest will be developed. Conversions of agricultural land to forest in the west are expected to offset losses of forests to urban uses in the eastern part of the region, resulting in an overall westward shift in forest area as well as changes in shares of forest types. In addition, population growth in rural areas portends the further fragmenting of remnant forests. The fragmentation of forests in turn means increasing limitations on forest management options, such as prescribed burning, that are necessary to maintain productive and healthy forests. Like its predecessors, the fourth forest will be shaped by the competing interests of its many users and dependents but will differ because it will be subjected to greater scientific and social scrutiny than ever before.

JAMES G. LEWIS
*Forest History Society*

Don Burdette, *Alabama's Treasured Forests* (Fall 1995, Winter 1996, Spring 1996, Summer 1996); Thomas D. Clark, *The Greening of the South: The Recovery of Land and Forest* (1984); David N. Wear and John G. Greis, eds., *Southern Forest Resource Assessment: Technical Report* (2002), *Southern Forest Resource Assessment: Summary Report* (2002); Michael Williams, *Americans and Their Forests: A Historical Geography* (1989).

## Gardens and Gardening

The South has long been noted for beautiful antebellum homes with lovely gardens, spacious lawns, majestic large trees, and masses of flowering shrubs. With many attractive native and introduced plants to use in landscaping and one or more botanical or public display gardens in nearly every southern state offering workshops, the southern gardening tradition continues.

A large proportion of the ornamental plants used throughout the southern states are broadleaf evergreens. These are far more predominant than the deciduous plants or the narrow-leaved evergreens such as junipers and dwarf hemlock pines. Once southern gardens consisted primarily of the magnolia (the handsome, large, evergreen, southern magnolia), camellias, azaleas, boxwood, gardenias, groundcovers of English ivy, liriope, crape myrtle, and daylilies for summer color. This is now changing as gardeners use exciting deciduous and evergreen plants such as elaeagnus, hollies, hydrangeas, flowering quince, and viburnums. Interest in native plants such as native azaleas and many herbacious plants has also increased; some of these are grown by specialty nurseries.

The *Camellia japonica* was introduced to Europe from Asia in the 18th century. An old but popular variety, Alba Plena, was displayed in Belgium in 1811 and arrived in the northeastern United States in 1880. Throughout the Northeast camellias were grown as tub plants for the greenhouse or conservatories and are still popular for this use. Large collections of camellias were a part of plantation life near port cities in South Carolina, Alabama, Louisiana, and Mississippi. In the late 1840s camellias were planted at Magnolia Gardens near Charleston, S.C. The first plants probably came from greenhouses in Philadelphia and other northern cities. Later they were imported directly from Europe. The glossy-foliaged camellias range from large shrubs to small trees and are grown in shaded gardens from North Carolina southward to eastern Texas. The large flowers bloom from October to April and vary from white to pink to red or variegated. The American Camellia Society offices are surrounded by a large camellia garden and greenhouse near Marshallville, Ga. The *Camellia sasanqua*, which flowers in autumn, is also important to the landscape. Despite popular legend, the plant is not as cold-hardy as *C. japonica*, yet the colorful single to double flowers often suffer little if any fall damage, unlike some of the later-flowering *C. japonica*.

Azalea gardens are a spectacular feature of the southern landscape. The large-flowered, evergreen Southern Indian hybrid azaleas were first introduced from Europe to the United States as Belgian Indian hybrids. The hybrids were developed in England and Belgium as greenhouse plants from several species native to Japan and China. Like camellias, they were used as tub plants in greenhouses and conservatories in the northeastern states before figuring as landscape plants in the South. In the 1840s they were introduced to Magnolia Gardens and proved to be hardy to the Deep South; they were soon popular throughout the Gulf Coast area. The hardier Belgian Indian hybrids in the South became known as the Southern Indian hybrids. The famous Fruitland Nursery in Augusta, Ga., played an important role in introducing azaleas, camellias, and many other ornamental plants to the South. A catalog of 1883 listed more than 50 varieties of azaleas; unfortunately, many of these old varieties are no longer available.

Southern cities such as Mobile, Savannah, and Charleston are famous for their azalea trails, roadside plantings, and special gardens lined with huge, colorful masses of such Southern Indian azaleas as the purplish-red Formosa, the Fielder's White, and the pink Pride of Mobile.

The small-flowering Kurume azaleas were known in Japan over 300 years ago and were introduced to the United States in 1915. Their hardy plants survive in −5 to −10°F as far north as Kentucky and Maryland. More than 300 varieties of the Kurume azalea are still known in Japan, and some gardens in the South have 50 or more named varieties. Over 20 Kurume azaleas are commonly grown in commercial specialty nurseries. Many of these plants were given English names after their introduction from Japan. Some of the favorites are Christmas Cheer (Imashojo), Hino (Hino de-giri), Pink Pearl (Asumakagami), Coral Bells (Kirins), Snow, and Salmon Beauty.

Other evergreen or persistent-leaved azaleas are noted in the South for flowering from early spring to May and June. These include the Glenn Dale hybrids (over 400 named varieties), the Back Acres hybrids (over 50 named varieties), and the late-flowering Satsuki hybrids, with more than 600 varieties grown in the United States. The interest in growing and hybridizing new azaleas continues throughout the South, and seven chapters affiliated with the American Rhododendron Society and/or the Azalea Society of America exist in the southern states.

The South is also known for its attractive evergreen boxwood hedges and large, compact specimen plants. Two species are frequently discovered in southern gardens. *Boxus sempervirens*, the common box, was introduced from Europe and is especially popular in the South. There are many selected varieties, however. *Suffruticosa* is a popular dwarf plant known as the "true dwarf box" and is prominent in the gardens of Williamsburg and Mount Vernon. *Boxus microphylla*, from Japan, is much hardier and lower in growth and is fond of the warmer areas of the Gulf states.

The handsome *Magnolia grandiflora*, or southern magnolia, is typical of the South and native from North Carolina to Texas. A large tree (to 100 feet) with glossy evergreen leaves six to eight inches long, its oversize white flowers are borne in mid- to late spring and add a delicate fragrance to the garden.

Other broadleaf evergreens noted in southern gardens include the fragrant gardenia, tea olive, and elaeagnus. Numerous hollies are used, such as the common American holly (*Ilex opaca*), the popular *Ilex cornuta Burfordii* holly, and Japanese hollies (*Ilex crenata*). Other common broadleaf evergreens include mountain laurel, cherry laurel, leucothe, and osmanthus. Of the many deciduous ornamental plants in the South the crape myrtle is the best known. The crape myrtle (*Lagerstroemia indica*) is a large shrub or small tree known as the "lilac of the South." It is noted for its smooth, strong trunk formation and is frequently used as a street tree. The large, pyramidal clusters of white, pink, red, or purple flowers appear in early to late summer. Many named varieties are available, and two favorites are Watermelon Red and Near East, a pale pink.

Other deciduous ornamental shrubs and small trees include the flowering quince or "japonica" (*Chaenomeles speciosa* [*lagenaria*]), pearl bush (*Exochorda racemosa*), hydrangeas, Bradford pear, redbud (*Cercis canadensis*), and native flowering dogwood (*Cornus florida*) and its many colorful varieties.

Two outstanding native shrubs are the oakleaf hydrangea and the many species of native azaleas often referred to as "wild honeysuckle." The fragrant native azaleas include the white to pink forms of rhododendron *R. canescens* (Piedmont azalea), *R. periclymenoides* (*nudiflorum*) (pinxterbloom azalea), and *R. alabamense* (Alabama azalea); the pink *R. vaseyi* (pinkshell azalea); the white *R. arborescens* (sweet azalea) and *R. viscosum* (swamp azalea); and the yellow *R. austrinum* (Florida azalea).

The nonfragrant azaleas include the orange to red *R. flammeum* (*speciosum*) and *Oconee azalea*, the yellow to deep orange flame azalea (*R. calendulaceum*), and the rare, late-flowering plumleaf azalea (*R. prunifolium*).

The South has a tradition of public gardens, many of which are associated with historic places such as Williamsburg, Mount Vernon, Monticello, Middleton, Hermitage, and numerous other plantation locales. Dumbarton Oaks, Biltmore, Bayou Bend, and the Elizabethan Garden represent spectacular gardens on private estates. Other well-known gardens include Callaway, Bellingrath, Cypress, Hodges, Magnolia, and Brookgreen. Botanical gardens at Fairchild in south Florida and the Plant Introduction Station at Savannah experiment with new plants to test their appropriateness to the southern environment. Southern writers have had private gardens that are now open to the public. William Faulkner, for example, acquired Rowan Oak in 1930, naming it for the mythic Rowan trees that Celts believed had special powers or protection. Faulkner kept a line of cedar trees along the drive leading to the house, planted narcissus, restored the magnolia garden, and added a scuppernong arbor and a rose garden. Fellow Mississippian Eudora Welty was an avid gardener at the home she shared with her mother in Jackson. Her mother established the garden, and

Eudora worked for years to keep it up. The garden included a perennial border, a woodland garden, a rose garden, a collection of camellias, and trellises and latticework. The names of flowers and plants from her garden appear often in Welty's writings. The garden has recently been restored to its high point, the years between 1925 and 1945.

Journalists and naturalists have long written about southern gardening, bringing out the distinctive climatic and environmental context. Elizabeth Lawrence (1904–85), for example, wrote for the *Charlotte Observer* between 1957 and 1971. Lawrence earned a degree in landscape architecture from the North Carolina State College School of Design, the first woman to do so. Her gardens in Raleigh and Charlotte provided material for her columns, which blended garden lore, horticultural advice, and personal experiences to engage readers and encourage their own gardening.

Flower gardening, at a different level, has always had special meaning for the southern poor. Flowers offered an aesthetic dimension to the sometimes drab rural life, and women as far back as the 1600s set out ceramic flowerpots along porches or on steps in yards. One North Carolina mill town woman, Ida L. Moore, who was interviewed in the 1930s, was probably typical of many women in saying that "no place seems like home without a few flowers." Her husband made flower boxes out of old car gas tanks and painted them red. She grew petunias, phlox, and the simple but popular zinnias. "It's nice settin' on the porch when they's somethin' to look at besides a red, ugly hill," she said.

Writer Alice Walker has perhaps best captured the cultural importance of flower gardening for the poor, especially southern black women. She points out that, although circumscribed in much of what they could do in society, black women in the South expressed their artistic creativity, indeed their human spirituality, through such seemingly simple activities as gardening. In Walker's novel *The Third Life of Grange Copeland* (1970), the character Mem decorates with flowers the rundown houses she has to live in. Walker's own mother in Georgia did the same, ambitiously planting gardens of 50 or so varieties that would bloom from early March until November, bringing color to the lives of her family. "Because of her creativity with her flowers," writes Walker, "even my memories of poverty are seen through a screen of blooms—sunflowers, petunias, roses, dahlias, forsythia, spirea, delphiniums, verbena."

FRED C. GALLE
*Hamilton, Georgia*

Patti Carr Black, ed., *Eudora Welty's World: Words on Nature* (2005); James C. Bonner, *Landscape* (Spring–Summer 1977); Ben A. Davis, *The Southern Garden: From the*

*Potomac to the Rio Grande* (1971); Fred C. Galle, *Azaleas* (1974); Catherine Howell, *Landscape Journal* (Spring 1982); William L. Hunt, *Southern Gardens, Southern Gardening* (1982); Lu Ann Jones, *Mama Learned Us to Work: Farm Women and the New South* (2002); Lee May, *In My Father's Garden* (1995); Felder Rushing, *Gardening Southern Style* (1987); John Wedda, *Gardens of the American South* (1971); Richard Westmacott, *African-American Gardens and Yards in the Rural South* (1992); Brooks E. Wigginton, *Trees and Shrubs for the Southeast* (1963).

## Indians and the Environment

The ecology of the South was well suited to Indian occupation, and large populations inhabited the river valleys of the interior as well as the coastal plains at white contact in the 16th century. These native people were highly successful at exploiting their ecosystem, drawing subsistence from a combination of hunting, farming, and gathering. When necessary, they purposely changed the environment, employing technologies that scholars only recently have begun to understand. Such economic diversity made Native American lives relatively secure. The southern Indians possessed an unusually sophisticated understanding of the environment, which provided virtually everything they needed for survival.

The largest concentration of Indian population in the western part of the South was in the Mississippi Delta and along the rivers east of it. Here the ancestors of the modern Choctaws and Chickasaws began building cities centuries before the voyage of Columbus. With the Spanish invasion, disease spread throughout the countryside, killing at times 80 percent of the Indian occupants and leaving but a scattered remnant of people by 1600. To the west of the Mississippi River, Caddoan groups survived in well-protected villages, whereas on the river itself the Natchez were the dominant urban dwellers. To the east, Europeans found the Choctaws, who lived in towns along the Big Black, Pearl, Tombigbee, and Yazoo rivers. To the north of the Choctaws lived their distant relatives, the Chickasaws. Hunters predominantly, the Chickasaws held the region from north-central Mississippi to the Ohio River and eastward to the Tennessee and Cumberland rivers.

Farther east, the river valleys of Mississippi and Georgia were occupied by the Creek Nation, a loose confederacy with various subtribes, including the Seminoles. The Creeks maintained some 50 to 60 towns after the initial decline in population brought about by European invasion. Related linguistically to the Chickasaws and Choctaws, the Creek populations were the largest in the eastern half of the South. The lands they occupied were part of an almost unbroken forest, with villages located generally along navigable streams such as the Alabama and Chattahochee. The Cherokees lived north and east of the Creek towns in the more rugged landscapes of western Georgia, North and South Carolina, and eastern Tennessee. North and west of the Cherokees, in the Upper South, were the Shawnees, hunters of considerable skill, and eastward on the Atlantic Coast smaller tribal groups could be found, such as the Virginia tribes, often called Powhatan's Confederacy, the Tuscarora, Catawba, Yamassee, Westos, and finally, in Florida, the Timucua.

The forest environment of the South had an important impact on all the nations of the region, fostering unique skills needed for survival. Nearly every southern tribe turned to the hunt in November to begin the subsistence cycle, stalking the whitetail deer. The herds were approached by hunters during the rutting season, when they were less inclined to run; hunters surrounded and killed the deer with bow and arrows. On occasions, thick underbrush and forest were set on fire to flush deer out, creating intermittent parklands across the South that allowed for better browsing. The winter hunt went into January, with large amounts of meat being smoked for later use. Some estimates suggest that deer provided 50 to 80 percent of the protein used in the diet of southern Indians. Other game animals that contributed were bear and turkey.

The opening of farms followed the hunt in spring, with various varieties of corn, squash, and beans being planted on scattered fields, usually opened in the fertile floodplains of river valleys. Women took charge of the planting after men had cleared the wild cane and trees. This slash-and-burn agriculture left scars; large trees were seldom removed but, rather, girdled and left to die. The Indians planted their crops in hills, a practice that limited erosion. Planting sticks and shell hoes were used to break the ground. About a half-dozen seeds were placed in each hill, necessitating some thinning when the seedlings came up. Although more food probably came from hunting and gathering, corn was a substantial part of the native diet, and all accounts suggest that yields were high. Because fertilizer was not used, however, towns had to move occasionally in order to find new land capable of sustaining crops.

Gathering provided the third means of subsistence. The list of edible foods found in the South was extraordinary, including nuts and seeds and many species of roots. Some wild plants, such as sweet potatoes, were semidomesticated, in that natives regularly burned off regions so that the chosen plants might better compete with the surrounding fauna. Fishing was another form of gathering. Inland tribes depended less on fish for food than did coastal groups, but both stalked catfish, a southern delicacy. The fish were collected in V-shaped rock fishtraps, constructed at considerable effort, in fast-moving streams. The end of the V was pointed downstream so that the current forced fish into the enclosure. The Florida Indians were most adept at fishing and coastal food gathering. Sea life became a primary food source for them, and they carried on the hunt for various edible sea creatures throughout the year. Everything from oysters to whales was taken, with men stalking the larger animals and women and children working primarily as gatherers. Even sharks were hunted, although the technique used to take them is still unclear. Apparently they were clubbed while in shallow water.

The obvious diversity in subsistence forms of southern Indians led to a keen perception of nature and environment. Indian religion and social organization evolved around this economic relationship with nature. Cherokee hunters, for example, carefully disposed of the bones of animals they had taken, not wanting to offend their spirits. Florida tribes also treated with respect the remains of whales and fish. The planting of corn and the harvest were occasions for careful thought and celebration. Southern Indians manipulated the ecosystem to its fullest, changing the natural environment when necessary to suit needs but living within its bounds more fully than most other civilizations in history.

GARY CLAYTON ANDERSON
*University of Oklahoma*

Robert S. Cotterill, *The Southern Indians: The Story of the Civilized Tribes before Removal* (1954); Frederick Hodge, ed., *Handbook of American Indians North of Mexico*, 2 vols. (1971); Charles M. Hudson, *The Southeastern Indians* (1976); Jack Temple Kirby, *Mockingbird Song: Ecological Landscapes of the South* (2006); Shepard Krech III, *The Ecological Indian: Myth and History* (1999); Lewis H. Larson, *Aboriginal Subsistence Technology on the Southeastern Coastal Plain during the Late Prehistoric Period* (1980); Wilcomb E. Washburn, *The Indian in America* (1975); Richard White, *The Roots of Dependency: Subsistence, Environment, and Social Change among the Choctaws, Pawnees, and Navajos* (1983); J. Leitch Wright Jr., *The Only Land They Knew: The Tragic Story of the American Indians in the Old South* (1981).

## Insects

Imagine southerners living in a world without the flicker of the firefly, the chirp of a cricket, the buzz of the honeybee, or the flutter of a swallowtail butterfly. They would probably prefer to live in a world without the bite of a mosquito, the itch of a chigger, the sting of the wasp, or the invasion of cockroaches. Southerners cannot escape the influence of insects. As a group, insects comprise the largest and most diverse form of animal life on earth, a fact southerners can easily believe on summer nights.

Most people enjoy products like silk and honey that are made by insects. Southerners have been especially successful at the business of raising bees. They sell packaged bees—including a queen and her workers—to northerners, whose bees die during the cold winters if left outdoors. A common sight for travelers in the South is people by the side of the road selling jars of such local honey flavors as sourwood, tupelo, and orange blossom.

Shellac and carmine dyes are also products of insects, and many foods are available only because insects pollinate the plants from which they are produced. Although unknown perhaps to most people, significant benefits accrue from the lives of literally hundreds of insect species, which prey on or parasitize other insects.

Throughout history insects have been well known for their ravages of humans and their domesticated animals, crops, and other material possessions. A negative image has resulted. One interested in learning more about how insects have influenced humans through the ages might begin with biblical accounts of swarms of flies or locust (grasshopper) plagues (Exodus 8:24, 10:4, and 10:13), and any text on the history of Europe will give a detailed account of the Black Plague.

American history is equally rich in its accounts of insect-human relationships. Indeed, settlement of many areas of the southern United States was greatly influenced by mosquitoes. Mosquitoes infested the early English colony at Jamestown and contributed to the diseases of the 1808 "starving time," which almost destroyed the colony. Later, southerner Walter Reed discovered that the mosquito (*Aedes aegypti*) transmits the yellow fever virus, and he helped to end a great plague in the region.

Fire ants (*Solenopsis invicta* and *Solenopsis richter*, the red and black imported fire ants) are pests common throughout the South. The red imported fire ant arrived from Brazil more than 60 years ago, apparently entering the South through wood off a freighter at Mobile. By 1985 these ants had caused nearly $59 million in damage to soybean crops, and one study by the Mississippi Cooperative Extension Service estimated that 744,000 people are stung annually in that state. The Mediterranean fruit fly has periodically endangered the South's citrus fruit industry, the screwworm has been costly for cattle growers to combat, the Texas cattle tick devastated cattle in years past, and the pine bark beetle is currently threatening the region's trees.

Perhaps no insect alien has gained greater notoriety than the boll weevil, originally a native of Mexico and Central America, because of its devastating effect on cotton culture during the early 1900s. In 1919, though, the citizens of Coffee County, Ala., erected a large monument to the boll weevil on the town

The Boll Weevil Monument, Enterprise, Ala. (Series VII.1, Photographs, box 7.1/3, file "II. Photographs—Boll weevil monument, Alabama," USDA History Collection, Special Collections, National Agricultural Library)

square of Enterprise as acknowledgment of its influence on the economy of the region. The boll weevil was credited with causing farmers to pursue more profitable ventures like peanuts and livestock in the southern states.

Many insects that humans label as pests became pestiferous because of the alteration of environments to suit human needs. Southerners live in heated homes, thus creating a somewhat tropical habitat for formerly tropical creatures such as cockroaches; southerners drained floodplains and planted them with crops, creating vast "food tables" for literally hundreds of native and imported insect species; and as Americans learned to travel over increased distances by land, sea, and air, they ignored insect "hitchhikers" like the Hessian fly, the European corn borer, and the smaller European elm bark beetle.

Insects have been the subject matter for a variety of cultural expressions in the South. Insect life is portrayed through folk sayings such as the old rule for planting corn: "One for the cutworm, One for the crow, One to rot, and Two to grow." Because of the sheer numbers of places that insects inhabit, southern language is graced with such expressions as "finer than a gnat's eyeball!" and "snug as a bug in a rug." Vernacular names chosen for many common insects reveal that nonentomologists can be good observers of nature. Such names as devil's horse for the praying mantis, dung roller for the adult dung beetle, snake doctor for any of the numerous species of dragonflies, and chicken choker for the larva of the tiger beetle are not the common names accepted by professional entomologists, but they are accurate statements about each insect's behavior.

On the other hand, certain vernacular names, such as waterbug for the oriental cockroach and locust for the dog-day or 13- and 17-year cicadas, have come about from observations but convey misconceptions about the insect's ecology. Vernacular origins were likely for many of the accepted common names of insects, including the tumblebug, hornworm, blisterbug or blister beetle, stinkbug, water strider, cabbage worm, ladybug or lady beetle, plant louse, head louse, crab louse, bluebottle fly, housefly, stable fly, horsefly, deerfly, bedbug, mayfly or fishfly, May beetle, and June beetle.

Southern literature and music reflect the human-insect interaction. James Agee recalled in his short vignette "Knoxville, Summer, 1915" lying in the yard of his family's house after supper, listening to "the dry and exalted noise of the locusts" and that of the crickets, which was "of the great order of noises." Like many a southern child, he chased fireflies—or lightning bugs, as they are called in the vernacular. Preacher Will Campbell titled his autobiographical memoir about growing up in Mississippi *Brother to a Dragonfly* and used an image of that insect to convey his moving relationship with his brother. In a more humorous vein, Harper Lee made a rollicking scene in *To Kill a Mockingbird* when

Burris Ewell inadvertently disrupted the school classroom by carrying a head louse—a cootie—on his head to school.

"Just looking for a home, just looking for a home" is a verse from the boll weevil ballad, one of the most popular southern folk songs. Kokomo Arnold sang the "Bo-Weevil Blues." Bobbie Gentry's song "Bugs" is a veritable compendium of good-natured human annoyance with insects, evoking images of a "granddaddy long legs" creeping up a screen, of boll weevils in the cotton, of dirt daubers and red wasps swooping out of the sky, of yellow jackets buzzing around one's head, and of shooing flies from the table and avoiding chiggers in the blackberry bushes.

Women in the South made spider leg quilts, in tribute to a close relative of insects; the pattern had 12 to 16 strips arranged like the limbs of a spider. Finally, one university, Georgia Tech, has made an ultimate modern southern tribute to an insect: the mascot for its football team is the Yellow Jacket.

T. J. HELMS
*Mississippi State University*

W. J. Holland, *The Moth Book: A Popular Guide to a Knowledge of the Moths of North America* (1903); Jim Howell, *Hey, Bug Doctor! The Scoop on Insects in Georgia's Homes and Gardens* (2006); Maurice T. James and Robert F. Harwood, *Herm's Medical Entomology* (1969); Robert E. Pfadt, ed., *Fundamentals of Applied Entomology*, 4th ed. (1985).

## Invasive and Alien Species (Floral and Faunal)

The American South, like every other region of the nation and the globe, is increasingly subjected to the problems and consequences created by biological invasions of alien flora, fauna, and pathogens into native biotas—plants, animals, and other living organisms of a specific region. The invasion of nonnative species into an existing biota frequently presents the invaders with a natural system in which they can flourish without the competition of the natural enemies they had known in their original environment. The immunity of time, distance, and the geographical barriers of oceans, deserts, and mountains, which in earlier eras slowed the march of nonnative species into new environments, declined exponentially as population growth, commerce, and transportation diminished the boundaries of the globe. The American South has not escaped the effects of these changes.

Growing populations in the South, with consequent increases in per capita consumption and production, required even more agricultural activities, industrial expansion, growth of cities, and the construction of highways, docks, and airports. All of these activities led to the disturbance and fragmentation of natural habitats, and it is within these disturbed systems that invasive species have their most success. From the 17th century to the present, no southern state has been immune to the decline in biodiversity created by bio-invasions and by the habitat alteration and destruction created by them. The appearance of non-native species is a major factor in species extinction and species endangerment in this region. The consequences for the southern economy and public health have been immeasurable.

Although many nonnative plants and animals create havoc with existing ecosystems, the nation's food supply is based on nonnative plants, such as rice, wheat, and corn, that have been introduced as food crops, and on nonnative animals, such as cattle, sheep, goats, and chickens, introduced as livestock. In-deed, most food consumed in the United States comes from nonnative, intro-duced species. The larger the animal or plant, the more likely that it was delib-erately introduced by human action. More than 25,000 species of nonnative plants have been brought to America's shores to grace individual gardens, to grow in arid regions, to augment a region's flora, to provide food or fiber, to become a cash crop, and to add beauty to an existing landscape. Perhaps 20 percent of these consciously introduced plants have escaped human control and have become a threat to the South's ecosystems, both managed and wild. By the beginning of the 21st century, approximately 50,000 plants, animals, and microbes had invaded American ecosystems.

Early Europeans, in particular, were agents for the spread of "virgin soil epi-demics" of measles, smallpox, malaria, and yellow fever, which reduced the populations of the lands they were seeking to seize and settle. Surprises occur daily for scientists who study the diverse pathways by which nonnative species enter new ecosystems. By 1701 the mosquito, *Aedes aegypti*, had entered French Louisiana. Brought originally from Africa to the Caribbean, when it arrived in Louisiana on slave ships, it became a pathway for carrying the yellow fever virus to humans. New Orleans experienced more than 100,000 deaths to yellow fever between 1796 and 1905. The Asian tiger mosquito entered the port of Houston on ships carrying scrap tires from Asia in the early 1980s. Until these mosqui-toes were discovered in Houston in the summer of 1985, they had not been found in North America. Reproducing in standing water, difficult to kill, and an aggressive biter, this mosquito is an excellent vector (mechanism or agent for spreading a disease) for a number of viruses that are harmful to humans and animals. Now found in 17 states, the tiger mosquito has also been accidentally introduced into the Dominican Republic, Brazil, Bolivia, Colombia, Nigeria, Albania, Italy, New Zealand, and Australia. Since 2000, the West Nile virus has become another exotic invader and dangerous disease vectored by mosquitoes in southern states.

The most agriculturally intrusive nonnative species for southern agriculture has been the boll weevil, which became a destructive invader in the 1890s. From its home in Mexico and Central America, it became an uncontrollable pest that severely damaged the cotton economy in the early 20th century. Assessing its economic impact is imprecise, but figures for its devastation are estimated as high as $14 billion. Other studies suggest that the annual impact of the boll weevil could have been as high as $300 million a year. Fire ants, while an invasive species and a significant problem in the region, have not produced the level of economic devastation caused by the boll weevil.

Nonnative plants, frequently introduced through human action, have become a significant problem in the South. Water hyacinths were brought from their home in the Amazon Valley in the last decades of the 19th century because of the beauty of their lavender flowers. Displayed and distributed in 1884 at the World's Industrial and Cotton Centennial Exposition held at New Orleans's Audubon Park, water hyacinths soon escaped human control and have become an enduring problem in southern waterways, lakes, and rivers. With the capacity of doubling the area they cover every 12 days, water hyacinths have become the South's leading aquatic plant problem. An acre of open water may contain 200 tons of this plant, which can block canals, cover lakes and ponds, destroy fishing sites, and clog intakes at power and hydroelectric plants. Some success in limiting its growth has been obtained through the use of mechanical, chemical, and biological agents, but the expense and difficulties of totally eliminating this aquatic invader have prevented its eradication.

Few who have lived in the South have failed to be amazed by the prolific growth of the Japanese vine kudzu. James Dickey, in his poem "Kudzu," observed,

> In Georgia, the legend says
> That you must close your windows
> At night to keep it out of the house.

Others have noted that this plant, which can grow a foot a day, expands with such vigor that you can hear it spreading as it covers trees, power lines, and abandoned buildings. It was first displayed at the 1876 Centennial Exposition in the oriental garden constructed by the Japanese government. The attractive, aromatic blooms and large leaves of the kudzu made it one of the most popular plants displayed at Philadelphia. Charles and Lillie Pleas, Florida nursery owners, popularized its use not only as an ornamental but also as livestock forage in the 1920s. Kudzu was even sold through the mail. During the Great Depression, it was promoted by the government for soil erosion control and was planted by the Civilian Conservation Corps. In the 1940s government support programs paid $8 an acre to farmers for the planting of kudzu. Resistant to drought, frost, and insects and ideally adapted to the southern climate, kudzu has become an uncontrollable plant in this region, with more than 2 million acres covered by this legume. It alters habitat for wildlife, destroys forests and watersheds, lessens agricultural productivity, and reduces biodiversity. Attempts to control kudzu reached more than $6 million a year by 2001.

The 19th century was a period that witnessed the enthusiastic introduction of other nonnative plants for agricultural and ornamental purposes. Japanese honeysuckle, Chinese privet, purple loosestrife, and Chinese tallow tree (popcorn tree) were imported species from the 18th and 19th centuries that have become problem flora for the contemporary South.

Seeking a tree that would grow in the wetlands of southern Florida, in 1906 a forestry professor at the University of Miami imported from Australia the seeds of the melaleuca tree (*Melaleuca quinquenervia*). Reaching heights of 80 feet, this tree seemed ideally suited for Florida wetlands, where it would grow in the Everglades, help dry out the swamps, and provide a habitat for birds and bees. For five decades it enjoyed varying degrees of popularity as it was sold in Florida as an ornamental tree for landscaping, fencerows, and windbreaks. In the 1960s melaleuca became a problem in the Everglades, covering hundreds of thousands of acres, degrading the "river of grass," and altering the habitat for many other species. Countless other plants that have played and are playing a role in shaping the natural history of the South include the giant salvinia, leafy spurge, Johnson grass, and hydrilla, to name but a few.

Florida has often been the center for invasive species disasters, and the southern tip of this state has become a case study for ecological misbehavior by the pet trade and pet owners. In a region that has an almost tropical environment with high levels of rainfall and mild temperatures, released pets have become a significant problem. Boa constrictors, African monitor lizards, monkeys, and potbellied pigs are now found in the Everglades. Burmese pythons are breeding there. Reaching lengths of fifteen feet, these pythons have become an unexpected challenge for Everglades wildlife managers.

Louisiana and Florida, more than any other southern states, have frequently suffered from accidental introductions of invasive species. Invasive species in the southern states have been a problem since European settlement, and there is no reason to expect that they will be less of a problem in the future. Wise resource utilization and wildlife management policies dictate that for economic, aesthetic, and health considerations the citizens of the South must become better stewards of the land, water, and air in which invasive species establish themselves through invitation or accident.

PHILLIP DRENNON THOMAS
*Wichita State University*

Chris Bright, *Life out of Bounds* (1998); Albert E. Cowdrey, *This Land, This South: An Environmental History* (1983); George W. Cox, *Alien Species in North America and Hawaii: Impacts on Natural Ecosystems* (1999); Alfred Crosby, *The Columbian Exchange: Biological and Cultural Consequences of 1492* (1972), *Ecological Imperialism* (1986); National Research Council, *Predicting Invasions of Nonindigenous Plants and Pests* (2002); Daniel Simberloff, D. C. Schmitz, and T. C. Brown, eds., *Strangers in Paradise* (1997).

## Land Use

The South has historically had a large arable area in relation to its small population, resulting in two centuries of widespread land exploitation. As historian Lewis C. Gray put it, "Planters bought land as they might buy a wagon—with the expectation of wearing it out"; the wave of farmers that swept from Virginia to Texas planting corn and cotton thus "passed like a devastating scourge." Poor husbandry, stemming from lack of motivation rather than ignorance about fertilizers or crop rotation, brought about soil exhaustion and erosion before the Civil War. In 1850 the South was basically a mixed farming region. Plantations, most of which grew cotton, represented 18 percent of holdings. The remainder took the form of farms whose size was greater than the national average; improved land was average, but value of holdings fell below the average. Livestock numbers were higher in the South, where 60 percent of U.S. swine, 90 percent of mules, about 50 percent of meat cattle, and a third of the country's sheep were run.

During Reconstruction the character of agriculture remained constant. After 1900, however, diversification and specialization and the shift away from cotton and corn began. Land planted in crops peaked in the 1920s, then declined. The years from the end of World War II to 1980 saw especially dramatic changes in land use. Texas, which had the largest harvested area, dropped from 30.6 million acres in 1930 to 22.2 million acres in 1960 and 19 million acres in 1970, a 35.5 percent decline. Farm numbers also tumbled 30 percent between 1950 and 1960 and 9 percent in the 1970s, to a total of 159,000, or 7 percent of the nation's total. Less cultivation, fewer farms, and more specialized crops have been the trend in many southern states.

By the 1970s approximately 27 percent of the land area of Mississippi, Louisiana, and Arkansas; 26 percent of Texas and Oklahoma; and 16 percent of the Southeast were used for crops and pasture. These averages, varying from 36 percent in Oklahoma to 11 percent in Florida, placed the South behind corn belt states and the northern plains' wheat belt, but ahead of the Northeast, mountain states, and the West as an agricultural region. Today former Confederate states account for approximately 20 percent of the nation's cropland harvested, with 62 percent of all land area in the South forested.

Irrigation agriculture has boomed. In 2003 almost one-quarter of Texas's 20 million acres of harvested cropland was irrigated. Of the southern states, Arkansas ranked next with 4 million acres of irrigated cropland; Florida, third with 1.5 irrigated acres; and Mississippi, fourth with 1.2 million.

Rice requires heavy drafts of water and is concentrated in the South. Arkansas grew more than 1.5 million acres of rice in 2002, Louisiana exceeded 500,000 acres of rice planted, and Mississippi and Texas grew more than 200,000 acres each.

Horticulture, drawing upon irrigation, is pronounced. South Carolina ranks second in peaches, and Georgia is third. In 2003 Florida was the nation's leading state in production of oranges, grapefruit, and tangerines, with Texas another southern state leader in citrus production. Large-scale beekeeping to bolster pollination has a strong foothold with the growing season and varied subtropical and warm temperate produce. Florida has the most bee colonies in the South, followed closely by North Carolina, Texas, and Tennessee. Other specialized crops are tobacco, canola or rapeseed, sunflowers, peanuts, and soybeans. Tobacco has been a particularly notable crop in the Upper South. North Carolina produced 12 million pounds of tobacco in 1850, triple that in 1900, and 12.5 times that by 1950. In 2002 the yield in North Carolina was 348 million pounds of flue-cured tobacco and 9.5 million pounds of burley tobacco. Tobacco accounts for 12 percent of total agricultural production in North Carolina, and in 2002 tobacco covered 169,500 acres of North Carolina cropland. Kentucky came in second that year with a total tobacco acreage of 112,300.

Cotton has historically been an abundantly grown crop in the South. In 2002, 12.728 million acres of cotton were grown in southern states, representing 88 percent of the 14.728 million acres of cotton grown in the United States that year. Texas consistently leads the South and nation in cotton acreage, with 5.82 million acres planted in 2002. Georgia ranked second nationally with 1.5 million acres; Mississippi, third with 1.2 million; and Arkansas, a close fourth with 1 million.

The growing of peanuts was an important crop diversification in the 20th century. In 2002, Georgia had 550,000 acres of cropland in peanuts. Texas was second in the nation with 425,000 acres, followed by Alabama (200,000), North Carolina (100,000), and Florida (100,000). Today, virtually all the acres planted in peanuts are in nine southern states. In 2002, Georgia produced 40 percent of the U.S. peanut crop, with the Georgia crop that year valued at $230 million.

Between 1950 and 1980 soybean acreage grew fourfold nationally, and soybeans remain a major southern crop. Arkansas had about 4.7 million acres, or 65 percent of the cropland, in the 1970s and today produces 96 million bushels. The Midwest dominates in acreage, but Mississippi, Louisiana, Tennessee, and Alabama are important. These four states have a combined 75 percent of their croplands in soybeans.

Two factors explain the decline in the use of land for agriculture in the 20th century. First, woodland is extensive, accounting for two-thirds of Alabama and Georgia and more than one-half of South Carolina, Florida, Mississippi, Arkansas, Louisiana, and Virginia. These states possess roughly 30 percent of forest area in the nation and have supplied 38 percent of the timber. Peak years of production were 1916 and 1925, but output declined to a steady 20 percent, mostly softwood timber. In the early 1900s the South's timberlands were so open because of logging, fire, and cattle grazing that you could see a white mule a mile away in the woods. Crop intensification, however, has released marginal lands back to native vegetation, and forest development, producing stands of even-age, quick-growing trees, has extended pinelands; but these account for only 11 percent of the South's forests. At the end of the 20th century, the South's forest cover had increased by 5 million acres to 215 million acres. Most of this forestland (71 percent) is owned by private landowners.

Second, one-third of the American population now resides in the 15 states termed the Sunbelt. Urban and other special-use categories have increased to reflect the population growth there. Florida, Georgia, and Texas are more than 80 percent urban, and neighboring states have sizable urban populations. Much of Florida falls into the urban industrial category, and the Texas-Louisiana "oil patch," cities in Oklahoma, and the manufacturing belt in the Southeast are expressions of metropolitan land use in the region.

ROBIN W. DOUGHTY
*University of Texas at Austin*

ROBERT L. IZLAR
*Warnell School of Forest Resources*
*University of Georgia*

Thomas D. Clark, *The Greening of the South: The Recovery of Land and Forest* (1984); H. Ken Cordell and Christine Overdevest, *Footprints on the Land: An Assessment of Demographic Trends and the Future of Natural Lands in the United States* (2001); Kenneth P. Davis, *Land Use* (1976); Donald B. Dodd and Wynelle S. Dodd, *Historical Statistics of the South, 1790–1970* (1973); Lewis Cecil Gray, *History of Agriculture in the Southern United States to 1860*, 2 vols. (1933); Robert G. Healy, *Land Use and the States* (1976); Sam B. Hilliard, *Hog Meat and Hoecake: Food Supply in the Old South, 1840–1860* (1972); Aldo Leopold, *For the Health of the Land* (1999); U.S. Census Bureau, *Statistical Abstract of the United States* (2006); U.S. Department of Agriculture, *Agricultural Statistics, 1980* (1980), *Economic Service, Major Uses of Land in the United States: Summary for 1969* (1969); David N. Wear and John G. Greis, eds., *Southern Forest Resource Assessment* (2002).

## Marine Environment, Fish and Fisheries

The shores of the southern United States are caressed by the warm waters of the Gulf of Mexico and the Atlantic Ocean. These bodies of water provide transportation, recreation, jobs, and food and have a profound effect on the culture of southern coastal communities. The Gulf of Mexico is the largest gulf in North America, covering approximately 400,000 square miles and having about 2,500 miles of coastline. The southern states of Texas, Louisiana, Mississippi, Alabama, and north and west Florida reap rich rewards from this body of water. The U.S. southern Atlantic Coast is approximately 1,300 miles in length and comprises the states of Maryland, Virginia, North Carolina, South Carolina, Georgia, and the east coast of Florida. The warm water of the Gulf Stream, a large current that flows northward along the east coast of the United States, significantly affects the coastal climate there, creating a warm, temperate environment farther north than would otherwise be predicted. Approximately 55 percent of the U.S. population lives in coastal counties, with a great percentage residing in southern coastal areas.

The earliest communities of the southern United States—Charleston, Savannah, St. Augustine, Mobile, and New Orleans—were located along the coasts primarily because of the proximity of water for transportation, sustenance, and protection. These cities have played no minor role in the history of the entire United States. The marine waters of the South have provided inspiration for countless works of art, song, poetry, and prose—Walter Anderson's visual art, the "shrimp boat rock" of Jimmy Buffet, and the sea stories of Ernest Hemingway, to name a few.

The waters of the southern United States are blessed with an amazing abundance and bewildering diversity of marine life. The Gulf of Mexico has more than 500 different species of shore fishes and many more species of deepwater fish and shellfish. However, the average coastal southerner would be likely to encounter only those species that might be found on the dinner plate. The importance of seafood to southern coastal residents cannot be overstated. The Cajun and Creole dishes of south Louisiana utilize local southern seafood: shrimp, crab, oysters, crawfish, and various species of fish. Similar to the clambake of the U.S. East Coast, shrimp, crab, and crawfish boils are not simply a meal; they are an event. Some of the more exotic marine/coastal species found on the dinner table include alligator, shark, garfish, and stingray cleverly disguised as scallops. A delicacy that is enjoyed by many southern coastal residents is smoked mullet. Some contend that the best-tasting mullet in the world is found in the big bend area of Florida, around Panacea and Cedar Key. Mullet are also used in sporting events in some coastal areas. The "mullet toss," a competition involving the distance a mullet can be thrown, is an annual event at the Flora-Bama Lounge located on the Florida-Alabama state line.

In economic terms, the marine environment is extremely important to southern communities. For example, in the Gulf of Mexico the landings of fish and shellfish are valued at more than $669 million. Remarkably, the Gulf of Mexico shrimp industry is the most valuable fishery in the entire United States, averaging about $450 million per year. It is estimated that saltwater sport fishing infuses $31 billion into the U.S. economy, and about 83 million pounds of fish are landed by recreational fishers in the Gulf of Mexico each year. The great abundance, value, and ready availability of fish and shellfish have permeated practically all aspects of southern community life, particularly in the many coastal communities whose very existence depends on fishing.

Some coastal communities are dominated by either recreational or commercial fishing, although these are not always mutually exclusive. Destin, Fla., for example, caters primarily to sport fishers. Party boat, charter boat, pier, and surf fishing are all available, and the Destin Fishing Rodeo offers prizes totaling $100,000. The oldest and largest fishing tournament in the nation is the Alabama Deep Sea Fishing Rodeo held on Dauphin Island. Other fishing tournaments of note include the Mississippi Deep Sea Fishing Rodeo in Gulfport, the Grand Isle Tarpon Rodeo in Grand Isle, La., and the Pompano Beach Fishing Rodeo in Pompano Beach, Fla. Some of the most popular recreational fish species include red snapper, snook, spotted seatrout, red drum, tarpon, king mackerel, Spanish mackerel, cobia, mahi mahi, bonefish, various species of grouper, various species of shark, and amber jack.

Commercial fishing communities of the Gulf Coast include Bayou LaBatre, Ala., Port St. Joe, Fla., and Biloxi, Miss. Important commercial species are shrimp, blue crabs, red snapper, menhaden, and grouper. While sport fishing is a very important component of the tourist industry in some coastal communities, commercial fishing communities tend to be blue collar. Tarpon Springs, Fla., was heavily influenced by Greek sponge divers and their families who settled in the area at the turn of the 20th century when sponges were commercially harvested from the waters offshore. Commercial fishing is considered to be the most dangerous and underpaid job in the nation, which might contribute to the religiosity of many commercial fishermen (i.e., the Blessing of the Fleet celebration) and to some being superstitious (i.e., never take bananas on a commercial fishing vessel). Other commercial interests include the thousands of sport diving shops that offer scuba diving trips and opportunities to swim with rays or dolphins.

The effect of the marine environment on southern communities is also seen in aesthetics. Who among us has never stood on the beach and marveled at the power and immensity of the sea? Sunset in many coastal communities (Key West and St. Petersburg Beach, Fla., for instance) will find residents gathered to watch the play of light on the ocean surface or perhaps catch a glimpse of the elusive "green flash," an intense flash of green light that is seen just as the sun dips below the ocean's surface. Some coastal residents are so smitten by the marine environment that they have chosen to live onboard their vessels. Commercial fishers, sailing enthusiasts, houseboat owners, and others have adopted the "life aquatic" full time. These counterculturalists are found at practically any marina, harbor, or dock. It comes as no surprise that the most valuable coastal homes are those that have a view of the sea.

Development of coastal areas in the United States and worldwide has been increasing at an alarming rate. In the South, many natural areas have been seriously degraded or completely destroyed. Although only one marine fish species is endangered (the smalltooth sawfish), many more species are in decline. Continued coastal development will no doubt lead to increased degradation of marine and coastal environments, unpredictable and deleterious changes in marine ecosystems, and parallel changes in southern coastal communities.

GLENN R. PARSONS
*University of Mississippi*

NOAA, National Marine Fisheries Service, Fisheries Statistics Division, 1315 East-West Highway, Silver Spring, MD 20910; Glenn R. Parsons, *Sharks, Skates, and Rays of the Gulf of Mexico* (2006).

## Natural Disasters

Natural disasters suddenly convey the vulnerability of human life and the fragility of civilization. They violently disrupt the fabric of society and create human misery as well as social dislocation. In the South most natural disasters are caused by weather-related phenomena: violent thunderstorms, tornadoes, floods, and hurricanes. The complex mechanics of warm, moisture-laden air from the Gulf of Mexico combining with the cool, drier air from the North spark violent thunderstorms that often engender short-lived tornadoes that tear unforgivingly across the landscape. Tropical weather patterns also spawn depressions that often evolve into hurricanes that threaten the Gulf and Atlantic coasts from June to November. Most of the South is also subject to heavy, anomalous rainfalls that push rivers beyond their banks, transforming towns and farms into a surreal watery landscape. The following cases illustrate the capricious forces of nature that often overwhelm the puny efforts of humankind to provide safe, comfortable habitats.

Thunderstorms are common natural occurrences of uncommon power and energy. A typical storm might be three miles across its base, tower 50,000 feet into the air, contain a half-million tons of condensed water, and release 10 times the energy of the atomic bomb dropped on Hiroshima. Tornadoes are the most devastating result of thunderstorms. Although they occur throughout the world, the American South and Midwest experience more tornadoes than anywhere else on earth. Southeastern tornadoes tend to be more deadly than those in the Great Plains and Midwest. Twisters in this region strike more often at night, are usually obscured in clouds and heavy rain, and are less prone to early detection than those that often are observed miles away on the plains. In fact, from 1916 to 1974 more tornado-related deaths—1,091—occurred in Mississippi than in any other state.

Tornadoes sometimes break out in large patterns. In the so-called super outbreak of 2–3 April 1974, a record 148 tornadoes swept across the Upper South and lower Midwest. Entire communities such as Xenia, Ohio; Brandenburg, Ky.; and Guin, Ala., were almost totally devastated. Losses totaled 315 dead, 6,142 injured, and $600 million in property damage. More than 9,600 homes were destroyed, and 27,590 families suffered to some degree. The combined length of the tornadoes' paths was an incredible 2,598 miles.

A series of tornadoes also sliced through Mississippi and Georgia on 5–6 April 1936. At Tupelo, Miss., a huge tornado mangled the city's residences and business district, destroyed its municipal water reservoir, killed 216 persons, and injured 1,500. The next morning two tornadoes ripped through Gainesville, Ga., and ignited a large fire. Deaths totaled 203, and injuries from the funnels and fire reached 934. Gainesville, like other communities, suffered multiple tornado strikes. A 1903 twister claimed 28 lives, and another in 1944 took 44.

Hurricanes develop over southern portions of the North Atlantic as well as over the Gulf of Mexico and the Caribbean Sea, usually during the "season" that lasts from 1 June to 31 October. On average, 8 to 10 storms a year are large enough to be named by the U.S. Weather Service and carefully monitored as possible risks to mainland areas. The worst hurricane season on record was the 2005 season with 21 named hurricanes and unnamed ones Alpha through Gamma. The combination of great size (hurricanes average 100 miles in diameter) and long life compounds their destructive powers. They are the most damaging of all geophysical disasters because they produce heavy rainfall, high winds, and flash floods as well as powerful storm surges and tides, and they spin off tornadoes.

The first written account of a hurricane in the South recorded the destruction that occurred at Jamestown, Va., on 27 August 1667. The "dreadful Hurry Cane" produced "such violence that it overturned many houses, burying in the ruins much goods and many people. . . . The sea swelled twelve foot above the normal height drowning the whole country before it."

Hurricanes occur along the Atlantic Coast, but the seaboard of the Gulf of Mexico is more prone to these violent attacks. Gulf Coast hurricanes usually follow a track toward the northeast and dump heavy precipitation across large areas of the South, causing widespread flash floods.

At the turn of the 20th century, Galveston, Tex., was a thriving, prosperous community that boasted the fastest-growing port in the United States. Much of the city was built on a barrier island, with the highest point only 20 feet above sea level. When a hurricane struck the morning of 8 September 1900, a ship broke from its moorings and crashed through the three bridges to the mainland, cutting off any chance of escape. Tides soon rose 20 feet above normal, tearing apart homes and buildings and reshaping them into a two-story-high mass of debris that was driven inland by the storm surge. An estimated 6,000 of Galveston's 20,000 residents died, a weather catastrophe unequaled before or since. Because of the threat of disease, masses of bodies were piled into trenches and burned—an acrid postlude to the worst natural disaster in the nation's history.

As the Miami, Fla., area developed in the 1920s, the fertile muck lands surrounding Lake Okeechobee became a source of produce for Florida's urbanites. Hundreds of small shantytowns arose near the lakeshore to house fieldworkers, and long mud dikes were built to mitigate flooding. On 16 September 1928 a hurricane with winds estimated at 160 miles per hour drove the lake waters across the flat landscape, collapsing dikes and drowning hundreds of people. The final death toll was estimated between 1,800 and 2,500, the second-worst hurricane disaster in American history. After the storm, the federal government funded a massive flood control program for some 12,000 square miles of the Lake Okeechobee Everglades area to prevent future disasters.

Until 2005, Hurricane Camille (14–22 August 1969) was by far the most powerful hurricane of recent times. It devastated the Louisiana, Mississippi, and Alabama Gulf Coast with winds over 170 miles per hour and gusts up to 200. Storm surges reached almost unbelievable proportions, including an estimated 25-foot height at Pass Christian, Miss. (The National Weather Service estimates that storm surges cause 9 of 10 hurricane-related fatalities.) Camille caused 152 deaths in Mississippi and Louisiana and, after passing over the Southeast, dumped unusually heavy rains on the mid-Atlantic region. Some 21 inches of rain fell within 24 hours over parts of Virginia and West Virginia, causing serious flash floods.

Hurricane Katrina has been termed the worst natural disaster in U.S. history. It hit between New Orleans, La., and Pass Christian, Miss., in the early morning of 29 August 2005. The economic damage was estimated to be as high as $100 billion. The city of New Orleans was particularly hard hit, and the levee system failed, causing extensive flooding, property damage, and loss of life. Estimates of the dead were placed at about 1,000, with some 6,400 missing in the entire area. High storm surges and winds caused enormous damage to the Mississippi Gulf Coast.

Because of relatively heavy rainfalls, much of the South is prone to flash, general, and backwater flooding. The propensity of people to farm, build, and live on former floodplains poses hazards to lives and property. Flood control measures such as levees, dams, pumping plants, and channel improvements have reduced these threats in many areas. For example, the Mississippi River and portions of its tributaries are now being controlled by the massive Mississippi River and Tributaries Project authorized by Congress in 1928 and still only 76 percent complete. The project was developed in response to the catastrophic 1927 flood that caused crevasses in levees and sometimes spread out nearly 100 miles. The statistical dimensions of the tragedy were nightmarish: 16.6 million acres flooded, 162,000 homes inundated, as many as 500 people killed, and 325,500 people cared for in refugee camps. Then secretary of commerce Herbert Hoover headed a relief effort that included 31,000 volunteers.

Some parts of the South have also experienced major seismic activity. The most violent and prolonged series of earthquakes in U.S. history occurred in the supposedly seismically quiet Mississippi Valley, far from the great faults of the West. During the early morning of 16 December 1811, a series of tremors centered near New Madrid, Mo., literally tore apart the landscape. Cabins and houses creaked and groaned, huge waves capsized boats on the Mississippi, trees swayed and snapped, and huge fissures opened in the earth. The shocks were felt over two-thirds of the United States and continued intermittently until 7 February 1812. An estimated 150,000 acres of timberland were destroyed, and new lakes were created in Arkansas (Lake Francis) and in Tennessee (Reelfoot Lake). In addition, thousands of acres of farmland were transformed into swamps through settling. So severe was the damage that in 1815 Congress passed the first national disaster relief act, which enabled owners of ruined property to obtain equal tracts of land elsewhere.

The South's other major seismic event occurred near Charleston, S.C., the evening of 31 August 1886. Felt as far away as Boston and Bermuda, the earthquake destroyed or badly damaged most of the city's major buildings, caused more than $5 million in damage, and claimed some 111 lives.

In the past quarter-century the life-threatening potential of some disasters has been reduced by improved weather forecasting, flood control, hurricane protection projects, and highly effective emergency management programs developed by federal, state, and local agencies. Nevertheless, property damage will probably escalate as the Sunbelt continues to grow.

MICHAEL C. ROBINSON
*U.S. Army Corps of Engineers*
*Lower Mississippi Valley Division*
*Vicksburg, Mississippi*

ROBERT L. IZLAR
*Warnell School of Forest Resources*
*University of Georgia*

Allen H. Barton, *Communities in Disaster: A Sociological Analysis of Collective Stress Situations* (1969); James Cornell, *The Great International Disaster Book* (1976); Gordon E. Dunn and Banner I. Miller, *Atlantic Hurricanes* (1960); Walter J. Fraser Jr., *Lowcountry Hurricanes: Three Centuries of Storms at Sea and Ashore* (2006); Kendrick Frazier, *The Violent Face of Nature* (1979); Gary Jennings, *The Killer Storms: Hurricanes, Typhoons, and Tornadoes* (1970); David Ludlum, *Early American Hurricanes, 1492–1870* (1963); James Penick Jr., *The New Madrid Earthquakes of 1811–1812* (1976); Ted Steinberg, *Acts of God: The Unnatural History of Natural Disasters in America* (2000).

## Natural Resources

Because gold and silver are not produced to any degree in the 11 states of the old Confederacy, there is a tendency to consider the South a region short of natural resources. Nothing could be further from the truth. If natural resources are defined as forms of wealth or potential wealth supplied by nature, then the South always has been blessed. Even though some of these treasures have been abused, they remain the region's greatest hope for a bright and prosperous future.

The South's most basic natural resources are high humidity and warm weather. With from 45 to 70 inches of rainfall a year and temperatures reaching 90°F more than 50 days annually, most of the region enjoys a nine months' growing season.

In much of the South soils were originally rich and productive. The earliest white Virginians grew tobacco, followed by corn and wheat. South Carolina soil, in combination with large quantities of water, produced rice, and an excellent short-staple cotton was grown above tidewater in the Carolinas, in the Black Belt of Georgia and Alabama, and in the rich Mississippi Delta between the Mississippi and Yazoo rivers. The land was surely abused, leached, eroded, and often made sterile, but with conservation measures and intelligent husbandry, it can and, indeed, has come back. Whether one speaks of the Tidewater South along the Atlantic, the Piedmont above the fall line, the Appalachian Highlands, the Kentucky bluegrass, the Gulf Coastal Plain, or the red clay hills of north Georgia and Alabama, the land has always borne foodstuffs in abundance.

The first white explorers initially exploited the most prevalent natural resource, the wild game. Deer, bear, buffalo, turkeys, passenger pigeons, bass, catfish, and other game, birds, and fish were killed in abundance. In the late 1600s more than 54,000 deerskins were shipped annually from Charleston, S.C. Even today sportsmen consider the South a paradise for hunters and fishermen.

When pioneer agriculturalists entered the South, they exploited the game but also attacked another great natural resource: the great forest covering much of the land with both hardwoods and softer conifers. In the 19th and early 20th centuries much of the hardwood was cut. So favorable was the South to the growth of timber, however, that tree farming of soft woods, especially for papermaking, is today one of the region's major industries. More than 200 million acres are currently forested.

A consequence of the high rainfall is the veining of the southern countryside with deep, sluggish rivers. In the early days settlers were attracted to the river valleys because canebrakes filled them and stretched for hundreds of miles along the stream banks. Settlers' cattle could graze on the leaves of the cornlike stalks, and the destruction of the cane and replacement by fields of grain or cotton were easier than clearing the forest and preparing it for planting.

Rivers range from the Potomac and James in Virginia and the Savannah and Altamaha down the Atlantic to the Suwannee, Apalachicola, Pearl, and Alabama along the Gulf and, in the Upper South, the Kentucky, Cumberland, and Tennessee. These rivers have always been, and remain, liquid highways of commerce; in the 20th century they also furnished immense quantities of electric power. Greatest of all is, of course, the mighty Mississippi, immortalized by Samuel Clemens.

The rivers carry rich nutrients into the bays of the Atlantic and the Gulf of Mexico, feeding schools of edible fish and seafood including scallops, oysters, and shrimp. Apalachicola Bay, off the north Florida coast, is one of the world's richest bodies of water, providing fish and seafood for markets as far away as Japan.

Precious metals are rare in the South—although gold was discovered at Dahlonega, Ga., and in small quantities elsewhere—but other useful minerals have been found. Texas, Arkansas, Louisiana, and Mississippi are leading producers of petroleum and natural gas; some sulfur is also mined. Alabama, Tennessee, and Virginia (including West Virginia) produce bituminous coal. Within the South are found in quantities suitable for exploitation stone, cement, sand and gravel, and phosphates.

RICHARD A. BARTLETT
*Florida State University*

Raymond Arsenault, in *Paradise Lost? The Environmental History of Florida*, ed. Jack E. Davis and Raymond Arsenault (2005); Thomas D. Clark, *The Greening of the South: The Recovery of Land and Forest* (1984); Henry Hill Collins, *Complete Field Guide to American Wildlife* (1959); Albert E. Cowdrey, *This Land, This South: An Environmental History* (1983); Donald Edward Davis, *Where There Are Mountains: An Environmental History of the Southern Appalachians* (2000); Gilbert C. Fite, *Cotton Fields No More: Southern Agriculture, 1865–1980* (1985); Charles B. Hunt, *Physiography of the United States* (1967); Howard W. Odum, *Southern Regions of the United States* (1936); Stephen J. Pyne, *Fire in America: A Cultural History of Wildland and Rural Fire* (1982); Mikko Saikku, *This Delta, This Land: An Environmental History of the Yazoo-Mississippi Floodplain* (2005).

## Naturalists

Colonial Europeans were overwhelmed by the richness of the flora and fauna they found in the American wilderness. Until the middle of the 19th century and the development of specialization in science, those interested in examining the topography, geology, native peoples, and plant and animal life were amateurs—planters, ministers, teachers, mariners, and physicians—who had limited, if any, scientific training in a specific field of natural history. Most of them were self-taught. They generally focused their energies on the collection of data, the classification of that data into a systematic framework, and the development of a scientific nomenclature that would permit the integration of newly discovered scientific species and phenomena into a larger framework of knowledge. The knowledge they gained on the flora, fauna, peoples, and geography of this continent permitted the development of scientific specialization into distinct disciplines. Although botany was the dominant interest among field naturalists in America until the middle of the 19th century, the most original contributions of Americans to science were in zoology and paleontology.

The American South lacked the libraries, gardens, and herbaria to permit the systematic study of natural history, but its varied topography and rich flora and fauna attracted many naturalists. As early as the 16th century, Thomas Harriot and John White chronicled and illustrated the plants, animals, and native peoples found near Sir Walter Raleigh's ill-fated Roanoke settlement. Harriot's *A Briefe and True Report of the New Found Land of Virginia* (London, 1588), which recorded the author's travels into the interior of Carolina and possibly Virginia, distinguished between the geology of the Coastal Plain and the Piedmont, identified the mineral resources of the coastal region, commented on the agricultural practices of the Indians, identified their crops, and recorded 28 species of mammals, 86 species of birds, and the presence of oak, elm, ash, walnut, fir, cedar, maple, witch hazel, willow, beech, and sassafras trees. His description of the American *Cervidae*, with its distinction between the deer of America and Europe, would not be surpassed for two centuries. Nevertheless, Harriot's scientific knowledge was limited, and his work provided generally accurate descriptions but little analysis. John White's delicate watercolors, housed in the British Museum, complemented Harriot's work and became the basis for the engravings that accompanied Harriot's published *Report*, the first work in English to describe the New World's natural history.

In the 17th century, individuals living in Virginia and other southern colonies served as correspondents for the Royal Society of London and provided Europeans with information ranging from the abundance of oyster shells in the soil to the proliferation of nettles, spinach, rattlesnakes, and turkey buzzards. As a result of such communications the Philosophical Transactions of the Royal Society began to publish accounts of New World phenomena. John Clayton and John Banister were particularly conscientious in providing English naturalists with field observations from America in the last decades of the 17th century.

John Lawson, surveyor-general for the lords proprietors of the province of North Carolina, traveled widely in North Carolina, and he published the results of his 1700–1701 reconnaissance as *A New Voyage to Carolina*. Two-thirds of this volume examined the natural history of the region and provided a description of 93 birds, 28 mammals, 70 fish, and 4 species of pine. Some of the information he provided was curious, for he classified tortoises, alligators, and snakes among insects; maintained that snakes charmed their victims and their bites could be cured by snakeroot; recorded that whales seldom washed ashore with their tongues intact; and noted that some American Indians hunted whales by climbing on a whale's back and plugging up its spout. His ornithological observations and his comments on Indian life in North Carolina were more carefully prepared and are important sources for that period. Lawson provided James Petiver, a Fellow of the Royal Society and patron of John Banister, with information and specimens from North Carolina. Captured by Tuscarora Indians while on an expedition up the Neuse River, Lawson was slain on 22 September 1711.

Lawson's work was eclipsed by the endeavors of Mark Catesby. English by birth, Catesby had studied under the distinguished naturalist John Ray and became the most experienced naturalist to work in America up to that date. In 1712 he came to Virginia to live with his sister and her family to satisfy, as he notes in the preface to his major work, "a passionate Desire of viewing as well the Animal as Vegetable productions in their native countries; which are strangers in England." For seven years Catesby collected materials in Tidewater Virginia, made trips west into the Blue Ridge Mountains, and voyaged to Jamaica and the islands of Bermuda. He became an experienced field collector before returning to England in 1719. The variety of his collections and the knowledge he had gained of American flora and fauna won support in both England and America for his proposed study on American natural history. In 1722 he returned to America to conduct additional studies. For three more years he conducted field studies, made drawings, and collected specimens from North Carolina to Georgia and Florida and west into the Piedmont. Under conditions of poverty, Catesby labored to complete his work on American natural history. In 1731 his *Natural History of Carolina, Florida, and the Bahama Islands* began to appear in sections. The two volumes were completed in 1743. With their colored plates containing 220 illustrations, they became the most attractive works on American natural history published for the next century. Although Catesby's taxonomy was weak, Linnaeus utilized Catesby's work and frequently incorporated Catesby's descriptions and binomial names of birds, fishes, and plants in his work. Catesby's *Hortus Britanno-Americanus*, published in 1737, with its description of 85 southern trees and shrubs, was the first study in English dedicated to the trees of this continent.

As a descriptive ornithologist, Catesby surpassed the standards of his time and concerned himself with enduring problems that are still studied. Although the plates in his work have been criticized as being on occasion too brightly colored, he was a talented and influential scientific illustrator. Catesby developed the practice of portraying on one plate an ornithological, zoological, or botanical specimen in a balanced natural habitat with the appropriate ecological setting of trees, shrubs, grasses, or other animals. Alexander Wilson and John James Audubon followed Catesby's practice of including floral and faunal specimens on one plate. Through his correspondence, his collections, and his magnificent folio volumes, Catesby stimulated an interest in American natural history in America and England and on the continent.

Natural history in the South was further enhanced by the endeavors of the first native-born American naturalist, John Bartram. Praised by Linnaeus as one of the world's greatest natural botanists, this diligent and meticulous field naturalist made numerous expeditions to collect seeds and specimens for his English friend and patron, Peter Collinson. Always interested in the promotion of natural science in America, he established a major botanical garden on the banks of the Schuylkill River, corresponded with numerous European scientists and collectors, suggested to Benjamin Franklin the need for the exploration of the western reaches of the continent, contributed substantively to the understanding of southern flora and fauna, and was honored by King George III with appointment as "Botanist to the King."

With his son William, an able illustrator, naturalist, and author, he journeyed south in 1765 through Georgia and Florida with instructions from the English crown to find the sources of the St. Johns River. In the fall of 1765 they discovered along the banks of the Altamaha River a new species of small tea tree, which they named in honor of Benjamin Franklin, *Gordonia pubescens Franklinia*, today *Franklinia altamaha*. By the end of the 18th century this species was no longer found in the wild. The attractive specimens of this flowering tree, which can still be seen today in American gardens, are all descendants from specimens maintained by the Bartrams in their Pennsylvania garden. A new species of anise, *Ilicuim parviflorum*, was also discovered on this expedition, and observations were made on soils, trees, fossils, and plants. Since John Bartram's vision was declining, this was the 66-year-old naturalist's last expedition. Details of his experiences were published in 1767 in *An Account of East Florida*.

William Bartram maintained an interest in Florida and in 1773 embarked on a five-year exploration of the natural history of Georgia, eastern Florida, the Carolinas, and Alabama. Named Pucpuggy, the "Flower Hunter," by Indians, he wandered patiently and alone through the southern wilderness studying and observing plants, animals, and Indians. Captivated by the richness and abundance of the area's natural history, he made the first detailed study of the American alligator and provided important early information on the reptiles, amphibians, birds, Indians, and plants of this region. His study contains many elements of a modern ecological survey. While Bartram's *Travels through North and South Carolina, Georgia, East and West Florida* (1791) contributes substantively to southern natural history, the wealth of romantic and exotic imagery in the *Travels* nourished the creative muses of Samuel Taylor Coleridge, William Wordsworth, François-René de Chateaubriand, and other authors of the Romantic movement. "Kubla Khan" and "The Rime of the Ancient Mariner," as well as other works, bear the distinct intellectual imprint of the imagery of Bartram's *Travels*.

Science has traditionally developed in cities, and the lack of cities in the South impeded scientific development there. Charleston's momentary eminence in the development of southern natural history is related to the city's prominence as an urban area in the late 18th and early 19th centuries. Charleston physicians and planters nourished interest in natural history and provided an intellectual milieu attractive to visiting naturalists. The French naturalists André and François Michaux established a nursery near Charleston in 1787. André Michaux had been commissioned by the French monarch Louis XVI to ascertain which of America's trees, particularly the oaks, could be profitably grown in France. In 1801 he published the handsomely illustrated *Histoire des Chénes de l'Amerique*, the first major study of American oaks. From their base near Charleston, André and his son, François, collected specimens in the Carolina mountains, the southern Appalachians, Florida, and the Bahamas. André's posthumously published *Flora Boreali-Americana* (1817–19) was the first systematic study of North American flora and included valuable information about southern flora.

Thomas Jefferson's *Notes on the State of Virginia* (1785) presented a perceptive assessment of the resources and natural history of that state with clear descriptions of the Indians, animals, plants, minerals, climate, and topography found there. Jefferson took the opportunity to refute French naturalist Comte de Buffon's contention that the same species of animals and humans grew smaller in America than in Europe. Less disciplined than Jefferson in scientific interests, Constantine Rafinesque was as comprehensive as the Virginian in his activities. Born in Constantinople, he became an ardent, if occasionally unfocused, student of this nation's natural history. From 1819 to 1826 he collected specimens and studied plants, fishes, shells, fossils, and Indian mounds while a professor at Transylvania College in Lexington, Ky. Although he traveled widely and published profusely on these topics in a variety of journals, he failed to make a substantive contribution in any specific area.

John James Audubon also led a life of wide wanderings. Born in Santo Domingo, he traveled through many of the southern states in his quest to capture through his paintings the birds of America. Much of his life was characterized by economic failures and frustrations, but he labored almost without ceasing from 1827 to 1838 to complete his monumental *Birds of America*. To obtain specimens for study and to observe birds in their natural habitats, he traveled to South Carolina and Florida and to the Keys in 1831. Friends in Washington provided him with government schooners so that he could more comfortably conduct his studies on the St. Johns River and in the Keys. On this trip he made the sketches and studies for the great white heron and brown pelican, which appear in his *Birds of America*. In 1837 Audubon journeyed along the Gulf Coast to Galveston, Tex., but few significant studies resulted from this trip.

In the three decades immediately preceding the Civil War, science became more specialized. The economic advantages of natural resources began to be of concern to southern states, and in North Carolina, South Carolina, Tennessee, Virginia, Alabama, Mississippi, Texas, and Florida state geological surveys were established. The increasing pace of scientific advancement and the development of more sophisticated theoretical assumptions about the methodologies of a scientific discipline reduced, in the last half of the 19th century, the contributions that naturalists and natural historians could make to understanding the natural resources of the South. Although the age of naturalists was waning, the great variety of the South's flora and fauna would continue to attract the attention of scientists.

PHILLIP DRENNON THOMAS
*Wichita State University*

Whitfield J. Bell, *Early American Science: Need and Opportunities for Study* (1955); Albert E. Cowdrey, *This Land, This South: An Environmental History* (1983); Victoria Dickenson, *Drawn from Life: Science and Art in the Portrayal of the New World* (1998); Robert Elman, *First in the Field: America's Pioneering Naturalists* (1977); John C. Greene, *American Science in the Age of Jefferson* (1984); Brooke Hindle, *The Pursuit of Science in Revolutionary America* (1956); William Martin and Mabel Sarah Coon Smallwood, *Natural History and the American Mind* (1941); Amy R. W. Meyers and Margaret Beck Pritchard, *Empire's Nature: Mark Catesby's New World Vision* (1998); Sue Ann Prince, *Stuffing Birds, Pressing Plants, Shaping Knowledge: Natural History in North America, 1730–1860* (2003); Kathryn Hall Proby, *Audubon in Florida, with Selections from the Writings of John James Audubon* (1974); Richard Rhodes, *John*

*James Audubon: The Making of an American* (2004); Henry Savage Jr., *Discovering America, 1700–1875* (1979); Raymond Phineas Stearns, *Science in the British Colonies of America* (1970); Shirley Streshinsky, *Audubon: Life and Art in the American Wilderness* (1993); Leonard Warren, *Constantine Samuel Rafinesque: A Voice in the American Wilderness* (2004).

## Parks and Recreation Areas

Preservationists did not arrive in the South until most of the parks and recreation areas were already designated. At the turn of the 20th century, when men like John Muir first decried the loss of natural places, the South still longed for more development. The National Park Service (NPS), established in 1916, immediately became responsible for 14 new parks, and only Hot Springs, Ark., was available for designation in the Southeast.

The boomtowns created by Yellowstone National Park first attracted the attention of city boosters in Knoxville, Tenn., and Asheville, N.C., in the early 1920s. Although wealthy patrons from the Tidewater cities already sent their families to mountain resorts in hot weather to avoid epidemics, no one had considered scenery as key to development or civic pride. The mountains, city people thought, lagged behind the rest of the state for a reason: poor people lived there on poor land. And so automobile clubs, civic boosters, and resort owners pushed to bring a national park to the South. To be sure, a few preservation-minded hikers joined them, but they did not constitute a movement. By the time Secretary of the Interior Hubert Work appointed the Southern Appalachian National Park Committee in 1924, promoters across the South competed to prove that they had the most beautiful mountains in the land. When the committee reached Gainesville, Ga., for example, 60 men showed up to convince them that north Georgia had the most scenic mountains in the region. In the Smoky Mountains of Tennessee, David Chapman, owner of a drug company in Knoxville and leader of the park movement there, went hiking for the first time in his life with Work's committee.

Work recommended that the Shenandoah Valley of Virginia become the first national park in the southern mountains. Buoyed by a spirit of competitiveness, Chapman and his Great Smoky Mountains Conservation Association pushed their congressmen to designate a park in Tennessee and North Carolina as well. Others followed suit. In 1926 Congress actually authorized three parks—Shenandoah, Great Smoky Mountains, and Mammoth Cave (Ky.)—but provided none of the funding. For the next 10 years, southern states scrambled to raise money and to deal with the complex issues of land title and ownership.

Logging and mining companies owned much of the unpopulated land, and park boosters faced bitter opposition and price gouging as well as local fears that parks would eliminate jobs and cut the tax base. Primarily urban folk, park fund-raisers did not see mountain residents as a realistic obstacle; as one Shenandoah official put it, a lack of "independence and resourcefulness" explained their rejection of modernity—and parks. In the Smokies, North Carolina and Tennessee gained the power of eminent domain to remove 5,665 people from 1,132 small farms; in Shenandoah, 600 families were "resettled" with the help of the Federal Homestead Corporation. As the Great Depression descended, both parks had endless problems with squatters who had no place to go and elderly people who refused to leave their homes. In 1934 the park service declared that certain "aged and especially meritorious" individuals could continue to live on their farms in the national parks; these "lifetime leasers" remained until the 1970s as objects of curiosity to many tourists.

Even in the midst of the Depression, Shenandoah and the Smokies brought tourism dollars, which encouraged Texas to promote Big Bend in 1935, a "fabulous corner of the world" that could "excel Yellowstone." As with the Smokies and Shenandoah, slow fund-raising during the 1940s combined with the complex purchase of small ranches made land acquisition something of a nightmare. Big Bend still includes inholdings, where residents stalk game or graze livestock, surrounded by national park lands. As early as 1929 Ernest F. Coe, a Yale-educated landscape architect, got the NPS interested in an Everglades National Park, but the old problems of fund-raising and byzantine land titles delayed dedication until 1947.

During the 1930s a New Deal relief program for young people, the Civilian Conservation Corps (CCC), also stimulated interest in southern parks. Charged with conservation work, the CCC employed young men to plant trees, stock fish, conduct fire prevention work, and build recreation facilities in the nation's over-harvested forests. Because they had new national parks that sorely needed this kind of development, Tennessee, North Carolina, and Virginia at first picked up the majority of CCC camps. Federal funding, however, inspired other southern states to start their own park departments, usually under a fledgling forestry or conservation division. South Carolina alone initiated 15 parks in the decade, buying land at Depression-era prices and promptly requesting CCC workers to build the needed trails and amenities. Alabama built 14 state parks on 21,769 acres of land with the help of the CCC and first began management of these lands when the CCC left. After World War II, southern states began to claim a stronger urban middle class whose members wanted to travel by automobile to parks for family camping. No one had to explain parks to their congressman any more. Virtually all the southern states extended their state park systems in response to 1950s travel. Governor Marvin Griffith of Georgia actually ran on a platform of granting "every county a state park."

Since they followed the National Park System, southern state parks borrowed NPS standards for everything from scenic landscape design to the use of seasonal employees. Both federal and state properties in the South, however, bowed to local segregation laws, providing separate facilities for white and black citizens, or no facilities for African Americans. A brochure from Georgia in the 1950s shows three state parks "for Negroes." In 1961 South Carolina, civil rights leaders filed a class-action suit against the state for failing to integrate the parks; the state attorney general responded by closing all the parks in 1963. They did not return to full operation until 1966.

At the national level, the U.S. Department of Interior pushed for a new classification, national recreation area, which would meet the demand for outdoor recreation without the special "scenic and historic" qualities found in national parks. Some of the same problems of land acquisition resurfaced; not surprisingly, rural residents did not welcome the loss of their land by eminent domain for city folks to enjoy. During the 1970s the Tennessee Valley Authority (TVA) pushed to make a national recreation area out of the land between the Kentucky Dam and the Barkley Dam, called the Land between the Lakes. The TVA did not want the management issues associated with the land, so they billed this as a development boom for the area. Many of the 900 families who lived there, however, had small tourism-related businesses and did not see their removal as a benefit.

Preservationists became a notable force in public policy finally in the 1970s. The Sierra Club organized the citizens of South Carolina to push for national park designation of the Congaree Swamp. Many environmentally minded people in the South have no idea, however, that their heritage rests on civic boosters and economic development. Recent issues related to parks include air pollution, water pollution threats, and the opening of some public lands to economic development.

MARGARET LYNN BROWN
*Brevard College*

Margaret Lynn Brown, *The Wild East: A Biography of the Great Smoky Mountains* (2000); John Jameson, *The Story of Big Bend National Park* (1996); Charles L. Perdue and Nancy J. Martin-Perdue, *Appalachian Journal* (Autumn–Winter 1979–80).

## Plants

To early colonial explorers and settlers accustomed to the relatively low plant diversity of Europe, the plants of the New World were one of its greatest wonders. The immense botanical diversity of the South has played, and continues to play, an important role in both the commerce and the culture of the region. Indeed, no other part of the country has such a strong association of its culture with plants. Native magnolias, Spanish moss, and longleaf pine and introduced plants such as indigo, rice, cotton, tobacco, peanuts, collards, okra, and kudzu elicit historical, political, economic, and culinary associations all of a regional nature.

Although the inland hardwood forests of the southern piedmont and mountains were generally similar in appearance to the deciduous forests of eastern North America and northern Europe, the first colonial settlements were in coastal areas that, in the South, are typified by forests of broad-leaved evergreens—magnolia, bay, live oak, and cherry laurel—which were quite unfamiliar. For the first two centuries after the discovery of America by the Europeans, these exotic evergreen trees, often shrouded in gray wisps of Spanish moss, typified the South. The associations remain even today a part of both actual and legendary southern culture.

Many of the early colonists truly had to "live off the land," and they depended on the variety of native trees, shrubs, and herbs for basic needs of food, shelter, fuel, and medicine. Some southern plants that maintain a visible role in southern culture and commerce are the pecan (*Carya illinoensis*), persimmon (*Diospyros virginiana*), sassafras (*Sassafras albidum*), and muscadine grape (*Vitis rotundifolia*), all of which provide food and/or beverage; the various species of pine for pulp, timber, turpentine, and solvents; the white oaks for timber and cooperage; and an array of other native hardwoods for furniture manufacture, paneling, and other specialized use. In addition, a number of native plants, such as magnolia, azalea, rhododendron, bayberry, and holly, are of horticultural value.

During the 18th century naturalists began to collect and describe the wealth of plants available in the South. Among these naturalists were Virginian John Clayton (1657–1725), whose collections of native plants were carefully studied and published as *Flora Virginica* in 1739–43 by J. F. Gronovius of Holland; Mark Catesby (1682–1749), an English naturalist who spent the years from 1712 to 1726 in Virginia and the Bahamas and then returned to England to publish, in 1731 and 1743, his remarkably illustrated *Natural History of Carolina, Florida, and the Bahama Islands*; André Michaux (1746–1802), a French botanist who established a garden at Charleston, S.C., and whose botanical explorations of much of eastern North America were the basis for his *Flora Boreali-Americana*, published in 1817–19; the father and son naturalists John (1699–1776) and William (1739–1823) Bartram of Pennsylvania, whose active botanical exploration, writing, and plant exchange program provided the strongest botanical link between Britain and America during the middle of the 18th century and led to the 1791 publication of William Bartram's classic *Travels through North and South Carolina, Georgia, East and West Florida*; and the Englishman Thomas Walter (1740–88), who settled along the Santee River in South Carolina and from the surrounding area of 500 or so square miles collected the varied plants that formed the basis for his *Flora Caroliniana*, which was published in 1788.

Of special interest to the many professional and amateur European naturalists of the 18th century were the various species of insect-catching or "carnivorous" plants native to the moist, sandy, open Coastal Plain savannas of the South. Indeed, worldwide interest in these fascinating and often colorful plants continues even today, and overexploitation of the native populations has brought a number of these species to the verge of extinction. The greatest variety of insectivorous plants to be found in North America can still be observed, however, on protected lands in the vicinity of Wilmington, N.C. Here, with diligent searching in appropriate habitats one can find four species of pitcher plant (*Sarracenia* sp.), four species of sundew (*Drosera* sp.), nine species of bladderwort (*Utricularia* sp.), three species of butterwort (*Pinguicula* sp.), and the widely known Venus flytrap (*Dionaea muscipula*), which was first brought to the attention of botanists in 1759 by Governor Arthur Dobbs of North Carolina and which Charles Darwin called "the most wonderful plant in the world."

Wildflowers have long been a beloved part of the southern rural landscape. Tourists and natives alike have frequently commented on their growth along the roadside, in meadows, and in fields. They are hardy plants, adapting to a variety of climate and soil conditions. One sees buttercups in spring, Queen Anne's lace in summer, and goldenrod in fall. There are bloodroots, black-eyed Susans, yellow lady's slipper orchids, bee balms, mayapples, atamasco lilies, bird's-foot violet, rue anemone, and Jack-in-the-pulpits. In the modern South the natural heritage is reinforced through human efforts. Texas has launched a major program to promote wildflower growth, especially the state's floral emblem, the bluebonnet, making the state's highways more attractive. Now, most southern states have followed Texas's lead with wildflower planting projects along interstate highways. Regionally oriented magazines such as *Southern Living* and gardening books tell southerners how to cultivate wildflowers as parts of planned suburban gardens. Organizations such as the Plant Rescue Volunteers at the

North Carolina Botanical Gardens in Chapel Hill collect endangered plants and grow plants from these specimens.

The southern states acknowledged the cultural significance of plants in the early 20th century when they adopted state flowers—goldenrod (Alabama, 1927; Kentucky, 1926; North Carolina, unofficial), apple blossom (Arkansas, 1901), orange blossom (Florida, 1909), Cherokee rose (Georgia, 1916), magnolia (Louisiana, 1900; Mississippi, 1900), yellow or Carolina jessamine (South Carolina, 1924), iris (Tennessee, 1933; earlier the passion flower or maypop), American dogwood (Virginia, 1918), and bluebonnet (Texas, 1901). Florida's nickname is the Flower State because of its abundant plant life.

Over the past 200 years natural plant migrations and continued introductions have added many species to the varied flora of the South. In succession, corn, then cotton, and finally soybean have been dominant cash crops in the region. Sugar in Louisiana, rice in low-lying terrains of the coast and river areas, tobacco in the Upper South, and hemp in Kentucky—all represent cultivated plants of economic importance in specific regions within the South. The study of these native and naturalized plants is still of considerable scientific interest, and their role in commerce, medicine, and recreation is of growing importance. The wise use and realistic conservation of the South's natural plant resources are issues that are also of growing relevance to the future of the region.

Plants not only add beauty to the environment and interest to a culture but are the world's only renewable resource that can reasonably be expected to supply the growing needs of humans for food, fuel, and fiber. Because the milder climate, longer growing season, and generally adequate rainfall characteristic of much of the South are often the primary factors in optimal plant growth, the plants of southern fields and forests will likely continue to play an important role in the economy, politics, and culture of the area for many years to come.

C. RITCHIE BELL
*North Carolina Botanical Gardens*
*University of North Carolina at Chapel Hill*

ROBERT L. IZLAR
*Warnell School of Forest Resources*
*University of Georgia*

William Bartram, *Travels of William Bartram*, ed. Francis Harper (1967); Ben A. Davis, *The Southern Garden: From the Potomac to the Rio Grande* (1971); Blanche E. Dean, Amy Mason, and Joab L. Thomas, *Wildflowers of Alabama and Adjoining States*

(1973); Wilbur H. Duncan and Leonard E. Foote, *Wildflowers of the Southeastern United States* (1975); Wilbur H. Duncan and Marion B. Duncan, *Trees of the Southeastern United States* (1988), *Wildflowers of the Eastern United States* (1999); Ron Lance, *Woody Plants of the Southeastern United States* (2004); James H. Miller and Karl V. Miller, *Forest Plants of the Southeast and Their Wildlife Uses* (2005); Albert E. Radford, Harry E. Ahles, and C. Ritchie Bell, *Manual of the Vascular Flora of the Carolinas* (1968); Harold W. Rickett, *Wildflowers of Southeastern States* (1967); J. K. Small, *Manual of the Southeastern Flora* (1933).

## Plant Uses

In addition to making economic use of cultivated plants, southerners have long utilized wild plants in a variety of ways. The pattern was set long ago by southeastern Indians. Plants were an important part of their belief system. The Indians believed that humans, animals, and plants were interrelated and that a balance between these forms should exist to keep nature properly functioning. The boundary between the animal and plant realms was blurred by plants such as the Venus flytrap and the pitcher plant, which trapped and "ate" insects. This kind of anomaly was of particular interest to southerners and took on symbolic significance in their oral traditions, which attributed extraordinary powers to the roots of these plants.

Native Americans made plants part of their ritual life. The cedar, pine, spruce, holly, and laurel ranked at the top of the Cherokee belief system in terms of ritual purity. Tobacco smoking preceded council meetings of chiefs, and "black drink" was a ceremonial beverage regarded as essential for these occasions. The Indians in their own language called it "white drink," because it symbolized purity, happiness, and harmony. The Europeans labeled it "black drink" because of its color. Made from the leaves of a variety of holly (*Ilex vomitoria Ait.*), black drink was a tea with a bitter taste and high caffeine content. To make it, the Indians dried leaves and twigs and parched them over a fire to a deep brown color. The product of this process was then boiled in water, producing a dark brown liquid. It was a stimulant and a diuretic, and the Indians also used it as an emetic. Early European colonists used black drink as a stimulant but gave it up after coffee and tea became more available in the later 1600s.

Wild vegetables were important as a food source for southeastern Indians. Women, the elderly, and children gathered vegetables, fruits, berries, seeds, and nuts, all of which were plentiful through much of the Southeast. Roots and tubers were the most valuable wild vegetables in the Indian diet. The big, tuberous roots that grow on various species of a green shrub called smilax L., which twines itself around trees, were especially popular. The taproot of the "wild sweet potato," or wild morning glory (*Ipomoea pandurata L.*), can weigh as much as 20 to 30 pounds. "Swamp potatoes" were collected in low-lying marshlands from the root of arrowhead (*Sagittaria L.*). The crunchy roots of the Jerusalem artichoke were gathered in fall and winter. The southeastern Indians enjoyed the persimmon and collected muscadine grapes and scuppernongs. They also ate wild cherries, papaws, crab apples, and wild plums. The summer months saw them feasting on gathered blackberries, strawberries, gooseberries, and raspberries, and they picked from trees the huckleberries, black gum berries, mulberries, serviceberries, and palmetto berries. Nuts were especially important in the southeastern Indian diet. In autumn, Indians collected chestnuts, chinquapins (a small variety of chestnuts), pecans, hickory nuts, black walnuts, and the acorns of the live oak, white oak, chestnut oak, and others. They ground seeds from cockspurgrass (*Echinochloa Beau V.*), the nulumbo, and chenopodium (*Chenopodium ambrosioides L.*) to make meal to be used in cooking.

Herbs were crucial in the Indian medicinal system. The Creeks, for example, used "red root," made from the bark of the root of a willow tree, to treat rheumatism, nausea, fever, malaria, and other health problems. Creeks used "button snakeroot" to treat neuralgia, kidney troubles, and snakebite and as a spring tonic. The roots of ginseng (*Panax quinquefolium L.*) were boiled in water and used as a potion to help with shortness of breath, to heal a wound, and to keep ghosts away. Among the other main Creek herbs were angelica, wormseed, red cedar, spicebush, and horsemint—a typical list for other tribes as well.

The southeastern Indians had a multitude of other uses for wild plants: they made clothing from Spanish moss; used the bottle gourd (*Lagenaria siceraria*) for water vessels, dippers, ladles, cups, bowls, birdhouses, rattles, and masks, among other things; and made baskets of bark, grass, and, especially, strips of the outer covering of cane.

Rural southern blacks and whites followed in the paths of the southeastern Indians and used wild plants as food, drink, cosmetics, and medicine and in their arts and crafts. Much understanding of the uses of plants was also brought from Europe and Africa by early settlers. Medicine has made particular use of plants. Yellow root, tree bark, and sassafras have long been used by southern blacks as home remedies; traditional healers, or "root doctors," are still consulted to cure ailments such as headaches, loss of memory, itching, and exhaustion. Specialists are sought who deal with particular ailments. Among North Carolina root doctors, for example, mint tea is known as the treatment for hysteria; sassafras, for stomach pains; and jimson tea, for constipation. Allen Eaton, in a 1937 volume on the southern highlands, reported that one local root doctor in Tennessee had a list of 52 herbs that he used. The list included bloodroot, a spring tonic; blacksnake, to calm the stomach; blackberry root, for diarrhea; boneset, for colds; butterfly root, for female troubles; buckeye, for rheumatism; calamus, for an upset stomach; crab apple bark, for asthma; dandelion root, for the blood; heart leaf, good for "weak hearted persons"; larkspur tincture, for hair trouble; mullein, for coughs; persimmon bark, a salve; pennyroyal, good for bedbugs and colds; redroot, to ease the bowels; stone root, good to ease kidney stone pain; slippery elm, to treat sore eyes; wild comfort, "a manhood medicine"; and redbud roots, to clean the teeth. In Louisiana sarsaparilla tea was drunk each spring in hopes of purifying the blood; a poultice of wild potato plant leaves was said to relieve boils and inflammation; copal moss, when soaked in hot water with whiskey, was an effective drink for general "miseries."

Rural whites and blacks used extracts from wild plants to color yarns, threads, baskets, and textiles. The most important dyes used by Appalachian women were indigo and madder, which provided the blue and red colorings used in many blankets and quilts. Indigo comes from the plant indigofera; it produces yellow flowers in late summer, and the boiled plant makes a blue dye, which was popular because it was a highly permanent natural dye and also subject to a variety of shades. Madder was both native and cultivated in the mountains, where pioneer women used the huge roots to produce a range of shades, from a deep red to a delicate pink, on both cotton and wool. Other natural vegetable dye colors used by southern blacks and whites included browns, blacks, and grays from walnuts; grays and tans from sumac berries; pinks and lavenders from pokeberries; yellows from hickory bark; yellow and orange from wild coreopsis; pink-yellow from sedge grass; and green from pine needles. The time of the year in which the roots, barks, hulls, fruits, nuts, leaves, seeds, stems, or whole plants are gathered can produce different shades.

During the Civil War, southerners relied on plants in various ways. They used caffeine-bearing holly berries to make tea, and they parched rye, acorns, beets, and sweet potatoes to make a coffee substitute. Chinaberries were used to make a shoe-blacking paste, Spanish moss became an ingredient in rope, and cork was made from cypress "knees." Children were set to work puncturing poppies to obtain opium-bearing droplets for use as a medicine for the wounded.

Southerners used plants and their products in folk arts and crafts. Pine needles and straw, white oak strips, palmetto fronds, and other plant materials were essential ingredients in basketry. Mountain women gathered native barks, cones, grasses, seeds, leaves, pods, berries, and acorns to make home decorations for interiors or to sell to tourists and collectors. Gourds were used as sounding boxes for homemade fiddles and banjos, for decorative purposes, and for birdhouses.

Southern writers and artists have frequently used plants to establish the sense of a distinctive place. Scholar Earl F. Bargainnier has noted that in literary portrayals of the myth of "moonlight and magnolias," "the aroma of magnolias—or honeysuckle, oleanders, or roses—is thick in the warm evening." William Faulkner titled a short story "An Odor of Verbena" and described many plants, but his favorite must have been wistaria. "It was a summer of wistaria," says Quentin Compson in *Absalom, Absalom!* (1936). Quentin recalled the "sweet and oversweet" smell of "twice-bloomed wistaria" at Rosa Coldfield's house, and when he was a student at Harvard he still thought of the plant's "odor, the scent." Folk artist Theora Hamblett of Oxford, Miss., painted the calamus vine, recalling later that the morning after her stroke in 1964 she would close her eyes and see a vision of long vines and golden leaves. She had never actually seen a calamus, but she painted her vision and later discovered the actual plant it was. At a more popular level, southerners of all social classes and groups decorate their homes with paintings and ceramics of local flowers: magnolias in Mississippi, bluebonnets in Texas, and orange blossoms in Florida.

CHARLES REAGAN WILSON
*University of Mississippi*

Judith Bolyard, *Medicinal Plants and Home Remedies of Appalachia* (1981); Anthony P. Cavender, *Folk Medicine in Southern Appalachia* (2003); Allen Eaton, *Handicrafts of the Southern Highlands* (1937); Wayland Hand, ed., *American Folk Medicine: A Symposium* (1976); Charles M. Hudson, *The Southeastern Indians* (1976); Clarence Meyer, *American Folk Medicine* (1973); Kay Moss, *Southern Folk Medicine, 1750–1820* (1999); Newbill Niles Puckett, *Folk Beliefs of the Southern Negro* (1926; 1969); Virgil Vogel, *American Indian Medicine* (1970); Eliot Wigginton, *The Foxfire Book* (1972).

## Pollution

When a national commission mapped the "pollution belt" in 1939, it omitted the southern states. Since the South was a rural region, many considered it pristine and bucolic, but it has its own distinct pollution history. Before the early 1970s, states held the primary pollution control authority, and during that time, southern state governments were slow to embrace policies to protect the environment. Southerners, however, consistently voiced objections to pollution that damaged natural resources. As a spate of federal environmental laws in the 1970s called for greater national consistency, southern states gradually came in line with the rest of the country.

The Ducktown copper basin in eastern Tennessee became industry's first dramatic "sacrifice zone" in the South. Copper smelters that rapidly expanded in the late 19th century fouled the air with toxic sulfurous emissions that, along with intensive deforestation to secure fuel, left a sterile and denuded landscape and a string of lawsuits from neighbors. Tennessee courts acknowledged a nuisance but declined to order an injunction. When the emissions spilled over into Georgia, landowners there initiated lawsuits that rose to the U.S. Supreme Court in 1904. The high court ultimately secured agreements that the smelters would pay damages to Georgia residents and begin recovering sulfur from the emissions to produce sulfuric acid. Nonetheless, smelter pollution left a virtual "moonscape" some 50 square miles in extent, with larger areas suffering less extreme impacts. Restoration of the most severely damaged countryside continued into the 1990s.

In more recent years, phosphate mining and processing in Florida characterized the tendency of southern states to limit enforcement against new industries that brought jobs and tax revenue, along with pollution. Growth of phosphate processing in the 1940s released unprecedented amounts of fluorine into the air that harmed neighboring agricultural operations. Despite complaints from farmers, a potent political voice, the state response was slow and ineffective. Legislators eventually authorized a pollution control commission, but it was reluctant to confront a powerful industry. Citizen appeals to federal authorities spawned debates among competing experts but brought no resolution. By the 1960s, farmers began winning lawsuits against the polluters, and the courts forced manufacturers to compensate their neighbors for harm to crops and livestock. Despite government tolerance for industrial pollution, Florida residents vigorously objected to undesirable conditions and eventually found relief through legal means.

In the shadows of the mighty petrochemical refineries along the lower Mississippi River, atmospheric emissions have prompted a considerable environmental justice movement. Large numbers of rural African Americans reside adjacent to chemical processing plants that make Louisiana a national leader for combined toxic releases. The majority of these producers cluster in what local residents refer to as "cancer alley." Opposition has arisen among communities of color, and despite an often reluctant state government, citizen pressure has secured some improvements in air quality. Manufacturers have also purchased the homes of some residents who live in the path of pollution and otherwise would not be able to evacuate. Sometimes successful citizens' groups have earned a national reputation for their environmental justice efforts.

One of the first great southern conflicts between landowners and water-polluting industries occurred in the east Texas oil fields. Producers conveniently dumped waste brine into streams after separating it from the crude oil. Drought conditions during the 1930s, in conjunction with massive saltwater releases, produced objections from downstream landowners. Working with the producers, the state encouraged a solution that would reinject the brines into underground formations and thereby reduce discharges to waterways. Reinjecting brines represents an effort to protect water resources, but equally important it helped producers extract more oil and worked as a mineral conservation technique. Its efficiency, as much as its pollution-reducing capabilities, ensured its application by the oil industry across the country.

Other natural resource–based industries overwhelmed waterways in the South. Paper mills produced particularly objectionable wastes across the great pine belt. One North Carolina manufacturer avoided regulation for decades by releasing its wastes into Tennessee, which had no legal authority to intervene. In Louisiana, fishermen and farmers objected to conditions produced by paper mills. Responding to their protests in the 1950s and 1960s, federal investigators encouraged plants to improve their waste treatment techniques. With little regulatory authority, agency personnel relied on cooperative solutions to pollution problems. The distinctive element of southern pollution control, epitomized by the objections to paper mill discharges, sought to protect aquatic life while largely ignoring public health concerns. With a smaller percentage of urban residents relying on river water than in the country's manufacturing core, pressure to prevent foul-tasting or disease-producing pollution was less prominent in the South.

Mississippi River pollution reflects the shift from natural resource concerns to public health priorities in both the nation and the South. A major fish kill occurred on the Mississippi River during the winter of 1963–64. In the wake of Rachel Carson's *Silent Spring*, a critique of pesticide use and a powerful impetus behind the national environmental movement, some officials feared agricultural chemicals were the cause. Federal investigators determined that industrial waste, not chemical runoff, was responsible. Ultimately, the producer diverted its wastes to a land disposal site—an example of the "search for the ultimate sink" to resolve the problem. A decade later, environmental organizations identified the Mississippi as a leading cause of cancer to people who drank its water, and the river became a prominent symbol of degraded waters. The U.S. Environmental Protection Agency reported 60 major sources of toxic organic chemicals that could enter New Orleans's drinking water supply, and this revelation heightened concern with the nation's sewer as a public health threat. Putting the Mississippi in the national spotlight contributed to the passage of the Safe Drinking Water Act in 1974, which fundamentally changed the focus of water pollution legislation from raw water quality to drinking water supplies.

Since the late 19th century, oystermen and other fishermen have fought to protect the Chesapeake Bay. Their early battles focused on deflecting Baltimore's sewage, which could introduce disease-causing bacteria to the oysters. Although Baltimore began treating its sewage in 1912, other metropolitan areas were slower to adopt technological fixes. As "the nation's river," the Potomac received regular investigations that documented the impact of sewage on water quality in the 1930s and 1950s. In 1940 the states that drained into the bay formed one of the first interstate compacts to coordinate pollution control efforts. Nonetheless, pollution continued, and in 1983 the EPA helped form the Chesapeake Bay Program with a goal to protect the bay and to ensure its restoration for the aquatic life that is central to the local society and economy. Efforts reach from the coal-mined headwaters to the sewage treatment plants in the metropolitan centers along the tidal bays. Basinwide restoration aims have not been achieved yet, but conditions have been improving in recent years with the aid of interstate cooperation.

Land pollution has been a source of contention in the South as well. The infamous "Valley of the Drums" in rural Kentucky was one of the high-profile sites prompting, in 1980, the passage of federal legislation that created programs to clean up the most severely contaminated disposal dumps. The Superfund Act helped focus attention on land pollution. The South's large African American population, who sometimes shouldered an inordinate risk of exposure to hazardous materials, has rallied to secure environmental justice and clean up superfund sites. Responding to state plans to open a toxic waste landfill, rural North Carolina residents drew on their experience and contacts in the civil rights struggle to oppose the impending project. Although ultimately unsuccessful, their efforts spawned a nationwide environmental justice movement that seeks to ensure that all people, regardless of race or income, receive equal treatment under the law in terms of waste disposal facilities. In direct succession of their North Carolina counterparts, residents in Anniston, Ala., protested the accumulation of tons of toxic substances in their community and the local landfill from 40 years of polychlorinated biphenyl manufacture. Activation of many community groups and the adoption of federal policies to oversee equitable administration of environmental laws have contributed to the cleanup of toxic sites across the South. In addition to major petrochemical plants that have created toxic waste sites, many smaller creosote operations typify the damages to land caused by resource-based industries in the South.

While state officials were slow to respond to citizen protests to pollution problems, the South now follows the national policies to abate environmental degradation. In recent years, the source of pollution opposition has shifted from white sportsmen and farmers who desired to protect their fishing grounds and livestock to black community members who seek environmental justice.

CRAIG E. COLTEN
*Louisiana State University*

Richard A. Bartlett, *Troubled Waters: Champion International and the Pigeon River Controversy* (1995); Christopher G. Boone, *Historical Geography* (2003); Robert D. Bullard, *Dumping in Dixie: Race, Class, and Environmental Quality* (1994); John Caper, Garrett Power, and Frank Shivers Jr., *Chesapeake Waters: Pollution, Public Health, and Public Opinion, 1607–1972*; Chesapeake Bay Program, *Twenty Years of Progress—Remaining Challenges* (2003); Craig E. Colten, *An Unnatural Metropolis: Wresting New Orleans from Nature* (2005); Scott H. Dewey, *Journal of Southern History* (August 1999); Hugh Gorman, *Redefining Efficiency: Pollution Concerns, Regulatory Mechanisms, and Technological Change in the U.S. Petroleum Industry* (2001); Gerald Markowitz and David Rosner, *Deceit and Denial: The Deadly Politics of Industrial Pollution* (2002); Eileen McGurty, *Environmental History* (1997); M. L. Quinn, *Technology and Culture* (1993); U.S. Department of the Interior, *The Nation's River* (1968).

## Reclamation and Irrigation

Inseparable concepts in the arid American West, reclamation and irrigation differed significantly in the South. Farmers in Dixie received 40 to 60 inches of annual rainfall and understood reclamation to mean the drainage of swamps and marshes, not the watering of deserts. Efforts to transform wetlands into property suitable for agriculture or housing were common, but irrigation was not. Most southerners found their crops adequately watered by nature. Rice growers were the great exception and remained the region's major irrigators for more than two centuries. Irrigation increased dramatically and reclamation virtually reversed course as agribusiness and environmentalism gradually gained prominence in southern life after World War II.

In the late 1680s, South Carolina colonists established rice as a money crop in a narrow strip of plantations along the Atlantic Coast. Expanded to include coastal Georgia in the 1760s, these farms produced millions of pounds of rice annually until the end of the 19th century. The rice plant grew best with periodic flooding. Plantation owners and slaves devised irrigation technology that took advantage of tidal rivers. Incoming ocean water lifted the lighter freshwater in the rivers high enough to enter floodgates that opened to a complex maze of canals, holding ponds, and rice fields. Trapped and distributed by workers or drained back through the floodgates at low tide, river water irrigated rice crops in the Lowcountry for over 200 years. The industry survived the disruptions of the Civil War, but declining profits and competition from new rice farms in Louisiana, Texas, and Arkansas virtually ended rice growing along the Atlantic Coast by 1910.

The second and present southern rice industry began in southwestern Louisiana in the 1880s. Like their Lowcountry predecessors, these farms were large operations requiring significant investments. Transplanted midwestern wheat farmers used their mechanical threshers and cultivators to grow rice on the flat fields of the coastal prairie with great success. Annual production rose from millions of pounds of rice in the 1880s to hundreds of millions in the 1890s. Irrigation using rainwater stored by farmers in holding ponds quickly gave way to an intricate system of bayous, canals, and pumps managed by water companies servicing the rice industry. With wells often providing water in the absence of bayous, rice farming spread rapidly from Louisiana to Texas and Arkansas. These three states produced a $1.1 billion rice crop in 2005.

Rice production was a large-farm undertaking from its earliest days, but cotton, tobacco, corn, and other crops could be grown for marginal profit on acreage of any size. Mired in poverty and mule-driven sharecropping, most farms in the South remained small for decades after Reconstruction. In the 1930s Franklin Roosevelt's New Deal programs brought cash and electricity to southern farmers, jump-starting mechanization and corporate agriculture. Home front support work during World War II brought an influx of people and more cash, setting the stage for the southern agribusiness boom in the last half of the 20th century. This led to the growth of supplemental irrigation through-out the region for virtually all crops. Supplemental (or conservation) irrigation maximized crop yields by distributing water during droughts or periods of light rainfall to ensure uninterrupted plant growth. Costly and impractical for small operations, supplemental irrigation offered increased profits and commonsense crop insurance to owners and managers of large, highly mechanized farms.

The 1930 U.S. irrigation census included only those states in which irrigation was customary: the 17 western states (including Texas) covered under the 1902 Reclamation Act, plus Louisiana and Arkansas. In 1940 Florida was added to the census, and in 1957 the Soil Conservation Service jumped on the bandwagon and published *Conservation Irrigation in Humid Areas*, a step-by-step manual explaining the mysteries of ditch linings, pumps, sprinklers, and perforated pipes to farmers east of the Mississippi River. Over the next 50 years southern farmers learned to spray, drip, and seep supplemental water to crops ranging from sugarcane and tomatoes to peanuts and oranges. By the end of the 20th century, 34 percent of the 38.7 million agricultural acres in the South were irrigated, removing more than 6.8 billion gallons of water from surface sources and 18.2 billion gallons from aquifers every day. Total irrigation water withdrawals of 25 billion gallons daily exceeded the combined withdrawals for public water supply and industrial use by 4.2 billion gallons. This extraordinary hydrological change contributed to the development of unprecedented regional water shortages and legal fights between southern states comparable to long-standing water wars in the West.

By the year 2000, Florida, with 16 million people and 8.1 billion gallons of freshwater used per day, became a water-shortage poster child for the ecological consequences of booming population growth. But irrigation accounted for 52 percent of the freshwater withdrawals in the Sunshine State, where lowered water tables promoted sinkholes and saltwater intrusion into aquifers. Irrigated sugarcane production and runaway urbanization shared responsibility for the near-destruction of the Everglades ecosystem through pollution and water deprivation. This environmental catastrophe prompted Congress to launch the Comprehensive Everglades Restoration Project, a billion-dollar effort led by the U.S. Army Corps of Engineers to reverse decades of corps reclamation work designed to replace the Everglades and other Florida wetlands with farms and subdivisions.

Reclamation projects were widespread in the South throughout most of its history. Common wisdom condemned wetlands as useless and unhealthy, and all efforts to "reclaim" them for the benefit of humans were applauded. Colonial planters in Louisiana built levees to hold back the Mississippi River's periodic flooding, and their counterparts in South Carolina drained swamplands to create rice fields. George Washington participated in a failed 1763 scheme to drain the Great Dismal Swamp in coastal Virginia and North Carolina, and untold numbers of less famous southern landowners attempted similar projects on smaller scales. Federal legislation encouraging the destruction of wetlands began with the Swamp Land Acts of 1849, 1850, and 1860 that gave 15 water-challenged states 64.9 million acres of marshes and swamps to be sold and drained. Five southern states—Louisiana, Arkansas, Alabama, Florida, and Mississippi—received nearly two-thirds of this land, but revenue from sales proved to be far less than the cost of reclamation. State governments and pri-

Large-crop irrigation system (Peggy Greb, U.S. Department of Agriculture, Washington, D.C.)

vate developers proceeded with drainage programs at a dishearteningly slow pace, but support for wetlands reclamation became established federal policy in the mid-19th century. Over the next hundred years a combination of federal programs for flood control, soil conservation, forestry, and drainage provided millions of dollars for the reclamation of wetlands throughout the United States.

After the Civil War, officials in the Mississippi River states pinned their flood control and reclamation hopes on the national economic importance of the Big Muddy. With the establishment of the federal Mississippi River Commission in 1879, flood control money disguised as federal funds for navigation improvements gradually began flowing to southern levee and drainage canal projects. In the 1870s and 1880s Florida officials supported private developers' partially successful efforts to drain Lake Okeechobee and millions of surrounding wetland acres by digging canals from the lake to the Atlantic Ocean and the Gulf of Mexico. Governor Napoleon Broward revived this vast reclamation effort in 1905, and in 1913 the Everglades Drainage District was established. Thousands of Everglades acres were converted to sugarcane fields and housing tracts, setting the stage for the great hurricane and flood of 1928 that drowned 400 people south of Lake Okeechobee. Congress responded, and the Army Corps of Engineers built the Hoover Dike, a massive barrier nearly surrounding the great lake that guarded against floods and greatly aided further reclamation. After passage of the Flood Control Act of 1936, the Army Corps of Engineers became fully engaged in the war against the wetlands in Florida, across the South, and throughout the nation.

The opening of Everglades National Park in 1947 signaled a shift in American attitudes toward swamps and marshes, but change came slowly. The 1955 *Yearbook of Agriculture* devoted 91 pages to a "Drainage of Fields" section that included a "Drainage of Peat and Muck Lands" chapter in which Everglades reclamation was praised. The same U.S. Department of Agriculture publication included a "Drainage in Forestry Management in the South" chapter that focused on North and South Carolina wooded wetlands. Despite the rise of environmentalism in the 1960s, reclamation work continued at a breakneck pace. In the decade following passage of the 1972 Clean Water Act, the beginning of federal wetlands protection in the United States, North Carolina lost 1.2 million pocosin acres.

From an estimated 99.4 million acres in 1780, southern wetlands were reduced to 55.5 million acres by the mid-1980s, with most losses coming after 1936. Reclamation slowed nationwide in the 1990s as environmental activists changed the public image of wetlands and federal legislation increasingly restricted land development. Reversing course, the Corps of Engineers and other federal agencies began trumpeting the "restoration" of wetlands destroyed in past reclamation projects. This new version of reclamation included the much-publicized Everglades Restoration Project and the "creation" of artificial wetlands to replace swampland and marshes destroyed by ongoing development.

GARY GARRETT
*Houston, Texas*

Nelson M. Blake, *Land into Water—Water into Land: A History of Water Management in Florida* (1980); Henry C. Dethloff, *A History of the American Rice Industry, 1685–1985* (1988); Gilbert C. Fite, *Cotton Fields No More: Southern Agriculture, 1865–1980* (1984); Lewis Cecil Gray, *A History of Agriculture in the Southern United States to 1860*, 2 vols. (1933); Martin Reuss and Paul K. Walker, *Financing Water Resources Development: A Brief History* (1983); Soil Conservation Service, *Conservation Irrigation in Humid Areas* (1957); U.S. Army Corps of Engineers, *The Comprehensive Everglades Restoration Plan 2005 Report to Congress* (2005); U.S. Department of Agriculture, *The Yearbook of Agriculture 1955: Water* (1955); U.S. Department of the Interior, *The Impact of Federal Programs on Wetlands*, vol. 1 (1988) and vol. 2 (1994).

## Rivers and Lakes

From the Potomac to the Rio Grande, the South is blessed with rivers flowing, with few exceptions, to the Atlantic and Gulf coasts. Fed by an average annual rainfall of 40 to 50 inches, with even greater amounts in the Appalachians and along the Gulf Coast east of New Orleans, the rivers of the South have bountiful flows except in drier west Texas, and the warm southern climate keeps the streams free of ice during most of the year. Because the rains fall abundantly in the winter and spring, however, the rivers often flood during those seasons, and they sometimes dwindle to trickles during summer and autumn droughts. Although uneven flows have at times hampered their usefulness, rivers provide southerners, in varying regional proportions, with fertile floodplains for agriculture, convenient routes for trade and travel, power to turn mills and produce electricity, water to drink, and many fish and waterfowl for dietary variety. The history of southern rivers has been marked by cooperative efforts to make the rivers better serve those purposes, and in the field of water resource development the South has most eagerly sought federal assistance.

Along the Atlantic Coast, Virginia has the Potomac, James, and Rappahannock rivers; North Carolina, the Roanoke, Neuse, and Cape Fear; South Carolina, the Pee Dee, Santee, and Edisto; Georgia, the Savannah and Altamaha; and Florida, the St. Johns River. All except the latter have sources in the mountainous western sections of the states. Estuarine near their mouths and easily navigated to the head of tidal influences, the rivers were ascended by explorers and colonists penetrating through the forests, into the interior. The earliest plantations and settlements were located along the lower reaches of the rivers where the colonists cooperated in the construction of wharves and later in port development to maintain trade and contact with their homelands by water. Port cities such as Charleston and Savannah arose there. At the fall line dividing the Atlantic Coastal Plain from the hilly Piedmont and marking the head of navigation for larger vessels, waterpower for mills was available for manufacturing, and the transfer of commodities from small craft navigating the upper rivers to larger vessels was necessary. Cooperative efforts to develop that waterpower and to transfer the commodities from one vessel to another around the falls often contributed to the founding of cities at the fall line; Alexandria and Georgetown on the Potomac, Richmond on the James, and Augusta on the Savannah River are examples.

In the absence of railroads and highways, rivers became the southern arteries of travel and commerce, vital for the transport of bulky commodities—hogsheads of tobacco, sacks of rice and sugar, bales of cotton—to settlements at the falls and mouths of the rivers for use or for sale in foreign markets. Some of the earliest legislation enacted by colonial and state governments was therefore aimed at preventing the obstruction of navigable rivers and in some cases providing for cooperative efforts to remove those obstructions.

Pioneers pushing west from the coastal settlements also followed the rivers, ascending to their sources and crossing the Appalachians through water gaps to rivers leading farther west. In western Virginia the pioneers followed the Clinch and Holston and New rivers and in western North Carolina the French Broad and Little Tennessee. Those streams funneled the pioneer migration northwest into Tennessee, Kentucky, and the Ohio Valley, but not directly west into Alabama and Mississippi. This explains in part why Kentucky and Tennessee were settled earlier than Alabama and Mississippi, though factors such as Indian resistance were perhaps more significant.

A similar settlement pattern developed along the Gulf Coast, explored by the Spanish and French who planted their first settlements at Pensacola, Mobile, Biloxi, and New Orleans near the mouths of rivers flowing into the Gulf and then ascended the streams for exploration and Indian trade. In addition to the great Mississippi River in Louisiana, the major rivers emptying into the Gulf are the Suwannee, Apalachicola, Choctawhatchee, and Escambia in the Florida panhandle; the Mobile and Alabama river system; the Pearl and Pascagoula rivers of Mississippi; and the Sabine, Nueces, Trinity, Brazos, and Rio

Grande of Texas. Only Arkansas and Tennessee in the Old South had no direct outlet to the Gulf or Atlantic coasts, but they used the Cumberland and Tennessee rivers and the Arkansas, St. Francis, and White rivers flowing to the Mississippi as their outlets to markets.

The Mississippi River, draining a 1.245-million-square-mile area covering all or parts of 31 states and two Canadian provinces, is the largest river in North America. Together with its tributaries, it funneled commercial navigation downstream to New Orleans from western New York state on the east to Montana on the west and Minnesota at the north. The lower Mississippi, the thousand miles of serpentine channel downstream of Cape Girardeau, Mo., was bordered by a 35,460-square-mile alluvial floodplain, initially settled by the French and Spanish at Natchez and New Orleans before Americans crossed the Appalachians into the central South. Called the "Father of Waters" by Indians, the Mississippi had a central role in the socioeconomic and cultural history of the South.

After settlements and plantations had been established in the fertile floodplains where ample water supply and fish and wildlife were available, southern pioneers built mills at falls on the streams for grinding grain, sawing lumber, and supporting other manufacturing purposes. They marketed the products of those mills and the produce of the floodplains via the waterways using unpowered craft at first and, after 1811, when the first steamboat reached New Orleans, adapting the steamboat to shallow river navigation. Able to rely chiefly on rivers for transport, southern states seldom undertook the elaborate canal and turnpike projects of the sort built in the North in the early 19th century, the significant exception being Virginia, where the falls on the Potomac and James rivers were bypassed by canals extending upriver. More common were local cooperative projects to clear the rivers of snags and boulders and the organization of port authorities to dredge and improve harbors at such ports as Charleston, Mobile, and New Orleans.

The southern concern for waterways navigation was reflected in Congress. Although southern statesmen often questioned the propriety of federal funding for road and canal projects, they tended to support such aid for river and harbor improvements. During the presidential administrations of Andrew Jackson of Tennessee, John Tyler of Virginia, and Zachary Taylor of Kentucky and Louisiana, substantial federal appropriations were approved for clearing the channels of inland rivers, the Ohio and Mississippi especially, and for dredging the coastal entrances to the mouths of rivers. Southerners after the Civil War avidly sought federal waterways project funding; small indeed was the southern river that was not improved for navigation during the late 19th century.

Log rafting, Levisa Fork of the Big Sandy River, Johnson County, Ky., c. 1910
(Photographic Archives, University of Louisville [Kentucky])

Vigorous southern support for navigation projects continued in the 20th century. Both the Gulf and Atlantic coasts were lined with intracoastal waterways, and elaborate systems of locks and dams to provide navigation uninterrupted by droughts and low-water flows were built on many rivers, making possible navigation by powerful diesel towboats and barge tows. Locks and dams on the Arkansas and Red rivers, for instance, opened Arkansas and Louisiana to barge navigation into Oklahoma, and locks and dams on the Cumberland and Tennessee rivers supported barge traffic in northern Alabama and Tennessee to the western slope of the Appalachians. A canal for the movement of towboats and barges from the Tennessee River to Mobile, Ala., known as the Tennessee-Tombigbee Waterway and ranking in size with the Panama Canal, established a route other than the Mississippi River for shipment of commodities from the Upper South to the Gulf.

The pioneers settling in the floodplains also undertook cooperative efforts at an early date to protect their settlements and plantations from inundation by flooding, especially along the Mississippi River, where the first levee for flood protection was constructed by the French at New Orleans in 1727. Southerners organized local- and state-funded levee districts in the early 19th century and lined the Mississippi and other streams with earthen walls to hold out floods. Contending that flooding was a national problem because the Mississippi poured northern floodwater onto southern lands, southern statesmen ushered through Congress the 1850 Swamp Lands Act, used to assist levee construction, and the 1879 act establishing the Mississippi River Commission, which would assist local levee districts with levee construction. With vigorous southern support Congress enacted flood control legislation in 1917, 1928, and 1936, authorizing federal participation in an immense program for building levees and also for creating floodways and constructing multipurpose reservoirs for flood control, hydroelectric power generation, water supply, and recreation. That program converted the South into a land of lakes.

Because the South was unglaciated, it had far fewer natural freshwater lakes than the North and none comparing with the Great Lakes except Florida's Lake Okeechobee, a shallow lake in the Everglades covering 730 square miles and ranking second to Lake Michigan as the largest lake entirely within the borders of the United States. Lakes Pontchartrain and Borgne near New Orleans are brackish embayments of the Gulf rather than freshwater lakes. The other natural southern lakes are chiefly ponding areas in swamps, oxbows of abandoned river meanders, lakes in the Florida limestone region, and Reelfoot Lake in Tennessee, created by the 1811 earthquake.

By the 1980s, however, cooperative water resource development along the South's rivers had dotted the map of the region with many lakes, some built by private power and utility companies for hydroelectric power production and water supply but most constructed by the Tennessee Valley Authority in the Tennessee River basin and by the U.S. Army Corps of Engineers throughout the remainder of the South. Those lakes harnessed rivers for many purposes, impounding flooding to protect downstream areas, furnishing pools for commercial navigation, producing economical hydroelectric power, supplying water for community and industrial uses, and offering recreational opportunities equal to those of the natural lakes of the North. Southern lakes, especially those built near the inland Atlanta, Nashville, and Dallas–Fort Worth urban areas, consistently ranked tops in the nation in terms of their use for recreation.

The Old South stereotypes in fiction and film portraying the plantation aristocracy and chattels greeting steamboats at the landings or picturing heroic struggles to save mansions and cotton fields from crevasses in the levees do not reflect the diversity of southern experience, yet they properly illustrate the paramount role of rivers in the history of the South. The relationship of rivers to exploration and settlement patterns and to the agricultural, urban, and industrial development of the South is noteworthy. Equally significant is the cooperative effort of southerners to improve and manage their rivers, for that effort belies the image of the South as the bastion of individualism and states' rights. At early dates, southerners cooperated to improve their rivers for navigation and to achieve a measure of flood protection, eagerly seeking federal assistance even before the Civil War and acquiring it in full measure during the Reconstruction years and afterward. As a result, southern rivers have been developed to an extent exceeding that of any other section of the United States.

Pollution of rivers remains an ongoing problem. Farmers rely on pesticides to eradicate the boll weevil in cotton country, with water quality impaired as toxic pesticides wash into nearby waterways. Nitrogen from farms and residential areas that use fertilizers along the upper Mississippi River causes pollution in the lower Mississippi. Most recently, the growth of industrial hog farming in North Carolina has severely polluted waterways adjacent to the farms. Other pollutants to rivers and lakes include waste materials from oil and gas production, sediments from deforestation, and waste from strip-mining.

LELAND R. JOHNSON
*Hermitage, Tennessee*

Bill Belleville, *Rivers and Lakes: A Journey on Florida's St. Johns River* (2000); Stanley J. Folmsbee, *Sectionalism and Internal Improvements in Tennessee, 1796–1845* (1939); Robert H. Haveman, *Water Resource Investment and the Public Interest: An Analysis of Federal Expenditures in Ten Southern States* (1965); Institute for Water Resources, *National Waterways Roundtable: Proceedings, History, Regional Development, Technology, a Look Ahead* (1981); Leland R. Johnson, *Engineers on the Twin Rivers: A History of the U.S. Army Engineers, Nashville District* (1978); Jack Temple Kirby, *Mockingbird Song: Ecological Landscapes of the South* (2006); Mikko Saikku, *This Delta, This Land: An Environmental History of the Yazoo-Mississippi Floodplain* (2005); Jeffrey K. Stine, *Mixing the Waters: Environment, Politics, and the Building of the Tennessee-Tombigbee Waterway* (1993); Charles L. White, Edwin J. Foscue, and Tom L. McKnight, *Regional Geography of Anglo-America* (1974).

## Roads and Trails

From preindustrial times to the automobile age, elaborate networks of roads and trails have crisscrossed the South and made commerce, political activity, and cultural exchange possible. The locations of these routes were determined in many cases not entirely by men and women who built them but by previous inhabitants who had already carved their own trails out of the landscape. These ancient trails served as a blueprint for later road-building efforts, and an unmistakable continuity exists between the trails established by early Native American residents of the South and the roads and highways built later by whites.

Long before humans inhabited the South, however, animals had worn a permanent system of trails to food supplies, watering holes, and all-important salt deposits. Salt licks like those in Mason and Boone counties, Ky., for example, attracted countless buffaloes and other animals, which, over thousands of years, tramped lasting routes to these locations. These particular trails served 18th-century white settlers who crossed the frontier south of the Ohio River to establish interior settlements in Kentucky. Animal trails were also a part of the elaborate arterial network of Indian traces throughout the South.

Indian trails paralleled water routes like the Alabama, Altamaha, Apalachicola, Mississippi, Mobile, Pascagoula, Santee, Savannah, Tennessee, and Tombigbee rivers. Others avoided parts of the terrain that were either too rugged, dense with undergrowth, or swampy, although the Indians did establish dugout canoe trails in the Okefenokee Swamp. These overland trails stretched across the South for hundreds of miles and made trade possible with Native American cultures in remote parts of the region as well as other reaches of the country. The Natchez Trace, which ran from central Tennessee to Chickasaw towns in northern Mississippi, and the Great Indian Warpath, which began in the Creek country of Alabama and Georgia, traversed Cherokee settlements in eastern Tennessee, and after dividing near Kingsport, Tenn., branched off to the northeast through Virginia and into Pennsylvania, were two of the more famous. Some Indian trails, notably the Natchez Trace in Tennessee and Mississippi and the famous Warriors' Path in Kentucky, served whites, who used them for exploration and trade and as military and wagon roads. Spaniards Pánfilo de Narváez, Álvar Núñez Cabeza de Vaca, Hernando de Soto, and Tristán de Luna y Arellano explored parts of the 16th-century South over Indian trails. In his invasion of Creek territory in 1813, Andrew Jackson also made use of existing Indian trails, as did other American militiamen who, about that time, constructed a series of outposts along the Georgia and Alabama frontiers to protect white settlers.

As white pioneers pushed into the South, both animal and Indian trails provided the beginnings for the construction of wagon roads, private turnpikes, post roads, and railroad rights-of-way. Although Daniel Boone built most of the historic Wilderness Road, which ran from Moccasin Gap in southwestern Virginia through the Appalachian Mountains to the fertile Bluegrass region of central Kentucky, portions of the route followed old Indian trails. Within the state of Kentucky, animal and Indian trails determined many lines of transportation and settlement patterns. In the construction of the Cincinnati, New Orleans, and Texas Pacific Railway in Tennessee and southern Kentucky; the Tennessee Central Railroad from Rockwood to Cookeville, Tenn.; and the Western and Atlantic Railroad from Chattanooga south to the Chattahoochee River, engineers followed parts of extant animal and Indian trails.

Post roads, which the federal government began constructing during the early 1800s, also facilitated the settlement of the South. After the United States acquired the Louisiana Territory, interest in opening a line of communication between the District of Columbia and New Orleans developed. Already existing was a 1,500-mile circuitous route over the Appalachian and Blue Ridge mountains to Knoxville and Nashville and on to New Orleans across the unsettled wilderness west of the Georgia frontier. Congress decided to continue use of this route rather than build a shorter one, but not before Isaac Briggs, a government surveyor, had laid out a road to New Orleans through southern Alabama and Mississippi, which early 19th-century settlers used extensively. Despite Indian hostilities, post road construction continued in the South until by 1823 a network of routes radiated from six mail distribution points located at Augusta, Savannah, and Creek Agency, Ga.; St. Stephens and Huntsville, Ala.; and Natchez, Miss. And once mail service began over these and other post roads, the South became more attractive to settlers.

Aside from post roads, the federal government did not commit itself until 1921 to public road construction on a large scale within the United States. After the 1820s, southerners had adamantly opposed federal aid for internal improvements. Spokesmen for the South argued that Congress had no right of eminent domain or police powers necessary to build bridges, canals, or roads. They claimed that the Constitution only specifically authorized post road construction and that any attempt on the part of Washington to engage in road building would violate the rights of individual states. This states' rights point of view prevailed throughout the 19th century, and except for post roads built after 1896 in conjunction with the Rural Free Delivery program, the only roads constructed in the United States before 1921 were built either privately or by state and local governments.

Long-distance travel in the 19th-century South took place over post roads, privately built and maintained turnpikes, and stagecoach roads. By 1850, for example, there were approximately 180 turnpikes in Virginia, and a network of stagecoach roads, with Milledgeville as its hub, linked Georgia with neighboring states. These roads were good enough to accommodate Civil War cavalry and foot soldiers, but they proved completely inadequate for 20th-century automobile travel.

Poor roads were a nemesis to automobile travel in the South throughout much of the first half of the 20th century. Before the end of World War I, few automobilists braved the uncertainty of travel over the South's treacherous roads. R. H. Johnson, an Ohio automobile executive, was one of the earliest to do so. In 1908 Johnson blazed two motor routes over the largely unmapped and often impassible roads of the South. His first trek lasted 25 days and took him from Ohio south to Lexington, Louisville, Nashville, Huntsville, Chattanooga, Atlanta, and finally Savannah. To determine the correct directions between towns, Johnson relied on information he gleaned from Civil War documents. His second trip in 1908 opened an auto route that connected the cities of Savannah, Atlanta, Anderson, Spartanburg, Charlotte, Winston-Salem, Roanoke, Staunton, Philadelphia, and New York. Johnson mapped these routes and published them commercially as the first official automobile guides to the South.

As automobile ownership increased in the United States, more and more Americans chose to vacation in the "Sunny South." Southerners responded by developing a system of motor routes, which, like the ancient Indian trails, connected their region with the rest of the nation. By the early 1920s, 12 officially recognized automobile highways ran through the South to Florida from various parts of the country. They included the Dixie Highway, the (Robert E.) Lee Highway, the (Andrew) Jackson Highway, the Dixie Overland Highway, the Mississippi River Scenic Highway, and the Old Spanish Trail. When the federal government, as a result of the Federal Aid Highway Act of 1921, assumed the responsibility for building and maintaining a national network of highways, these roads lost much of their regional identity. The Dixie Highway, for example, which connected Sault Sainte Marie, Mich., and Miami, Fla., became U.S. 41 and U.S. 441. The Bankhead Highway, named after the Alabama senator who had persistently advocated federalization of highways in the United States, became U.S. 29, and the old Capital Highway, the first north-south interstate route to be proposed that connected the national capital with the state capitals of Virginia, North Carolina, and South Carolina, received the distinction of becoming U.S. 1.

The construction of these first interstate automobile highways linked parts of post roads, county highways, and privately built turnpikes, which had com-

Highway 61 between Clarksdale and Tunica in the Mississippi Delta, 1968 (William R. Ferris Collection, Southern Folklife Collection, Wilson Library, University of North Carolina at Chapel Hill)

prised the 19th-century network of roads in the South. Some automobile highways, like much of the motor route from Augusta, Ga., to Petersburg, Va., were originally trails and roads used by Indians and early white settlers. During the automobile age, however, as road-building technology improved, construction engineers were able to ignore the established, well-traveled routes of earlier generations. Speed of movement became the premium, and it was as technologically feasible to build a highway through a mountain as around one. Witness the modern multilane superhighways that now shuttle travelers in and out of the South. In 1956 Congress set up the highway trust fund to pay for 90 percent of the Eisenhower National Defense Highway System (interstate highway system), and today the 42,500-mile system is complete.

These modern interstate highways have erased the continuity that existed between generations of road builders in the South, and they have so homogenized travel that much of the uniqueness of the South has been exchanged for a uniformity manifest in motel accommodations and fast-food restaurants. Although earlier roads and trails in the South helped export southern culture to other parts of the nation, the modern superhighway has done much to destroy it. To be sure, some roads have enduring regional significance because national and regional culture celebrates them. Country music and trucking lore paint images of I-40 going into Nashville; labor union literature refers to I-85, or the "Textile Highway," in the Carolinas; and blues singers and even Bob Dylan have celebrated Highway 61, which runs through the Mississippi Delta, north to Chicago. Nonetheless, perhaps more than any other medium, interstate highway travel has eroded sectional differences and helped forever nationalize the South.

HOWARD PRESTON
*Spartanburg, South Carolina*

ROBERT L. IZLAR
*Warnell School of Forest Resources*
*University of Georgia*

Peter A. Brannon, *Alabama Highways* (April 1927); Richard T. T. Forman et al., *Road Ecology: Science and Solutions* (2003); Robert F. Hunter, *Technology and Culture* (Spring 1963); Wheaton J. Lane, in *Highways in Our National Life: A Symposium*, ed. Jean Labatut and Wheaton J. Lane (1950); William E. Myer, "Indian Trails of the Southeast," *42nd Annual Report of the Bureau of American Ethnology, 1924–25* (1928); U. B. Phillips, *The History of Transportation in the Eastern Cotton Belt to 1860* (1908); Douglas L. Rights, *North Carolina Historical Review* (October 1931); Randle B. Truett, *Trade and Transportation around the Southern Appalachians before 1830* (1935).

## Shellfish

The South has both recreational and industrial shellfish resources, all of which have been exploited as far back as the earliest aboriginal inhabitants. Shellfish may be categorized as mollusks or crustaceans found in either fresh or salt waters. Important mollusks include clams, mussels, oysters, scallops, and snails. Valuable crustaceans are crabs, freshwater crayfish, shrimps, and spiny lobsters.

Aboriginal settlements are often located by the presence of shell mounds, or middens, adjacent to inland rivers. Native Americans ate copious quantities of mussels (family *Unionidae*) and coveted those with pearls and lustrous mother-of-pearl inner shells for ornaments. European settlers ate few mussels but exploited them for the mother-of-pearl used in buttons. Even today, many tons of southern mussel shells are shipped to the Orient, where small pieces are used for nuclei of cultured pearls. As much as 4,500 tons of mussel shells were harvested in 1993 from the eastern half of the United States. More recently, less than 1,500 tons of mussel shells have been harvested, primarily in Tennessee, because Oriental pearl farmers have started using artificial pearl nuclei. In estuarine areas surrounding the South, inhabitants have used clams and oysters as foodstuffs and their shells for building materials. Many mollusks, especially in Florida waters, are so beautiful that they are the subject of world-famous shell-collecting industries. Major offshore scallop resources have provided sustained yields of the sweet-meated bivalves. Mollusks are also valuable. In 2003 more than 13.369 million tons of oysters worth more than $76.429 million were taken from southern waters, while scallop harvests accounted for at least 1.44 million tons worth in excess of $1.88 billion.

Oysters deserve special attention. Most are cultivated in what represents the oldest form of American mariculture. Today's oyster farmer commonly relies on natural nursery beds where larval oysters settle. These so-called spat attach to old shells. Nursery beds are usually located in less productive, low-salinity waters so that the spat must be moved to prime, high-salinity growing beds. Low, squat white oyster boats are constantly relocating and/or harvesting oysters in Gulf coastal waters. In the Chesapeake Bay, sail-powered skipjack oyster boats relocate and harvest oysters in waters where rival oystermen from Maryland and Virginia fought pitched sea battles over oyster grounds in the late 1800s. Fresh oysters are available in all months, but quality is somewhat poorer in warm months when they spawn. Oyster dishes vary from salted, raw, and live oysters on the half-shell to savory stews and the always popular fried oysters, including oysters en brouchette (wrapped with bacon and fried). The New Orleans oyster "poor-boy" (pronounced "poe boy") sandwich on French bread is a favorite of oyster lovers who visit the Crescent City.

Over the course of the past decade, mariculture of clams (genus *Mercinaria*) has developed dramatically in Florida's coastal waters. Changes in fisheries regulations closed down traditional finfish and shrimp industries, and clam mariculture became an alternative for displaced commercial fishermen. Larval clams are cultivated in hatcheries and cultivated on sea bottoms. In 2003, 4,441 tons of clams worth $6.367 million were harvested from southern waters.

All southern coastal states have major shrimp and crab fisheries. White, brown, and pink shrimp (genera *Litopenaeus* and *Penaeus*) spawn at sea, but larvae are nurtured in the fragile coastal wetlands before returning to sea to mature and spawn. Shrimp boats with high masts festooned with trawl nets are common sights along all coasts, and annual blessings of local fleets are gala festivities. Blue crabs (genus *Callinectes*) generally remain in estuaries, growing, as do all crustaceans, by shedding their hard shells periodically. The crab boil is a southern coastal tradition, but soft-shelled crabs command the highest prices and are cultivated throughout the region. Spiny lobsters (genus *Panulirus*) are a legacy of south Florida and are so valuable that the fishery is intensively regulated. Prawns, pandalid shrimps, are important as fish bait, especially the one- to two-inch grass, or glass, shrimp (genus *Palaemonetes*). Thriving fisheries once existed for the clawed, lobsterlike *langostina* species (genus *Macrobrachium*) in estuarine areas, but these have been largely displaced by pollution, habitat destruction, and man-made changes in hydrology. In freshwater, crayfish (genus *Procambarus*) are the crustacean kings. Although exploited throughout the South by Native American communities, they became important food sources only in French Louisiana. There the inventive Acadians, or Cajuns, have even learned to cultivate the "ecrevisse" in earthen ponds during the cool months, often in a unique rotation with rice, which is grown in the warm months. However, as a consequence of dramatic increases in production from crawfish ponds, the Cajun spring crawfish boil is now being widely enjoyed in areas remote from southern Louisiana, including Dallas–Fort Worth, St. Louis, Atlanta, Raleigh, and points in between.

In 2003 the marine shrimp harvest in south Atlantic and Gulf of Mexico waters was 119,604 tons worth more than $380 million, with most coming from Gulf waters. The southern blue crab harvest in 2003 was 77,338 tons worth more than $153 million. While the spiny lobster catch was only 1,937 tons in 2003, it was worth $18.871 million. Southern crayfish production exceeded 80 million pounds in 2004 and was valued at more than $46.5 million.

Southern shellfish resources are threatened by both physical and economic problems. Stream channelization, draining of wetlands, and pollution have destroyed many productive freshwater shellfish habitats. All southern coastal waters are polluted to some degree. Each state monitors edible mollusks for signs of sewage pollution to avoid health problems like hepatitis, which is contracted by eating raw, contaminated mollusks. Estuaries are hit especially hard by all forms of water pollution because contaminants are dropped there when freshwater runoff reaches the sea. The problems of suffocating silt and toxic chemicals are obvious, but inorganic fertilizers and organic matter fuel microbial activity that strips bottom waters of oxygen and severely restricts habitat and productivity in once-fertile waters. Overexploitation of freshwater mussel populations to supply mother-of-pearl nuclei has led to imposition of strict control on commercial exploitation of such populations and the identification of threatened and endangered species that cannot be harvested. However, competition and/or shell fouling by introduced exotic mollusks, including the

Asian clam (genus *Corbicula*) and zebra mussels (genus *Dreissena*), have become major threats to native freshwater mussels over the past decade. Coastal development in the form of recreational centers and fossil-fuel exploitation has destroyed thousands of acres of productive marshes. Loss of wetlands caused by long-term elevation of sea level, subsidence, and erosion all affect nursery areas for shrimp, crab, and mollusk resources.

Because much labor is involved in harvesting and/or cultivating and processing mollusks and crustaceans, various commercial ventures in the South are vulnerable to competition from the importation of low-cost foreign products. Since the mid-1990s, shrimp, crab, and crawfish industries have all suffered severe economic damage as the result of the importation of very large volumes of frozen products—both peeled meat and whole boiled—from southeast Asia, especially the People's Republic of China.

Vigilance and environmental education as well as coastal restoration programs are beginning to produce significant and measurable improvement of conditions in southern waters and must continue to ensure that future generations will share in the South's bountiful shellfish resources.

JAY V. HUNER
*University of Louisiana at Lafayette*

R. Tucker Abbott, *Seashells of North America: A Guide to Field Identification* (1968); Jay V. Huner and E. Evan Brown, eds., *Crustacean and Mollusk Aquaculture in the United States* (1985); James A. Michener, *Chesapeake* (1979); Fred Ward, *National Geographic* (February 1985).

## Soil and Soil Conservation

Soils are natural bodies, the result of unique interactions of soil-forming factors. Once soils were thought of as merely the residuum from rocks. Parent material is indeed an important factor in soil formation, or soil genesis, because it is the source of many elements needed for plant growth. As parent material is exposed at the earth's surface, it is altered by processes that can be related to climate, topography, and living organisms and the amount of time the material remains near the land surface before being dissolved, eroded, or buried. Soil properties have always placed limitations on food production. With limited ability to transport plant nutrients or food, indigenous people focused on the relationship of soil to plant growth, native vegetation as well as domesticated plants.

Soils of the South are regionally diverse. Over small areas such as on a farm, soil differences can be significant for agricultural uses or for location of a house.

Regional generalizations about soils are useful for considering the interaction of soil with southern history. For example, plants require carbon, oxygen, and nitrogen that are available in the atmosphere. Hydrogen is acquired from the uptake of water. Atmospheric nitrogen needs to be converted to reactive nitrogen, which the plant can utilize. Under natural conditions this conversion is accomplished by lightning, the work of microorganisms, or legumes. Plants also need phosphorus and three elements known as bases—calcium, potassium, and magnesium—in rather large quantities. Plants also need small quantities of at least seven other elements that can come only from soil minerals. Food grains, because of their rapid growth and seed production, require much more rapid uptake of these elements than native vegetation. When used for human food, these elements are removed from the site. Replenishment from weathering of minerals is too slow for food crops but usually fast enough to support slow-growing natural vegetation. The distribution of essential elements among soils is so uneven that some soils can produce low levels of agronomic crops and sustain the export of nutrients for a very long time (consider the long-term experiments at the University of Illinois and Rothamstead Experiment Station). Phosphate- and calcium-poor mineral material such as the granite present in many Piedmont and Coastal Plain soils would produce only a few crops before failing to make available sufficient quantities for rapid food-crop growth. In the era before commercial fertilizer, the content of calcium, magnesium, and available phosphorus in the soil therefore defined the prime agricultural areas of the South.

Two soil-forming factors, age and climate, are frequently overemphasized in discussing southern soils. Soils developed in granitic rock of the Piedmont and the coastal sediments—formed from their geologic erosion—are among the most infertile in the continental United States. Although humid conditions leach and acidify soils, not all of the soils in the South are poor in these essential elements. Base-rich igneous rock as well as sedimentary sources such as limestone and calcareous materials developed soils that are notably more fertile than soils formed from granite and granite-derived sediments on the Coastal Plain.

Native Americans as well as European colonists found the alluvial soils along rivers, not the interfluves, to be the preferred setting for agriculture. The recurrent overflows deposited valuable plant nutrients: phosphorous, potassium, and calcium as well as nitrogen bound up in the organic matters. The most fertile were along the Mississippi River, where Native Americans of the Mississippian culture developed a highly effective economic and agricultural system, often located on alluvial terraces. The system spread to other small river systems.

Soil erosion, Natchitoches Parish, La., 1967 (Soil Conservation Service,
U.S. Department of Agriculture, Washington, D.C.)

Town Creek Indian Mound, a historical site in North Carolina, would be one
such example. In the base-poor Piedmont section of Virginia, North Carolina,
South Carolina, and Georgia, fertile, base-rich soils are scattered in a north-
south pattern formed in mafic rock, high in ferromagnesian minerals. Naturalists find remnants of native prairies here. Indians would have likely found these
areas to be better hunting ground; the calcium and phosphorus are conducive
to animal growth, and Native Americans used fire to provide hunting grounds.
Further, the Native Americans established a transportation route along the

patterns of base-rich soils. European migrants later used the route south and called it the Great Wagon Road. De Soto found Native Americans growing corn in Florida, not on the coastal flatwoods, but along the central ridge where phosphatic sands provide nutrients. Undoubtedly the early explorers and traders learned by the actions of the Native Americans where the best lands lay.

Native Americans and the Europeans, when they arrived, coped with low-fertility, acidic soils by felling and burning trees and brush. Burning made available, in the upper soil surface, nutrients taken up by the deep-rooted trees and stored in the trunks and limbs. While Native Americans did plant some crops, they also utilized fire to provide browse for game and created the open, parklike landscape that early travelers often observed. The export of nutrients in agricultural crops quickly removed the nitrogen, phosphorus, potassium, calcium, and magnesium, elements that the deep-rooted trees had taken up and stored in trunks and limbs over several decades. These elements were released in plant-available form as trees were burned or rapidly decomposed in cultivated fields. Then the system needed to be repeated. It required that natural, slow-growing vegetation be allowed to grow for several years before enough nutrients were contained in its biomass to fertilize a food crop when the biomass was cut and burned. Before commercial fertilizers were available, most crops were grown in widely spaced, cleanly tilled rows that, combined with intense rainfall and rolling terrain, led to erosion. Unlike many northern and midwestern soils, most southern soils could not sustain continuous crop production and therefore prompted migration to the West. The disparity between the potentials of the southern soils and midwestern soils to support continuous cultivation and a dense rural population was apparent in the numbers of rural youth available to fight the Civil War. In 1860 Alabama, Georgia, and Mississippi supported an average 17.3 rural residents per square mile, while Ohio, Indiana, and Illinois had an average 37.5 rural residents per square mile.

Other soils of the South were better favored, at least agriculturally. Soils developed in limestone beds are often higher in the bases: calcium, potassium, and magnesium. In many cases they will include more phosphorous, derived from the skeletal remains of organisms. Limestone-derived soils are found in the Shenandoah Valley, the Ridge and Valley province, the Kentucky bluegrass country, and the Nashville basin. Some of these high-base soils may be shallow to bedrock, but they are valuable for pasture grasses and domesticated grasses such as corn, and for wheat and other grains. The appellation "Breadbasket of the Confederacy" aptly fit the Shenandoah Valley. Soils of the Shenandoah made possible a style of agriculture often associated with conservation, sustainability, and good husbandry. But the soil properties have to provide the opportunity, and not all soils of the South provided the possibility of this type agriculture. Many Germanic, Swiss, and English migrants to this area came from base-rich soils of Europe that permitted continuous cultivation with proper care. Soil properties had created much of the agricultural methods and preference that the Europeans brought to the New World.

The primary horse-breeding areas of the South developed in soils with copious quantities of both calcium and phosphorus for large-boned animals. The primary areas were the Virginia horse country based around Loudon County, the Kentucky bluegrass, the Nashville basin, and later the area of phosphatic sands on the Florida ridge.

Other base-rich southern soils played a larger role in southern agriculture—especially the plantation economy. The Black Belt of Alabama and Mississippi and the blackland prairie of Texas developed along the shoreline of an ancient inland sea. The soils are rich in the bases derived from the skeletal remains of organisms. The Black Belt developed into Alabama's primary cotton and cattle area. On the blackland prairie of Texas, farmers produced cotton for decades on the bases and nitrogen accumulated in organic soils. Farmers in these areas were not as dependent on commercial fertilizers as their neighbors on the base-poor lands. The clays in these two groups of soils are similar to the soils of the Mississippi Delta. Clays developed in calcareous materials often have more layers than the clays developed in the granites of the Piedmont. Such clays have a great capacity to hold both bases and water. The capacity to swell and then shrink, dependent upon wetness, gives soils their reputation for cracking. The soils of the Mississippi Delta were greatly influenced by the glacial materials from the upper Midwest that were transported by the Mississippi River. They too were base-rich and noted for their productivity. Western Tennessee and the east banks of the Mississippi and Yazoo rivers are capped by wind-deposited loess, primarily silt-sized particles. The cotton culture around Natchez predated the westward migration of cotton. The base-rich loess hills supported the plantation economy, but loess is highly erodible. Erosion eventually proved the undoing of this once prosperous region.

Reformers tried to adjust southern agriculture to the region's environment. One of them, Edmund Ruffin, promoted marl ostensibly to correct the acidity problem of southern soils, but it had other advantages not always recognized. Marl, deposited in an aquatic environment, included phosphorus. Also, in a low-base environment the application of calcium carbonate made more of the bases and phosphorus available to the plant. Raising the pH level enhances microorganisms, which take up bases. As the microorganisms die off, they release bases and phosphorous that the plant takes up. However, the low content of bases and phosphorus in the soil minerals ultimately limited the efficacy of marl. Southerners of a later era learned to apply lime along with other elements necessary for plant growth.

Commercial fertilizers eventually became of immense importance to southern agriculture and its economy. One could argue that developments in technology and sciences related to plant growth benefited the South as much as or more than the base-rich areas of the Midwest—though both came to rely on commercial fertilizers. Fertilizers permitted denser rural populations. The mental image of a southern landscape, especially the Piedmont, dominated by small cotton farms is more a creation of the fertilizer era than of natural soil qualities. Among the Americans, southerners led the way in importing guano, ostensibly for the nitrogen supply, but the guano included other nutrients as well. In the late 19th century southerners imported Chilean nitrates and mined southern deposits of phosphorus. The Haber-Bosch process of fixing nitrogen, developed in Germany around World War I, provided nitrogen at an affordable price. The availability of fertilizers increased the value of the soils of the Coastal Plain in the farmer's eyes, since the nitrogen, potassium, phosphorus, and lime could now be supplied economically. Also, these soils had better tillage properties for mechanized farming than did many Piedmont and Black Belt soils. With a supply of plant nutrients, southern farmers could now take advantage of other geographical and climatic advantages by raising crops that required a longer or earlier growing season.

Since European settlement, erosion has been a problem in the South. Native Americans had developed a sustainable system in the prefertilizer era. Fire recycled nutrients to provide game habitat and allowed for a very limited amount of cropland. The region had the highest intensity and duration of rainfall in the continental United States. Climate, combined with an affinity for cleanly tilled, widely spaced rows on sloping hillsides, unleashed erosion. Subsequent loss of topsoil, the growing medium, was to be lamented. But many southern topsoils and especially the subsoils were not loaded with nutrients, as the historical literature too often assumes. Topsoil "richness" was very limited to the nutrient content of rotting vegetation and/or the ash that could be obtained from burning the biomass that took several years to grow. The amount of nutrients exported in food crops quickly removed the nutrients (the phosphorus content of 150 bushels of corn is approximately equal to the amount of phosphorus in a 20-year-old stand of pine trees). Many historians had adopted the shibboleth that modern technology and farming methods cause more erosion than small, animal-powered farming methods of the past. The exact opposite is true. Farmers no longer plant steep hillsides, once accessible with mules or horses. Herbicides and tractor-powered conservation tillage permit one to keep the ground clothed continuously in growing plants or crop residues. Fertilizers make possible more pasture and small grain, conditions that retard erosion. Most importantly, fertilizer and plant breeding produce quick-growing, closely spaced plants that form a canopy rapidly. The denser crops permit less erosion than the sparse plant populations of old.

DOUGLAS HELMS
*Natural Resources Conservation Service*
*Washington, D.C.*

Stanley W. Buol, ed., *Soils of the Southern States and Puerto Rico*, Southern Cooperative Series Bulletin No. 174 (1973); Douglas Helms, *Agricultural History* (Fall 2000); Daniel D. Richter Jr. and Daniel Markewitz, *Understanding Soil Change: Soil Sustainability over Millennia, Centuries, and Decades* (2001).

## Streams and Steamboats

Waterways help explain much of the demographic, economic, and social history of the South. The Potomac, Ohio, and Missouri rivers formed a rough boundary for the slave states and the Confederacy. Seven thousand miles of the Mississippi River system with its tributaries from the Ohio and Tennessee southward to the Big Black and the Red rivers flow through the central agricultural region of the South. Smaller river systems from the Trinity at Galveston Bay to the Alabama at Mobile Bay and the Suwannee in Florida drain the Gulf Coast states. On the Atlantic seaboard, 20 river systems from the York and James to the Cape Fear, from the Pee Dee to the Broad, and from the Savannah to the St. Johns have offered transportation from fall line towns to tidewater ports. Few southerners in the past acknowledged that the Ashley and Cooper rivers joined at Charleston harbor to form the Atlantic Ocean, but almost all farmers recognized the opportunities existing in fertile river valleys. *Niles Weekly Register* reported in 1818 that two-thirds of South Carolina's farm exports were grown within five miles of a river and that all of the market crops were produced within 10 miles of navigable water.

More than 12,000 miles of navigable rivers flowed through the South. Henry Hall, reporting on American boat building in the tenth census (1880), noted that southern rivers were seldom closed by snow or ice and that the "noble" Tennessee alone provided a transportation route of more than 800 miles. Although most southern rivers were "subject to variations in depth," Hall emphasized that they were "all good highways." He could have added that captains of small boats, boasting that their steamer could make way on a "heavy dew" or on the "foam from a barrel of beer," converted innumerable shallow streams into back roads, if not good highways.

Rafts, flatboats, and keelboats transported farm produce downstream from the early colonial period to the mid-19th century. Only an occasional keelboat on narrow rivers or a sailing vessel on broader sheets challenged the currents until the steamboat *New Orleans* reached its name city in 1811 and thereby inaugurated a new era in transportation. Steamboats, whether the grand floating palace or the meanest little workaday "trade boat" peddling notions and necessities along shallow rivers, served the South for more than a hundred years. Regardless of size or opulence, steamers brought the sound of modernity to southerners along the meandering rivers. The loud puffing of the tall chimneys, the clanging bell, the steam whistle, and an occasional calliope interrupted the quiet farm life and transformed sleepy river towns and landings into centers of excitement and activity.

The commercial activity associated with steamboats in New Orleans is well known. But the same activity, although reduced in scale, occurred at thousands of landings. The antebellum cotton port of Apalachicola, Fla., is representative of the excitement. Sail and steam vessels brought cargoes to Apalachicola merchants in the late summer and early fall. As autumn changed into winter, the *Apalachicola Commercial Advertiser* (1844) dreamed of the "busy scenes which will ensue when the [steamboats] come booming down the river with their tall chimneys just peeping over the bales of cotton." When winter rains raised the Chattahoochee River, the newspaper announced, "The river is riz—the boat bells are ringing, ships are loading, draymen swearing, Negroes singing, clerks marking, captains busy, merchants selling, packages rolling, boxes tumbling, wares rumbling, and everybody appears up to his eyes in business." During the remainder of the cotton season, "steamboat follows steamboat—each wharf has its pile—every merchant his business—every clerk his duty—loafers are out of fashion." The "River News" column of newspapers throughout the South reported similar activity. Steamboats provided farms and plantations, river towns, and rural hamlets with news, gossip, and accommodations for travelers; boats came loaded with necessities, tools, and luxury goods and backed from the landing loaded with outgoing farm produce. The steamers provided a way to the outside world and brought the sights and sounds of the outside to the river valleys.

The everyday business of steamboating sometimes became dramatic. During the 1836 Creek Indian War, the little frontier settlement of Roanoke, a few miles south of Columbus, Ga., was attacked by Indians. The steamer *Georgian* touched at the landing, rescued the settlers, and escaped when the crew threw sides of bacon into the fires to get up steam and speed. During the 1848 Christmas season, William and Ellen Craft, making an exciting escape from slavery, traveled in disguise aboard steamboats from Savannah to Charleston and then to Wilmington, N.C., in their successful bid for freedom. During the Civil War, Robert Smalls, a slave pilot in Charleston harbor, escaped to freedom by taking a Confederate steamer, the *Planter*, to the Union fleet standing offshore. During flood seasons throughout the South, steamers rescued stranded farmers from dangerous situations, and in a yellow fever epidemic along the Yazoo River, steamboats brought medicine and supplies to ravaged towns and took panic-stricken citizens to safer ports. Steamboat fires and explosions saddened southerners when they lost relatives, friends, cargoes, or just a favorite boat. The worst steamboat disaster, the explosion of the *Sultana* in 1865 with more than 1,500 casualties, shocked the nation. Accidents and disasters only temporarily diminished southern reliance on, or affection for, the glamour and excitement of steamboats.

Many boats on southern rivers, especially steamers in the St. Louis to New Orleans trade, were floating palaces. Historian Louis C. Hunter described the elegance as "steamboat gothic" and regarded it as an "aesthetic experience" for many backwoods farmers. He noted that the *Eclipse* (363′ × 36′) was built for the lower Mississippi River in 1852 and offered an elegance surpassing "many of the best hotels in the country." By 1850 steamers had adopted a standard arrangement for passenger service. The main cabin of large steamers was 150 to 200 feet long, with staterooms of 50 to 100 square feet flanking each side. The ever-present barroom, the boat's office, and the pantry were at the fore end, with the ladies' cabin aft. The main cabin was the showpiece. Often lavishly appointed with white paneling, gilded decorations, richly colored carpets, ornate chandeliers, stained glass skylights, polished furniture, gleaming tableware, and snow white linen, the saloon was the center of social activity, providing dining facilities for as many as 200 passengers. Smaller boats engaged in passenger service tried to offer a comparable degree of elegance reduced only in scale.

The decade beginning in 1850 constituted the golden age of American steamboating, but the golden age for steamers in the southern passenger and cotton trade came after the Civil War. Some of the fastest, the most luxurious, and the largest boats steamed between New Orleans and St. Louis. The *R. E. Lee* raced the *Natchez* in 1870, with both boats making about 17 miles an hour on the lower Mississippi. Henry Hall reported on two "remarkably handsome vessels" that made their maiden trip to New Orleans in 1878. The *Ed. Richardson* (303′ × 48.5′) cost $125,000, while the *J. M. White* (321′ × 48′) cost $220,000. The 233-foot main cabin of the *J. M. White*, flanked by staterooms and with a polished bar forward and the ladies' cabin overlooking the stern, could seat 250 guests for dinner. In addition to cabin passengers, this fine steamer could transport 2,600 tons of freight or 10,000 bales of cotton. Everything about the boat seemed oversized: the magnificent bell weighed 2,500 pounds.

When such fine steamers as the *Natchez* or the *J. M. White* and hundreds of smaller boats faced increased competition from southern railroads, steamboats changed to meet the challenge. The foredeck of steamers was first squared to accommodate barges; then the bow was further changed to handle larger tows. As tows increased, speed and passenger service diminished, and once steamboats completed the change to towboats, the magic was gone. In 1902 the giant *Sprague* (276′ × 61′), with a tow of 67,000 tons in 60 barges covering nearly seven acres, could not generate the excitement of the grand packets of the golden age of southern steamboats. Even before the Howard Boatyards at Madison, Ind., built their last steamboat in 1934, railroads, towboats, and the internal combustion engine ended the age of steamboats on southern rivers. Today only three steamboats—the *Delta Queen*, the *Mississippi Queen*, and the *American Queen*—continue to travel the Mississippi.

HARRY P. OWENS
*University of Mississippi*

Charles P. Fishbaugh, *From Paddle Wheels to Propellers: The Howard Ship Yards of Jeffersonville in the Story of Steam Navigation on the Western Rivers* (1970); Charles H. Fitch, "Report on Marine Engines and Steam Vessels in the United States Merchant Service," *Tenth Census of the United States*, vol. 22 (1880); Michael Gillespie, *Come Hell or High Water: A Lively History of Steamboating on the Mississippi and Ohio Rivers* (2002); Henry Hall, "Report on the Ship-Building Industry of the United States," *Tenth Census of the United States*, vol. 8 (1880); Forrest P. Holdcamper, ed., *Merchant Steam Vessels of the United States, 1807–1868* (1952); Louis C. Hunter, *Steamboats on the Western Rivers: An Economic and Technological History* (1949); T. C. Purdy, "Report on Steam Navigation in the United States," *Tenth Census of the United States*, vol. 4 (1880); George Rogers Taylor, *The Transportation Revolution, 1815–1860* (1951).

## Swamps

Swamps—technically, wooded wetlands—bear a complex relationship to southern culture. While not unique to the South, swamps are much more common in southern states than in the rest of the nation; the South features the highest concentration of wetlands in America. Also, southern wetlands differ in type from those elsewhere. While New England tends toward relatively tractable and arable coastal marshes, southern wetlands are more likely to be densely and picturesquely wooded, a difference that has given them a distinct place in the popular imagination. Swamps have always been powerfully linked with images not only of the southern landscape but also of southern culture in a variety of widely disparate and sometimes directly contradictory ways.

Traditionally, swamps have been associated with all manner of foulness, and even evil. Their initial negative associations to an aristocratic southern culture built around the cavalier myth, which claimed that the southern gentleman could master nature by sheer force of will, came from their seeming indomitability. Until the late 19th century, efforts to clear and drain swamps met overwhelmingly with failure. Most conspicuous (and potentially symbolic) among these efforts was the project of the Great Dismal Swamp Company, in which George Washington was a principal investor. Beginning in the 1760s the Dismal Company spent over 40 years attempting to clear and drain the Great Dismal Swamp and ultimately failed resoundingly, their only income generated by the inexhaustible timber produced as they chipped away negligibly at its edges. Another practical problem that the swamp posed for white aristocratic southerners was its usefulness as shelter to persons excluded from or victimized by mainstream southern society. A number of slave narratives, notably those of Harriet Jacobs and Nat Turner, describe the ease with which slaves could vanish into the seemingly ubiquitous southern swamps to elude capture. Further, the swamps were home to cultures and groups—Native American tribes, the exiled Acadians, poor whites subsisting on the swamps' natural bounty—that the dominant aristocracy either feared, scorned, or both. Early southern accounts and depictions of the swamp, then, tend toward profound negativity.

The swamps were initially obstacles to the cultivation necessary to realize the southern agrarian ideal. Eventually, the swamps' practical intractability and real dangers mixed in the popular imagination with an array of wild tropes and exaggerations. Admittedly sometimes dangerous swamp fauna were imagined as supernatural predators in rumor and fiction. Fears of leviathan-like alligators and venomous serpents were compounded by misguided beliefs about pestilence and contagion. It was long believed that malaria, for example, was caused by simple respiration of swamp miasma. Racial fears played a role in the developing swamp mythology as well. The image of the Swamp Maroon, an archetypal savage, elementally powerful escaped slave, dwelling animal-like in the heart of the swamp, took strong hold in the American imagination in the wake of stories about slaves escaping into swamps. Although nonsoutherners tended to view the swamps differently from southerners—writers like Henry David Thoreau, Walt Whitman, and Quaker naturalist William Bartram celebrated the swamps' elemental wildness—the dramatic negative tropes connected to the swamps made them powerful rhetorical tools for abolitionists attacking southern society. Daniel Webster and Harriet Beecher Stowe, among others, made effective use of the swamps as a metaphor for southern corruption and immorality and characterized the entire region as a vast, swampy morass of pestilential evil. All of these images mingled with superstition and decades of artistic embellishment to render the swamps classic locales for stories of ghosts, monsters, and devils, originating in antebellum oral and literary tradition and persisting in comic-book and B-movie representations even today.

With the end of the 19th century, though, a slow rehabilitation of the swamps' image began—a rehabilitation that, tragically, coincides with the beginnings of widespread deforestation and wetland loss throughout the South. Curiosity about the mysterious, exotic swamps brought waves of northern tourists to Florida in the 1870s and 1880s in what David Miller has called a "swamp vogue." Harriet Beecher Stowe, who exploited the image of the swamp as metaphor for festering southern evils to the fullest in her novel *Dred*, praised the unspoiled beauty and wildness of the southern swamps in her later work *Palmetto Leaves*. New appreciation for the swamps and their cultural significance inflected southern writing as well. During the era often referred to as the Southern Renaissance, southern writers began looking at their culture in new ways, questioning or breaking out of wistful evocations of romanticized plantation life to render a more complex and multicultural South. William Faulkner explores the swamp as a space for intercultural encounters and as a site of alternative southern heritage removed from the legacy of slavery in his novel *Go Down, Moses*, while Lillian Smith, in *Strange Fruit*, depicts an interracial relationship that can only thrive in the swamps, removed from judgmental civilization. Harlem Renaissance writers like Jean Toomer and Zora Neale Hurston reexamined the swamps' significance for southern African Americans, acknowledging in fiction the swamps' status as African American home ground in the midst of a civilization built on racist precepts. As writers like these reexamined and redefined southern culture, the swamps experienced a kind of culturewide redemption. Instead of being depicted as obstacles to southern culture, they began to be venerated as pure, distinctive spaces, removed to some extent from the troubling legacies of Old South society.

Even as this rehabilitation of the swamps' image was under way, physical swamps were being cleared at alarming rates. While the influx of northerners into the South in the aftermath of the Civil War led to a new sense of appreciation for swamps, it also paved the way for their destruction. New technologies made clearing the swamps—so long a mocking impossibility for southern planters—relatively easy, and timber barons harvested the vast southern wetlands with abandon, leading to large-scale deforestation and the beginnings of an ecological crisis that would not be widely recognized as such until the dawn of a focused environmental movement in the mid-20th century. During the New Deal era, government programs treated the swamps in radically contradictory ways. As the Civilian Conservation Corps worked to stop wetland loss in the interest of flood control, the U.S. Department of Agriculture encouraged swamp drainage as a way to jump-start the agricultural economy in the wake of the Great Depression. Typical of this contradictory approach to swamp conservation were the efforts of the Army Corps of Engineers, who carried on concerted efforts first to drain the swamps and then to conserve them over the course of the 20th century. Before the dawning of the environmentalist movement in the 1970s, more than half the total wetlands in the United States had been destroyed.

While environmental consciousness has been a bit slower to develop in the South than in other parts of the nation, a southern environmentalist movement combining traditional ecologists, conservationists, and academics with sportsmen, hunters, and fishermen—so-called Bubba Environmentalists—has developed over the past few decades, and now organizations like the Georgia Wildlife Federation and Ducks Unlimited work energetically to advance the cause of wetland preservation. Swamps in the contemporary South are now, for the most part, protected by federal mandate.

Swamps have a complex relationship with contemporary southern culture. In most contemporary southern writing, the traditional divide between swamps and human culture has been replaced by a strong, often nostalgic sense of how powerfully swamps have influenced life in the South. While the superstitions and tropes that marked them as sinister and forbidding have faded, those elements still fascinate the tourists who support the booming swamp tour industry in Louisiana, where attractions like the "Haunted Night Swamp Tour" and "Voodoo Swamp Tour" mix appreciation for nature with fantasy menace. Although a few members of some traditionally swamp-dwelling cultures—notably the Acadians of south Louisiana—still live among the swamps, the majority of the wetlands not on private property are now wildlife reserves and state and national parks. Nevertheless, throughout the South, wetlands remain threatened by pollution, erosion, and development. So long regarded as antithetical to mainstream southern culture, the eminently vulnerable, vanishing swamps now threaten to take with them a valuable part of the South's beauty and distinction.

ANTHONY WILSON
*LaGrange College*

Jack Temple Kirby, *Poquosin: A Study of Rural Landscape and Society* (1995); David Miller, *Dark Eden: The Swamp in Nineteenth-Century American Culture* (1989); Charles Royster, *The Fabulous History of the Dismal Swamp Company* (1999); Ann Vileisis, *Discovering the Unknown Landscape: A History of America's Wetlands* (1997); Anthony Wilson, *Shadow and Shelter: The Swamp in Southern Culture* (2006).

## Tennessee Valley Authority

The 50th anniversary of the signing of the TVA Act by President Franklin D. Roosevelt was 18 May 1983. In that half-century the Tennessee Valley Authority played a major role in transforming one of the most underdeveloped and poverty-stricken areas in the nation into one centrally involved with critical problems besetting the South, the nation, and the world in the waning years of the 20th century. Senator George Norris's vision of "taking the Tennessee River as a whole and developing it systematically, as one great enterprise, to bring about the maximum control of navigation, of flood control, and of the development of electricity" was realized along with other major environmental accomplishments before Norris's death in 1944. And by the end of World War II the agency already was involved with matters that transcended the initial vision of its creators.

On 8 October 1945, President Harry Truman dedicated Kentucky Dam, the last of the on-river dams to be constructed and the 16th dam built by the TVA within the seven states (Tennessee, Alabama, Georgia, Kentucky, Mississippi, North Carolina, and Virginia) encompassed by the drainage system of the Tennessee River, an area roughly the size of Scotland and England. The president in his remarks quoted those spoken by Roosevelt on 18 April 1933: "The usefulness of the entire Tennessee River . . . transcends mere power development; it enters the wide fields of flood control, soil erosion, reforestation, elimination from agricultural use of marginal lands, and distribution and diversification of industry." Truman then made the obvious point that Roosevelt's prophecy had been fulfilled, "for in the TVA the Congress has provided for a tying together of all things that go to make up a well-rounded economic development." With the goal of well-rounded economic development in mind, the TVA in its first decade, through planned development, modified the environment in remarkable ways to achieve its mission.

In 1933 throughout the valley, unemployment was endemic, mountains had been slashed and burned, a barter economy was widespread, and spring flooding was taken for granted. By constructing 16 dams within 12 years, the TVA put thousands of people to work and provided untold opportunities for the development of skills among a largely untutored rural workforce. To further assist its workforce, the TVA encouraged the establishment of unions and collective bargaining with its employees. It also pursued a policy of working with landowners to increase the production and use of trees in ways that would assist in erosion control and watershed protection. And, as it generated electricity, rates came down so that electricity became easily available.

Through the Electric Home and Farm Authority, the TVA facilitated the purchase of low-cost appliances. Before the advent of the TVA, 97 percent of the people had no electricity; within three decades thereafter, it was universally available. In helping to ease the lives of an undernourished, deprived, rural population, the TVA helped create opportunities for a better life that agency officials as well as many in government hoped could be emulated elsewhere.

The TVA also pioneered in the development of rural regional libraries and helped to improve county school systems and to create parks throughout the region. Plans, ordinances, and codes developed in villages constructed by the TVA at various dam sites were usually adopted by the councils of these communities as they were absorbed into the structure of county government. Many practices, notably the TVA's emphasis on uniform accounting, were adopted by municipalities and other local and state government agencies.

One of the notable changes the TVA accomplished, initially through the slight raising and lowering of water levels at various dams, was the eradication of malaria, previously considered endemic throughout a large portion of the valley. Before the TVA came into the valley, at least a third of the people suffered from malaria. By making the river navigable; by providing a nine-foot channel from Knoxville to Paducah, where it entered the Ohio River; and by providing cheaper electricity, the TVA helped to make cities and surrounding areas attractive to commercial and industrial ventures, furthering the economic development of the valley states. Moreover, research conducted at the TVA National Fertilizer Development Center at Muscle Shoals, Ala., developed and encouraged the use of inexpensive phosphate fertilizers, thereby assisting farmers in the valley, throughout the nation, and in other countries as well to increase their yields and to combat erosion of their soils. Through various programs the TVA encouraged valley farmers in organizing cooperatives to bring electricity to their farms and in weaning them away from an agriculture largely based on cotton and corn.

The devastating flooding that occurred throughout the Ohio and Mississippi river valleys in 1937 brought to national attention the fact that flood control on the Tennessee River was already quite effective. At that time, only 3 dams and reservoirs were in operation. By 1980 there were 9 dams on the Tennessee River itself, 5 major dams on headstreams, 12 smaller impoundments, 7 steam plants, and an equal number of nuclear plants in operation or in various stages of construction. The dams and impoundments provided the Tennessee River Valley with the nation's most effective flood control system. Moreover, the various TVA structures—dams, powerhouses, bridges, and generators—were widely proclaimed as magnificent functional structures. In most instances, they blended harmoniously with the environment, imaginatively utilized building materials, and successfully coordinated the science of engineering with the art of architecture. They quickly gained national and worldwide attention as models of public architecture, a successful team effort in one of the largest construction projects in the world.

With the outbreak of World War II and America's participation in it, the TVA put increased emphasis on the production of electricity to assist plants in the valley manufacturing aluminum for aircraft and for the installation at Oak Ridge utilizing uranium 235 to produce atomic weapons. The Muscle Shoals fertilizer program was set aside for the production of phosphates and nitrates for munitions. During these years, the capacity of the TVA's power system more than doubled from a little less than a million kilowatts in 1940 to more than 2.5 million in 1946. By 1980 TVA installations had a generating capacity of more than 100 billion kilowatts.

The last figure indicates that the TVA in the postwar years continued to play a leading role in the economic development and transformation of the valley. During these years, the TVA focused its attention on tributary area development and enhanced energy production, including nuclear energy. As a result, by 1980 Decatur, Ala., for example, had 20 Fortune 500 companies within the Tennessee River environs. Barges on the river were moving more than 30 million tons of freight. A more balanced economy, agricultural and urban, had been established in large part through the efforts of the TVA. In a half-century, the valley had been transformed from a deprived, eroded, flooded area where the per capita annual income was $168 to a modern region with an income nearly 80 percent of the national average. The towns of the region, in contrast to those of neighboring central Appalachia, had an air of solid prosperity.

All these changes did not come easily, and in the postwar years the TVA was the butt of increasing criticism. At the outset blacks found much to complain about in the racism and discriminatory practices of the agency, some of which went beyond those prevailing in various parts of the valley. Black leaders noted that little rehabilitation for blacks was included in the programs and policies espoused by the T VA. In addition, population removal was a serious problem as almost a million acres were flooded by T VA reservoirs. The agency, after several years, developed procedures to provide adequate compensation for displaced people. These became models for emulation in other parts of the country. Whenever possible the T VA rebuilt or replaced roads, bridges, and other structures. It tried to move churches and cemeteries. But not everyone was satisfied. Farm families not owning the land on which they lived received no compensation and were placed in dire straits.

Moreover, the T VA was never exempt from political pressures, legal challenges, and internal controversies. Investor-owned utilities at first challenged its constitutionality and later succeeded in preventing any expansion of the area the T VA could serve. In the postwar years, as the institutional apparatus of the states and counties throughout the Tennessee Valley became more sophisticated, some resentment against the T VA developed as various agencies of state and local government claimed that their prerogatives had been usurped or ignored.

In the late 1960s environmentalists in the valley and throughout the nation criticized various aspects of the T VA's operations. They successfully challenged the T VA's purchasing most of its coal for its 63 coal-burning steam-generating plants from strip-mine operators in eastern Kentucky. They correctly charged the T VA with being one of the worst despoilers and polluters in the region and prompted the agency to mend its ways by installing scrubbers to reduce the emission of sulfur from its coal-fired plants as well as cooling towers to lower the temperature from its coal-fired and nuclear plants. Their interest in a then-endangered species, the snail darter, delayed the completion of Tellico Dam on the Little Tennessee River. By the next decade, however, the T VA's concern for conservation had markedly improved.

By the end of the 20th century the T VA engaged in a broad range of environmental projects to improve the quality of life for the more than 3 million ratepayers served by the agency and the local distributors of its power. As ratepayers increased, so too did steam generation increase its coal burn, surpassing over 30 million tons by the 1970s. The T VA endeavored to create a society of both economic plenty and environmental quality in a region where industry now was the principal employer, where farms were too small and supported too many people, and where older patterns of commerce experienced hard times.

As part of this effort, the first nuclear plant operated by the T VA at Browns Ferry came online in the early 1970s just as electric rates began to rise. The costs of nuclear plants became so prohibitive that the TVA could not provide saleable power from them. All but four were dismantled, leaving the agency to rely more heavily on coal-fired steam plants. As a result the TVA faced legal challenges from both the Nuclear Regulatory Commission and the Environmental Protection Agency for polluting both the air and the water throughout the seven-state area. Its reign as the region's undisputed federal agency was challenged. Public confidence diminished, congressional support turned to critical scrutiny, and the media, which historically supported the TVA, now at times severely criticized it. There was a noticeable erosion of confidence among TVA employees. And the states now could provide many of the services and amenities the TVA initially provided, thereby reducing the agency in the view of growing numbers of citizens to that of a monopolistic public utility.

By the 1980s the TVA had ceased to serve a significant national mission. It was no longer cited as a symbol of progressive government. It was part of no national agenda. It was not grounded in a regional political or legislative process that could set goals. No institutional linkages existed to ensure accountability. Rates were determined solely by the TVA. No public service commission or oversight agency existed to challenge rate decisions and call the TVA to account. The TVA had to change and define a mission for itself in tune with its original overall mandate to promote the welfare of the people in the valley. It needed a perspective and strategy for development within a democratic framework.

In 1978 the TVA signed a consent decree with the Environmental Protection Agency and thereafter began to renew itself. In 1986 the TVA agreed to accept an independent inspector general, and it strengthened valley ties with citizen advisory committees, opened board meetings, and enhanced public participation. A regional industrial council now meets periodically to share information and opinions related to individual development issues. In addition, the TVA launched efforts to conserve energy and reduce acid rain and thereby provide yardsticks for the nation.

In the last decades of the 20th century the TVA forged a new sense of mission beyond that of a utility company, with area residents something more than ratepayers. Serving more than 3 million customers, the TVA provided planning assistance, economic research, and engineering know-how to facilitate development throughout the valley. The TVA carefully considers the impact its proposed actions may have on the environment. Using advanced technology, for example, the TVA is now able to locate and map specific areas where there is a high probability of water pollution from soil erosion, animal wastes, septic tank systems, and other types of diffuse contamination, thereby helping to reduce pollution and improve water quality throughout the 201 counties of the Tennessee Valley region. The TVA at the outset of the 21st century has the potential once again to make real the values of family and community cooperation, sharing, and creativity by appropriately using the technology and resources at its disposal.

RICHARD LOWITT
*University of Oklahoma*

North Callahan, *TVA: Bridge over Troubled Waters* (1980); Walter L. Creese, *TVA's Public Planning: The Vision, the Reality* (1990); Wilmon H. Droze, *High Dams and Slack Waters: TVA Rebuilds a River* (1965); Erwin Hargrove and Paul Conkin, eds., *TVA: Fifty Years of Grassroots Bureaucracy* (1983); David E. Lilienthal, *TVA: Democracy on the March* (1944); R. C. Martin, ed., *TVA: The First Twenty Years* (1956); Michael McDonald and John Muldowny, *TVA and the Dispossessed: The Resettlement of Population in the Norris Dam Area* (1982); John Robert Moore, ed., *The Economic Impact of TVA* (1967); Martha E. Munzer, *Valley of Vision: The TVA Years* (1969); Phillip Selznick, *TVA and the Grass Roots: A Study in the Sociology of Formal Organization* (1949); William Bruce Wheeler and Michael J. McDonald, *TVA and the Tellico Dam, 1936–1979: A Bureaucratic Crisis in Post-Industrial America* (1986).

## Trees

William Faulkner's story "Delta Autumn" talks of Mississippi Delta land that is an "impenetrable jungle of water-standing cane and cypress, gum and holly and oak and ash." Trees have been both a natural and a cultural resource for southerners. A great forest has covered much of the South since the region's human history began. Pine forests paralleled the Atlantic and Gulf coasts, hardwoods were found in the uplands, mixed pine-hardwood growth occurred in the low-lying swamps and river valleys, and the mountains produced appropriate high-altitude hardwoods. The slopes of the Appalachian Mountains and the Ozarks have been especially rich with tree life.

Oaks found in the South include the chestnut oak (*Quercus acuminata*) in the Mississippi River Valley, the cinnamon oak from North Carolina to Texas, Durand's oak from Alabama to Texas, the laurel oak (*Q. laurifolia*) from Virginia to Florida, the swamp white oak along southern creeks and riverbanks, and the myrtle oak from South Carolina to Florida. Strips of white oak are used by Deep South basket makers, and the bark from red oaks is commonly used by rural southerners to make a tea believed to cure backache, rheumatism, diarrhea, toothache, and chills and fever. The live oak, which figures prominently in southern literature and regional imagery, has been an important source for the American shipbuilding industry and is popular in landscape design throughout the region.

Evergreens are coniferous trees, with tough, needlelike leaves; they remain verdant throughout the winter months. The yellow or shortleaf pine (*Pinus echinata*) grows naturally in the Coastal Plain of the South, as does the longleaf, or Georgia, pine (*P. palustrisis*), which is hardy from Tampa Bay west to the Mississippi River and north to Virginia. The loblolly pine can grow to 170 feet in its native southern habitat, where it can adapt to either swampland or more barren highlands. The red spruce keeps to the uplands of the Carolinas and Georgia, whereas the white cedar (sometimes called a juniper) ranges along the Atlantic and Gulf coasts, growing up to 80 feet in height. One also sees the Carolina hemlock, the cherry laurel, and the evergreen magnolia. The Cherokee Indians regarded the red cedar, an aromatic wood resistant to the damp southeastern climate, as the most sacred of all trees. The litters on which their honored dead were carried were made from cedarwood. It also has been important to the regional furniture industry.

In 1936 Howard W. Odum pointed out that the South grew more than a third of all the peach trees in the nation, a third of the orange trees, and four-fifths of the grapefruit. Today, delicious apples are abundantly grown in North Carolina and Virginia, the Japanese plum is found throughout the South, and the fig tree can be grown as far north as southern Virginia, with Florida, Georgia, South Carolina, Louisiana, Texas, and Mississippi among the largest producers of figs in the nation. The South grows a variety of pears as well. In terms of nut trees, the pecan is native throughout the Mississippi River Valley, but its special home is Texas, which adopted it as the state tree in 1927. The English walnut (*Juglans regia*) also thrives in the Southeast.

The southern Appalachians are noted for their hardwoods. The sweet gum (*Liquidamber styraciflua*), which is also called red gum in places, has massive branches and a light gray bark and is seen from the Upper South down to the Gulf of Mexico. In autumn it is a glorious sight, with brilliant colors, described by one naturalist as running "the gamut in hues from kingly yellow, through bright orange and red, and on to a deep bronze." Hickories are abundant in the South, sturdy, tough trees that gave a nickname to President Andrew Jackson, who lived among them in the uplands.

The South has always had a number of flowering trees that have captivated the southern imagination. In particular the dogwood (*Cornus florida*) is identified with the imagery of the region. In Atlanta a million dogwoods were once planted in a campaign to beautify the city. Red and white flowering dogwoods grow wild through most of the region and can reach 30 feet tall. They are slow growers, and their leaves are glossy, pointed, grayish-green in color, turning to a deep red in autumn. Dogwood festivals throughout the South attest to its popularity among southerners. Other flowering trees include the Texas ash and tulip trees.

Other trees in the South that are particularly associated with the region include the black willow, the red birch, the yellow birch, palm trees in Florida and along the Gulf Coast, and the blue ash (seen to best effect in the Great Smoky Mountains). The mimosa, or silk tree, is a somewhat fragile-looking tree that grows as far north as northern North Carolina. It has attractive colorings and delicate foliage. It belongs to the *Mimosaceae* family, is native to warm, tropical regions, and can grow to 40 feet. When flowering, it shows an array of whites, yellows, and reds. Chinaberry trees (*Melia azedarach*) are popular throughout much of the Deep South as flowering shade trees. They bear in the early spring, producing a pale pink flower slightly tinged with purple. Members of the Lester family in Erskine Caldwell's *Tobacco Road* were frequently lurking behind a chinaberry tree, and the tree crushed to death a character in Eudora Welty's "Curtain of Green."

CHARLES REAGAN WILSON
*University of Mississippi*

William C. Coker, *Trees of the Southeastern States, including Virginia, North Carolina, South Carolina, Georgia, and Northern Florida* (1937); Charlotte H. Green, *Trees of the South* (1939); Ellwood S. Harrar and J. George Harrar, *Guide to Southern Trees* (1962); F. Schuyler Mathews, *Familiar Trees and Their Leaves* (1903); Gary O. Robinette, *Trees of the South: Collected and Organized by Gary O. Robinette* (1985); John K. Small, *Florida Trees: A Handbook of the Native and Naturalized Trees of Florida* (1913).

## Water Use

Stretching from the soggy Dismal Swamp of Virginia to the semiarid Llano Estacado of western Texas, the diverse southern geography and the associated climatic differences create the need for a variety of approaches to the utilization and management of southern water resources. Found in lakes, streams, and aquifers, these resources have both blessed and cursed the South. Watercourses provided the means by which early Europeans moved westward to settle the southern Coastal Plain and Piedmont. Traversing the Appalachian Mountains, other pioneers sought the fertile valleys of the Tennessee and Cumberland rivers and the access they gave to farther movement westward. Representing a temporary impediment to westward movement, the Mississippi River became the chief waterway to the southern states. Crossing the "Father of Waters," settlers moved up its lush and boggy tributaries until they reached the dryer areas that foretold of the arid West.

As the settlers moved westward from the Atlantic Coast, they discovered that southern rivers did not provide a reliable means of transportation. Periodic low water alternated with floods to make water travel difficult, while rapids and other impediments added to the difficulty and danger of southern waterways. Early southerners focused on making southern streams more navigable. During the James Monroe administration, Secretary of War John C. Calhoun gave serious consideration to the Muscle Shoals, Ala., rapids as an obstruction to navigation on the Tennessee River. After the administration of Andrew Jackson such projects were considered primarily state rather than federal responsibility.

Both the federal and state governments, however, struggled with improving navigation and controlling floods on the Mississippi River. In the antebellum era a government engineer, Charles Ellet, emphasized the need for scientific data on water flow and suggested that a relationship existed between stream flow and other conditions within a river's watershed. In suggesting the construction of tributary reservoirs to regulate the river's flow for navigation as well as to control floods, Ellet anticipated later engineering principles. The concepts of another pair of engineers, Andrew A. Humphreys and Henry L. Abbot, had a more immediate influence on attempts to control Mississippi waters by stressing the use of levees, outlets, and cutoffs.

As far as swamps and coastal wetlands were concerned, few people prior to the Civil War had much understanding of their value. In the Swamp Lands Acts of 1849 and 1850 the federal government ceded much of this area to the states to be reclaimed by drainage.

During the Gilded Age the attempts to reclaim wetlands and to prevent flooding in the Mississippi basin continued as a practical matter. Only later in that period did such attempts merge as part of the conservationists' river basin development concept, with its implications for federal action on a regional basis. Responding to projects he had seen in Europe, Louisiana congressman Randall L. Gibson proposed in 1876 to establish a commission for supervising developments on the Mississippi. When President Rutherford B. Hayes signed Gibson's bill for the Mississippi River Commission (MRC) in 1879, he implicitly committed the federal government for the first time to flood control on an American river.

In the following decades members of the MRC debated not only the best technology for controlling floods on the Mississippi but also the question of the constitutionality of federal aid for flood control. When the commission adopted a "levees only" policy as the primary solution for Mississippi flooding, the results often aggravated problems of control. The constriction caused by levees not only forced the river to rise higher during flood stage, but levees encouraged expensive developments in the floodplain. Some scholars, particularly the geographer George P. Marsh, pointed to the dangers inherent in relying solely on levees for flood control. He considered headwater reservoirs of equal importance in solving the complicated problem of flooding.

During that same period both geographers and other social scientists developed the philosophy of approaching a river basin as an ecological unit for planning purposes. Advocates of this concept readily incorporated the idea of reservoir control as part of their philosophy. Among the promoters of the regional planning philosophy was the Scot Patrick Geddes, whose ideas influenced American conservationists and politicians. John Wesley Powell and W. J. McGee of the Geological Survey promoted the principle of treating a river system as a unit, finding strong support for their ideas with politicians such as U.S. Forest Service chief Gifford Pinchot and Theodore Roosevelt. Congressional approval of the Reclamation Act of 1902 reinforced the idea of multipurpose water developments under federal authority. In establishing the Inland Waterway Commission, President Roosevelt instructed the group to consider a comprehensive plan for all the watersheds in the United States as well as the integration of varied water uses. Perhaps Roosevelt's most important single contribution to the future development of the nation's water resources was his resounding veto whenever Congress attempted to allow private development of waterpower sites without proper government supervision. His boldest statement of the government's duty to protect the public interest in power development came in the James River (Missouri) Dam veto of 1909, thus reserving a southern river for federally supervised development. Passage of the Weeks Act in 1911 recognized the association between forest conservation and watershed protection, an important element of river basin planning. The federal government took a major step toward acceptance of the idea of comprehensive watershed planning with passage of the Federal Water Power Act of 1920.

The first extensive proposal for multipurpose water planning within a river basin was made for a southern river, the Tennessee. Concerned primarily with establishing federal responsibility for water development and interested in public power development, Senator George W. Norris of Nebraska proposed that the government continue to develop the hydroelectric potential at Muscle Shoals on the Tennessee River. Although government support for developing electric power at Muscle Shoals had been associated with the nation's war effort,

Norris proclaimed that the government should retain the project to produce cheap electricity for the region and cheap fertilizer for the farmer. Eventually the senator incorporated into his proposal the multipurpose and river basin planning ideas that had already become current in some bureaucratic and academic circles. The noted North Carolina geologist and engineer Joseph H. Pratt recognized the need for an interchange system of electricity, and he also envisioned the possibilities for development that hydroelectric production offered the South. Beginning in 1917 George Norris consistently favored financing of reservoirs on the Missouri River, claiming they would contribute to flood control on the lower Mississippi and would also provide irrigation water for parts of the arid West from whence the senator came. As early as 1913 he endorsed federal development of hydroelectric power on the Potomac River.

The congressional debates over Muscle Shoals continued throughout the 1920s. While Congress deliberated over government control of Muscle Shoals, it passed other legislation essential to water resource development. Significantly, the River and Harbors Bill, passed by Congress in February 1925, embodied many of the principles of multiple use of water resources, which implied the need for integrated planning in developing each watershed.

The congressional debate about disposal of the Muscle Shoals property revealed that power production would be the project's primary importance. As this fact became more evident, Norris gained greater support from southern congressional representatives. Progressive politicians from the arid West who supported government operation of the Boulder Dam project joined in support of government ownership of Muscle Shoals. Norris's campaign for multipurpose river development also gained support as a result of disastrous floods on the Mississippi River in the spring of 1927. Ironically, the Corps of Engineers' report a year earlier had ignored concepts of tributary control and had maintained that all was well with the levees and channel works on the lower reaches of the river.

The year 1928 proved to be crucial for advocates of water resource development. In May Congress passed a flood control act providing for a comprehensive study of water resources of the nation's major streams for purposes of flood control, irrigation, power, and navigation. The act included many of the ideas of comprehensive and integrated water resource management, although on the same day Congress approved a plan for flood prevention on the lower Mississippi that completely ignored tributary control.

In late May 1928 Congress passed Norris's bill calling for government ownership and operation of the Muscle Shoals property for purposes of improving navigation and controlling floods on the Tennessee as well as for producing electric power, but President Calvin Coolidge failed to sign the bill. By the beginning of the special session of Congress in the spring of 1929, many groups in the South more openly and firmly supported the comprehensive development of the Tennessee Valley by the central government as best for the economic and social well-being of the region. With a few minor changes, in May 1929 Norris reintroduced his bill for government ownership and distribution of power. After intense debate in both houses of Congress and in conference committee, Congress approved a compromise version in February 1931. The bill allowed the president either to choose Norris's concept of government operation or to lease the property to a private chemical company. Southern congressmen and legislatures urged Hoover to sign the legislation. On 3 March the president issued a resounding veto of the bill, basing his rejection primarily on opposition to government distribution of power.

During the Muscle Shoals debate another controversy arose concerning a southern river that held great significance in settling the larger question of the government's right to promote comprehensive development of navigable streams and their tributaries. The issue arose when the Appalachian Electric Power Company asked for a "minor part" license to build a power dam on the New River, a tributary of the Kanawka, located in Virginia. Although Virginia granted permission, the Federal Power Commission (FPC) refused to approve the request in 1927. The question arose as to whether the federal government had jurisdiction over a nonnavigable tributary of a navigable river located entirely within one state. In 1931 the courts upheld FPC jurisdiction over the New River under the Water Power Act. Eventually in the 1970s President Gerald Ford incorporated the New River as a part of the National Wild and Scenic Rivers System, ending a decades-long conflict between conservationists and development groups.

When the principles of planning and regionalism became more widely known and supported, the Muscle Shoals debate took on new vigor. Whereas previously it had been backed almost entirely by conservationists and public power advocates, by 1932 professional planners paid more attention to it as an opportunity for practical application of many of their theories. Franklin D. Roosevelt's nomination as the Democratic candidate for president in 1932 proved crucial to achieving Norris's goals for the Muscle Shoals project. An ardent conservationist and tree farmer, Roosevelt already understood the interrelationship of various conservation measures, such as reforestation, water control, and soil erosion.

The economic emergency of 1932 aided in creating a favorable atmosphere for the acceptance of Norris's proposal for integrated water resource development and Roosevelt's broader concepts of planning. During his campaign Roosevelt endorsed the Norris proposal for multipurpose development, declaring that conditions in the Tennessee Valley offered an opportunity to set an example of planning for the whole country. Roosevelt's election to the presidency resulted in the launching of an experiment in river basin planning as embodied in the Tennessee Valley Authority Act signed on 18 May 1933.

Most southern states established agencies to collect data concerning water resources, but such agencies seldom had authority to develop or enforce water plans. By the end of the 1920s, some southern states had begun to experiment with the river basin concept of water resource planning. In 1929 Texas established the Brazos River Conservancy and Reclamation District. The New Deal further spurred interest in water development and management throughout the South. With encouragement from the federal government, some southern states developed river basin projects and established water planning agencies.

The Mississippi River continued to receive attention from both state and national governments during the 1930s and 1940s. The destructive flood of 1927 brought demands for action. The Corps of Engineers responded by deepening the Atchafalaya tributary, which left the main channel near its joining with the Red River. Acting as a safety valve for the Mississippi floods, the Atchafalaya channeled excess waters into the swamplands surrounding its course. In the process of deepening and straightening the Atchafalaya, the corps blocked drainage into 22 tributary bayous, thus restricting the Atchafalaya's capacity to absorb Mississippi floodwaters. Eventually the corps constructed an extensive, complicated levee system to hurry floodwaters through the Atchafalaya to the Gulf. This constriction of the floodwaters raised the ground level within the levees higher than that of the surrounding basin, reducing the capacity of the basin to absorb floods while creating a greater potential for disaster if the levees were ever breached. Controversy raged over this project, intensifying in the environmental debates of the 1970s and 1980s. Environmentalists not only questioned the effectiveness of the system as a flood control measure but condemned the ecological changes it wrought.

Pressure created by rapid expansion of water use during World War II highlighted the need for coherent water plans in the southern states. During the war both federal authorities and state governments attempted to develop desirable water policies in the South, but many southerners remained suspicious of federal efforts except when directly affected by floods or when water developments promised immediate economic benefits.

The period from the end of World War II until passage of the National Environmental Protection Act of 1969 represents a significant stage in the history of southern water development. As in other areas of the United States, in the South in the 1950s and 1960s residents evolved from the older conservation ethic to new principles of environmentalism, with their emphasis on quality of life as well as wise use of resources for development purposes. In the post–World War II period older concepts of water management were increasingly challenged by new environmental coalitions.

Like most other Americans, the majority of southerners believed that there would always be an adequate supply of water. Throughout the history of water management, the resource had been directed most often toward developmental use. During the 1950s and 1960s, for the first time, conflict arose in many areas of the South over priority of water use, since the usable water supply was no longer adequate to accommodate all demands. Little thought was given to environmental protection until the 1970s, when it was supported by actions of the federal government such as passage of the National Environmental Protection Act, the Water Quality Act, and the Clean Water Act. As a result, many southern states established water development and water quality boards, but the thrust of their efforts has often been more toward development than protection. Some state boards, such as Georgia's, made serious efforts to protect water quality while others, such as the Texas Water Quality Board, did little that might retard economic growth. In 1973 one study indicated that at least 60 major industrial sources were contaminating the waters of the lower Mississippi with significant quantities of 89, often highly toxic, organic compounds.

Since 1969 environmental groups have challenged many of the traditional water projects in the South, especially the grandiose, very expensive proposals funded by the federal government and enthusiastically supported by local development groups. Each region of the South had advocates of such projects. In the Arkansas Valley, politicians and local support groups promoted development of a navigable waterway that would make Tulsa, Okla., a port city. Its critics called it wasteful and unprofitable. When Texans attempted to get the national government to fund channelization of the Trinity River for barge traffic to Dallas and Fort Worth, a decades-long controversy ensued. Local environmental groups joined fiscal conservatives to defeat the project for ecological and financial reasons. In Mississippi and Alabama a similar controversy raged around the Tennessee-Tombigbee Waterway, which was eventually built.

One of the most spectacular proposals that engendered intense support and opposition was the plan in Texas to pump water from the wet regions of the east to the arid regions of the west. Severe water depletion on the High Plains threatened the irrigated agriculture of that area. The plan recommended taking water from as far east as the Mississippi River and transferring it more than a thousand miles westward. This suggestion encountered opposition not only from Louisiana and Arkansas but also from local environmentalists and fiscal conservatives, a combination that again stalled action on the plan. Even the Tennessee Valley Authority came under scrutiny by environmental groups.

The wetlands of the South, especially the coastal areas, have increasingly engaged the attention of environmentalists. The human population has made numerous demands on nature's resources in many of these areas. Traditionally, Americans viewed swampy and marshy lands as undesirable areas to be altered for the benefit of humans. By the 1980s, scientists and others had become aware of the crucial nexus that this transitional area between land and sea represents. The federal government encouraged action in preserving the ecology of the South's coastal regions with passage in 1972 of the Federal Coastal Zone Management Act. With federal urging, many southern states established coastal management programs.

The conditions in southern Florida represent the complexity of water resource management in the wetlands and coastal zones of the South. In 1971, 21,000 acres of land south of Lake Okeechobee burned simultaneously. This situation resulted from decades of human alteration of the water conditions in southern Florida. The lake acted as a great reservoir for maintaining the marshes and swamps of the Everglades, essential to survival of the wildlife and the ecological balance of the region. Settlers in the area considered the wetland unproductive unless drained so that the fertile muck that remained could be cultivated. When dry, however, the muck was also flammable.

Canals were dug in the region to service the growing tourist centers of the east and west coasts of Florida, further altering the ecology of the wetlands. Some envisioned canals cutting across the state through the Okefenokee Swamp to shorten the barge route around the peninsula. In 1971 President Richard Nixon halted construction by the Corps of Engineers on the Cross Florida Barge Canal project, the first time a president had ever stopped work on a public works project for environmental reasons. The state of Florida also turned away from its policy of encouraging drainage and canal building. With toughened laws the state inaugurated a program to protect and preserve its remaining wetlands.

The water problems of the Florida coast have parallels throughout the South: in South Carolina, where citizens prevented the construction of a chemical plant on their coast; in Savannah, Ga., where the people have demanded that polluting industries alter their practices and even stopped the tradition of dyeing the Savannah River green on St. Patrick's Day; along the Texas coast, where environmental groups insist on balancing clean water and air with industrial development. In 2005 the South still possessed more undeveloped islands and more productive wetlands than any region in the contiguous United States. The question for the future was how resort and industrial developments would affect the wildlife, commercial fishing industry, recreational opportunities, and the existing culture of these vital and attractive areas of the South.

J. B. SMALLWOOD
*North Texas State University*

ROBERT L. IZLAR
*Warnell School of Forest Resources*
*University of Georgia*

Nelson M. Blake, *Land into Water—Water into Land: A History of Water Management in Florida* (1980); Albert E. Cowdrey, *This Land, This South: An Environmental History* (1983); Stephen E. Draper, ed., *Model Water Sharing Agreements for the Twenty-First Century* (2002); James M. Fallows et al., *The Water Lords: Ralph Nader's Study Group Report on Industry and Environmental Crisis in Savannah, Georgia* (1971); Donald E. Green, *Land of the Underground Rain: Irrigation on the Texas High Plains, 1910–1970* (1972); Martin Reuss, *Louisiana History* (Spring 1982); Jeffrey Rotherfelder, *Every Drop for Sale* (2001); Thomas J. Schoenbaum, *The New River Controversy* (1979); *Southern Exposure* (May–June 1983); Sara Warner, *Down to the Waterline: Boundaries, Nature, and the Law in Florida* (2005).

# Wetlands

Wetlands were long regarded as sources of locally valuable materials, but modern treatment of wetlands as wastelands ignores the historically significant roles these waterlogged areas have always played in civilization. The rich accumulating sediments of lake, river, or ocean shores frequently capture and sometimes preserve remnants of the past. The pair of footprints from the Laetoli site in East Africa, for example, may verify the upright stance and bipedal walk of human ancestors more than 3.7 million years ago.

Bogs and lake sediment retain pollen grains that paleontologists use to understand the floral composition of antiquity and to reconstruct the prehistory of recent geological climate change. The significance of rice and papyrus, two wetland crops, in Asian and African civilizations is an indication of the centrality of wetlands in preindustrial civilization. Paper was crafted from both of these wetland plants. Also trapped within a wetland's mud layers are artifacts that suggest the recurrent uses of wetlands for a variety of subsistence and commercial purposes, contradicting the modern view of marshlands as wastelands. Looking at wetlands as a cache of artifacts suggests that these borderlands are

Cypress/tupelo wetland entered in the Wetlands Reserve Program in central Mississippi
(Photo by Lynn Betts, USDA Natural Resources Conservation Service)

anything but wastelands. Items uncovered from the surrounding areas or adjacent watersheds help us piece together the significant clash between incompatible uses of wetlands. Against this backdrop of cherishing and despising wetlands, a keener understanding of wetlands' many roles has emerged. These ecological services include flood protection; nurseries for endangered fisheries, birds, and mammals; sanitation through nitrogen and phosphorus absorption; and water storage.

Early American settlers utilized marshes for sources of food, fuel, and forage but found that these low-lying lands drastically slowed land and water travel. The earliest seat of government in the South, Jamestown, was moved to less swampy and higher ground in Williamsburg during the 17th century. The mouth of the Mississippi River fostered early disputes between the older tradition and the emergent progressive belief of engineers that suggested wetlands be drained and rivers lined with levees. Levees are designed to keep the water in a river bed from flowing over into an adjacent wetland. In 1717 French engineer Dumont de la Tour proposed that New Orleans, after early 18th-century flooding, be protected by such a levee system. A campaign to ring the Mississippi with walls began prior to the Civil War. Today, New Orleans, south Florida, and St. Louis are protected by expensive levee systems and extensive wetland drainage.

By 1993 the great flood of the upper Mississippi proved to many the necessity of extensive wetlands in addition to spillways and walls to protect particularly vulnerable populations downstream of riparian narrows. Contemporary arguments over the values and uses of wetlands must be understood in this longer historical context because these archaeological discoveries reveal the inherent value of wetlands as a potential source for flood protection and both useful commercial alteration and aesthetic appreciation. It remains certain that the economic value of wetlands as high-water buffers and as sanitary engineering properties assures their continued existence, if in modified form. The experiences of engineers in New Orleans led to similar approaches throughout the South, West, and Midwest. Chicago, like many cities, grew over a drained swamp. Wetland reclamation fully transformed California's central valley and reached a national crescendo during the Great Depression. Converting wetlands continued in Florida with the extensive draining of the Everglades after World War II, and in Virginia and Maryland until the 1980s, when the process threatened water quality and fisheries in the Chesapeake Bay.

While many writers have focused on the obstructing maladies posed by wetlands to civilized progress, discoveries concerning the importance of swamps in the life and lore of southern regions suggest that indigenous people, settlers, and their slaves all recognized a deeper importance of wetlands. From Joel Chandler Harris's stories to Walt Kelly's comic characters from the Okefenokee Swamp, wetland imagery and wildlife have been used to convey important stories concerning persistent human follies. Southern ecologists and brothers Eugene and Thomas Odum, in their quantification studies of Silver Springs and, later, the Georgia Sea Islands (1950s), established the scientific credibility necessary to the protection of estuaries and wetlands (1970s). Research has uncovered that physical, chemical, and biological features of wetlands together engender an enriched venue where scientists have measured levels of natural productivity greater than in any other comparable ecosystems.

Wetlands are anomalous frontiers where water gives way to land or land subsides into water. The ecological processes comprise a situation referred to as an "edge effect" in wetlands where species from adjacent territory overlap along the edges or boundaries of these saturated frontiers. In addition to migratory fish and birds, resident species of coastal and interior wetlands attract fishers and hunters. So important were wetlands to colonial subsistence patterns that constitutional provisions were crafted to allow residents access to wetlands and shorelines to navigate, fish, and hunt for a living. Larger wetlands have formed legal borders, such as the Dismal Swamp in North Carolina and Virginia or the Okefenokee Swamp in Georgia and Florida. From ancient and medieval practices of walking around the boundaries of property, called rogations, wetlands were avoided and thus formed common borderlands between property owners or along rivers. Under federal law, promoted by southern and western states, extensive title to wetlands was given to states under the Swampland Acts of the 1850s. Throughout the South and the Mississippi River Valley thousands of wet acres were granted to owners who promised to drain these wetlands.

Sugar cultivation made the extensive drainage of Louisiana and Florida wetlands desirable. But rice cultivation in the Carolinas actually required the periodic flooding of these acres, called "paddies," for germination. The North Carolina naturalist Edmund Ruffin, before the Civil War, commented on the freshwater flooding of rice marshes as a corollary in the spread of malaria. In seasonally inundated wetlands or vernal pools cattle grazing was a viable use of emergent vegetation.

Extensive forests also persist along with grasslands or wet prairies in southern wetlands. Cypress trees are common from Florida and Louisiana to Maryland and Delaware, and cottonwoods, maples, and sweet gums appear in the interior valleys. Lumbering of rot-resistant woods in wetlands occurred with increasing intensity in the 18th, 19th, and 20th centuries. Land-use practices that require wet conditions during all or part of the vegetation's life cycle promote the protection of wetlands.

Competing land-use practices that promise greater economic returns than do forestry or agriculture often lead to reclamation, or the removal of water for a more intensive use of the landscape. Drainage was considered the principal means of combating malaria and yellow fever that were epidemic in the humid summer months south of Philadelphia. So tormented were coastal populations that seasonally the upland areas of the Appalachians and Ozarks gave rise to health spas such as Hot Springs in Arkansas or White Sulphur Springs, originally in Virginia.

While it is easy to see the removal of wetlands as a signal of progress, the southern poet Sydney Lanier was moved in the 19th century to recognize the enduring qualities of wetlands. Lanier wrote that the Georgia Sea Islands possessed vast marshes whose deeper value for the perceptive observer lay in their evocative expansiveness. He wrote in *The Marshes of Glynn*, "Oh like the greatness of God is the greatness within the range of the marshes." Lanier spoke of these south Georgia coastal borderlands with northern Florida as "tolerant plains. How candid and simple. And free."

The recent Western view of wetlands runs counter to the ancient—preindustrial—heritage because it encompasses many disconcertingly contradictory uses that undermine the biological productivity of submerged land. What people think of wetlands depends on what is known about their physical, biological, and social conditions. What we do with wetlands is influenced by the crops that sustain our economic institutions. The history of rice alone suggests that wetlands have been critical in shaping the foundations of civilization because of the technical skills, organizational arrangements, and cultural significance of this staple for half the world's people.

Regardless of prejudices for or against wetlands as valuable commodities, they remain repositories of the artifacts needed to reconstruct knowledge of the past. V. S. Naipaul, the award-winning Trinidadian novelist, reminds us there is built in, on, or around a wetland "always a shanty town, and always growing, spreading over the hills." Whether wetlands are viewed as measures of land reversal or renewal, or thought of as nurseries or trash heaps, historically they hold the shards of ancestors. They are places to jog our memories and to assure us that we are but momentary users of the land regardless of our pretensions about permanence and progress. Wetlands are a witness of our antiquity and in some sense a measure of the planet's geographical diversity, richness of species, and vulnerability to alteration. In wetlands resides enduring evidence of the Earth's nurturing qualities.

JOSEPH V. SIRY
*Rollins College*

Nelson M. Blake, *Land into Water—Water into Land: A History of Water Management in Florida* (1980); Alexander C. Brown, *Dismal Swamp Canal* (1946); Archie Carr, *The Everglades* (1973); Malcolm L. Comeaux, *Atchafalaya Swamp Life: Settlement and Folk Occupations* (1972); Albert E. Cowdrey, *This Land, This South: An Environmental History* (1983); Gay M. Gomez, *A Wetland Biography: Seasons on Louisiana's Chenier Plain* (1998); Bevil Knapp and Mike Dunne, *America's Wetland: Louisiana's Vanishing Coast* (2005); Cecile H. Matschat, *Suwannee River: Strange Green Land* (1938); Joseph V. Siry, *Marshes of the Ocean Shore: The Development of an Ecological Ethic* (1984); Bill Streever, *Saving Louisiana: The Battle for Coastal Wetlands* (2001).

## Air-Conditioning

"Let us begin by discussing the weather, for that has been the chief agency in making the South distinctive." This was the opening line of U. B. Phillips's 1929 classic *Life and Labor in the Old South*. In Phillips's day, environmental determinism was a powerful force in American social science; it was the age of Ellsworth Huntington and Walter Prescott Webb, when the link between climate and culture was thought to be a simple relationship of cause and effect, when the southern climate in particular was credited with producing everything from plantation slavery to the southern drawl. Such determinist views are no longer fashionable, but the connection between regional culture and climate remains an intriguing subject, one that has taken on a new dimension since the advent of air-conditioning. Ask any southerner over 30 years of age to explain why the South has changed in recent decades, and he or she may begin with the civil rights movement or industrialization. But sooner or later the subject of air-conditioning will arise. For better or worse, the air conditioner has changed the nature of southern life.

The age of air-conditioning, in the broadest sense of the term, was initiated by Dr. John Gorrie, an Apalachicola, Fla., physician who began experimenting with mechanical cooling in the 1830s. In an attempt to lower the body temperatures of malaria and yellow fever victims, he blew forced air over buckets of ice suspended from a hospital ceiling. Gorrie eventually patented a primitive ice-making machine, but the world's first true air conditioner—

a machine that simultaneously cools, circulates, dehumidifies, and cleanses the air—was not invented until 1902, when Willis Haviland Carrier installed an experimental system in a Brooklyn publishing company. Carrier's invention soon spread to the South, thanks to the efforts of two young southern engineers, Stuart Cramer and I. H. Hardeman. Cramer actually coined the term "air-conditioning" in 1906, and later the same year Hardeman helped Carrier design and install the region's first air-conditioning system, at the Chronicle Cotton Mills in Belmont, N.C. By 1920 the new technology was being used as a quality-control device in a number of southern cotton and rayon mills, paper mills, cigar factories, tobacco stemming rooms, breweries, and bakeries. Prior to the 1920s air-conditioning in the South was restricted almost entirely to industrial uses. The major exceptions were a Baltimore hotel and Montgomery's elegant Empire Theatre.

This situation began to change in 1923 when Carrier's invention of the centrifugal compressor ushered in the age of "comfort cooling." By the mid-1930s air-conditioned movie theaters and railway cars had become common. But the movement of air-conditioning into other areas of southern life was more gradual. Although a sprinkling of air-conditioned department stores, office buildings, homes, hospitals, drugstores, barbershops, and restaurants could be found across the region by the late 1930s, air-conditioning remained an oddity until after World War II. During the 1950s air-conditioning became an immutable part of southern life. After the air conditioner invaded the home (the inexpensive, efficient window unit appeared in 1951) and the automobile, there was no turning back. By the mid-1970s air-conditioning had made its way into more than 90 percent of the South's high-rise office buildings, banks, apartments, and railroad passenger coaches; more than 80 percent of its automobiles, government buildings, and hotels; approximately two-thirds of its homes, stores, trucks, and hospital rooms; roughly half of its classrooms; and at least a third of its tractors. The South of the 1970s could claim air-conditioned shopping malls, domed stadiums, greenhouses, grain elevators, chicken coops, aircraft hangars, crane cabs, offshore oil rigs, cattle barns, steel mills, and drive-in movies and restaurants. Even the Alamo had central air, and in Houston alone the cost of air-conditioning in 1980 exceeded the gross national product of several Third World nations.

Not all southerners live in air-conditioned homes, ride in air-conditioned cars, or work in air-conditioned buildings. Among rural and working-class blacks, poor whites, migrant laborers, and mountaineers, air-conditioned living is not the norm. Nevertheless, in varying degrees virtually all southerners have been affected, directly or indirectly, by the technology of climate control. Air-conditioning has influenced everything from architecture to sleeping habits and has contributed to the erosion of several regional traditions, most notably cultural isolation, agrarianism, romanticism, poverty, neighborliness, a strong sense of place,

and a relatively slow pace of life. The net result has been a dramatic decline in regional distinctiveness. In combination with other historical forces—the civil rights movement, advances in communication and transportation technology, and economic and political change—the air conditioner has greatly accelerated what John Egerton has called "the Americanization of Dixie."

To begin with, the air conditioner has helped to reverse an almost century-long southern tradition of net out-migration. It was more than a coincidence that in the 1950s, the decade when air-conditioning first engulfed the South, the region's net out-migration was much smaller than in previous decades, and that in the 1960s, for the first time since the Civil War, the South experienced more in-migration than out-migration. The 1970 census, according to the *New York Times*, was "The Air Conditioned Census." "The humble air conditioner," the *Times* concluded, "has been a powerful influence in circulating people as well as air in this country. . . . Its availability explains why increasing numbers of Americans find it comfortable to live year round in the semitropical heat." The 1960s was only the beginning; between 1970 and 1978, 7 million people migrated to the South, twice the number that left the region. By the end of the decade, the Sunbelt era was in full swing. Abetted by millions of tourists, northern migrants brought new ideas and new lifestyles to the Sunbelt South, disrupting the region's long-standing cultural isolation. Thanks in part to air-conditioning, the southern population became increasingly heterogeneous, and the concept of the Solid South—long a bulwark of regional mythology—all but faded from view.

Air-conditioning has also played a key role in the industrialization of the modern South. In addition to bringing new factories and businesses to the region, it has helped to improve working conditions and increase productivity. Economic growth, partially induced by a better work environment, has led to a rising standard of living for many southern families; per capita income in the South has risen from 52 percent of the national average in 1930 to approximately 95 percent today, and air-conditioning is one of the reasons why.

Air-conditioning has also fostered the urbanization of the South by encouraging industrialization and population growth; by accelerating the development of large public institutions, such as universities, museums, hospitals, sports arenas, and military bases; by facilitating the efficient use of urban space and opening the city to vertical, high-rise development; and by influencing the development of distinctively urban forms of architecture. Without air-conditioning, skyscrapers and high-rise apartments would be less prevalent, urban populations would be smaller, cities would be more spread out, and the physical and architectural differences between inner cities and suburbs would be less striking. Although the region's agrarian legacy is still a force to be reckoned with, in the air-conditioned South the locus of power and activity has moved to Main Street.

In a related development, climate control has altered southern attitudes toward nature and technology. Air-conditioning has taken its toll on the traditional "folk culture," which as David Potter once pointed out, "survived in the South long after it succumbed to the onslaught of urban-industrial culture elsewhere." The South has always been an elemental land of blood, sweat, and tears—a land where personalism and a curious mixture of romance and realism have prevailed. But climate control has taken the edge off this romantic element. As the southern climate has been artificially tamed, pastoralism has been replaced by technological determinism, and human interaction with the natural environment has decreased significantly. To confirm this point, one has only to walk down almost any southern street on a hot summer afternoon, listen to the whir of compressors, and look in vain for open windows or front porch society.

In many cases, the porch is not simply empty; it is not even there. To the dismay of many southerners, air-conditioning has impinged upon a rich tradition of vernacular architecture. From the "dogtrot cabin" with its central breezeway to the grand plantation with its wraparound porch to the tin-roofed "cracker" house up on blocks, traditional southern architecture represents an ingenious conspiracy of passive cooling and cross-ventilation. The catalog of structural techniques developed to tame the hot, humid southern climate is long and varied: high ceilings, thin walls, long breezeways, floors raised three or more feet off the ground, steeply pitched roofs vented from top to bottom, open porches with broad eaves that blocked the slanting sun, massive doors and windows that sometimes stretched from floor to ceiling, louvered jalousies, transoms placed above bedroom doors, dormers, groves of shade trees blanketing the southern exposure, houses situated to capture prevailing breezes, and so on. Historically these techniques have been an important element of a distinctively southern aesthetic and social milieu. But with the proliferation of residential air-conditioning, vernacular architecture has given way to the modern tract house, with its low ceilings, small windows, and compact floor plan.

Residential air-conditioning has not only affected architectural form; it has also influenced the character of southern family life. As families have withdrawn into air-cooled private spaces, interaction with grandparents, aunts, uncles, and cousins, not to mention friends and neighbors, has often suffered. As more than one observer has noted, the vaunted southern tradition of "visiting" has fallen on hard times in recent years.

The air conditioner has also had an impact on the basic rhythm of southern life. To a significant degree air-conditioning has modulated the daily and seasonal rhythms that were once an inescapable part of southern culture. Thanks to air-conditioning, the "siesta mentality" has declined, and the summer sun is no longer the final arbiter of daily and yearly planning. In addition to these mundane changes, the declining importance of climatic and seasonal change may have profound long-term consequences, eventually dulling the sense of time and perhaps even the sense of history of the southerner.

A more immediate threat is the air conditioner's assault on the South's strong "sense of place." Southerners, more than most other Americans, have tied themselves to local geography. Their lives and identities have been rooted in a particular county, town, neighborhood, or homestead. Yet in recent years, thanks in part to air-conditioning, the southern landscape has been overwhelmed by an almost endless string of look-alike chain stores, tract houses, glassed-in high-rises, and perhaps most importantly, enclosed shopping malls. The modern shopping mall is the cathedral of air-conditioned culture, symbolizing the relative placelessness of the 21st-century South. In some measure, the region retains a distinctive cultural heritage based on history and place-bound experience, but how long this will last remains an open question. Perhaps the southerner's special devotion to myth and tradition will eventually turn back or at least place limits on the technological insurgency of air-conditioning and related technologies of comfort and convenience. But this will not be easy in a land where General Electric has proved a more devastating invader than General Sherman.

RAYMOND ARSENAULT
*University of South Florida at St. Petersburg*

Marsha Ackerman, *Cool Comfort: America's Romance with Air-Conditioning* (2002); Raymond Arsenault, *Journal of Southern History* (November 1984); Raymond B. Becker, *John Gorrie, M.D.: Father of Air Conditioning and Mechanical Refrigeration*

(1972); Daniel Boorstin, *The Americans: The Democratic Experience* (1973); Gail Cooper, *Air-Conditioning America: Engineers and the Controlled Environment* (1998); Robert Friedman, *American Heritage* (August/ September 1984); Margaret Ingalls, *Willis Haviland Carrier: Father of Air Conditioning* (1952); Tom Shactman, *Absolute Zero and the Conquest of Cold* (1999).

## Alligators and Crocodiles

The American alligator (*Alligator mississipiensis*), one of only two remaining species of alligator, inhabits the rivers, swamps, and marshes of the southeastern United States as far west as Texas and along the Atlantic seaboard up through North Carolina. The name "alligator" is an Anglicization of the Spanish *el legarto*, "the lizard." The American crocodile (*Crocodylus acutus*), an extremely endangered species, is limited to the southern tip of Florida.

Eighteenth-century accounts and drawings by explorers and naturalists in the American South elevated the alligator to a symbol representing America in European cartography and art. William Bartram's *Travels through North and South Carolina, Georgia, East and West Florida* (1791) and his drawings of "the alegator of St. Johns" burned into both American and European imaginations the image of a fearsome, aggressive, bellowing man-eater.

White southerners have alternately hunted and been hunted by the alligator. Until the Civil War, alligator hunting was a sport common enough to decimate the alligator population in the lower Mississippi. The use of alligator hides for shoes, belts, and purses began in the 1850s and for the next century accelerated the hunt, as the value of the hides grew astronomically. In the 1940s the southern states outlawed the killing and trapping of alligators, and the 1970 U.S. Endangered Species Act banned the international sale of hides and products. Despite continued poaching, the protected alligator population had so replenished itself that in 1981 selling the hides became legal once more.

Stories of encounters with alligators, especially deadly attacks on children and dogs, have been common throughout the South since the 18th century. The belief that alligators are especially prone to attack blacks began in early slave ship accounts and persists as a motif in white southern fiction and humor and on postcards and souvenirs from the early decades of the 20th century. Turning the tables, African American folktales portray the alligator as the victim of a trickster animal such as the rabbit, with whom blacks identified.

Boosters for Florida tourism and land sales in the late 19th century appropriated the alligator as the symbol of that state's wild nature, marketing the Florida Everglades as America's "last frontier." Photographers in Jacksonville, St. Augustine, and Miami took studio portraits of neatly dressed visitors posed with stuffed alligators, and by the 1920s the tourist could see live alligators at a variety of alligator farms and attractions around the state. Alligator wrestling has thrilled countless tourists, but alligator wrestling never was a Seminole native custom; it was invented by white entrepreneurs who wanted to combine the

display of Seminole Indians and alligators.

The Seminole Indians of Florida
have had a relationship to alligators
similar to that of the Plains Indians to
the bison. Both African Americans and
Native Americans have incorporated
the alligator into their foodways. Southern magical medicine employs alligator
teeth and oil in treatments for pain,
as antidotes for poison, and as charms
against witches. A Cajun superstition
alleges that an alligator crawling under
one's house is a portent of death.

Commercial alligator farming began
in Louisiana and Florida in the 1970s,
and by the turn of the century this
multimillion-dollar industry provided
skins and meat far beyond the legal wild
harvest by hunters. Alligator meat now
is commonly available at restaurants in
the South.

Traditional alligator tourist attractions have been joined by ecotourism
aimed at giving the visitor a close-up
look at the alligator in its natural habitat. The centuries-old human fascination
with this prehistoric, man-eating reptile
continues to fuel the imaginations and
economies of the South.

JAY MECHLING
*University of California, Davis*

Dick Bothwell, *The Great Outdoors Book of
Alligators and Other Crocodilia* (1981); C. C.
Lockwood, *The Alligator Book* (2002); Sher-
man A. Minton Jr. and Madge Rutherford
Minton, *Giant Reptiles* (1973); Wilfred T.
Neill, *The Last of the Ruling Reptiles: Alliga-
tors, Crocodiles, and Their Kin* (1971).

## Anderson, Walter Inglis
(1903–1965) ARTIST.

Walter Anderson was born in New
Orleans on 29 September 1903, the
second son of George Walter Anderson,
a grain merchant, and Annette Mc-
Connell Anderson, an artist who taught
him a love of art, music, and literature.
He grew up valuing the importance of
art in everyday life and developed what
would become a lifelong interest in
mythology. He attended grade school in
New Orleans, went to boarding school
in New York, and was later trained at
the Parsons Institute of Design in New
York (1922–23) and the Pennsylvania
Academy of Fine Arts (1924–28). He
received a scholarship that enabled
him to study and travel in Europe. He
read broadly in history, natural science,
poetry, art history, folklore, philosophy,
and epic narratives of journeying.

After he returned to the United
States, Anderson worked with his
brother on earthenware at Shearwater
Pottery in Ocean Springs, Miss. He mar-
ried Agnes Grinstead Anderson in 1933
and fathered four children. His developing interest in murals coincided with
his work on Works Progress Administration mural projects in Ocean Springs
during the 1930s. The late 1930s saw the
onset of mental illness, for which he was
hospitalized for three years. Then he and
his family moved to his wife's family
estate, the Oldfields Plantation, in Gau-
tier, Miss. He had long been interested
in nature, but at Oldfields natural scenes
begin to appear in his watercolors and
tempera paintings and in the large lino-
leum block prints he created.

In 1947 he secluded himself in a

cottage at Shearwater, where he wrote, painted, decorated pottery for the family business, and carved. Increasingly he rowed the 12 miles to Horn Island, one of the barrier islands off the Mississippi coast. This unspoiled natural landscape became his home for long stretches of time during the last decade and a half of his life. "So much depends on the dominant mode on shore," he wrote, "that it was necessary for me to go to sea to find the conditional. Everything seems conditional on the islands." Anderson's paintings and drawings captured the numerous species of flora and fauna in this pristine environment, as he illustrated birds, insects, animals, flowers, trees, shrubs, and any other natural life he saw in his exploration through the wild underbrush and coastal lagoons. He used the term "realization" to suggest his hope of becoming at one with the natural species he observed. In one episode, he tied himself to a tree during a hurricane and experienced the fury of nature. He documented everything he saw, from the life of a spotted frog to the near-extinction of the brown pelican, because the effects of the pesticide DDT in the 1940s and 1950s reached even this isolated island. Anderson kept 90 journals and logs recording what he experienced, writings mostly for himself that drew from his broad artistic and philosophical knowledge.

Walter Anderson died of lung cancer in New Orleans in 1965. During the centennial of his birth in 2003, the Smithsonian Institution honored Anderson's work with a major exhibit. The Walter Anderson Museum was established in Ocean Springs in 1991. Much of Anderson's work is there, but his family compound at Shearwater also housed many of his watercolors, paintings, and ceramics, which were damaged or destroyed as a result of Hurricane Katrina, which hit the Mississippi coast in 2005. Conservators are working to save and restore his work.

CHARLES REAGAN WILSON
*University of Mississippi*

Christopher Maurer, *Fortune's Favorite Child: The Uneasy Life of Walter Anderson* (2003); Patricia Pinson, ed., *The Art of Walter Anderson* (2003); Redding S. Sugg Jr., ed., *The Horn Island Logs of Walter Anderson* (1985).

## Appalachian Coal Region

The South is a region of vast mineral wealth, and the Appalachian coalfields have been a major energy source for the nation. Mining companies began exploiting the land and the people of Appalachia in the 19th century, leaving an indelible mark on the region. Coupled with that history are the faces of people and a scarred environment.

The Appalachian mountain region in the southeastern United States is full of predominantly bituminous coalfields, some of the largest of which are in West Virginia, Kentucky, and Alabama. In the 19th century, as wood supplies dwindled in the East, people began to turn to coal to supply their energy needs. Bituminous fields run through the Appalachians from Pittsburgh, Pa., to near Birmingham, Ala. Part of the success of the fields had to do with the fact that they were spread out through such a large region, and once transportation networks found their way to the major fields, the production grew.

The iron manufacturing industry discovered in its early use of coal that bituminous was superior to anthracite for their processes. At the beginning of the Civil War the iron making industry began using coal from the Appalachians on a steady basis. The 1890s saw the first large mining companies filter into the southern Appalachians. At first, industry utilized the fields closest to the East Coast, but southern boosters had other designs. The coalfield near Birmingham, at the end of the Appalachian line, was so prolific that city fathers set up the community specifically to exploit the coal resources. The lack of a railroad line kept the business enterprise down until the late 1870s, but soon the region became a powerhouse of coal and iron. In 1870 the Birmingham field produced only 13,000 tons of coal, but by 1900 it produced almost 141,000 tons. The city's ties to the iron industry combined with its prodigious coal production helped make it the leading industrial city of the South.

The bituminous coal industry continued to grow rapidly until the 1910s, when too much internal competition and the meteoric rise of petroleum as an energy source cut into coal's market share. Use for the black rock peaked in 1920 with over half a million tons mined in the United States, much of it bituminous. By 1940 oil and natural gas surpassed coal as the dominant fuel for the country. However, even though coal was no longer king, it still commanded almost half of the total market share, and in 1944 miners took from the ground the largest amount recorded in U.S. history up to that time. Most of that went to generating electricity, railroads, steel manufacture, and heating.

The coal mines had significant economic difficulties through the Great Depression. During most of the 1930s, coal did not show a profit, a fact that the ever-present labor strife exacerbated. Things were so difficult for the industry that the economic woes and labor issues almost bankrupted the entire operation. Miners throughout Appalachia suffered dramatically from the collapse. Almost half a million miners could not find work during the Depression, and many who could find work attempted strikes in order to offset the horrible conditions. However, because so many people needed work, the strikes had limited success. By the time it emerged from the Depression, king coal could scarcely operate without government assistance.

Coal mining in Appalachia has been a poorly paid and dangerous job. In much of the region mine operators have exploited the area for its mineral resources and taken the profits elsewhere, leaving local residents impoverished. Despite a higher wage than most of industry by the 1920s, the lack of steady work in mines limited the real income. Many miners only worked about 200 days a year and spent most of those days in dangerous working conditions. They faced horrors ranging from invisible gases that could kill without warning to mine collapse. Labor unions, notably the United Mine Workers, attempted to deal with these issues with some success.

Miners suffered from a variety of

abuses at the hands of owners during the early 20th century. Many operators felt that the local citizens were racially inferior, and they used that racism to justify treating the miners poorly. Workers were abused and subjugated. The isolation of many coalfields enabled mine owners to create company towns. These towns had their own company police forces that suppressed civil liberties and limited the mobility of miners in and out of a community. Mine owners required residents to purchase goods and lease property from the company. This ensured that laborers remained in debt and tied to the corporation for their subsistence. Company towns persisted in areas of the South until the early 1920s. Workers organized in an attempt to improve their quality of life, and their action, through bitter work stoppages with violent repercussions, eventually achieved results. Their perseverance helped create a lasting tradition of labor solidarity in the region.

The character of the workforce was diverse, even from the earliest days. From the Civil War to the 1890s, mine owners used predominantly white labor, but blacks soon became the majority in the Deep South fields. Even so, mines farther north used African American labor as well. Operators realized in the early 19th century that local mountain people alone could not meet their labor demands. By 1910 southern blacks filtered into West Virginia coal mines with other new immigrants to the United States.

Labor issues, competition from other energy sources, and new technology encouraged operators to fully implement a devastating technique to get at coal seams—the strip mine. Coal mining in general damages the local environment, but strip-mining brought the devastation to an entirely different level. The 19th century saw mine owners attempt to utilize strip-mining in Kentucky, but they had limited success because the technology at that point was limited. Real mechanized strip-mining did not get under way in Appalachia until after World War II.

Coal mine owners were eager to find ways to compete with oil, and strip-mining presented an economic solution. A few men could do the same job with a few machines that hundreds of men used to do using traditional techniques. Strip-mining gradually accounted for more and more of the annual mined tonnage of coal. In 1920 the total was around 9,000 tons, but by 1950 the tonnage was close to 124,000. Through the 1960s strip-mining grew to be a preferred method of extraction. During the same period operators developed the technology to a point that miners could literally remove the entire top of a mountain to get to the coal seams. Despite the region's close affiliation with the mining industry, many areas have protested the practice. Kentucky produced the first protests toward this technology during the 1960s. Citizens recognized that strip-mining was a threat to the culture of Appalachia because the method had the potential to destroy the land around them.

Traditional and strip coal mines throughout the Appalachians polluted the region to the point that some might consider the area sacrificed to industry.

By the late 20th century, traditional mines damaged almost 7,000 miles of streams by allowing mine drainage containing toxic substances to filter into Appalachian waterways. Strip-mining is an ugly process that leaves a visible mark on the landscape. Operators often left their mines open to the elements despite calls to reclaim the land. This neglect resulted in massive soil erosion and water pollution. Mud and mine waste from the open strip mines polluted waterways by choking them with solid materials and toxic runoff. In many circumstances strip-mining caused landslides that disturbed local communities in addition to the natural environment. Many areas have experienced an almost 20 percent population drop as a direct result of strip-mining.

Coal continues to be an important energy source for the United States, and the Appalachian coal region supplies a prodigious amount of that need. In the 1970s electricity generators continued to use coal in half of their facilities. Natural gas took over a portion of that, but coal still accounts for a considerable amount of total usage. Coal from Appalachia will definitely remain an important energy source for the nation and perhaps the world. As petroleum supplies dwindle, energy consumers are reminded of the value of coal, and the Appalachian coal region promises to have a stake in supplying future demand. Hopefully, the industry will have learned to be more environmentally friendly and more accommodating to the needs of labor.

JOSEPH STROMBERG
*University of Houston*

Edwin L. Brown and Colin J. Davis, eds., *It Is Union and Liberty: Alabama Coal Miners and the UMW* (1999); Barbara Freeze, *Coal: A Human History* (2003); Martin V. Melosi, *Coping with Abundance: Energy and Environment in Industrial America* (1985); Chad Montrie, *To Save the Land and Its People: A History of Opposition to Surface Coal Mining in Appalachia* (2003); Stephen H. Norwood, *Strikebreaking and Intimidation: Mercenaries and Masculinity in Twentieth-Century America* (2002).

## Appalachian Mountains

This extended mountain system stretches from the St. Lawrence Valley in Canada to central Alabama. It includes a series of ranges, and those in the South include the Allegheny Mountains, the Blue Ridge, the Black Mountains, the Great Smoky Mountains, and the Cumberland Plateau. Composed of sedimentary rock, the beds of insoluble material in the southern mountains have resisted erosion, resulting in the South's having the highest ranges of the series. Mount Mitchell (6,684 feet) in the Black Mountains is the highest peak in the Appalachians. The Blue Ridge Mountains run upward into Pennsylvania and represent the eastern escarpment of the southern Appalachians. They are a maze of coves, hills, and spurs, resulting from gradual erosion of a mound of irregular rock. The Appalachian Valley lies between the Blue Ridge Mountains on the east and the Great Smoky Mountains on the west. It is a series of river valleys, including the Coosa, Tennessee, Shenandoah, and Cumberland.

Paleo-Indians lived in the Appalachian Mountains by about 10,000 B.C.

Native tribes established villages in mountain valleys with rich soil, and hunting parties traveled into the Great Smoky Mountains to search for game. The Appalachian Mountains represented a barrier to the advance of the frontier in the colonial era but were being crossed by the time of the American Revolution. Germans, Scots, Irish, and Quakers were among the diverse settlement groups at this time. Folk songs such as "The Cumberland Gap" and stories of Daniel Boone and other frontiersmen preserve the memory of this phase of southern history. Comparatively small and diffuse coves, gorges, basins, and hollows developed population centers that remained isolated until the late 19th century. The mountains were a source of Unionist sentiments in the South during the Civil War, and the Great Valley of Virginia was the scene of General Philip Sheridan's raids, one of the most dramatic chapters of the military struggle. In the late 19th century commercial interests began the exploitation of such mountain resources as coal, gas, petroleum, iron, and timber found abundantly in the mountains. Bituminous coal beds existed under 63,000 square miles of the Appalachians and became the basis for one of the region's main industries, whose story included some of the most violent labor history in the South. Throughout the 20th century the area was the scene for some of the nation's worst poverty, with Lyndon B. Johnson's War on Poverty including special programs aimed at southern mountain economic and social development. The natural resources of the Appalachian

Mountains support tourism and recreational sports. Aaron Copland's *Appalachian Spring* conveys in music the beauties and mysteries of the mountains, and photographer Eliot Porter's *Appalachian Wilderness* (1973) captures their rhythms in visual images.

CHARLES REAGAN WILSON
*University of Mississippi*

Thomas L. Connelly, *Discovering the Appalachians: What to Look for from the Past and in the Present along America's Eastern Frontier* (1968); Thomas R. Ford, ed., *The Southern Appalachian Region: A Survey* (1962); Clark Hubler, *America's Mountains: An Exploration of Their Origins* (1995); Karl B. Raitz and Richard Ulack, *Appalachia: A Regional Geography: Land, People, and Development* (1984); Charlotte T. Ross, ed., *Bibliography of Southern Appalachia* (1976); Scott Weidensaul, *Mountains of the Heart: A Natural History of the Appalachians* (2000).

## Armadillo

The armadillo is an armored mammal about 30 inches long, including a tail of about 12 inches, usually weighing about 10 pounds. The body is enclosed by a three-sectioned shell. One section in the front protects the shoulders; another section in the rear protects the pelvic region. In the middle section between these two are a number of movable bands. The vulnerable underside is without armor, but it is protected by a tough skin covered with coarse hair.

Collectively, armadillos are distributed throughout South America and north to Texas and into the Deep South. Because the early explorers had not seen the animal in Europe, it was natural for them to identify the "New Animal" with the "New World." Gradually this identification became so fixed that the armadillo took on the nature of a symbol. It was widely used in such symbolic contexts as decorative map frames in the 1500s and 1600s.

In 20th-century America there was special interest in a single species: the nine-banded armadillo, which is known formally as *Dasypus novemcinctus mexicanus*, or informally as the Texas armadillo. In modern times the nine-banded armadillo has become identified with Texas just as strongly as the armadillo once was identified with America. This identification is somewhat emotional and symbolic because in fact the armadillo is not at all confined to present-day Texas. Indeed, there are large numbers of armadillos in Louisiana, Mississippi, and Florida.

The armadillo usually comes out only at night. It lives on insects and worms. The animal is basically harmless to people and does not put up a fight when captured. In fact, its peaceful nature invited its use by antiwar protesters as a symbol during the 1960s. In 1968 self-styled hippie artist Jim Franklin, asked to come up with a design for a poster for a free concert in a park in Austin, drew an armadillo smoking a marijuana cigarette, and after that the armadillo became the visual symbol of the Texas youth culture.

In the early 1970s a group of counterculture businessmen started an Austin music hall called the Armadillo World Headquarters in an abandoned armory. The music hall became the center of

"redneck rock," a fusion of country and western with rock and roll.

The popularity of the new music catapulted the armadillo into high status at the University of Texas. The armadillo was soon rendered in orange and white, the university's colors. In 1971 the student senate voted to change the school's mascot from the longhorn to the armadillo, but the change was never made official.

The armadillo became familiar in Austin through the musical scene and was reinforced by posters and handbills, stories, and jokes. The connection between the armadillo and Texas youth culture may fade since the last concert at the Armadillo World Headquarters was on 31 December 1980. The building has since been torn down.

ANGUS K. GILLESPIE
*Rutgers University*

Larry L. Smith and Robin W. Doughty, *The Amazing Armadillo* (1984).

## Assateague Island National Seashore

Assateague Island is a wild natural barrier island encompassing 19,000 acres surrounded by oceanic and estuarine waters. It is approximately 37 miles long and one-quarter to two and a half miles wide. Its name is thought to derive from a American Indian word meaning "the marshy place across." Barrier islands are a natural phenomenon, a temporary formation created by the buildup of sand close to the continental coastline by storms, winds, and ocean tides. The waters of the earth's oceans are fed by the polar ice caps, which have been slowly melting since the ice age 18,000 years ago. As the tides slowly rise, the barriers retreat toward the coast. These islands, common along the U.S. Atlantic coastline from Massachusetts to Texas, are the longest in the world. Assateague Island straddles the coastline of Virginia and Maryland, located with Delaware on the northeast Delmarva Peninsula. Twenty-two miles lie on the Maryland coast, and the remaining 15 are on the Virginia side. Three public entities are established on the island: Assateague Island National Seashore (managed by the National Park Service), the Chincoteague National Wildlife Refuge (680 acres managed by the U.S. Fish and Wildlife Service), and Assateague State Park (managed by the Maryland Department of Natural Resources).

The island is a place of environmental extremes. Nevertheless, wildlife abounds on the barrier landscape whose main features typically include salt marsh, a band of trees running down the mid-length of the island, sand dunes, and beach grasses. Despite impermanence, barrier islands form resilient ecosystems that adapt to climatic fluctuation. Assateague is no exception. This island has been stable long enough for forests to develop. Much to the delight of scientists and researchers, the island and much of the Delmarva Peninsula escaped the rampant northeastern urbanization of the late 19th and 20th centuries. An abundance of wild horses, whitetail deer, foxes, raccoons, and humans coexist with buried species of crabs, sand hoppers, and other marine forms. Over the decades the

habitats and behaviors of many plant and animal species have been studied and documented. Of particular interest are the feral horses, a nonnative population thought to have been introduced by humans in the 17th century. Generations of visitors have enjoyed the mystique of horses running wild on the beaches; scientists today are interested in their long-term impacts on the fragile land environment.

The island area was once home to enormous waterfowl populations. Numbers dwindled rapidly with the conversion of wetlands for agriculture, private development, illegal gaming, and capture of birds for food and feathers. The Chincoteague refuge was established in 1943, protecting a prime Atlantic Flyway habitat. Terns, pipers, plovers, herons, gulls, egrets, warblers, hawks, falcons, snow geese, mallards, and sea ducks migrate through the area. Long-term management programs are needed to document and promote the well-being of high-profile species, such as the plover, as well as lesser-known resident plants and insects and transient bird species.

In 1933 a hurricane created an island inlet at Ocean City on the Maryland side. Stone jetties were constructed to take advantage of the breach for navigation. This set in motion a series of disruptions, extending more than nine miles south of the inlet, affecting the natural cycles of the land, including sand accumulations on the Fenwick Island side, an offset of more than a half-mile between the two islands, alteration of beach heights, and erosion of critical beaches and dune habitats. Erosion rates were calculated at 10 feet per year, one of the highest in the nation. On 16 September 2002 the U.S. Department of the Interior announced a coastal restoration plan representing a partnership with the National Park Service, the U.S. Army Corps of Engineers, and the Minerals Management Service. In the first phase, 18 million cubic yards of sand were dredged from Great Gull Bank to be used as fill for the Assateague beaches. Redistribution of sand from the inlet to the island will continue on a biennial schedule for a period of 25 years.

In 1934 the National Park Service initiated a study of 20 areas along the Atlantic, Gulf, Pacific, and Great Lakes shorelines for preservation. In 1955 the U.S. Park Service published *The Vanishing Shoreline*, documenting the loss of untrammeled shorelines caused by real estate and commercial development. These issues were not uncommon on Assateague Island, where housing, ditches, and concrete were already endangering the fragile ecosystem. In 1962 the Outdoor Recreation Resources Review Commission affirmed the need for more national seashore recreation areas. The Ash Wednesday hurricane of March 1962 put an immediate end to seaboard development plans on Assateague Island. On 21 September 1965, after years of congressional disagreement, President Lyndon Johnson signed and approved Public Law 89-195. The lengthy debate over private versus public lands and the complexities of interagency engagement in creating a national seashore on a transboundary

site is meticulously documented in an administrative history prepared by Barry Mackintosh for the National Park Service and can be accessed on the park service Internet site.

VICTORIA M. GARCIA
*Houston, Texas*

Dorothy Camagna and Jennifer Cording, *Chincoteague Revisited: A Sojourn to the Chincoteague and Assateague Islands* (2004); Linda Firestone, *Virginia's Favorite Islands: Chincoteague and Assateague* (1982).

## Atchafalaya Basin Swamp

The Atchafalaya Basin Swamp is in south Louisiana. It is North America's largest river basin swamp, containing about 2 million acres. It is traversed by the Atchafalaya River, a distributary of the Mississippi River. The Atchafalaya River carries away a considerable portion of the Mississippi River flow (about 30 percent) and brings large floods to the Atchafalaya Basin in late winter and early spring. On either side of the Atchafalaya River, several miles from the stream, are large man-made levees that confine these waters to a "floodway," the largest in the world (about 820,000 acres). This floodway is designed to relieve New Orleans and south Louisiana from extreme floods by allowing water from the Mississippi to take another route to the Gulf of Mexico. The entire area is forested and laced with bayous, rivers, and lakes; it is one vast swamp.

The Atchafalaya Basin Swamp is the most productive swamp in the world. Throughout the 20th century this natural paradise produced a vast amount of products. Many millions of pounds of crawfish were taken from the swamp annually, as were fish, pelts, frogs, crabs, turtles, Spanish moss, lumber, and alligators. Today there is no lumbering or alligator hunting, but all of the other products are still gathered and sold in communities surrounding the swamp. And oil production is now very important. Unlike in the past, few people today live in the swamp. Those that exploit the area live in small communities that surround it and commute to the heart of the swamp in boats. Whenever there are boom times in the economy, many of these swamp dwellers have jobs beyond the swamp, but when the economy sours, they return to the swamp to earn livelihoods or to supplement incomes.

The Atchafalaya Basin is steeped in controversy. The main goals of the Corps of Engineers are flood prevention and preventing the Mississippi from diverting and following the Atchafalaya River route to the Gulf of Mexico. The Atchafalaya Swamp is now tightly controlled by the corps, but no one is satisfied. The corps (beginning in the early 1970s) tried to develop a consensus as to what was to happen to this swamp. Competing interests include agriculture, river navigation, flood control, recreation, sport fishing, commercial fishing, oil and gas exploitation, and owners of large tracks of land within the swamp. Environmental activists want to keep this area as pristine as possible, while on the other extreme are those who want to drain and develop the area. There are many competing interests, and no long-term agreement has been reached as to how the swamp is to be managed for

future generations. So the controversy continues.

MALCOLM L. COMEAUX
*Arizona State University*

John M. Barry, *Rising Tide: The Great Mississippi Flood of 1927 and How It Changed America* (1997); Malcolm L. Comeaux, *Atchafalaya Swamp Life: Settlement and Folk Occupations* (1972); John McPhee, *The Control of Nature* (1989); Martin Reuss, *Designing the Bayous: The Control of Water in the Atchafalaya Basin, 1800–1995* (1998).

## Audubon, John James

(1785–1851) NATURALIST AND ARTIST.

Although Audubon's observations of wildlife extended from Labrador to the Florida Keys and from New Jersey to the Missouri River country, his works are particularly rich in material gathered in Kentucky, Louisiana, Mississippi, and Florida. During the years when these southern frontiers abounded in birds, he was able to compile an extraordinary record in paintings and journals.

The illegitimate son of Captain Jean Audubon and Jeanne Rabine, a French servant, Audubon was born 26 April 1785 on his father's plantation in Aux Cayes, Santo Domingo. Brought up in Nice, France, as the adopted son of Captain Audubon and his legal wife, the boy received very little formal schooling but did have some instruction in painting and music. In 1804 the 18-year-old Audubon came to America, where he lived for a time on a Pennsylvania farm belonging to his father. From 1808 to 1819 he attempted to make a living as a frontier trader in Kentucky. He had some success operating a store and sawmill in Henderson but had to declare himself bankrupt in 1819. After this failure he concentrated most of his energies on hunting and painting birds, activities in which he had spent his happiest hours since first coming to America. He occasionally earned a few dollars practicing taxidermy, painting portraits, and teaching drawing and music, but his remarkable wife, Lucy Bakewell, often had to support herself and their two sons by tutoring while Audubon was ranging the wilderness. He traveled extensively in the Mississippi Valley and lived briefly in New Orleans and West Feliciana Parish, La.

In 1826 Audubon's portfolios contained some 400 paintings of birds, done in watercolor and pastel. Unsuccessful in getting support for his work in America, Audubon carried his appeal to the British Isles, where he managed to interest important savants and wealthy people. With this backing he was able to arrange for the reproduction of his paintings in color by Robert Havell, a skillful London engraver. Through persistent effort Audubon signed up enough subscribers for the publication of *The Birds of America* (1827–38) in four beautiful volumes, "double elephant" or 39 1/2″ × 29 1/2″ in size. No more than 200 complete sets were issued, and surviving copies now command very high prices in the rare book market.

Audubon's restless energy found many outlets. In 1831–32 he extended his knowledge of the South by hunting birds in the St. Augustine region and the Florida Keys. With the help of scientific collaborators and his own artist sons,

John and Victor, he published *Ornithological Biography* (5 vols., 1831–39), a cheaper edition of *The Birds of America* (7 vols., 1840–44), and *The Vivaporous Quadrupeds of North America* (2 vols., 1845–46). He died 17 January 1851 at Minnie's Land, his estate on Manhattan Island near the Hudson River.

During his lifetime Audubon had to contend with the jealousy of other naturalists, and he defended himself vigorously against charges of plagiarism and mendacity. Modern critics have applauded the originality, general accuracy, and beauty of his work, including his documentation of an important phase of southern wildlife. Contemporary southern authors such as Eudora Welty and Robert Penn Warren have celebrated Audubon in their own works as a significant southern artist.

NELSON M. BLAKE
*Syracuse University*

Annette Blaugrund, *John James Audubon: The Watercolors for the Birds of America* (1993); Alice Ford, *John James Audubon* (1964); Duff Hart-Davis, *Audubon's Elephant: America's Greatest Naturalist and the Making of "The Birds of America"* (2004); Francis H. Herrick, *Audubon the Naturalist: A History of His Life and Time* (1938); Kathryn Hall Proby, *Audubon in Florida, with Selections from the Writings of John James Audubon* (1974); Richard Rhodes, *John James Audubon: The Making of an American* (2004).

## Azaleas

Azalea is the name for a group of colorful deciduous shrubs now usually classified with their evergreen relatives in the genus *Rhododendron*. Although native primarily to the acid soils and more temperate climates of the southeastern United States and southeastern Asia, many botanical species and horticultural varieties of azalea are widely grown in other areas of the world that have comparable soils and climates. Indeed, although azaleas were among the first North American shrubs to be sent back to England in the early days of colonial exploration, their general association with the South stems primarily from the extensive plantings of horticultural forms in some of the major southern show gardens during the early to mid-20th century. Many of the varieties now grown in the South were introduced from Asia. Azaleas grow in mounds from three to eight feet tall and as wide, with leaves from one to three inches long.

From the impact generated by colorful spring displays at such gardens as Bellingrath, near Mobile, Ala.; Orton, near Wilmington, N.C.; and the Magnolia and Middleton gardens near Charleston, S.C., azaleas have come to be associated with the South. The association is greatly strengthened by the brilliant spring display of the native flame azalea (*Rhododendron calendulaceum*) along the Blue Ridge Parkway in Virginia and North Carolina and by the intense, spicy fragrance of swamp honeysuckle (*R. viscosum*), another attractive native shrub, which grows in bogs and along stream margins over much of the South. Southern Indian hybrid azaleas are large shrubs including such varieties as the Formosa (rosy purple), pride of Mobile (watermelon red), fielder's white, and George Lindsey Tabor (pink and white).

These are not cold hardy in the Upper South. Kurume azaleas are more tolerant than other azaleas of climatic extremes. These include such popular varieties as coral bells (pink), snow (white), and Christmas cheer (bright red).

The azalea has also increasingly become a resource for luring tourists. Mobile, Ala. (also known as the Azalea City), Lafayette, La., and Charleston, S.C., among many other cities, sponsor azalea trail tours.

C. RITCHIE BELL
*North Carolina Botanical Gardens*
*University of North Carolina at*
*Chapel Hill*

CHARLES REAGAN WILSON
*University of Mississippi*

Ben A. Davis, *Azaleas, Camellias, Gardenias* (1950), *The Southern Garden: From the Potomac to the Rio Grande* (1971); Fred C. Galle, *Azaleas* (1974); William L. Hunt, *Southern Gardens, Southern Gardening* (1982); Felder Rushing, *Tough Plants for Southern Gardens* (2003); L. Clarence Towe, *American Azaleas* (2004).

## Bartram, William

(1739–1823) NATURALIST, EXPLORER, ARTIST, AUTHOR.
Bartram was the third son of the Quaker botanist and horticulturalist John Bartram and his second wife, Anne Mendenhall. He was born and raised at his father's horticultural garden in Kingsessing, Pa., on the outskirts of Philadelphia. As a teenager, he attended the Academy of Philadelphia for four years and joined his father on a series of collecting trips. Although William clearly loved nature and the outdoors, his father worried that locating, pre-

*Pl. 4.*

*Great Soft-shelled Tortoise*

Illustration of the Great Soft-shelled Tortoise from the 1792 London edition of
Travels through North and South Carolina, Georgia, East and West Florida.

paring, sketching, and selling natural history specimens offered little hope of secure employment for his otherwise unfocused son.

Following an apprenticeship with a Philadelphia merchant, in 1761 William established a trading post at Cape Fear, N.C., the home of his paternal uncle. His heart was never in the business, however, and five years later, when his father announced that he was heading south on an extended botanical expedition to British East Florida, William jumped at the opportunity to close up shop and accompany him. Immediately taken with the lush subtropical landscape he encountered in Florida, William convinced his father to finance a small rice and indigo plantation on the banks of the St. Johns River. The enterprise soon floundered, however, for William proved completely unfamiliar with the crops he was hoping to grow and temperamentally unsuited to supervising slaves. Dispirited, William soon returned home, where he eked out a living by various means, including a series of commissions to draw natural history specimens received from British collectors. His most important patron was the Quaker physician John Fothergill, who offered to pay him £50 per year, plus expenses, to collect southern plants.

To fulfill the terms of this generous commission, in March 1773 William Bartram set off on a four-year journey across the southeastern region of North America. Much of the time he traveled alone through the sparsely settled wilderness, collecting natural history specimens, making drawings, and keeping copious notes on the flora, fauna, and Native Americans he found. He returned to Kingsessing in January 1777 and spent the remainder of his life close to home, drawing natural history specimens, writing, laboring in the family nursery business, and greeting the many naturalists drawn to Bartram's Garden.

After several years of delay, in 1791 Bartram finally published a lengthy account of his southern rambles. In vivid, exuberant prose, Bartram's *Travels through North and South Carolina, Georgia, East and West Florida* celebrated the southern landscape and the Native American peoples its author had encountered there. The popular book—which was not only soon reissued in several American and British editions but also translated into Dutch, German, and French—offered a powerful source of inspiration and imagery for Samuel Taylor Coleridge, William Wordsworth, and other Romantic writers who sometimes incorporated whole passages from it into their own work. Readers today continue to be entranced by the book, and since 1976 an organization known as the Bartram Trail Conference has worked to locate and mark Bartram's route while commemorating his life and achievement.

MARK V. BARROW JR.
*Virginia Polytechnic Institute and State University*

Bartram Trail Conference website, <www .bartramtrail.org>; William Bartram, *The Travels of William Bartram: Naturalist's Edition*, ed. Francis Harper (1958); Whitfield J. Bell Jr., in *Dictionary of Scientific Biography*, ed. Charles C. Gillispie (1970); Thomas P. Slaughter, *The Natures of John and William Bartram* (1996).

## Big Bend National Park

According to Indian legend, when the Great Spirit had finished making the Earth, he dumped all of the leftover rocks in what is now Big Bend country. Some time later, yet still more than a hundred years ago, a Mexican cowboy described Big Bend country as a place "where the rainbows wait for the rain, and the big river is kept in a stone box, and water runs uphill and mountains float in the air, except at night when they go away to play with other mountains."

What is now Big Bend National Park sits on the U.S.-Mexican border along the Rio Grande and covers 801,000 isolated acres of southwestern Texas. The Rio Grande, the Chihuahuan Desert, and the Chisos Mountains comprise the three distinct geological divisions within the park, and because of these diverse areas the park's climate is one of extremes. Altitudes range from 1,800 feet at the river to more than 7,800 feet in the Chisos Mountains (highest point is Emory Peak, 7,832 feet). During the summer, ground temperatures in the Chihuahuan Desert can reach 180°F. Winters are normally mild, with temperatures hovering around a balmy 80°F. The Chihuahuan Desert is a geologically young desert, only around 8,000 years old, and despite its extreme heat, it is lush and green, receiving around 10 inches of rainfall annually.

Most of the exposed rock within the park is sedimentary, consisting mostly of limestone, sandstone, and shale formed during the Cretaceous period 145 to 65 million years ago. Average rainfall in the Chisos Mountains reaches 20 inches, creating a vast diversity between plant and animal life in the mountains and on the desert floor. Because of the range's relative isolation, several species of plants and animals can be found only in the Chisos Mountains. The Chisos oak, which grows only in the high country, is one such plant. While cacti and wildflowers carpet the desert, the flora changes to grasslands as one approaches the mountains. As the elevation continues to increase, taller plants such as the evergreen sumac, mountain mahogany, and the Texas marone replace leafy shrubs and bushes.

The Rio Grande forms 118 miles of border between the United States and Mexico through the Chihuahuan Desert. The name of the park is derived from the U-turn the river takes on its border, redirecting the river's southeasterly flow northeastward. Canyons made by the river long ago include the Santa Elena, Mariscal, and Boquillas, and garfish and turtles that live in the river illustrate the evolutionary record that extends back 50,000 years to when the area was a lush, swamplike savanna.

Big Bend is home to over 1,200 species of plants, including pink and blue bluebonnets, yucca flowers, lechuguillas, and 60 species of cacti. Altogether, there are 3,600 species of insects, 450 species of birds, 75 species of mammals, and 67 species of amphibians and reptiles in Big Bend National Park. Animals include panthers, black bears, kangaroo rats, jackrabbits, roadrunners,

*Rio Grande, Big Bend National Park, Texas (Gary M. Stolz, photographer, U.S. Fish and Wildlife Service)*

rattlesnakes, tarantulas, and coyotes. Summer tanagers, painted buntings, vermilion flycatchers, and cardinals make up a colorful array of birds in the area. Other native birds include the sandpiper, killdeer, golden eagle, and cliff swallow.

Evidence suggests that humans have continually inhabited the park range since the Paleo-Indian period. Several Indian groups have inhabited the area since the beginning of the historic era, including the Chisos, Jumanos, Mescalero Apaches, and Comanches. The Spanish were the first non-Indian group to pass through the area. Álvar Nuñez Cabeza de Vaca began exploration of the area around 1535. Other Spanish expeditions in search of gold and silver soon followed, and before long the area became known as El Despoblado, or "the uninhabited land."

Anglo settlers began entry into the area after Texas declared its independence from Mexico. Mining brought these settlers to the area, and soon small communities such as Boquillas and Terlingua began to dot the landscape. In 1933 Texas Canyons State Park was established, and on 12 June 1944 it became Big Bend National Park.

Big Bend, because of it remoteness, is one of the least-visited national parks in the United States, attracting only

300,000 to 350,000 visitors annually. The entrance to the park at Persimmon Gap lies 70 miles from the nearest town. It is, however, one of the largest parks in the National Park System. It is popular with adventurous hikers and backpackers and offers more than 150 miles of trails for day hikes and backpacking. Some of the most popular trails include the Chimneys Trail, Marufo Veg Trail, Outer Mountain Loop, and Dodson Trail. Other attractions include the Santa Elena Canyon and Mule Ears Peaks, two impressive rock towers seemingly thrust upward from the middle of the desert floor.

JAMES G. THOMAS JR.
*University of Mississippi*

Arthur R. Gómez, *A Most Singular Country: A History of Occupation in the Big Bend* (1990); John Jameson, *The Story of Big Bend National Park* (1996); J. O. Langford, with Fred Gipson, *Big Bend: A Homesteader's Story* (1952); Ross A. Maxwell, *The Big Bend of the Rio Grande: A Guide to the Rocks, Landscape, Geologic History, and Settlers of the Area of Big Bend National Park* (1968); Roberto Suro, *New York Times* (3 March 1991).

## Big Thicket

A biological and historical subregion of southeast Texas, the Big Thicket once covered approximately 3 million acres, from the Louisiana border across the lower Neches and Trinity river basins westward to the San Jacinto River and its tributaries. This dense wilderness is now reduced to approximately 300,000 acres in Hardin and surrounding counties.

Biologically the Big Thicket is the southwesternmost extension of the Southern Evergreen Forest. Proximity to both the Gulf of Mexico and the dry Texas prairies accounts for the incursion of western and tropical species into its otherwise deep-southern ecology. Roadrunner and alligator, prickly pear cactus and water tupelo, and bluejack oak and subtropical orchid can be found there within sight of one another. Biologists have described this sanctuary for rare, scarce, and endangered species as the most zoologically and botanically diverse area of its size in the Western Hemisphere.

Historically the Big Thicket has long been famous as a refuge. Early pioneers entering southeast Texas in the 1820s found their way blocked by dense vegetation along innumerable streams. They detoured around the area, which they named the Big Thicket. Though it was never an unbroken jungle, civilization tended to bypass the thicket. During the Civil War, deserters and conscientious objectors from Texas and nearby southern states hid there. During World Wars I and II, descendants of some of the original fugitives hid there for the duration of the conflict. As late as the 1950s, prisoners from nearby state prisons were said to have a good chance of escape if they could reach the thicket ahead of their pursuers.

By the late 1950s it had become clear that, given current trends, the Big Thicket was not going to endure. Roads, urban sprawl, reservoirs, and a new clear-cutting technology employed by area lumber corporations were increasingly fragmenting the once-contiguous forest, extirpating indigenous species, and replacing diverse plant growth communities with pine monoculture. The result was an environmental controversy that lasted from the founding of the Big Thicket Association (1964) until the establishing of the Big Thicket National Biological Preserve (1974).

The 84,550-acre Big Thicket National Preserve, the first such designation in the history of the National Park Service, consists of nine units and three stream courses, including the Neches River Corridor. The units, which range from the diminutive Loblolly Unit (640 acres) to the sprawling Lance Rosier Unit (24,942 acres), contain examples of almost all of the topographies and plant growth communities in the region. Subsequently other nearby areas have also been environmentally protected. These include Nature Conservancy's Roy E. Larson Sandyland Sanctuary (5,600 acres), Village Creek and Davis Hill State Parks (1,054 and 1,734 acres, respectively), the Trinity River National Wildlife Refuge (10,033 acres), and numerous smaller sanctuaries, including many donated by forest products corporations. The end result is a complex of preserves, sanctuaries, and parks now termed the Big Thicket Environmental Area and requiring to be managed as a whole. The Big Thicket Preserve was designated an International Man and the Biosphere Reserve by the United Nations in 1981.

PETE A. Y. GUNTER
*University of North Texas*

Geyata Ajivsgi, *Wildflowers of the Big Thicket, East Texas, and Western Louisiana* (1979); Pete A. Y. Gunter, *The Big Thicket: An Ecological Reconsideration* (1993); Campbell Loughmiller and Lynn Loughmiller, *Big Thicket Legacy* (2002).

## Biscayne National Park

Located south of Miami, Fla., and approximately 20 miles east of Everglades National Park, Biscayne National Park was established as a national monument in 1968. A rare underwater unit in the park system, it originated from the initiative of a grassroots campaign to protect Biscayne Bay.

The beauty of the jade-colored bay, fringed by habitat-rich red and black mangrove trees, and the marine life that thrived in its coral-reef environment had always been the principal natural attraction at the southeastern tip of the Florida peninsula. The first people known to have established a civilization in the area are the Tequesta of the Glades culture; theirs was a sedentary existence that depended primarily on the bay's natural resources. Initial contact with Europeans came from the flotsam of wrecked Spanish ships that washed ashore the barrier islands between the bay and the Atlantic Ocean. Today, more than 40 shipwrecks rest within the national park's boundaries. After whites permanently settled the area following the Seminole wars, the bay became a favored location of bathers, boaters, skin divers, marine scientists, ornithologists, and sports and commercial fishermen.

By the 1960s, unbridled population growth and development in south Florida had brought the bay to the brink of ecological disaster. Raw sewage had been pouring into it since the city constructed the first wastewater system at the turn of the 20th century. Thermal pollution from Florida Power and Light's power plant was killing marine life in the shallow bay. Investors were planning to develop many of its barrier islands, which were favored nesting ground for sea turtles. A threat as ominous as any came from supertanker giant Daniel Ludwig. In 1962 his Ludwig Enterprises announced plans to build Seadade, a combination oil refinery and deepwater port, between Everglades National Park and John Pennekamp Coral Reef Preserve. The proposal included dredging a shipping channel through coral reef.

A small group of local citizens responded by organizing the Safe Progress Association (SPA). Its dozen or so male and female members were fishermen from the Izaak Walton League, birders from the Audubon Society, wildlife lovers from the Nature Conservancy, civic-minded individuals from local women's clubs, and scientists from the University of Miami. The SPA convinced a reluctant Metro Dade Commission, which supported Seadade, to pass a rigid pollution-control ordinance. The group also launched a bumper-sticker campaign and published *The Creeping Peril! Industrial Pollution and You*, a 19-page pamphlet warning that the proposed oil refinery risked turning a major tourist center into "the Smogville of the south." Member and writer Polly Redford brought national attention to the campaign with a *Harper's Magazine* article titled "Small Rebellion in Miami," and her SPA colleague Belle Scheffel gave speeches on the women's club circuit.

The turning point in the campaign came when SPA founder Lloyd Miller proposed the creation of an underwater federal preserve. Through the efforts of Nathaniel Reed, a south Florida native and environmental adviser to the governor, the idea won the support of Claude Kirk, Florida's first post-Reconstruction Republican governor and the first to establish an impressive environmental record. Department of the Interior Secretary Stewart Udall ordered a scientific study of the bay, and after a tour of south Florida he was convinced he had a worthy addition to the National Park System, which President Lyndon Johnson wanted to expand to full capacity. To help the cause, the Hoover Environmental Legal Defense Fund offered $100,000 toward the monument's creation. Employing the assistance of Joe Browder, National Audubon's southeastern representative based in Coconut Grove, U.S. Representative Dante Fascell maneuvered legislation for the national monument through Congress, and President Johnson signed it in 1968.

The activists who campaigned for the monument continued their struggle by challenging the other threats to the bay. Many went on to lead the ground-level fight against the construction of the world's largest airport in the Everglades, halted in 1970, and for the creation of the Big Cypress National Preserve, established in 1974.

The original Biscayne monument they championed totaled 100,500 acres, 95 percent of which lay under water. In 1980, after 81,000 acres were added, the monument received national park designation. The park today includes mangrove marshlands, tropical hardwood hammocks, scores of bird species, more than 200 varieties of fish, five species of sea turtles, and manatees. Biscayne is now on the National Parks Conservation Association's list of 10 most endangered national parks. Its coral reefs, sea grass, marine life, and coastline are threatened by overfishing, development, poaching, pollution, and increased ocean temperatures from global warming.

JACK E. DAVIS
*University of Florida*

Luther Carter, *The Florida Experience: Land and Water Policy in a Growth State* (1974); Scott Hamilton Dewey, in *Making Waves: Female Activists in Twentieth-Century Florida*, ed. Jack E. Davis and Kari Frederickson (2003); Jennifer Brown Leynes and David Cullison, *Biscayne National Park Historic Resource Study* (1998); *New York Times* (15 January 1967, 1 June 1969); Polly Redford, *Harper's Magazine* (February 1964); U.S. National Park Service, *Biscayne National Monument: A Proposal* (1960); *Washington Post* (13 September 1966, 5 October 1968, 12 January 1969).

## Blue Ridge Mountains

The Blue Ridge Mountains are the easternmost range in the southern Appalachians, extending from Pennsylvania to northeast Georgia. The oldest known rocks on earth are found in this range, on Roan Mountain, and are more than a billion years old. The characteristic rounded shapes of the Blue Ridge Mountains, which appear as progressively lighter blue waves on the horizon, were formed by eons of weather and erosion.

The earliest migrants to the Blue Ridge arrived around 8000 B.C. during the Paleo-Indian period, and evidence of their presence exists in Russell Cave, Ala. Their successors, referred to by anthropologists as the Archaic tradition, left behind one practice that very much shaped the landscape: small burial mounds. About 1000 B.C. Woodland Indians began to become more devoted to agriculture and so retreated to the river valleys of the area, and in A.D. 700 Mississippian Indians developed elaborate pottery and jewelry traditions as well as a strong relationship to the "three sisters," corn, beans, and squashes. Tobacco, native to South America, was traded north sometime during this period.

Although various Spanish explorers ventured inland, Hernando de Soto led the first extensive exploration of the Blue Ridge by white people in 1540. De Soto, a protégé of Francisco Pizarro, gained information through intimidation and torture from the Chalaque (the first usage of the word "Cherokee"), who not surprisingly sent him to the next valley. When two Englishmen, James Neeham and Gabriel Arthur, explored the Blue Ridge in 1693, they encountered Cherokees using objects traded with the de Soto expedition, such as cooking utensils, weapons, cloth, and beads.

For almost 150 years, the heavily forested Blue Ridge Mountains presented a barrier to white settlement, but environmental impact increased dramatically over this time through native dependence on the deerskin trade. Encouraging intertribal warfare for the enslavement of human beings, white traders prevented the development of alliances between Indian tribes. Relying heavily on metal goods, cloth, and liquor supplied by traders, the Cherokees and the Creeks rapidly depopulated the mountains of deer and beaver; then they were forced into treaties that included land cessions. After the French and Indian War, the English established the Proclamation of 1763 to prevent settlement west of the Blue Ridge. White settlers ignored it and pressed into the mountains.

The second great migration into the Blue Ridge included English, Highland Scots, Scots-Irish, Welsh, Irish, Dutch, German Protestants, and French Huguenots. Fleeing either religious or political persecution, these inhabitants of the backcountry remained skeptical and rebellious toward colonial and the subsequent state governments. They carried with them cattle and hog production, which shaped the land, and introduced English plants, such as plantain, and ethnic traditions, such as the log cabin from Germany. At the same time, settlers adopted native crops, including corn and beans, and often developed new uses for them, such as cornshuck mattresses and forage for animals. They co-opted native practices like using purple martin colonies to chase crows out of a graden, and they expanded the size of balds on the mountaintops in order to graze sheep and cows. Even the "long hunt"— months of winter travel to catch fur— which white people associate with the legendary Daniel Boone, is an adaptation of a Native American tradition.

After the American Revolution and the War of 1812, many soldiers received payment for services in the form of land grants, forcing further land treaties with native tribes. By the 19th century Boone and others had led settlement to Kentucky and parts farther west, and the Creek Wars and Indian Removal Act eliminated native peoples from the Blue Ridge, except in western North Carolina. The diverse people who remained on the land, supporting themselves with a combination of subsistence agriculture and localized market economies, created the folklife most often associated with the Blue Ridge.

Early 20th-century scholars either dismissed the isolated mountain folk as "hillbillies" or ennobled them as preservers of archaic Anglican speech and ballads. But folk proverbs, riddles, and storytelling owe as much to Scottish and Native American heritage as to English, and one story often proves to be influenced by more than one culture. Blue Ridge music includes authenticated English ballads but also the African American standard "John Henry." Likewise, the tradition of noncompliance with dominant Christianity led to a variety of Baptist sects proliferating in the mountains and with them full-immersion baptism, foot washing, and faith healing. Centuries of subsistence farming meant that all these customs and the handcrafts associated with them relied heavily on the environment— from a folktale about a bear to a fiddle made of black walnut to baptism in a creek.

Blue Ridge farming culture left as much as 90 percent of the land wooded

*Rocky Knob Recreation Area on the Blue Ridge Parkway, view of the valley from Belcher's Curve (photographer unknown, Library of Congress [HAER NC,11-ASHV.V,2-77], Washington, D.C.)*

in 1880, but the beautiful cove hardwood forests would meet the axe in just three decades. The most profound ecological change to the mountains and culture of the Blue Ridge came first with the great timber harvest of the early 20th century. Timber companies from the Northeast and Great Britain invested in narrow-gauge railroads and low-geared Shay and Climax engines, which made the most remote moun-

tains accessible. Heavy logging left the thin mountain soils susceptible to wind and weather; flooding and fires typically followed. When Congress passed the Weeks Act in 1911, authorizing the purchase of "forested, cutover, or denuded lands" for a forest reserve, the first major purchase occurred in the Blue Ridge Mountains of North Carolina (Pisgah National Forest).

Conservation opened the door on

a new path of land development: tourism. During the Great Depression, Franklin D. Roosevelt's New Deal aimed to uplift an economically depressed region by promoting a scenic parkway through the region. The state highway commissions paid just $30 per acre for the mountain land the parkway was to cross, and when they faced bitter opposition, they held the ultimate power of condemnation. Because the Blue Ridge Parkway barred commercial vehicles and prevented roadside development and advertising, the benefits to local communities were not as great as hoped. Today the 469-mile-long parkway is less popular with local communities than with tourists because of access issues, but it does promote national exposure and boasts 20 million annual visitors, as it is one of the most popular units in the National Park System.

MARGARET LYNN BROWN
*Brevard College*

Harley E. Jolley, *The Blue Ridge Parkway* (1969); Ted Olson, *Blue Ridge Folklife* (1998); Timothy Silver, *Mount Mitchell and the Black Mountains: An Environmental History of the Highest Peaks in Eastern America* (2002); Anne Mitchell Whisnant, *Super-Scenic Motorway: A Blue Ridge Parkway History* (2006).

## Cancer Alley (Louisiana)

Cancer Alley lies along a 100-mile stretch of the Mississippi River between Baton Rouge and New Orleans. The area has become a central case study for some of the most controversial and pointed issues in the modern environmental movement. The "Cancer Alley" moniker arose in the 1980s with the emergence of the environmental justice movement linking minorities and poverty to increased environmental hazards. Louisiana has a long-standing history of attempting to attract industry and business through tax incentives and plenty of available, cheap land. Cancer Alley, reflecting the monumental success of that policy, holds more than 300 industrial plants, as well as accompanying waste facilities. Many of the major petrochemical companies, including Texaco, Occidental Chemical, Chevron, Dow, and Du Pont, built plants in the area, which was historically a land of plantations. Blacks continue to live here, and the region is overwhelmingly poor. Although the chemical and industrial plants build with a promise to provide jobs to the surrounding communities, most local residents lack a high school diploma and fail to qualify.

Residents claim a high incidence of illnesses associated with their proximity to the chemicals. These illnesses range from various cancers like leukemia to stillbirths, miscarriages, birth defects, and a variety of respiratory difficulties. The high level of pollution of various types and perceived government neglect led many communities to take a stand against their neighboring corporations. For example, in the small, mostly black community of Convent, La., Shintech, a Japanese corporation, proposed a massive polyvinyl chloride plant in 1997. Convent, already suffering from high levels of toxins, organized to oppose the facility. The community achieved a small victory when it defeated the original Shintech proposal, although the company built a smaller facility nearby.

Children of Cancer Alley are intensely vulnerable to chemical contamination. In Gonzalez, La., a small community with a population of about 18,000, doctors discovered four cases of a very rare cancer, rhabdomyosarcoma, among children. The national rate for children with the disease rests at one in a million.

Although residents attempt to link the chemicals to ill health, industrialists and critics of the communities' theories, on the other hand, develop research to prove that the area's cancer rate closely approximates the national average. Other critics blame Cancer Alley's illnesses on the lifestyles of the residents, pointing to smoking and dietary habits. Overall, despite much evidence of illness among residents, communities have achieved very limited success against the chemical companies in the area. Cancer Alley remains one of the most polluted and poverty-stricken areas in the United States.

ELIZABETH BLUM
*Troy University*

Craig E. Colten, ed., *Transforming New Orleans and Its Environs* (2000); Laura Dunn, dir., prod., *Green* (Two Birds Film, 2000); Frank D. Groves, Patricia A. Andrews, et al., *Journal of the Louisiana State Medical Society* (1996); Barbara Koeppel, *Nation* (8 November 1999).

## Cape Lookout National Seashore

Cape Lookout National Seashore is a thin barrier island off the southeastern fringes of the Outer Banks of North Carolina's Atlantic seaboard. This narrow shore is 56 miles in length and includes the North Core Banks, South Core Banks, and Shackleford Banks on the southern rim. It runs the length of the southeastern coast from Ocracoke Inlet to Beaufort Inlet. Cape Hatteras, the nation's first national seashore, lies along North Carolina's northeastern seaboard. Two currents of water, the northern Labrador and the Gulf Stream, converge along their coastlines. For centuries these lands and turbulent waters have attracted unusual friends and foes. The infamous pirate Blackbeard tops the list of wanderers who found refuge in Cape Lookout's gnarled harbors. The remains of hundreds of other less fortunate travelers and warships lie buried off the treacherous coast of the Outer Banks, waters known as the Graveyard of the Atlantic.

The two contiguous seashores, a double barrier-island system, provide researchers and natural observers an ideal locale for comparative environmental studies. Major ecosystems include beaches, berms, grasslands, woodlands, fresh marshes, and salt marshes. The grasslands of Cape Lookout are the last remaining natives of the eastern seaboard. Of particular interest to researchers is the long-term impact of artificial dunes and other measures taken to stabilize the dynamics of the islands. In fact, these efforts have left developed islands more susceptible to degradation, including saltwater intrusion into freshwater inlets, unnecessary dredging, vehicular damage to sand and vegetation, and litter.

Cape Lookout, established as a national seashore on 10 March 1976, is prized for its isolation and relative inaccessibility. It has been a member of the Carolinian–South Atlantic Biosphere

Reserve since 1986. Here many species can be observed in relative seclusion. Since 1984 island officials have monitored the activities of nesting sea turtles. Data collected on observed nests, digs, and crawls is correlated to other activities such as floods, hurricanes, and vehicular access to the island. Bottlenose dolphins are a common estuarine marine mammal. Their activities are monitored using photo identification, allowing researchers to track individual migrations from New York to Florida. Land mammals are uncommon; the few native species include rice rats, rabbits, otters, and raccoons. Shackleford Banks is famed for its nonnative populations of wild horses, sheep, goats, and cows. On 22 July 1997 Congress approved the Shackleford Banks Wild Horses Protection Act.

Finally, thousands of shorebirds pass along the Atlantic seaboard flyway during seasonal migrations between North and South America. The North Carolina seaboard is unique because it is a year-round stopover for the piping plover. Pipers, an endangered species, no longer breed along the Great Lakes. Researchers at Cape Lookout observe the birds in and out of breeding seasons and have compiled data documenting the effects of development and human intrusion on their migratory patterns.

Researchers are impressed with the relative stability of these barrier islands. Despite dramatic upheavals caused by storms and climatic change, they have maintained the same ecosystems and general appearance for centuries. Natural processes are suppressed to some degree in land areas that have been artificially managed or developed. This indicates that further attempts at artificial control are impractical and should be discouraged.

VICTORIA M. GARCIA
*Houston, Texas*

Paul Godfrey, *Barrier Island Ecology of Cape Lookout National Seashore and Vicinity, North Carolina* (1976); David Stick, *The Outer Banks of North Carolina* (1958), *An Outer Banks Reader* (1998).

## Catfish

Southerners have never aligned themselves as closely with any cold-blooded creature as they have with the feline-looking catfish. Catfish are found elsewhere, to be sure. There are some 2,000 species throughout the world and more than two dozen in the United States alone. Southerners, though, have claimed the freshwater cat as their own. They have written the bewhiskered fish into their literature and sung songs and spun tales around it. And they have argued among themselves for years about which one tastes best and how it should be cooked.

The three major kinds, all of the family *Ictaluridae*, are the blue, the channel, and the flathead. Names change with locale, but none of the fish are particularly attractive. The flathead, in fact, looks like its head has been slammed in a car door. For long years, too, all three have suffered from the image of being a trash fish that would eat anything. Catfish were considered a lazy man's fish, a poor man's fish, and a black man's fish. Still, the size and exploits of the catfish—and the catfisherman—have become legend below the

Mason-Dixon line, and their image is beginning to change.

Reports still exist from the 19th century of catfish weighing 150 to 200 pounds or more regularly surfacing at the major fish markets along the Mississippi River. It has been a century since Huck Finn and Jim pulled a catfish as big as a man out of the Mississippi. Roughly the same amount of time has passed since Mark Twain also reported that a gargantuan catfish bumped into Marquette's canoe, almost prompting the French explorer to believe what Indians had told him about the river's roaring demon.

Today's equivalent is the omnipresent tale about car-sized catfish lurking below the dams of the South's major rivers, but like Twain's frequent references, these sightings have never been verified. Still, the catfish's association with the South persists—enough so that catfish were the subject of one rollicking song from a 1982 Broadway musical, *Pump Boys and Dinettes*, set somewhere near Frog Level, Ga. Mississippi writer Larry Brown's final novel was *A Miracle of Catfish*, suggesting the creature's wonders.

Although sizes are not consistently documented, plenty of catfish are caught—and bragged about—yearly by southern anglers. In earlier times, dynamite was sometimes used to kill a mess of cats. So was "telephoning" or electric-shocking, but both these practices are strictly illegal. Big, old catfish, however, are still caught in a variety of ways in the South, many of which are a legacy from the old days.

There are those who continue to work the banks with a cane pole, sinker, and handful of worms. A brave few carry on the practice of hand-grabbing in the warmer, sluggish rivers of late spring or summer. Sometimes called grabbling or noodling, this method consists of reaching into a submerged hollow log, grabbing a resident blue or flathead by the lower jaw, and hauling it out by hand like a suitcase.

Many fishermen use trotlines to hook cats. "Jugging" is a mobile version of trotlining. Anglers simply take a piece of line, tie a jug on one end and a baited hook on the other, and then follow the jug as it bounces the bait along a river's bottom. Snagging consists of just hooking the fish any way possible with bare treble hooks. It is not too sporting, admittedly, but it has brought in some flatheads weighing 130 pounds or more from Arkansas rivers.

The rod-and-reel fisherman in search of a good fight and a good meal began to modernize the image of the South's catfish. Casting with heavy rigs below the dams and using electronic equipment, southern fishermen are netting prize blues and flatheads of 38 to 55 pounds and more.

The channel catfish, too, has made another significant step toward revamping the tarnished image. Based in the South and Southwest, channel catfish farming is the nation's leading aquaculture industry. Since 1960 soybean and cotton fields in Mississippi, Alabama, Arkansas, and other southern states have been converted into catfish ponds. Fed on grain and carefully nurtured, the grown fish are trucked live from the ponds to processing plants, from which they are shipped out across the country. Supplying some 72 percent of the U.S. production, Mississippi currently leads the industry, yielding 660 million pounds of farm-raised catfish in 2003. Industry spokespersons swear that catfish is the best thing to hit the South since cotton.

Experts cite several reasons for the fish's growing popularity. Research is constantly improving the product, creating better strains of fish that are easier to raise. The channel cat's white, flaky-clean flesh is high in protein and low in fat and calories—a plus in an increasingly diet-conscious culture.

Recipes for dishes like soufflé-stuffed catfish, catfish amandine, and catfish Kiev style are appearing more and more often in magazines such as *Southern Living*, one of the South's self-proclaimed culinary bibles. The National Farm-Raised Catfish Cooking Contest, held in Mississippi, garners almost 1,000 recipe entries each year. One of the country's better-known fast-food chains, Church's Fried Chicken, has opted to add catfish to its standardized menu. When fried catfish was served to the world's leaders at the 1983 Williamsburg Summit Conference, not a single piece of the entrée, according to observers, remained as leftovers. The South's lowly catfish has finally swum uptown.

New image and all, however, the catfish will probably never leave behind its down-home connections. Every southern state proclaims at least one "catfish capital of the world." To name but a few, Mississippi boasts Belzoni, Tennessee has Paris, and Arkansas declares Toad Suck as the spot for catfish. Most of these places and many more still hold annual festivals to celebrate their own hometown favorite—the catfish. They batter and fry huge amounts of the fish and serve it swimming in catsup on plates heaped high with hush puppies, coleslaw, and french fries, usually to the beat of local bluegrass or country music. Most of these are all-you-can-eat affairs meant to be social occasions rather than gourmet experiences. Despite the changing image of the catfish, its use as a reason for a traditional southern celebration is not likely to change anytime soon.

DIANNE YOUNG
Southern Living

Larry Brown, *A Miracle of Catfish* (2007); Kenneth D. Carlander, *Handbook of Freshwater Fishery Biology*, vols. 1 and 2 (1969, 1977); Midori Kobayagawa and Warren E. Burgess, *The World of Catfishes* (1991); John Madson, *Smithsonian* (September 1984); Dianne Young, *Southern Living* (July 1984).

## Chesapeake Bay

This is the largest estuary in North America, stretching 200 miles from southern Virginia to northern Maryland and ranging from 3 to 35 miles in width. The bay includes 4,300 square miles of water and covers 8,100 miles of shoreline. There are 170 miles of channel connecting the bay to the island seaport of Baltimore. The Chesapeake Bay Bridge spans the narrowest point of the bay. The area has historically nurtured a distinctive culture of the Upper South and today continues to provide an economic and environmental context for many southerners.

The Chesapeake Bay was the site of the first permanent English colony in North America and gave rise to a cohesive society in the colonial South. Jamestown was founded in 1607 on the lower bay, on the James River. Captain John Smith called it "a faire Bay." "Heaven and earth never agreed better to frame a place for man's habitation," he wrote. Some 200 Algonkian Indian villages were already in the area when the settlers arrived, and the Native American influence survives in the names of such rivers as the Potomac, Patuxent, Patapsco, Rappahannock, Nanticoke, and Wicomico. The Algonquian word *Chesepioc*, meaning "great shellfish bay," gives a continuing Indian significance to the region. More than 10 major waterways feed into the bay, as well as 140 other rivers, creeks, and streams. The Susquehanna River is the bay's main artery.

Tobacco early became the dominant economic factor in the Chesapeake. The long shoreline and extensive system of navigable waterways encouraged the growing and exportation of staple crops, especially tobacco, for trade. In 1775 tobacco represented 75 percent of the total value of export from the Chesapeake area, was worth $4 million, and accounted for 60 percent of the colonies' total exports to England. Shipbuilding, another important economic activity dating back to the 1600s, reached a high point before the Civil War. The construction of canals in the 1820s and railroads in the 1830s and 1840s provided

a foundation for the region's economic expansion during the 19th century. The Chesapeake became part of a Middle Atlantic industrial seaboard area, with its ports in Baltimore, Norfolk, and Hampton Roads serving as centers of international commerce.

The Chesapeake Bay has immense environmental importance. It gives life to 2,700 species of animals, especially fish and shellfish. Clams, crabs, eels, sea trout, flounder, bluefish, croakers, shad, and herring are found in the bay, which produces 33 percent of the U.S. oyster catch and 50 percent of its blue crabs. Crisfield, Md., the self-styled crab capital of the world, sponsors an end-of-summer hard crab derby and a Miss Crustacean Beauty Pageant. Geese, ducks, swans, and other waterfowl can be seen in the bay, as part of their winter migration from the North. Baltimore journalist H. L. Mencken called the bay "a great big protein factory" because of its animal resources. The environment there also supports sport fishing and other recreational activities in the surrounding areas.

The Chesapeake region has grown enormously in recent decades and now supports almost 9 million people, with a 50 percent population increase from 1950 to 1984 in the bay's drainage area of six states (Virginia, Maryland, Pennsylvania, New York, Delaware, and West Virginia). This increased concentration of population, along with pollution from the factories and farms of the area, has brought a deteriorating environment and rising fear for the bay's future. The Susquehanna empties chemical pollutants from Pennsylvania industries into the bay, the Patapsco in Maryland carries refinery contaminants, and the James River holds waste from Richmond and Norfolk. Fertilizer run-off from farms is considered perhaps an even greater threat than industrial pollution. A significant decline of sea life has resulted. In the mid-1970s the bay produced more than 6 million pounds of striped bass, also known as rockfish, yearly, but that had declined to 600,000 pounds by the mid-1980s. The rockfish has recovered since then and is now fished in limited and regulated amounts. The federal government and the Chesapeake states announced a major cleanup program in September 1985. The Chesapeake Bay program reports progress in cleanup as a result of interstate agreements and targeted projects, in the face of continued residential and commercial developments along the bay.

CHARLES REAGAN WILSON
*University of Mississippi*

Carl Bridenbaugh, *Myths and Realities: Societies of the Colonial South* (1963); Chesapeake Bay Program, *The Chesapeake Bay Program: 20 Years of Progress—Remaining Challenges* (2003); Ernest M. Eller, *Chesapeake Bay in the American Revolution* (1982); Carolyn Ellis, *Fisher Folk: Two Communities on the Chesapeake Bay* (1986); William C. McCloskey, *National Wildlife* (April–May 1984); Arthur P. Middleton, *Tobacco Coast: A Maritime History of Chesapeake Bay in the Colonial Era* (1984); Thad W. Tate and David L. Ammerman, eds., *The Chesapeake in the Seventeenth Century: Essays on Anglo-American Society* (1979); William W. Warner, *Beautiful Swimmers: Waterman, Crabs, and the Chesapeake*

*Bay* (1976); John R. Wennersten, *The Chesapeake Bay: An Environmental Biography* (2001).

## Cumberland Island and Little Cumberland Island

Cumberland Island is a barrier island approximately three miles off the coast of Georgia near the Florida border. It is approximately 18 miles long and from one-half to three miles wide. Separated from it by coastal marshes and Christmas Creek is Little Cumberland Island, a part of the same barrier formation as its larger neighbor. Both islands are within the boundary of Cumberland Island National Seashore, established in 1972 by Congress as a unit of the National Park System.

The two islands are part of a vast system of barriers created by fluctuating sea levels and onshore movement of sedimentary material during the last 2 million years. Cumberland Island primarily consists of a Pleistocene beach ridge that reaches more than 100 feet in elevation, while Little Cumberland Island and much of Cumberland's Atlantic shore have formed from a Holocene ridge that welded onto the older formation during the last 10,000 years. The primary vegetation community is a maritime oak-pine forest with a dense understory of saw palmetto and other brush. Both freshwater and saltwater marshes are common and help support a rich faunal assemblage.

Native Americans began using the islands' resources at least 6,000 years ago, and by A.D. 1500 they had developed permanent villages and an economy of mixed agriculture and hunting and gathering. The Spanish built several small missions on Cumberland Island to serve the region's Native Americans, but threats from the British led to their decline in the early 18th century. The British then erected a pair of forts but abandoned them prior to the American Revolution. During the 19th century, Cumberland Island became a premier site for the production of Sea Island cotton. More than half of the original forest acreage on the larger island was converted to cotton fields during the 19th century. The plantation economy came to an abrupt end with the inauguration of the Civil War and the departure of nearly all the African American slaves.

In 1881 Thomas Carnegie, the brother and partner of industrialist Andrew Carnegie, purchased much of the island as a vacation homestead. He soon died, but his wife Lucy eventually acquired 90 percent of the island and raised nine children in wealth and luxury. She paid for several other mansions to be erected for her children, none of whom ever worked. Meanwhile, the northern tenth of the island developed hotels, a hunting club and, finally, an estate for the Candler family of Atlanta. After Lucy Carnegie's death, her Cumberland Island estate remained in a complicated trust until 1962. Thereafter her grandchildren were freed to sell, develop, or retain their segments of the island. Most of the heirs sold or donated land to the government to serve as a national seashore, with the stipulation that they could continue to live and drive on

the island. In the meantime, an association of conservation-minded people purchased Little Cumberland Island and developed it as a low-density, ecologically sensitive community. The National Park Service agreed to leave the smaller island in their hands.

Once established, Cumberland Island National Seashore faced a number of difficult planning and management issues. Agency planners sought substantial development for recreation, but island residents and environmental organizations blocked these plans and succeeded in having the northern two-thirds of the island established as a wilderness area. Once this area was mandated by law, the agency could not use vehicles to maintain the numerous historic resources on the island, especially the huge Plum Orchard mansion. After years of bitter recriminations and infighting between former wilderness allies, island residents succeeded in getting Congress to remove the historic road that runs the length of the island from the wilderness. Island residents also may drive on the Atlantic beach, so the slender wilderness is bracketed by automobile routes.

Cumberland Island is a popular destination that holds intact and ruined mansions, a postbellum African American settlement, a wide and seldom used beach, wild horses, and a mysterious tangle of maritime oak forest where the hiker can briefly experience wilderness. National Park Service limits on the number of visitors allowed on the island are continually challenged. Little Cumberland Island, which features a historic lighthouse, remains a private preserve that also portrays the untrammeled Georgia coast of centuries past.

LARY M. DILSAVER
*University of South Alabama*

Mary R. Bullard, *Cumberland Island: A History* (2003); Lary M. Dilsaver, *Cumberland Island National Seashore: A History of Conservation Conflict* (2004); Hilburn O. Hillestad et al., *The Ecology of Cumberland Island National Seashore, Camden County, Georgia* (1975).

## Cypress

Author Willie Morris, looking back on his childhood in the Mississippi Delta, recalled a vivid memory of the "cypresses, bent down like wise men trying to tell us something." The bald cypress (*Taxodium distichum R.*) is a common image in the literary and visual works of southerners who are well acquainted with the tree that grows in the Coastal Plain of the Gulf and Atlantic coasts, along inland swamps and rivers, and in pine-barren ponds. It is submerged during much of the year, often providing nearly total forest coverage of large wetland areas. Spanish moss is frequently seen draped over the cypress's heavy branches, and herons and water turkeys sometimes nest in its limbs.

Unlike most coniferous trees, the cypress sheds its foliage, leaving its gray trunk and its branches bare in winter months. This can create an eerie—and Gothic, in the mind of a romanticist—impression during the winter and early spring seasons. Known as the "wood eternal," it has survived since the Ice Age. The cypress can grow to be 100 feet high, but it grows slowly, typically expanding its radius by only one inch every 30 years. A stump eight feet in diameter was once found 30 feet underground in Florida. Such trees, which have been preserved in mud, are known as "Choctaw" cypress and are highly valued for their color and resistance to water. The cypress's distinctive "knees" are conical-shaped appendages rising into the air from the main roots; they help aerate the tree.

Cypress has played an important role in the economy of the Deep South. Its wood is highly durable and resists the humid climate of the Southeast. Builders value it for use as roof beams, flooring, and shingles. Southerners made cisterns, coopers' staves, and rail fences from it, and it was an essential material for the shipbuilding industry. As a result of the Swamp Lands Acts (1849–50), the region's best cypress lands near the Atchafalaya, Mississippi, and Red rivers ended up in the hands of lumbermen. They gained it through fraud involving surveyors and land agents and then proceeded to cut the land and to illegally clear nearby public land as well. After the Civil War, the cypress lands of the South were even more fully exploited, as the center of the nation's lumber industry moved south. Developers built railroads into swampy area, giving access for sawmills and disturbing the ecology of areas. They produced "pecky" cypress, which is charred and brushed with acids to produce an antique effect, and it became popular for use as interior beams, paneling, and doors.

CHARLES REAGAN WILSON
*University of Mississippi*

William C. Coker, *Trees of the Southeastern States, including Virginia, North Carolina, South Carolina, Georgia, and Northern Florida* (1937); Wilbur H. Duncan and Marion B. Duncan, *Trees of the Southeastern United States* (1988); Ellwood S. Harrar and J. George Harrar, *Guide to Southern Trees* (1962); Nollie Hickman, *Mississippi Harvest: Lumbering in the Longleaf Pine Belt, 1840–1915* (1962); John Hebron Moore, *Andrew Brown and Cypress Lumbering in the Old Southwest* (1968).

## Dogwood, Flowering

On his way to Mobile from Talasse (where the Coosa and Tallapoosa rivers meet), the 18th-century naturalist William Bartram encountered what he described as a "remarkable grove of Dog wood trees (*Cornus florida*), which continued nine or ten miles unalterable." According to Bartram, this stand of interconnecting trees "formed one vast, shady, cool grove, so dense and humid as to exclude the sun-beams, and prevent the intrusion of almost every other vegetable, affording us a most desirable shelter from the fervid sun-beams at noon-day." Bartram's fascinating description is all that remains of that early Alabama forest stand, but the mystique of the flowering dogwood remains firmly entrenched in southern culture even today.

For many, the flowering dogwood depicts an image of graceful beauty, with its cascading display of white flowerlike bracts, which emerge in early spring followed later in the fall by brilliant scarlet red fruit. Over the years, southerners transplanted countless flowering dogwoods because of the tree's natural beauty and form, including both George Washington and Thomas Jefferson, who planted flowering dogwoods around their homes in the 1700s.

The flowering dogwood's unique qualities combined with human ingenuity produced a variety of uses important to life in the South. Early Native Americans were known to have extracted a scarlet-colored juice from the twigs and roots for use as a dye. They also used the bark to make a weak tonic for treatment of fevers and stomach ailments and as an astringent and stimulant. Some chewed the ends of twigs to form a soft brush to clean teeth.

Early colonists adopted many of these Native American uses for the flowering dogwood and added a few of their own. In the South, flowering dogwood was used to treat malarial fever, chronic diarrhea, colds, and sores. Ripe berries were combined with brandy to make a tincture, which was common among country folk. The flower was also used as an occasional chamomile substitute. So prolific were the uses that one early colonist claimed that almost every part of the tree was used for some benefit "except the rustle of the leaves."

The flowering dogwood never became a timber source in the South. For those who made a living working in the forest, the dogwood's value was relegated to "firewood only when no better kinds are to be had." The quality of the tree's wood earned it a niche as a valuable raw material for small articles such as spindles, shuttles, hubs, golf club heads, and handles. Its close-textured, smooth wood meant that it suffered little wear with use. Today, new technology and plastics have reduced the

Dogwood blooms at Carolina Sandhill National Wildlife Refuge, S.C.
(Ginger L. Corbin, photographer, U.S. Fish and Wildlife Service)

flowering dogwood's commercial appeal. It is now limited to specialty uses and as a wood for handcrafters.

There are many interesting legends and folklore associated with the flowering dogwood. People who lived in the mountains of North Carolina, Tennessee, and Kentucky knew that a "dogwood winter" meant a bad spell of weather in May when the dogwoods were in full bloom. Other southern folk believed that if dogwoods were in bloom, you would catch fish by the sackful and it was time to plant tomatoes, early peas, and peppers. Perhaps the most common legend is rooted in the deeply religious southern culture. It states that the dogwood was once a large tree comparable to the oaks and was used as the timber for the cross to crucify Christ. Sensing the dogwood's sorrow, the legend claims, Jesus said the dogwood would never again grow large enough to be used as a cross. Instead, it would be slender, bent, and twisted, with blossoms in the form of a cross. For many years, a common tradition in rural southern communities would be to use flowering dogwood branches to decorate churches during Easter because of the crosslike blossoms.

W. NEIL LETSON
*Montgomery, Alabama*

William Bartram, *Travels of William Bartram* (1955); Overton W. Price, *Practical Forestry in the Southern Appalachian* (1901); U.S. Department of Agriculture, *Silvics of North America*, vol. 2, *Hardwoods* (1990).

## Dry Tortugas

The Dry Tortugas are a cluster of seven very small islands (totaling 104 acres) that represent the westernmost extension of a string of islands or "keys" that range from the southern edge of the Gulf of Mexico to the island of Miami Beach, Fla. They are roughly 70 miles west of Key West. Originally named Las Tortugas by early 16th-century Spanish explorers who found multitudes of large sea turtles on the islands, the Tortugas earned the appellation "dry" in later years in an effort to warn people that the islands have no freshwater. Given the very shallow seawater and abundance of coral reefs separating most of the islands, the region became a veritable graveyard for many oceangoing vessels dating back to the 16th century.

The U.S. government recognized the strategic importance of the Tortugas as guardians of the Gulf of Mexico in the early 19th century. In addition to erecting a lighthouse on Loggerhead Key and a harbor light on Garden Key (both of which still function today), the United States also built a fort that would become part of the nation's emerging coastal defense system. Construction began on massive Fort Jefferson (the largest 19th-century coastal fort) in 1846, and work continued for nearly three decades. The fort occupies virtually all of Garden Key. In spite of the fort's girth, development of the rifled cannon during the Civil War (which dramatically increased the fort's vulnerability), outbreaks of yellow fever, and periodic hurricanes combined to lead the U.S. Army to abandon the Tortugas in 1874. Indeed, during the Civil War, the Tortugas served mostly as a prison for Union deserters. Perhaps its most famous occupant was Dr. Samuel A. Mudd, the physician who treated John Wilkes Booth soon after he shot President Abraham Lincoln in 1861. Mudd was finally released from the Tortugas in 1869.

Used sparingly by the U.S. military during the Spanish-American War and again during World War I, Fort Jefferson became a national monument in 1935 thanks to a declaration by President Franklin D. Roosevelt. Such a designation led to the preservation and management of the fort, lighthouses, and underwater archaeological resources of the Tortugas. As the 20th century progressed, however, it became increasingly clear that in addition to the area's cultural resources, the Dry Tortugas had become a magnet for an increasing number of people who wanted to enjoy the area's remoteness and position in the midst of some of the most spectacular coral reefs in the United States. Accordingly, in 1992, Congress and President George H. W. Bush transferred the fort, seven tiny islands, and more than 64,000 submerged acres to the National Park Service, creating Dry Tortugas National Park. This action allows for the management of the region's cultural *and* rich biological resources.

The park now faces several challenges. To begin with, in spite of its remoteness (the Dry Tortugas are accessible only by boat or seaplane) the number of visitors each year has escalated dramatically over the past few decades.

The terrorist attacks of 11 September 2001 and hurricanes during 2004 and 2005 notwithstanding, survey research executed in 2002 revealed that people are starting to complain that the islands do not feel as remote as they should. Moreover, although neighboring coral reefs help reduce wave damage from hurricanes, the reefs offer no protection from wind or rusting metalworks that jeopardize the stability of Fort Jefferson. Finally, a few on-site National Park Service employees deal with an increasing number of private boaters who make their way to the Tortugas (and occasionally get stuck on coral reefs), and they must cope with approximately 1,000 Cuban refugees who make their way to the Tortugas each year.

CHRISTOPHER F. MEINDL
*University of South Florida at St. Petersburg*

Thomas Reid, *America's Fortress: A History of Fort Jefferson, Dry Tortugas, Florida* (2006); Thomas W. Schmidt and Linda Pikula, *Scientific Studies on Dry Tortugas National Park: An Annotated Bibliography* (1997); Donna J. Souza, *The Persistence of Sail in the Age of Steam: Underwater Archaeological Evidence from the Dry Tortugas* (1998).

## Florida Everglades

The Everglades, called Pa-hay-O-kee by its original inhabitants, form the largest Florida marsh and are like no other wetland on earth. Marjorie Stoneman Douglas said in 1947 that "the saw grass and water made the Everglades both simple and unique." This 435-square-mile drainage area stretches for 60 miles south of the Kissimmee River and Lake Okeechobee in south Florida. A 50-mile-wide marsh, covered up to 70 percent by saw grass (*Cladium jamaicensis*), slopes less than two inches per mile as it merges with saltwater swamp forests, defining the climate, geology, and availability of water for more than 6 million residents in 16 counties. Recent scientific findings concerning the ecology of this broad and shallow "grassy river" confirm Douglas's belief.

Recent studies have led research scientists to describe this frequently submerged grassland as an ibis-dominated, crayfish ecosystem where the quantity, quality, timing, and distribution of water flowing south from central Florida creates an ample landscape of periphyton algae and saw grass prairies perched atop a Pliocene limestone called marl. Scientists discovered that the ibis (*Eudocimus alba*), a wading bird, feeds on two crayfish species (*Procambarus sp.*), a freshwater crustacean that is sustained by the algae, grasses, and detritus from this rain-drenched and evaporative pan where only inches of water maintain a gentle sheet flow from less than five feet above sea level at Lake Okeechobee to Florida Bay 120 miles west-southwest. The periphyton composed of blue-green bacterium makes nutrients available to the saw grass, which is both flood and fire resistant, while the marl, a valuable construction material, is susceptible to subsidence when drainage occurs. Approximately one-third of the glade's original marshlands that had existed before the 1920s and 1930s remains. These marshlands are now the focus of lawsuits, congressional action, state plans, and Native American and regional water district efforts to improve water quality and restore seasonal periodicity of rainwater to the fisheries and wildlife of Everglades National Park.

Today we are witnessing the fourth of several stages in the ecological protection of the natural features and biological wealth of the wider Everglades. At the turn of the 20th century Audubon Society "rangers" were killed trying to protect breeding plume birds from market hunters on a then-wild frontier. During this initial stage of advocacy for protecting tropical hardwood trees and more than 200 million wading birds, local and national conservationists sought to set aside sufficient land to preserve mangrove seashores, mahogany forests, and freshwater marshes.

The second stage of protection came when Congress debated setting aside about one-third to one-fourth of the greater Everglades ecosystem as a national park in the 1930s; however, action was delayed by World War II. When Congress did establish the boundaries of the park, the original protected areas of America's only continental, offshore coral reefs and island mangrove swamps of the Florida Keys were omitted from the final bill. Thus the second stage of protection fragmented this intricate water-suffused and nutrient-enriched natural area.

Included in the protected areas are all three mangrove species of saltwater trees: white (*Laguncularia racemosa*), red (*Rhizophora Mangle*), and black (*Avicennia germinans*). This is also where saltwater crocodiles (*Crocodilus acutus*), West Indian manatees (*Trichecus manatus*), Florida panthers (*Felis concolor coryi*), black bears, swallowtail kites, frigate birds, crested caracaras, wood storks, and, of course, alligators (*alligator mississippiensis*) reside. Since 1947, when the shores of Florida Bay and the southern extremities of the Everglades were set aside by Congress as the nation's first wildlife and fishery park, the struggle to protect the tropical vegetation and wildlife of the region has drawn national and international attention.

The third stage has thus been characterized by a pervasive recognition of several profound failures, owing in part to a 90 percent decline in wading bird populations. Since the national park was established at the mouth of the river, as opposed to the source springs or upper watershed of the Everglades, all of the upstream pollutants and water diversions now deteriorate existing conditions in the park. Added to this difficulty, an initial error was a failure to consider the essential role of sufficient amounts of water in sustaining ecological conditions or services, agricultural production, and municipal needs. A second failure was due to extensive water diversion schemes that both polluted the river entering the national park and robbed the vegetation and invertebrate populations of water during the often-prolonged dry seasons. Removal of water or drainage led to fires in the dry season, disappearance of peat soils from oxidation, and subsidence of the marl underneath the accumulated peat. A third, and most controversial, failure has been the idea that historical water flow can be reestablished using the existing canal and levee system that has been responsible for decreasing the size of the Everglades by two-thirds because of drainage and reclamation.

Constructed by the Army Corps of Engineers at public expense and authorized by Congress, an intricate drainage canal system, only surpassed in extent of its hydraulic engineering by the Netherlands, was painstakingly built in response to several stimuli. Since 1906, early drainage efforts by Governor Napoleon Bonaparte Broward, devastating hurricanes of 1926 and 1928, a rapid growth of the population, and the even faster rise in the rate of water use per capita all propelled the corps and its supporters to build a sophisticated flood control and drainage operation. Because of an existing 1,400 miles of canals and levees, or raised earthen dams, stretching along the reclaimed banks of the glades, a considerable volume of water—from one-tenth to one-third of the natural flow resulting from rainfall—never reaches the interior. Instead, rainwater falls on urban and suburban development and moves as surface runoff into the bays and lagoons, altering the original brackish water quality and marine life of coastal estuaries such as Biscayne Bay.

The fourth phase of protection, referred to as the "restudy" began in 1993. Scientists and engineers in the 1990s proposed a plan to the South Florida Water Management District and the Army Corps of Engineers to remove polluted water, store otherwise misplaced freshwater, and revive the ailing ecological system of the national park. These current proposals to correct past mistakes and "rebuild" or replumb the glades from the ground up will cost from $7 billion to $9 billion of state and federal money over a 30- to 50-year period. As the momentum built among environmental groups, Congress, and the William Clinton administration to address water pollution in the national park, marine geological and coastal ecological studies revealed a disturbing pattern of saltwater creeping inland. While the causes of such watershed changes are complicated, two overriding continuing factors are the removal of groundwater for drinking or irrigation and the thermal expansion of the ocean leading to sea level rise. Studies reveal that developers in 1900 touted Cape Sabal at the southern extremity of the Everglades National Park as prime area for sugarcane cultivation. A century later, the same landscape is a mangrove forest interlaced by saltwater marshes with saw grass retreating inland. Along the southern rim of the park, saltwater-tolerant mangrove forests are advancing over several hundred acres where originally freshwater saw grass existed.

Recognized as an international biospheric preserve, different portions of the vast Everglades are both a protected place and a pricey agricultural reclamation area for growing tropical fruits and vegetables. Necessary for the water supply on which south Florida's economy thrives, the greater Everglades has become a contentious restoration project. Legislative actions and constitutional amendments in Florida, the fastest-growing large state in the country, amount to an ambitious and expensive land acquisition program trying to simultaneously protect water supply, species, and recreational needs. Stretching between densely populated Gulf and Atlantic coastal cities, protected parts of the Everglades ecosystem remain a refuge for genetically endangered panthers and recovering saltwater crocodiles, owing some measure to the loss of freshwater and encroaching marine water on this ever-shrinking "river of grass."

JOSEPH V. SIRY
*Rollins College*

Marjorie Stoneman Douglas, *The Everglades: River of Grass* (1947); Edward Fernald and Elizabeth Purum, eds., *Atlas of Florida* (1992); John Edward Hoffmeister, *Land from the Sea: The Geologic Story of South Florida* (1974); Adam Markham, "Trouble in Paradise: The Impacts of Climate Change on Biodiversity and Ecosystems in Florida" (World Wildlife Fund Report) (January 2000); Ronald L. Myers and John J. Ewel, eds., *Ecosystems of Florida* (1990); R. W. Tiner Jr., *Wetlands of the United States: Current Status and Recent Trends* (1984).

## Florida Keys

Florida's subtropical Keys, a beautiful string of lush, low-lying islands and coral reefs straddling the Atlantic Ocean and Gulf of Mexico, begin at Key Largo just south of Miami and end in the Dry Tortugas. They are famous today for the Conch Republic, Cayo Hueso, "Margaritaville," "parrotheads," bone fishing, fabulous diving areas in the Florida Keys National Marine Sanctuary, key lime pie, and the diminutive key deer. But there is much more to them and their long, rich history.

The Keys were originally inhabited by a people called the Calusas. Ponce de Leon made the European discovery of the Keys in 1513. Later, Bahamians, or "Conchs," settled the Keys. The Keys were well known as a navigation hazard from the days of the Spanish Main, and along with fierce hurricanes, they caused the loss of many treasure ships. After the U.S. acquisition of Florida via treaty from Spain in 1819, "wrecking" became a very profitable salvage business even into the early 20th century.

Key West was the center of the U.S. sponge industry for several decades in the 19th century. It also became the focus of cigar manufacturing and turtle harvesting. Turtle kraals for the canning factories were in use until the early 1970s. Now tourism is the economic driver.

The Keys are a wonderful natural resource with waters "as crystal as gin," as Stetson Kennedy quotes the Conchs. From the palm-lined beaches to the mangrove swamps to the pine inlands to the coral reefs, each key is different but part of a cohesive ecosystem. The Labor Day hurricane of 1935 was the first of several notable storms that have lashed the Keys in modern times, but hurricanes have always been a part of the natural forces shaping them.

While the Keys have been inhabited for centuries, it was the Florida East Coast Railroad and the extension of U.S. 1 to Key West that opened the area for tourism. John James Audubon, Tennessee Williams, Ernest Hemingway, and President Harry Truman all helped romanticize life in the Keys. Like many of the nation's great areas, the Florida

Keys face increasing pressure from development and overuse. However, residents and visitors alike are beginning to work together to conserve this magnificent resource.

ROBERT L. IZLAR
*Warnell School of Forest Resources*
*University of Georgia*

Joyce Huber and John Huber, *Adventure Guide to the Florida Keys and Everglades National Park* (2001); Stetson Kennedy, *Palmetto Country* (1942, 1982); Johnny Malloy, *From the Swamp to the Keys: A Paddle through Florida History* (2003); Walter C. Maloney, *A Sketch of the History of Key West, Florida* (1876, 1968).

## Florida Panther

Reflecting one of countless historical ironies in the American relationship with nature, the Florida panther, a member of the cougar family, acquired its subspecies name from a 19th-century gentleman naturalist who preferred hunting for sport as much as for science. Indeed, Charles Barney Cory liked to have his photograph taken with his trophies, and nothing was more prized from the Florida wild than *Puma concolor coryi*, which is slightly lighter in weight and darker in color and with longer legs and smaller feet than its seven North American subspecies counterparts. In Cory's time, the hunter's assault against the panther was similar to that mounted against the Florida black bear, alligator, and several bird species. Hunting was soon followed by habitat destruction from agriculture and development. When the Florida panther made endangered species lists late in the 20th century, disease, in-

breeding, and diminishing food sources were also reducing its population.

Panther numbers had already begun falling when Cory named the species. Scientists estimate that 1,360 panthers lived in Florida before European settlement. After the United States acquired Florida, the territorial legislature sanctioned eradication. In 1832 it instituted a bounty for panthers, and by the time Cory had begun carrying his gun into Florida in the 1880s, a hunter could collect five dollars from the state for each panther scalp. The home of the panther had once reached as far as Arkansas and the Carolinas before encroaching forces narrowed its habitat mainly to the environment of the Everglades.

But even there the panther was not protected. Believing the whitetail deer hosted a Texas cattle-fever tick, the Florida legislature passed a deer-eradication bill in 1937. With its main food source disappearing, the panther increasingly preyed on cattle, a turn of events that led to a concerted effort among ranchers to hunt panthers.

Some biologists expressed concern over "the doom of the panther in its last eastern stronghold." The establishment of Everglades National Park in 1947 provided the panther a degree of security, although a large part of its range, the Big Cypress Swamp, had been removed from the park's original proposed boundaries. Three years later the legislature took moderate steps toward protection by declaring the panther a game species that could be killed only during hunting season or when behaving as a nuisance. In 1958 the state placed the panther on its list of endangered

It is estimated that there are fewer than 50 Florida panthers remaining in the wild.
(*George Gentry, U.S. Fish and Wildlife Service*)

species, and the federal government followed suit nine years later. By that time, however, some observers believed the Florida species had become extinct.

Then in 1973 biologists treed and anesthetized a panther, arousing hope for its future. The next year Congress created the Big Cypress National Preserve, which considerably expanded protected animal habitat. Disease, inbreeding, and ever-expanding roadways, nevertheless, threatened Florida's few remaining panthers, estimated to number fewer than 50. Moved in part by the American public's growing concern for the natural environment and its diminishing wildlife, the state conservation and wildlife commission launched a recovery plan in 1981. The thrust of the plan involved tracking and studying the habits of panthers by anesthetizing and then collaring them with radio-monitoring devices, action that many animal-rights activists and environmentalists argued was more harmful than helpful. The recovery plan, however, led to the creation of the Florida National Wildlife Refuge for panther protection in 1989, the same year that a computer program convinced scientists that the animal had a 15 percent chance of averting extinction. That determination resulted in an equally controversial captive-breeding program instituted by the U.S. Fish and Wildlife Service. Six years later, as part of a genetic restoration program intended to help reduce instances of inbreeding, several cougars from Texas were released into the Everglades region.

By that time, the Florida panther had become a popular symbol of vanishing wild Florida. Schoolchildren chose the panther as the state animal. In 1991 Florida issued a panther automobile theme tag to provide proceeds for the Panther Research and Management Trust Fund. When Alligator Alley, traversing the Everglades, was converted into an extension of Interstate 75, the new roadway included wildlife underpasses for the panther.

Yet in the 21st century, the fate of the panther remains uncertain. The habitat range of the male averages 200 square miles, and development, including the placement of the state's newest university, Florida Gulf Coast University, in panther territory, continued to reduce the endangered species' living space. In 2001 alone, drivers killed 7 panthers, when their population still struggled at some ambiguous level below 50.

JACK E. DAVIS
*University of Florida*

Charles Fergus, *Science* (8 March 1991), *Swamp Screamer: At Large with the Florida Panther* (1998); W. J. Hamilton Jr., *American Midland Naturalist* (May 1941); David S. Maehr, *The Florida Panther: Life and Death of a Vanishing Carnivore* (1997); *Panther News* (Fall 1987).

## Galveston Bay

Galveston Bay is located on the southeast coast of Texas and is surrounded by five counties: Brazoria, Chambers, Galveston, Harris, and Liberty. By geological reckoning, the bay is a recent feature of the earth. It is a 600-square-mile estuary that formed in a drowned river delta. The bay complex is composed of four major subbays: Galveston, Trinity, East, and West bays. Each subbay has a different depth and salinity. Galveston Bay has a maximum undredged depth of 12 feet. Trinity Bay reaches 8 feet, and East Bay's depth ranges from 4 to 8 feet, with West Bay at 4 to 6 feet deep. This complex of minor bays creates the ecosystem known generally as Galveston Bay.

Two barrier bars, Galveston Island and Bolivar Peninsula, enclose the ecosystem. These barrier bars impede the flow from the Trinity and San Jacinto rivers and numerous bayous and streams as they drain into the Gulf of Mexico. The bay is a shallow estuary, a semienclosed transitional zone where freshwater mixes with saltwater from the Gulf. It is an ecosystem that is constantly changing in response to the daily tide cycles and seasonal weather patterns. The bay contains a wealth of plants and animals that tolerate fluctuating salinities and temperatures. For the past 200 years the fishing and seafood industries in the bay have played a major role in the economic growth of Texas.

Early in Texas history the small port on the eastern tip of Galveston Island became a major shipping port. By the mid-1850s a channel was dredged from the Brazos River through West Bay to the deepwater port of Galveston, and the natural channel from Buffalo Bayou to Galveston Bay was improved. Navigation up Galveston Bay to the inland ports on the Trinity and San Jacinto rivers and the port at Houston on Buffalo Bayou were historically hindered by two major bars: Red Fish Bar, which ran the width of the bay at its midpoint, and Clopper's Bar at Morgan's Point, where the San Jacinto River entered the bay. These natural features kept the port at Galveston the only deepwater port on the upper coast of Texas for many years. The primary inlet into Galveston Bay between Galveston Island and Bolivar Peninsula was constantly changing with the movement of the tides. By 1870 the inlet had silted in, and during 1872 a congressional proposal was made to remove the bar between Fort Point and Pelican Spit and deepen the channel over the outer bar to 18 feet. Jetties were to be built to prevent silting. Twenty years would pass before the jetties were finished, in 1897.

The city of Houston had been in a shipping competition with the city of Galveston from the beginning. In 1897 Congress directed a survey for a channel 25 feet deep and 100 feet wide from the Galveston jetties to Buffalo Bayou. In 1899 the channel project became the Galveston Ship Channel and Buffalo Bayou Texas. The tremendous hurricane known as the "1900 Storm" caused great destruction to the city of Galveston and the towns around the bay. It also gave Houston the advantage in the political struggle over shipping in Galveston Bay. By the Rivers and Harbors Act of 25 June 1910 the name of the channel project became the Houston Ship Channel. The channel from the Brazos River through West and Galveston bays became a part of the intracoastal waterway in 1902. The channel to the Texas City Terminal was begun in 1893.

By 1943 the last ton of shell was dredged from Red Fish Bar, and over the years the channels have been continually deepened and widened. Of all the human influences, the dredged shipping channels have caused the most permanent damage to the ecology of Galveston Bay. Economic growth has taxed the resources of the bay over the years as it has been utilized for agriculture, fisheries, shell, transportation, oil, gas, and petrochemical production. Residents and recreational users have also demanded a voice in the future of the bay. The Galveston Bay Plan of 1995 grew from the Water Quality Act of 1987 and the Galveston Bay National Estuary Program established in 1989. Today research continues to increase the knowledge of this valuable estuary and the long-term impact on its finite resources as government agencies, corporations, and citizen groups struggle to find a common vision for the future of Galveston Bay.

ALECYA GALLAWAY
*University of Houston, Clear Lake*

James Lester and Lisa Gonzalez, *The State of the Bay: A Characterization of the Galveston Bay Ecosystem* (2002); David G. McComb, *Galveston: A History* (1986); Marilyn McAdams Sibley, *The Port of Houston: A History* (1968).

## Great Smoky Mountains

A distinct family of mountains in the southern Appalachians, the Great Smoky Mountains of North Carolina and Tennessee may be the most biologically diverse place in North America. Heavy rainfall (80 inches per year on the peaks) here produces an omnipresent mist that makes them appear to give off steam—hence the nickname, "the

Smokies." The geology of the Smokies also contributes to their biodiversity, as the high peaks escaped the glaciers of the Ice Age; instead, they remained frozen in permafrost and tundra. When the earth warmed, the tops of the Smokies supported a spruce-fir forest, like an island of Canada in this very southern place. At 4,300 feet, the Smokies support northern hardwoods, such as maple and birch, and below that elevation lies the tremendously diverse cove hardwood forest, with over 130 species of deciduous trees alone.

First settled by the Cherokees about 4,000 years ago, the Smokies play a central role in the tribe's cosmology. Their creation myth mentions these mountains, and many stories describe specific locations in this sacred ground. The "Origin of Diseases and Medicine," for example, took place on Clingman's Dome (6,643 feet). Like all the tribes of the Mississippian era, the Cherokees depended on corn grown in cleared fields in the rich valleys. They fished for brook trout in the whitewater streams, managed the forests below 3,000 feet with fire, and used fire and bow and arrow to hunt deer. In the early 16th century, Spanish conquistador Hernando de Soto invaded the Southeast. Although he did not quite reach the Smokies, European diseases, plants, and trade goods certainly did. By the 18th century, English colonials had transformed the Cherokees' economy into one dependent on the deerskin trade. If elk were ever common in the Smokies, they vanished before the first white settler arrived; however, when the first white settlers arrived in Cades Cove in 1818,

deer and wolves still roamed the mountains.

Much of the 540,000 acres that comprise the Smokies became part of land grants given to soldiers as payment for their service in the American Revolution. Several large land speculators swooped up these grants and then sold them to individual settlers, often to squatters on the land before it was formally ceded by the Cherokees. A small settlement of very traditional Cherokees living along the Oconoluftee River separated themselves from the Cherokee Nation just before removal and, through legal work and political maneuvering, managed to avoid the Trail of Tears. They remain today on what is known as the Qualla Boundary.

For the rest of the 19th century, Cherokees and whites shaped the Smokies as a landscape of small farms with well-forested peaks towering above. What predators remained in the mountains were eliminated by state bounties, which put one dollar on the head of a wolf and one dollar on a fox. On the highest mountains, both Cherokees and whites grazed cattle and sheep, which together created the large Appalachian "balds" that so impressed the first hikers in the region. In the woods below, where the chestnut and oak trees created a rich supply of mast, farmers grazed hogs in the fall to fatten them for the winter kill. And in the valleys, of course, they expanded the fields started by Cherokee farmers yet relied on the same crops—corn, beans, and squashes.

Although small farmers engaged in market activities, such as collecting ginseng, selling surplus corn as moonshine, and cutting locust trees for railroad ties, industrial logging would transform the Great Smoky Mountains. Some two dozen lumber companies harvested 2.2 billion board feet of lumber, affecting 60 percent of the region. Attendant floods, fires, and erosion altered some areas so much that they still do not (100 years later) support the same level of diversity as areas that remained unlogged. At the same time, an imported fungus, *Cryphonectria parasitica*, or the chestnut blight, finished off the remaining chestnut trees. Scenic preservationists, alarmed at the loss of the forests, worked with tourism interests to sell the region as a national park.

Creating a national park out of a region so heavily affected by humans proved a Herculean task. With unprecedented powers of eminent domain, the state governments of North Carolina and Tennessee removed 5,665 people from the former farming communities and lumber camps. The first national park rangers arrived in 1931, and within a year of Franklin Delano Roosevelt's New Deal legislation, the Smokies had 17 Civilian Conservation Corps camps—more than any two national parks combined. The 4,350 young men who participated constructed 800 miles of trails and four major road systems; they built tourist amenities, stocked fish, and replanted roadsides with sensitivity to native species and scenic beauty, all in time for the president's dedication in 1940.

The environmental history of the Great Smoky Mountains defines many of the contemporary challenges that face the national park. Years of farming, logging, and hunting make reintroduction of many native species one of the park's greatest areas of innovation. The removal of so many people and the restructuring of their economy around tourism have shaped the park's relationship to the gateway communities and even with political forces in both states. And the tremendous biodiversity of the Smokies makes them the greatest example of restoration—not preservation—in North America.

MARGARET LYNN BROWN
*Brevard College*

Margaret Lynn Brown, *The Wild East: A Biography of the Great Smoky Mountains* (2000); Durwood Dunn, *Cades Cove: The Life and Death of A Southern Appalachian Community, 1818–1937* (1988); Daniel Pierce, *The Great Smoky Mountains: From Natural Habitat to National Park* (2000).

## Guadalupe Mountains National Park

The Guadalupe Mountains National Park, surrounded by the Chihuahuan Desert, is the westernmost of all of the South's national parks, located roughly 90 miles east of El Paso, Tex., and along the New Mexico border. The Guadalupe Mountains extend from Texas into southeast New Mexico and contain the highest summit in Texas, Guadalupe Peak (8,749 ft.) and the "signature peak" of west Texas, El Capitan (8,085 ft.). Open year-round, the park's remote 86,000 acres are chiefly accessible by hiking or horseback. More than 80 miles of hiking trails are available for the casual nature walker and the experienced outbacker alike. Elevations within in the park vary between 3,600 and

Guadalupe Mountains in 1899 as shown in a U.S. Geological Survey photo. El Capitan Peak is in the center of the photo, and Guadalupe Peak in the right background is the highest point in Texas. (Culberson County Texas. Plate 8-A in U.S. Geological Survey, Bulletin 794, 1928)

more than 8,700 feet above sea level, making the park a hiker's paradise.

The Guadalupe Mountains are part of a 250-million-year-old, 400-mile-long limestone fossil reef that was formed along a shelf in the Permian Sea. The Guadalupes, resting atop an immense earth fault, were lifted out of the sea 10 to 12 million years ago, exposing the reef to weather and erosion. The result was a wearing away of the soft, sedimentary rock that covered the hard limestone beneath.

The first humans came to the area between 10,000 and 12,000 years ago. Evidence of these hunter-gatherer peoples is still found in the park today in the form of rock art, projectile points, and pottery. The Mescalero Apache Indians may have lived in the region as early as the 1500s, and in the 1700s the Mescalero made the Guadalupes their homeland when they retreated to the mountains as a result of the war with Comanches. They sustained themselves by hunting elk, mule deer, and bighorn sheep and harvesting agave, sotol, and bear grass until the 1880s, when Texas Rangers ambushed and removed the last remaining Mescalero at Hueco Tanks. By then whites were traveling through the area in greater numbers, and the Butterfield Overland Mail Coach had begun its 2,800-mile Butterfield Route, which was traveled by government mail carriers between St. Louis, Mo., and San Francisco, Calif. Piney Springs Station was the midpoint meeting place for carriers, and El Capitan was often used as a landmark for Butterfield Stage drivers. Remnants of the Pine Springs Station still remain near the Pine Springs Visitor Center.

After the Civil War, African American soldiers in the U.S. Army, many recently emancipated and seeking employment, were sent to the Great Plains and the Guadalupe Mountains region to put down Indian hostilities. The name "buffalo soldiers" was given to these regiments by the Plains Indians, either because of the resemblance between their hair and that of the buffalo's mane or because of their fierce fighting style, reportedly much like that of the buffalo. These buffalo soldiers patrolled the Guadalupe Mountains and the area that is now the Guadalupe Mountains National Park, and they were among the first to explore and map the area.

By the 1900s the American Indian had all but disappeared from the Guadalupe Mountains, and a few, mostly unsuccessful, ranchers filtered into the wild area. It was the sale and donation of land to the National Park Service by two ranchers, J. C. Hunter Jr. and Wallace E. Pratt, that later provided for the establishment of the Guadalupe Mountains National Park on 30 September 1972.

Today nearly 180,000 people visit the park annually to experience the solitude, tranquility, and unique natural environment that the remote area offers. The flora within the park ranges between the low-elevation creosote, yucca, and prickly pear cacti and the higher-elevation Douglas fir and ponderosa pine. More than 60 species of mammals inhabit the Guadalupe Mountains National Park, including mountain lions, badgers, hog-nosed skunks, black bears, coyotes, black-tailed jackrabbits, and 16 species of bats. Rattlesnakes, numerous lizards, and the western box turtle are among the many reptiles that are commonly found there.

JAMES G. THOMAS JR.
*University of Mississippi*

John Barnett, *Guadalupe Mountains National Park: Its Story and Its Scenery* (n.d.); W. C. Jameson, *The Guadalupe Mountains: Island in the Desert* (1994); Don Kurtz and William D. Goran, *Trails of the Guadalupes: A Hiker's Guide to the Trails of Guadalupe Mountains National Park* (1978); David J. Schmidly, *The Mammals of Trans-Pecos Texas: Including Big Bend National Park and Guadalupe Mountains National Park* (1997); Alan Tennant, *The Guadalupe Mountains of Texas* (1997).

## Homer, Winslow

(1836–1910) PAINTER.
Among the 19th century's most prominent artists, Winslow Homer has been
praised for his engravings, genre paintings, and marine oils. Although the
details of Winslow Homer's reclusive
life and career are well known, his deep
attachment to the South, its people, and
its scenes is less frequently acknowledged. He was the quintessential New
England Yankee, but his development
as an artist was complemented by the
incorporation of southern and tropical
themes in his work. His bright, expres-
sive, and energetic watercolors in particular reveal the impact of his southern
experiences and differ substantively
in color and mood from his famous
marine paintings.

Homer's works began to appear in
*Harper's Weekly* in the 1860s. One of
his earliest engravings was of Abraham
Lincoln shortly before his inauguration. With the outbreak of the Civil
War, Homer became a special artist for
*Harper's*, and for a brief period, he was
with the Army of the Potomac during
the early phases of the Peninsular campaign. Numerous sketches were made
of the Union forces in the field, with
Homer frequently illustrating the monotony of military life. Essentially genre
paintings of daily incidents in a soldier's
camp life, the sketches and notes that
he made of the early phases of the Civil
War provided him with the themes
for his first oil paintings. Of these 20
paintings, only one focused on a battle.
Homer exhibited selections of these
early military paintings at the National
Academy in 1863, 1864, 1865, and 1866.

The most distinguished of these initial
oils was *Homer's Prisoners from the
Front*, which was exhibited at the Paris
International Exposition of 1867 and
later at Brussels and Antwerp.

During the Civil War, Homer became interested in blacks as a subject.
He was one of the earliest American
painters to portray blacks in a series of
oil paintings. His *Upland Cotton, Sun-
day Morning in Virginia*, and *Visit from
the Old Mistress* demonstrate his skill
in painting such subjects in a graceful, dignified, noncomic manner. His
later watercolors from the Bahamas
rejoiced in the physical abilities of the
black fishermen of those waters and
document his ability to define in art the
human anatomy. In his most famous
painting, *The Gulf Stream*, he captures
the raw energy of human conflict with
the sea as a black seaman drifts on a
dismasted sloop circled by sharks.

Although his Florida watercolors are
less graphic in the depiction of humans
confronting the elements, nature is still
a fundamental theme. Homer traveled
to Florida in the winters of 1885–86,
1890, 1903–4, and 1908. On each occasion he prepared watercolors of the area
he visited from the St. Johns River to
the Homosassa River to Key West. The
most striking and graceful of his Florida
watercolors are those he painted at Key
West. Key West was a favorite place
for Homer to work, and his marine
watercolors reveal his enthusiasm for
this region. In his beautiful depiction
of schooners and fishing boats at Key
West, he demonstrated his mastery of
the technical and pictorial skills appropriate to the medium and justified his

recognition as one of the nation's premier watercolorists.

PHILLIP DRENNAN THOMAS
*Wichita State University*

Philip C. Beam, *Winslow Homer* (1975), *Winslow Homer's Magazine Engravings* (1979); Nicolai Cikovsky, *Winslow Homer* (1990); James Thomas Flexner, *The World of Winslow Homer, 1836–1910* (1966); Lloyd Goodrich, *Winslow Homer* (1944); Patti Hannaway, *Winslow Homer in the Tropics* (1973); Miles Unger, *The Watercolors of Winslow Homer* (2001); Peter H. Wood, *Weathering the Storm: Inside Winslow Homer's Gulf Stream* (2006).

## Hot Springs National Park

Forty-seven hot springs flowing from the slope of Hot Springs Mountain in the foothills of Arkansas's Ouachita Mountains gained much attention in the early 19th century as immersion in their waters became known as a treatment for rheumatism and other ailments. Today, these naturally occurring springs serve as the centerpiece of Hot Springs National Park, one of the state's most popular tourist destinations.

Archaeological and other historical evidence suggests that Native Americans bathed in Hot Springs Creek prior to the arrival of Europeans. Before the Louisiana Purchase, the area surrounding the springs remained a virtually uninhabited wilderness; after that time, the thermal waters gained a widespread reputation for their healing, therapeutic qualities.

Early on, visitors flocked to the area in search of a cure. For example, in the 1820s the *Arkansas Gazette* reported 61 people representing seven different states at the springs "for health and pleasure." Belief in the thermal waters' efficacy in treating rheumatism and paralytic afflictions caused the valley's popularity to grow with each passing year.

In 1820 the Arkansas Territorial Assembly requested that Congress grant the site to the newly established Arkansas Territory, but Congress refused. Instead, on 20 April 1832, Congress created the Hot Springs Reservation by setting aside "four Sections of land including said Springs" for future use of the United States, making it the oldest area in the National Park System. This act intended to deny private landownership within a mile of the springs; but the government failed to enforce the measure, so the town continued to grow within the federally reserved area.

The uncertainty surrounding landownership in the area hindered progress. The population of Hot Springs increased little from the time of Arkansas statehood until the Civil War, reaching only 201 by 1860, but its fame as a health resort grew steadily. While the land dispute discouraged large investments or improvements for residents or visitors, a number of structures sprang up in the narrow valley alongside Hot Springs Creek. Bathing procedures remained primitive, and visitors utilized crude facilities throughout the antebellum period.

Following the Civil War, the place took on an entirely different character. Numbers of tourists increased dramatically as patrons from all parts of the country poured in to spend their money. After 1869 the number of visitors grew by about 50 percent each year, and by the early 1870s Hot Springs enjoyed widespread popularity across the nation as a health resort. When Garland County was established in 1873, the city of Hot Springs became the county seat. The town included 24 commercial hotels and boardinghouses, with a capacity of 1,500 to 2,000 visitors per day. After the U.S. Supreme Court finally vested title to the springs in the federal government in 1877 and allowed private ownership in the surrounding area, bathing facilities and services enjoyed even further expansion. The once sleepy little village rapidly acquired characteristics of a wide-open boomtown.

The government took an active interest in its Hot Springs Reservation in the late 19th century. Federal improvements helped transform the frontier town into a cosmopolitan spa: construction of a grand entrance to the reservation, mountain drives, elaborate fountains, and an arch covering Hot Springs Creek along Central Avenue all contributed to a more pleasing appearance. And government officials regulated activity involving the springs by establishing standards for bathing prices and related services.

For decades to follow, growth and development within the bathing industry paralleled growth and development of the city itself. Bathing reached a peak by the end of World War II, when more than 1 million baths per year were provided to patrons. As the industry reached its zenith during the first half of the 20th century, luxury accommodations dominated the town's landscape, and the city bristled with activity. The town gained a reputation as an entertainment-rich destination, complete with illegal gambling, thoroughbred racing, and an assortment of amusement parks. Everyone—movie stars, politicians, rich, poor, and even gangsters—frequented "The American Spa." The town's slogan, "We Bathe the World," rang true.

In 1916 Congress established the National Park Service, which assumed control of the Hot Springs Reservation. The reservation officially became Hot Springs National Park on 4 March 1921.

A combination of factors resulted in the sharp decline of Central Avenue and its bathing industry by the 1960s: improved medical techniques, a general trend away from downtown shopping, and the elimination of gambling all contributed to the downturn.

Hot Springs's Bath House Row was listed in the National Register of Historic Places on 13 November 1974. The most ornate of the Central Avenue structures, the Fordyce Bath House, became the National Park's visitor center, and only one of the eight existing bathhouses continues to offer baths today. The remaining six facilities sit vacant. Now, as the reservation approaches its 175th anniversary, park officials plan to offer leases of the other structures to the private sector for renovation and development in an attempt to revitalize Hot Springs National Park's world-famous Bath House Row.

WENDY RICHTER
*Ouachita Baptist University*

Orval Allbritton, *Leo and Verne: The Spa's Heyday* (2003); Dee Brown, *The American Spa: Hot Springs, Arkansas* (1982); Francis J. Scully, *Hot Springs, Arkansas, and Hot Springs National Park: The Story of a City and the Nation's Health Resort* (1966).

## Ivory-Billed Woodpecker

The magnificent ivory-billed woodpecker (*Campephilus principalis*) is the largest woodpecker north of Mexico and the third largest in the world. It possesses a beautiful jet-black body with large white patches on its wings, an impressive wingspan varying from 30 to 33 inches, and a prominent white beak that measures nearly three inches long. The male sports a bright red crest, while the female's crest is black. The imposing size and brilliant coloration of the ivory-bill led some locals to dub it the "Lord God Bird." Others called it the "kent," a reference to its distinctive toy-horn-like call. Casual observers have often confused it with the pileated woodpecker, which is smaller, much more common, and much more widely distributed.

Although never abundant, the ivory-bill once thrived in the extensive bottomland hardwood forests that graced much of the southeastern United States before the Civil War. Those mature forests were home to numerous dead and dying trees that attracted wood-boring beetle larvae, the bird's favorite food. The rapacious felling of those valuable trees in the decades following the war forced the species to retreat into ever-smaller areas. As the ivory-bill became rarer, the predations of bird collectors anxious to possess

its skin further hastened its decline. In 1942, following an extensive, multiyear search, the biologist James Tanner declared that fewer than two dozen ivory-bills remained. In fact, he had only observed five of the shy birds with his own eyes, all on the Singer Tract, in Madison Parish, La., along the banks of the Tensas River. Despite a campaign by the National Audubon Society to preserve the site, it too was logged; by 1944 the ivory-bills had apparently vanished.

For the next six decades most scientists believed the ivory-bill was extinct in the United States. Although there were credible sightings in Cuba, ornithologists stubbornly refused to accept evidence that the species might still exist in the South, despite repeated claims of encounters at numerous locations, a sound recording made by John Dennis in the Big Thicket region of east Texas (1966), and admittedly fuzzy photographs of the species taken by a sportsman in Louisiana (1971). Hope for the species was finally renewed in 1999, when an undergraduate forestry student at Louisiana State University named David Kulivan spotted an unfamiliar bird while turkey hunting in the Pearl River Wildlife Management Area. Kulivan provided such stunning details that he convinced local scientists he had seen the ivory-bill, leading to several extensive (and, as it turned out, unsuccessful) searches of the area.

Meanwhile, fresh reports of sightings out of eastern Arkansas led author and wildlife photographer Tim Gallagher to organize a trip with his friend Bobby Harrison and Gene Sparling, a kayaker who claimed to have caught a glimpse of an unusual woodpecker in Bayou de View, a section of the Cache River National Wildlife Refuge. On 27 February 2004, Gallagher and Harrison reportedly observed the large black-and-white bird soaring in front of them. That encounter led the Cornell Laboratory of Ornithology to mobilize a large-scale search of the area, which eventually yielded additional sightings, a four-second video of the bird, and numerous recordings of its call. The formal announcement of the ivory-bill's rediscovery in April 2005 electrified the birding and conservation communities, offering hope for the future of the species. By September 2006, numerous alleged sightings were reported as far south as the Florida panhandle, but as of 2007 there have yet to be any indisputably substantiated sightings proving the continued existence of the bird.

MARK V. BARROW JR.
*Virginia Polytechnic Institute and State University*

Tim Gallagher, *The Grail Bird: Hot on the Trail of the Ivory-Billed Woodpecker* (2005); Phillip Hoose, *The Race to Save the Lord God Bird* (2004); Jerome Jackson, *In Search of the Ivory-Billed Woodpecker* (2004); James Tanner, *The Ivory-Billed Woodpecker* (1942).

## Kudzu

Kudzu (*Pueraria lobata*) is a weedy vine with often rampant invasive growth (a foot or more in a single day) that, if not controlled, soon covers anything in its path—shrubs, trees, automobiles, or even small buildings. A native of Asia,

kudzu has been a useful plant to Orientals for 2,000 years. The Chinese made a medicinal tea from its roots and used it to treat dysentery and fever, and fibers from the vine were used to make cloth and paper. The Japanese as far back as the 1700s used starches from the plant's roots to make cakes. Kudzu powder is still used as a thickening ingredient in cooking and as a coating for fried foods. It is widely available in health food stores in the South.

Kudzu was introduced into this country at the Philadelphia Centennial Exposition of 1876, and it became known in the South through the Japanese pavilion at the New Orleans Exposition (1884–86). It was first used in the South as a shade plant on porches and arbors, but by the early 20th century some southern farmers were buying kudzu seeds and cuttings and planting them. Alabama Polytechnic Institute (Auburn University) led in the study of kudzu in this era. Florida farmer C. E. Pleas, beginning in 1902, devoted 50 years to singing kudzu's praises. He wrote a pamphlet, *Kudzu—Coming Forage of the South*, in 1925, and after his death a bronze plaque was erected near his agricultural center, announcing "Kudzu Was Developed Here."

The U.S. Department of Agriculture in the 1930s imported kudzu to help control erosion on bare banks and fallow fields throughout the South. The federal government paid as much as $8 per acre for farmers to plant kudzu, which became so popular during the ensuing years that kudzu festivals were held and kudzu beauty queens crowned.

*Growing up to a foot a day, kudzu can quickly shroud fully grown trees. (James G. Thomas Jr., photographer)*

Georgia farmer Channing Cope, sometimes called the "father of kudzu," wrote about it in the Atlanta *Constitution* from 1939 on, formed the Atlanta-based Kudzu Club of America in 1943, and published the *Front Porch Farmer* in 1949, urging southern farmers to plant the crop. "Cotton isn't king here anymore," he once announced. "Kudzu is king!"

Because the plant is a member of the bean family (*Fabaceae*), the bacteria in the roots fix atmospheric nitrogen and thus help increase soil fertility. Although the vines are killed by frost, the deep roots easily survive the relatively mild winters of the South and produce a new and larger crop of vines each growing season. They bloom in late summer, but the clusters of purple or magenta,

wistaria-like flowers, which have the fragrance of grapes, are usually hidden beneath the large, three-lobed leaves. Kudzu is rich in protein and is sometimes used as fodder for livestock in times of drought. When animals graze on it regularly, though, they tend to kill it. Kudzu today has become a danger to timberland, because its vine will envelop a tree and eventually choke it to death by shutting out the sun. Kudzu is now categorized as a weed, and it covers 2 million acres of forestland in the South.

Whatever kudzu's current practical value to the South, it has assumed almost mythic cultural significance. James Dickey's poem "Kudzu" portrays it as a mysterious invader from the Orient, hinting at foreign domination, scientific misjudgment, and the ineptitude of a federal government that encouraged its use among unsuspecting southerners. The poem is filled with a sense of danger, as the vine he portrays kills hogs and cows, hides snakes, and threatens humans.

> In Georgia, the legend says
> That you must close your windows
> At night to keep it out of the house.
> The glass is tinged with green, even
> so. . . .

Marjie Short's 1976 film *Kudzu* is an informative and amusing documentary containing a scientific discussion of the weed by botanist Tetsuo Kyama, Dickey reading from his poem and referring to the plant as the "vegetable form of cancer," and interviews with Jimmy Carter about his memories of the vine in South Georgia, with Atlanta resident James H. Jordan ("kudzu, city life, and mosketeers go hand in hand to make your life miserable"), and with Athens, Ga., newspaper columnist Tifton Merritt, who suggests that the government may eventually subsidize kudzu and then pay farmers not to grow it. There is also a visit with the 1930s Kudzu Queen (Martha Jane Stuart Wilson) of Greensboro, Ala., who said she was continuing the kudzu tradition "by spreading out in all directions."

There has been a southern rock band called Kudzu, a film titled *Kurse of the Kudzu Kreature*, and an underground counterculture newspaper from Birmingham, Ala., named *Kudzu*. Doug Marlette chose *Kudzu* as the name for his comic strip dealing with the South. Keetha DePriest Reed uses kudzu as a metaphor for memory in her book *Culinary Kudzu: Recollections and Recipes from Growing up Southern* (2002).

C. RITCHIE BELL
*North Carolina Botanical Gardens University of North Carolina at Chapel Hill*

CHARLES REAGAN WILSON
*University of Mississippi*

Juanita Baldwin, *Kudzu in America* (2003); William Shurtleff and Akiko Aoyagi, *The Book of Kudzu: A Culinary and Healing Guide* (1977); Larry Stevens, *Smithsonian* (December 1976); University of Alabama, Center for Public Television, *The Amazing Story of Kudzu* (video recording, 1996); John J. Winberry and D. M. Jones, *Southeastern Geographer* (November 1973); Henry Woodhead, *Atlanta Journal and Constitution* (19 September 1976).

## Lightwood

Pronounced "light'ood"—the *w*, particularly in the Deep South, having lost sound altogether—lightwood is the resin-saturated, naturally dried trunks, limbs, and knots of pine trees. It is important as a building and kindling material in areas of the South heavily forested with conifers. Not subject to replication by any known process, lightwood occurs only in nature. More often than not it begins with still-standing trunks of large trees killed by lightning strikes in the late spring, after sap has risen. Typically, an ensuing hot summer dries the moisture from the tree, leaving the resins free to permeate the wood before they solidify, a process that takes many years. The resulting material is extremely hard and brittle, practically impervious to bacterial rot or insect attacks, and readily ignitable, even when wet, by as little heat as that of a simple match. Similar in quality and color—dark red-black—to heart pine, lightwood differs from it in including the entire corpus of the tree, heart and pulp, all save the bark, thus providing much larger building members.

Found only rarely now, lightwood once served as a major product in the South. Trunks were used only whole or in short sections called "drums," for lightwood was too hard to rip lengthwise into boards or beams, though it can be cross-sawed. Lightwood drums, stood upright or laid on their sides (the preferred method, for in that position they were even less prone to deterioration), provided excellent, cheap, and convenient piers for log-and-frame structures, houses, and service buildings. Larger, finer houses in areas of the South where lightwood was easily available frequently had lightwood drums supporting the inner, unseen portions of the substructure, though they might have brick or stone piers on the periphery of the structure. Though whole lightwood tree trunks were sometimes used as sills for simple log houses and outbuildings, sills were usually hewn from the heartwood of new-felled trees. More often, whole lightwood trunks were stood upright in the ground to form tall pillars supporting whole structures, often quite large barns, storehouses, carriage houses, sheds, and shelters, as well as early "open-side" churches.

Lightwood as kindling was almost as important as its use in building. Limbs sawed into one-foot sections could,

because of their brittle nature, be easily split into half-inch, square splinters. Lightwood splinters, tied in small 8- to 10-inch bundles, were long a standard commodity in southern grocery, hardware, and seed stores. Lightwood knots, cut out of limbs or found in the woods where they had fallen, were too hard to split—hence the expression "hard as a lightwood knot." The knots were left for the country poor—or in antebellum times, slaves and, later, tenants and sharecroppers—to pick up, cart, or carry into town and peddle to the urban poor for important extra cash.

JERAH JOHNSON
*University of New Orleans*

Nicholas Minov, *The Genus Pinus* (1967).

## Live Oak

Few trees are as closely linked to southern culture as the live oak (*Quercus virginiana*). This magnificent tree grows naturally along a narrow strip starting along the Atlantic coastal region of southeast Virginia southward to Florida before wrapping along the Gulf Coast to central Texas. It grows in the driest sands of the Coastal Plain as a dwarf tree or in the rich fertile soils of hardwood hammocks as a dominant tree laden with Spanish moss.

Called live oak because of its evergreen foliage, it is as tenacious as it is stately. Highly resistant to salt spray, soil salinity, and hurricane-force winds, the tree is ideally suited to the climate and geography of its range. The low-spreading tree rarely tops 50 feet in total height, but its massive branches seem to defy gravity as they stretch outward as much as 125 feet in crown spread. The trunk normally grows between 8 and 12 feet in diameter, though some larger specimens can be found.

Live oak trees produce a prodigious annual crop of acorns that are highly favored by squirrels, turkeys, bears, and other animals. It is not uncommon for squirrels to bury the acorns and forget them, thus planting the next generation of live oaks. Early Native Americans are known to have used the live oak both for sustenance and to enhance quality of life. The English naturalist William Bartram reported seeing Native American homes and their inhabitants under the comfort of sheltering live oak canopies. According to Bartram, the Native Americans collected live oak acorns to derive sweet oil used to cook hominy, rice, and other foods. They also roasted acorns in hot coals and ate them much like roasted chestnuts.

Everything about the live oak indicates both power and toughness. Because of its great tensile strength, resistance to rot, tightly grained wood, and naturally curved branches, it was a highly prized timber used in building this nation's early wooden sailing fleets, especially from the 1700s until the emergence of iron and steel ships. New England shipwrights, called "live-oakers," traveled South each winter to harvest and form live oak timber into the much-needed ribs and frames of wooden ships of the northern shipbuilding industry.

During the 1820s heavy harvesting forced the U.S. government to purchase more than a quarter of a million acres of live oak forest preserves in Florida, Alabama, Mississippi, and Louisiana. This act is considered one of the nation's first efforts at natural resource conservation. A remnant of this original preserve still exists along U.S. Highway 98 near Gulf Breeze, Fla. Called the Naval Live Oak Area, more than 1,300 acres are now within the National Park Service and serve as both a recreational and an educational site. Eventually, the commercial value of the live oak declined along with that of the wooden shipbuilding industry.

Because of the live oak's stately endurance, many individual trees have been located that give glimpses into the South's history and culture. The Treaty Live Oak in Jacksonville, Fla., was used by Native Americans to transact treaties. In Goliad, Tex., the Hanging Live Oak was used in the early 1800s to carry out the sentences. In Baldwin County, Ala., the Jackson Live Oak was used by Andrew Jackson to address his troops during the time of the battle of New Orleans.

Today, the live oak's main value is as an ornamental tree. Throughout many southern coastal cities, long avenues of live oaks can be found along street rights-of-way, in parks, and on lawns. Many communities pass tree ordinances to protect the live oaks and other trees from misuse or loss. This relationship with the live oak has had a direct effect on the identity of many areas. The state tree of Georgia is the live oak. There is a Live Oak Road in every southern coastal state, and Florida, Louisiana, and Texas all have towns named Live Oak. Hurricane Katrina devastated the live oaks on the Mississippi beach, but

The magnolia, Mississippi's state flower and tree (James G. Thomas Jr., photographer)

many survived as a lone symbol of natural endurance.

W. NEIL LETSON
*Montgomery, Alabama*

William Bartram, *Travels of William Bartram* (1958); Elbert L. Little, *The Audubon Society Field Guide to North American Trees, Eastern Region* (1980); William Trelease, *The American Oaks* (1924); U.S. Department of Agriculture, *Silvics of North America*, vol. 2, *Hardwoods* (1990); Virginia S. Wood, *Live Oaking: Southern Timber for Tall Ships* (1981).

## Magnolia

In an otherwise grim portrait of life in the segregated South of the early 20th century, Mississippian Richard Wright in *Black Boy* (1945) remembered from his youth "the drenching hospitality in the pervading smell of sweet magnolias." "Could I write a book about the South without mentioning THE MAGNOLIA in some detail?" asks writer Ann Lewis. More than any other plant, the magnolia, a large tree with lustrous, dark green leaves and spectacular, white, fragrant flowers, is associated with the South.

The southern magnolia (*Magnolia grandiflora*), sometimes also known as "bull bay," is native to the southern Coastal Plain from Virginia to Texas. Of somewhat wider, but still essentially coastal, distribution is the closely related sweet bay (*Magnolia virginiana*), which is also an evergreen tree but has smaller leaves and flowers. Among other, and less known, native magnolias are three species with deciduous leaves: the umbrella tree (*M. macrophylla*), which has thin, pale green leaves up to three feet long and flowers more than one foot in diameter; the cucumber tree (*M. acuminata*), with attractive yellow flowers; and the mountain or Fraser magnolia (*M. fraseri*). In addition, two very attractive horticultural species from Asia have been widely planted in the South. These shrubs or small trees are the star magnolia (*M. stellata*) and the Japanese magnolia (*M. X soulangeana*). The attractive and commercially valuable tulip poplar, or tulip tree (*Liriodendron tulipifera*), of southern forests is not a true poplar but is rather a member of the magnolia family.

The magnolia is one of the prime symbols for the romanticized South of the plantation. The phrase "moonlight and magnolias" describes one of the South's central myths—the story of the charmed and graceful society of the Old South. It is an image that appears frequently in literature and in visual portrayals of the region. It has come to suggest an unrealistic attitude toward life, of a people blinded by beauty. Paul Oliver, a blues scholar, has written that blues lyrics are unsentimental, and magnolias do not appear in them. A group of liberal southerners chose *You Can't Eat Magnolias* for the title of a book of 1971 essays urging reform in the region.

The magnolia image is frequently applied to southern women. Words typically used to describe the southern lady are those also applied to the magnolia: "beautiful and graceful"; "delicate"; "a fragrant beauty"; "neatness, grace, and beauty"; and "a showy flower." The sensual aspect of the magnolia is also sometimes noted and applied to the South and its women. A *Time* magazine article on the South in 1977 mentioned, for example, "the aphrodisiac-soporific magnolia, more potent by far in midnight bloom than overblown fiction can convey." The region's environment, then, nurtured its sensual women. The 1989 film *Steel Magnolias* dramatized the strength of southern women, but Ann Lewis resists the term, noting that "the steely image is too cold, the contrast between metal and this luscious flower too severe."

The magnolia is particularly associated with the Deep South. It was officially adopted as the state flower of Louisiana and Mississippi in 1900; in the latter, schoolchildren were allowed to determine the choice through a statewide vote (the magnolia won with 12,745 votes, to 4,171 for the cotton blossom and 2,484 for the Cape jasmine).

C. RITCHIE BELL
*North Carolina Botanical Gardens University of North Carolina at Chapel Hill*

CHARLES REAGAN WILSON
*University of Mississippi*

Pearl Cleage, *Southern Magazine* (June 1987); Jim Gardiner, *Magnolias: A Gardener's Guide* (2000); Ann Lewis, *Confederate Jasmine and the Fat Tuesday Tree: A Poetic Herbarium* (1997); F. Schuyler Mathews, *Familiar Trees and Their Leaves* (1903); Brooks E. Wigginton, *Trees and Shrubs for the Southeast* (1963).

## Mammoth Cave National Park

Located in south-central Kentucky, Mammoth Cave National Park is the longest recorded cave system in the world, officially identified as the Mammoth Cave System. The national park

The Rotunda Room at Mammoth Cave (U.S. Geological Survey)

was established in 1941; it now encompasses 52,830 acres aboveground and
360 miles of mapped tunnels and passageways below, with newly found tunnels adding to that number yearly. Time
and water carved the caves and tunnels
out of Mississippian-aged limestone
strata 379 feet deep. A layer of sandstone
crowns the system and provides an extremely stable support structure above.

The history of the Mammoth Cave
region extends across several millennia—perhaps as far back as the Paleo-
Indians, who roamed the Mississippi

Valley more than 11,000 years ago. Little
is known about these nomadic people,
but spear points from the Paleo-Indian
period have been found in the national
park, suggesting they traveled through
the area. Evidence of humans existing
in the Mammoth Cave National Park
region can be found from every period
since the Paleo-Indian, with native
peoples beginning to explore Mammoth
Cave during the Late Archaic period
(3000–1000 B.C.). It is uncertain when
modern humans began exploring Mammoth Cave, but legend has it that John

Houchins first "discovered" the cave in 1797 when giving chase to a wounded bear while hunting; other accounts place its discovery before then.

The first person to map the cave system and name many of its features was Stephen Bishop. By the War of 1812, Mammoth Cave was mined for bat guano, which contains calcium nitrate, an ingredient used to make gunpowder. In the decades following the war, after the price of gunpowder had significantly fallen, the cave became one of America's first and most popular tourist attractions, and ownership of the cave changed hands a number of times. Eventually it was purchased by Franklin Gorin in 1838. Gorin, a slave owner, used his slaves as guides for tourists who wanted to explore the increasingly famous cave. Stephen Bishop, one of Gorin's slaves, was sold in October 1839, along with Mammoth Cave, to Dr. John Croghan. Through the 1840s and into the 1850s Bishop explored, mapped, and guided visitors through Mammoth Cave. Today, many features of the cave still bear the names that Bishop gave them, such as Pensacola Avenue, the Snowball Room, Bunyan's Way, Winding Way, Bottomless Pit, Great Relief Hall, and the River Styx.

Croghan attempted to turn portions of the cave into a sanitarium for tuberculosis patients, believing the vapors within the cave contained healing powers. Some of his patients died shortly after relocating to the cave; all the rest grew progressively worse. Within a year Croghan had abandoned his sanitarium experiment. In 1849 he died of the disease he was attempting

to cure, and Bishop, one year after his manumission in 1856, also died of tuberculosis at age 36.

By 1926 advocacy for the preservation of Mammoth Cave had grown among wealthy Kentuckians. Private citizens donated funds to purchase much of the land within the proposed park, and the right of eminent domain secured the remaining tracts. On 1 July 1941 Mammoth Cave National Park was officially dedicated, and the cave system below the park has continued to grow since then. As recently as 2005 a connection linking the Mammoth system to another cave system, Roppel Cave, was discovered east of the park. It is generally accepted that explorers will continue to discover new pathways in the coming years and that thousands of yet-to-be-discovered animal species exist in the cave system.

Today the wondrous subterranean world of Mammoth Cave is visited by nearly 2 million visitors annually. Tourists travel from all over the world to explore Mammoth Cave's labyrinthine passageways. Features of particular interest within these caverns are the 192-foot-high Mammoth Dome; the 105-foot-deep Bottomless Pit; conical stalagmites, stalactites, and walls sprinkled with sparkling white gypsum crystals; giant vertical shafts; the underground Echo and Styx rivers; and rare and endangered animal species such as the southeastern bat, the eyeless crayfish, and the Mammoth Cave shrimp. Although most visitors are attracted to the park to venture belowground, aboveground the 52,830-acre park contains lakes and rivers, a 300-acre old-growth forest, rolling hills, miles of hiking trails, and a complex and diverse ecosystem.

JAMES G. THOMAS JR.
*University of Mississippi*

James D. Borden and Roger W. Brucker, *Beyond Mammoth Cave: A Tale of Obsession in the World's Longest Cave* (2000); Roger W. Brucker and Richard A. Watson, *The Longest Cave* (1976); Horace Carter Hovey, *One Hundred Miles in Mammoth Cave in 1880: An Early Exploration of America's Most Famous Cavern* (1982); Johnny Molloy, *A Falcon Guide to Mammoth Cave National Park* (2006); Robert K. Murray and Roger W. Brucker, *Trapped! The Story of Floyd Collins* (1979); Bob Thompson and Judi Thompson, *Mammoth Cave and the Kentucky Cave Region* (2003); William B. White and Elizabeth L. White, eds., *Karst Hydrology: Concepts from the Mammoth Cave Area* (1989).

## Mississippi River

The largest river in North America, the Mississippi River was named by Indians the "Father of Waters" and created the central South both literally and figuratively. The lower Mississippi over geologic eons built a fertile valley and delta to which it adds even now from a drainage area of 1.245 million square miles including all or parts of 31 states and 2 Canadian provinces. The river system severed soil from the slopes of the Appalachians and Rockies, and from prairies and plains, and carried it downstream eventually to become the croplands, forests, and swamps of an alluvial valley with a 35,460-square-mile area bordering the 1,000 miles of the Mississippi downstream of Cape Girardeau, Mo.

Celebrated in fiction, film, and music, the Mississippi was the setting for many Old South stereotypes: of crinolined belles and riverboat dandies, of cheerful roustabouts toting bales to steamboats at the levees, and of colonnaded mansions and cotton fields saved by heroic fights against floods. Steamboat transport, starting with the *New Orleans* in 1811, once was vital to the economy of the central South, and there were indeed belles, dandies, roustabouts, and mansions; yet, the stereotypes did not convey the richness of the cultures blended by the river, the Native American, Spanish, French, British, and African threads that are part of the rococo fabric of the southern heritage.

The history of the river falls into two phases: efforts to secure strategic control of the stream and its hinterlands followed by efforts to control the river itself through engineering. In 1541 conquistador Hernando de Soto became the first European to see the Mississippi, and later he was buried in it; the French first settled the valley, building the first levee for protection against flooding in 1717. Through byzantine diplomacy and military raids, the Europeans wrested control of the river from the native tribes and from each other, the Spanish taking New Orleans and the British occupying Natchez after the French and Indian War in 1763. The Spanish and the Americans drove the British from its banks during the American Revolution, and the Americans purchased full control of the river from Napoleon in 1803, subsequently repulsing an effort by the British to retake it at New Orleans in 1815.

"The Father of Waters" (David Wharton, photographer)

Through construction of levees, Americans then wrested croplands from the rich floodplain, establishing an agricultural system made possible not only by the soils brought south by the river but also by flatboats crammed with midwestern foodstuffs and manufactures, barges of Pittsburgh coal for sugar refineries and steamship fuel, and thousands of steamboats funneling downriver the commerce of a network of waterways reaching as far north as St. Paul, Minn., as far west as Fort Benton, Mont., and as far east as Olean, N.Y.

The Mississippi also brought less-welcome guests south: northern soldiers in ironclad steamboats breaking the chain the Confederacy placed across the river, scalawags and rascals, and the floodwater from its immense watershed. Southerners lost the fights against both the soldiers and the floods but, through formation of the Mississippi River Commission in 1879, enlisted some of those soldiers in the efforts to control flooding and maintain navigation. Supplemented by floodways to sap the river's strength and by reservoirs to stop floods where they originated, the levee system was fortified after the 1927 flood. By 1972, 1,683.8 miles of the proposed 2,193.7 miles of levees had been completed, and they successfully withstood the record 1973 flooding.

Powerful diesel towboats pushing barges supplanted steamboats after 1930. The 1,832-mile navigation channel maintained between Baton Rouge and Minneapolis and the 12,350-mile network of connecting waterways bore a tonnage far larger than that carried by steamboats. The barges moved through the Illinois River to the Great Lakes and via the Gulf intracoastal waterway west to Houston and east to Tampa. The Tennessee-Tombigbee Waterway offers an alternative to the Mississippi for barge traffic, but it is not expected that tonnage moving on the Mississippi will significantly diminish.

LELAND R. JOHNSON
*Hermitage, Tennessee*

Stephen E. Ambrose, Douglas Brinkley, and Sam Abell, *The Mississippi and the Making of a Nation* (2002); John Barry, *Rising Tide* (1997); Benjamin A. Botkin, *A Treasury of Mississippi River Folklore* (1955); Hodding Carter, *Lower Mississippi* (1942); Marquis William Childs, *Mighty Mississippi: Biography of a River* (1982); Pete Daniel, *Deep'n as It Come: The 1927 Mississippi River Flood* (1977).

## Mockingbird

Atticus Finch in *To Kill a Mockingbird* (1960) told his children "it's a sin to kill a mockingbird" because, as Miss Maudie explained to them, mockingbirds "don't do one thing but sing their hearts out for us." The mockingbird has been, indeed, particularly tied to the imagery of the South. It is as close to being an official southern bird as any; five southern states (Arkansas, Florida, Tennessee, Mississippi, and Texas) have adopted it as their state bird. The legislative resolution in Florida naming the mockingbird as the avian emblem of the state referred to it as a "bird of matchless charm." "Song of Louisiana," which was adopted as the official song of that state in 1932, speaks of the "singing of the mocking bird, and of the blossoms of the flowers" in describing the natural wonders found there.

The mockingbird, whose Latin name, *Mimus polyglottos*, means "many tongued," has been a prominent part of the environmental landscape of the South. Discovered more than 250 years ago by naturalist Mark Catesby, who called it the "Mock-Bird of Carolina," it is now found from the eastern United States to California, but it is still particularly identified with the South. A renowned songbird, the mockingbird is an unequaled mimic, noted, as an Audubon Society writer says, for "rapturous singing on moonlight nights among magnolias and moss-covered live oaks of the South." The male sings by day or night, repeating a phrase several times before striking a new one. Its "whisper song" is particularly soft and haunting, but its call notes tend to be harsh, grating noises. It can mimic 39 birdsongs and 50 call notes, as well as the cackling of chickens, creaking of wheelbarrows, croaking of frogs, barking of dogs, and tinkling of a piano.

The appearance of the mockingbird is not particularly striking or colorful. Its predominant look is a dull gray, together with a faded white on its underside. It is slimmer than a robin and has long legs and a constantly twitching tail. It lives year-round in trees and shrubs and can be spotted on the edge of woods, in pastures, and on rail fences and farm hedges. In the Southwest, it nests in sage and cactus. Found in both suburban and rural gardens, the mockingbird feeds on insects (especially grasshoppers and beetles), seeds, and wild and cultivated berries.

Mockingbirds are aggressive by nature. Males are belligerent and courageous, especially while courting. They tolerate no one intruding on their territory, and they quickly attack anyone or anything seen as a threat. Males challenge each other through a highly ritualized dance, squaring off and rapidly bouncing sideways like boxers sparring, with heads held high and wings arched defiantly. Their imitative singing is their most effective way to keep other birds away from their territory.

CHARLES REAGAN WILSON
*University of Mississippi*

Robin W. Doughty, *The Mockingbird* (1988); *Southern Living* (September 1985); John K. Teres, *The Audubon Society Encyclopedia of North American Birds* (1980).

## Muhammad, Benjamin Franklin Chavis

(b. 1948) ACTIVIST.
Never shunning criticism or controversy, Benjamin Muhammad has combined his deep-seated religious beliefs with his strong commitment to civil rights justice over the course of his lifetime. Born Benjamin Franklin Chavis Jr. in Oxford, N.C., in 1948, Chavis participated in the civil rights movement in the late 1960s as a young man. He served as a youth coordinator for the Southern Christian Leadership Conference, working with Martin Luther King Jr. The United Church of Christ (UCC) sent active member Chavis to Wilmington, N.C., in 1971 to organize protests by high school students against racism in that city. Protests turned violent when a white-owned grocery store was firebombed, leaving two dead and one police officer wounded. As a part of the "Wilmington 10," Chavis was convicted in 1976 for his alleged part in the violence. After Chavis served four years in prison, officials set aside his convic-

tion. Radicalized by his prison term, Chavis founded the short-lived National Black Independent Political Party, explicitly rejecting both the Republican and Democratic parties.

Although disillusioned with the political system, he continued his work with the UCC, becoming a minister in 1980. From 1985 to 1993, Chavis led the church's Commission on Racial Justice (CRJ). During this time, he involved the organization in a variety of causes, including environmental issues. Widely credited with coining the term "environmental racism," Chavis popularized the idea that "people of color bear the brunt of the nation's pollution problem." Under his leadership, the CRJ produced *Toxic Waste and Race in the United States* (1987), one of the earliest studies linking race and pollution hazards. Chavis also continued his participation in civil rights demonstrations, notably in Warren County, N.C. When officials selected the mostly black, poor county for a PCB dump site, hundreds of demonstrators protested. After the arrest of more than 500, including Chavis, environmental racism (later referred to as environmental justice) became a national issue. Relentless publicizing of the cause by Chavis and others led President Bill Clinton to place the issue on the agenda of the Environmental Protection Agency. The UCC's and Chavis's work on environmental racism at this time played a pivotal role in igniting the debate over the role of race and class in environmental problems across the nation and around the world. The work also provided a foundation for many studies that followed.

Chavis left the CRJ in 1993, when the National Association for the Advancement of Colored People (NAACP) appointed him director. The relationship proved a rocky one. Chavis continued his long-standing emphasis on programs and assistance for black youth and yet also formed a close relationship with the controversial leader of the Nation of Islam, Louis Farrakhan. Farrakhan's organization drew considerable criticism for its leader's heavily anti-Semitic remarks as well as its hostility to female leadership. In 1994 the NAACP dismissed Chavis from his post for several reasons. First, the NAACP perceived Chavis as "a small part of a much bigger problem within the NAACP—the problem of inequitable treatment of females with regard to leadership positions, salaries and promotion." In addition, questions arose over Chavis allegedly using more than $300,000 of the NAACP's funds to settle a sexual harassment suit against him without board approval.

Chavis continued his close relationship with Farrakhan, leading his Million Man March in 1995. Later, in 1997, Chavis became a Black Muslim under the Nation of Islam. With his conversion, Chavis also changed his name to Muhammad. His conversion left few happy in his old church; the UCC removed his title of "Reverend" and reduced him to a layperson.

In 2001 Muhammad became the president and CEO of the Hip-Hop Summit Action Network, an organization dedicated to promoting hip-hop music's positive messages and political activism and voting among youth. Although the group vocally supports "equal justice for all," males dominate the visible leadership and membership of the organization, continuing a trend seen in Muhammad's life. Muhammad also stood behind Eminem, a white hip-hop artist, when criticism flew for the singer's use of racist and sexist language against black women.

Although occasionally controversial, Muhammad has continually demonstrated a commitment to civil rights justice through a wide variety of causes over his lifetime.

ELIZABETH BLUM
*Troy University*

Benjamin Chavis, in *Confronting Environmental Racism: Voices from the Grassroots*, ed. Robert D. Bullard (1993); Mark Dawes, *Jamaica Gleaner* (25 March 2003); Hip-Hop Summit Action Network website, <www.hsan.org>; Brian Taylor, *The Militant* (31 March 1997).

## Muir, John

(1838–1914) NATURALIST, ENVIRONMENTALIST, EXPLORER, WRITER.

Shortly after the end of the Civil War, the Scottish-born John Muir, traveling mostly on foot, made his way from Indianapolis, Ind., to Cedar Key, Fla. The 29-year-old began his journey on 1 September 1867, averaged 25 miles per day, and reached Florida on 15 October. In his record of this trip, *A Thousand-Mile Walk to the Gulf*, first published in 1916, we see both Muir's exaltation of the natural world and his frustration with humankind's misuse of that world.

Carrying little more than a plant press, a change of underwear, and three books—the *New Testament*, the poetry of Robert Burns, and Alphonso Wood's 1862 *Class-book of Botany with a Flora of the United States and Canada*—Muir, who grew up in Wisconsin under a severe and religious father, recorded his investigations of trees, mosses, snakes, wildflowers, caves, and ferns as well as his interactions with blacks and whites in the aftermath of war. Evidences of war, he noted, "are not only apparent on the broken fields, burnt fences, mills, and woods ruthlessly slaughtered, but also on the countenances of the people."

Muir climbed Kentucky's Cumberland Mountains and tasted the nearly dry Salt River, scrambled over "naked limestone," and passed through "noble forests" of oaks guarded by catbrier. He tramped through Tennessee and sailed on the Chattahoochee River, where he ate muscadine grapes that fell from overhanging vines. He waded and swam his way through Georgia, wondering at beauties like the striking purple liatris and the "dense radiant masses" of the state's longleaf pines. Singing the praises of the South's legendary Spanish moss, Muir traveled among cypress swamps and saw palmettos, caught his first sight of the "stately banana," and noted an increasing abundance of magnolia trees. He sometimes scorned what was new to his experience, particularly when he viewed a landscape as threatening rather than inviting. "Am in a strange land," he wrote. "I know hardly any of the flowers, & I cannot see any place for the solemn dark mysterious forest." Alert to even the smallest gradations of change, Muir arrived in a "watery and vine-tied" Florida whose palms and winds "severed the last strands of the chord that united me with home."

The delights he recorded are balanced by Muir's consistently negative criticism of the man-made: he "escapes" the squalid and repellent taverns, garrets, and farmhouses where he stayed overnight; deplored a "paltry" man-made garden; and pondered the illogic of Christian hunters he described as "vertical godlike killers."

Muir suffered through conversations disparaging blacks and championing the hunt, was assessed by a would-be robber on horseback, was offered aid by both blacks and whites, met an impressive gentleman who foresaw the future uses of electricity, and was closely questioned by homeowners "under the seal of war" who, more often than not, exercised an abundance of caution before opening their doors. He slept more happily in mossy beds, bushes, and caves; on hillsides; and even in leafy cemeteries. Throughout, his sympathy was with the innocent, the "enslavable" world of animals and plants. In a war between wild beasts and mankind, Muir commented, "I would be tempted to sympathize with the bears."

In rhapsodic incantations that bear witness to the influence of British Romanticism and American Transcendentalism, Muir used biblical imagery in setting out his own theology, a holy and prescient environmentalism that asserts the equality of all species. "Lord Man," he named those who believe that all of creation has been made for humankind's pleasure. Anticipating today's Deep Ecology movement, Muir wove throughout his journal a bright thread of disapproval for humanity's characteristic attitude toward the natural world, suggesting that perhaps man was created as "a tasty bit for the alligator," an animal he mentioned many times, though he saw it only once. The unfamiliar challenged Muir's worldview, one heretofore informed by places less enclosed.

He had yet to declare his theory of glacial sculpting, to champion the preservation of Yosemite, or found the Sierra Club, but in his 1867 observations we see the characteristic mental processes by which Muir reconciled his ambivalence regarding humans and nature, northerner and southerner, black and white, self and other. One recognizes the necessity for reconciliation that drove John Muir's lifelong dedication to saving what he loved.

SUDYE CAUTHEN
*Florida State University*

Michael P. Cohen, *The Pathless Way: John Muir and American Wilderness* (1984); Stephen Fox, *John Muir and His Legacy: The American Conservation Movement* (1981); Steven J. Holmes, *The Young John Muir: An Environmental Biography* (1999); John Muir, *Our National Parks* (1901), *The Story of My Boyhood and Youth* (1913), *A Thousand-Mile Walk to the Gulf* (1916); Frederick W. Turner, *Rediscovering America: John Muir in His Time and Ours* (1985); Linnie Marsh Wolfe, *Son of the Wilderness: The Life of John Muir* (1945).

## Natchez Trace

The Natchez Trace originated as Native Americans beat a path through swamps, dense wilderness, and hills, from the Natchez bluffs into the hunting grounds of the Cumberland River Valley. Tribes that settled along the trace used it as a link in a network of commerce. Europeans later used the well-worn path. Hernando de Soto traveled it on his way to the Mississippi River, while French explorers established trading posts at its extremities, Natchez and Nashville. During the American Revolution the road was a path of freedom as colonists fled southwest.

Though long and hazardous, the road acted as a sort of interstate highway in the new American republic. At its peak of use around 1810, literally thousands of travelers walked or rode horses along its path—eight feet wide at best—every month. Many of these were settlers in the Mississippi River Valley who took their products downriver on flatboats to New Orleans. There they sold their goods and the scrap lumber from their boats and then headed north on the six-week journey back up the trace, laden with profit from their sales. Poised to prey upon these hapless "Kaintucks" were poison ivy, mosquitoes, swirling rivers, and notorious highwaymen who lay in wait along "The Devil's Backbone."

Colorful characters traversed the road: traders, peddlers, pioneer families, gentlemen and ladies, trains of slaves, circuit-riding evangelists, and fortune hunters. The rich and famous came, too. French Camp was settled by Louis LeFleur, father of the Choctaw Chief Greenwood LeFleur. Meriwether Lewis died of a gunshot wound at nearby

Grinder Inn. Major General Andrew Jackson marched up the road victoriously after the battle of New Orleans.

Recognizing the potential for public service, the U.S. government designated the trace as a mail route in 1800 and hired people to widen and improve it. Horsemen carrying mail would leave Nashville and Natchez on the same day and meet two weeks later at midpoint to exchange pouches.

The heyday of the trace ended with the whistle of the steamboat, which defied the Mississippi's strong current and thus eliminated the need for overland travel homeward. By 1830 it had begun to revert to nature, though it experienced a brief revival as a strategic artery during the Civil War.

Modern interest in the trace began in 1909 as the Daughters of the American Revolution sought to mark the route of the Old Trace. A Natchez Trace Association was organized, and in 1934 the Department of the Interior, through the National Park Service, surveyed the trace and began construction of the Natchez Trace Parkway. Now a small, limited-access, continuous two-laned road spanning 444 miles, this "Highway of History" is a drive back in time where travelers encounter animals and forests, not trucks and traffic lights. A marker reads, "Walk down the shaded trail and leave your prints in the dust, not for others to see but for the road to remember." Parkway headquarters and a visitors' center are in Tupelo. The trace has figured prominently in southern literature, as an image of a wild, beastly South. Eudora Welty's novel *The Robber*

*Bridegroom* (1942) and a musical made from it evoke the place.

LUCIE R. BRIDGFORTH
*Northwest Mississippi Community College*

Robert M. Coates, *The Outlaw Years: The History of the Land Pirates of the Natchez Trace* (2002); Jonathan Daniels, *The Devil's Backbone: The Story of the Natchez Trace* (1962); William C. Davis, *A Way through the Wilderness: The Natchez Trace and the Civilization of the Southern Frontier* (1995).

## Nuclear Pollution

Since the early 1940s, the South has been deeply involved in the development and use of nuclear energy for military and civilian purposes. During World War II, scientists and engineers at the Manhattan Project's immense installation at Oak Ridge, Tenn., conducted investigations and produced materials that were instrumental in making the atomic bombs dropped on Japan in August 1945. After the war, Oak Ridge continued as a key site for nuclear production, research, training, and distribution of radioactive isotopes. In the early Cold War period, the government built another huge facility, the Savannah River plant near Aiken, S.C., to meet its requirements for plutonium and tritium for nuclear weapons.

After the 1954 Atomic Energy Act made nuclear technology available for widespread commercial applications, the South moved aggressively to explore the economic opportunities of peaceful nuclear energy. Within a short time, experimental power reactors were built at Oak Ridge and at Parr Shoals, S.C.

In 1966 the Tennessee Valley Authority provided an important impetus to the growth of nuclear power when it announced plans to construct two plants of unprecedented size at Browns Ferry, Ala. At the end of 2002, 41 of the 95 nuclear power plants licensed to operate in the United States were located in the South.

The operation of nuclear installations caused environmental problems in the South, some of which were serious and many of which were not. The worst offenses occurred at Oak Ridge and Savannah River. At Oak Ridge, liquid wastes that were contaminated with both low-level radioactivity and chemical pollutants were placed in holding ponds or sometimes discharged directly into streams or wells. Solid wastes, which included equipment, pipes, filters, clothing, and tools, were buried in trenches and covered with soil. Gaseous wastes were released into the atmosphere. Although Oak Ridge officials monitored levels of radioactivity to guard against excessive occupational or public exposure, the surrounding environment served as the major sink for wastes for decades. At Savannah River, the same practices were employed for low-level radioactive and chemical wastes. In addition, some 34 million gallons of high-level liquid radioactive waste from reprocessing reactor fuel that had accumulated by the 1980s, which was far more hazardous than the low-level wastes generated in other operations, was stored in 48 steel tanks. Several of the tanks leaked wastes into secondary barriers, and one overflowed

to allow seepage into the environment. In 1996 the U.S. Department of Energy opened a $2.5 billion plant at Savannah River to immobilize liquid wastes into glass canisters.

The impact of commercial nuclear power plants in the South placed a much lower burden on the environment and posed less of a threat to public health. Reactors release small amounts of radiation as a part of routine operations, but their emissions remained well within permissible limits set by the Environmental Protection Agency. Another problem that generated a great deal of concern in the late 1960s and early 1970s was thermal pollution from nuclear power. This can result from the condensation of the steam that drives the turbines in a large plant, coal as well as nuclear, if the condensate water is discharged directly into the environment. After considerable public debate and acrimony, this issue was largely resolved when utilities added cooling towers or cooling ponds to plants on inland waterways. One such controversy took place when the Florida Power and Light Company bowed in 1971 to pressure from the state government and environmental groups by agreeing to build a 4,000-acre cooling canal system at its Turkey Point nuclear facilities on Biscayne Bay.

The greatest danger to the environment from nuclear power would be a severe reactor accident that spewed large quantities of volatile forms of radiation into the environment. Such an accident has never occurred in the United States—even when the core melted at the Three Mile Island plant in Pennsylvania in 1979, only tiny amounts of the most hazardous radioactive "fission products" escaped outside the plant. A very serious fire at the Browns Ferry plants in 1975 disabled many of their safety systems, but it did not release radiation into the environment.

J. SAMUEL WALKER
*U.S. Nuclear Regulatory Commission*

Kevin D. Crowley and John F. Ahearne, *American Scientist* (November–December 2002); Terrence R. Fehner and F. G. Gosling, *Environmental History* (April 1996); J. Samuel Walker, *Containing the Atom: Nuclear Regulation in a Changing Environment, 1963–1971* (1992).

## Odum, Eugene P.

(1913–2002) ECOLOGIST.
Eugene "Gene" Pleasants Odum (born in New Hampshire in 1913, died in Georgia in 2002) was the eldest child of Anna and Howard Washington Odum. He was called the "father of modern ecology" largely because of his text *Fundamentals of Ecology*, published in 1953. This text focused on ecosystems and was the first book of its kind; it was influential in establishing the bases of ecology as a unique discipline. Odum was the visionary who founded the University of Georgia's Savannah River Ecology Laboratory, the Marine Institute on Sapelo Island, and the Institute of Ecology. Today, these institutions have international reputations for excellence in ecological research. Odum's publications included more than 300 manuscripts and 14 books, many of which are well known by ecologists. Throughout his career, Odum also wrote

for the general public to inspire environmental conservation by focusing on our life-support systems.

Odum received a zoology bachelor's degree in 1934 from the University of North Carolina at Chapel Hill. Two years later at the same institution, he completed a master's degree in zoology. At the time of these studies, Odum's father was a well-established scholar studying regions, a field referred to as regionalism. He encouraged his son to seek doctoral training elsewhere. Following this advice, Odum completed a Ph.D. in zoology, majoring in ecology, at the University of Illinois. Odum returned to his native South as an instructor in the University of Georgia's Department of Zoology in 1940. He quickly proposed teaching a course on ecology but was turned down, because ecology was not yet viewed as a science with its own set of principles. As a result, he embarked on writing *Fundamentals of Ecology* as a means to prove that ecology was indeed a unique scientific area that focused on the interactions within and across ecosystems. The text has been translated into over a dozen languages, and its fifth edition, coauthored by G. W. Barrett, was published in 2004.

Odum spent his entire career at the University of Georgia involved with multiple field studies in the Southeast and around the world. He was an elected member of the National Academy of Science, president of the American Ecological Society, and Fellow of the American Academy of Arts and Sciences. He served on numerous state and national advisory committees and was awarded the Tyler Ecology Award and Presidential Medal of Science, which were presented to him by President Jimmy Carter. In 1987 Gene Odum and his brother Howard Thomas "H. T." Odum shared the Swedish Crafoord Prize, considered ecology's equivalent of the Nobel Prize. Both brothers collaborated on multiple research projects and produced many still-cited manuscripts.

Gene Odum often referred to his father's studies, taking inspiration from his father as a scholar and academic leader. Odum would often remind readers in his numerous writings that the precursor to landscape ecology was his own father's regionalism. Odum saw his work as a continuation of his father's legacy, and he consistently included humans in his discussion of ecosystem ecology. Gene Odum expressed this interconnectedness between the natural and social sciences in his 1997 text *Ecology: A Bridge between Science and Society*. He argued that ecology was a paradigm that connected many sciences. His approach included both natural and social systems and separated Odum from other natural science scholars, who often ignore the human component of ecological systems.

KAREN SMITH-ROTABI
*University of North Carolina*

Betty J. Craige, *Eugene Odum: Ecologist and Environmentalist* (2001); Eugene P. Odum, *Fundamentals of Ecology* (1953), *Ecology: A Bridge between Science and Society* (1997).

## Offshore Oil Industry

In the 60 years since the end of World War II, the offshore oil and gas industry has been one of the most dynamic engines of investment, employment, and growth for the Gulf Coast region. From negligible production in 1945, offshore now produces about 34 percent of the world's crude oil and about 25 percent of the world's natural gas. Of all offshore provinces in the world, the northern Gulf of Mexico is the most explored, drilled, and developed. In 2005, in the continental shelf waters off Louisiana and Texas, there were nearly 4,000 active platforms servicing 35,000 wells, and 29,000 miles of pipelines. Output from the Gulf, providing close to one-third of U.S. oil and gas production, exceeded Texas's onshore output and was poised to surpass Alaska's.

In the late 1930s major oil companies, through the corrupt state leasing practices, obtained hugely profitable oil and gas fields in south Louisiana. The 1938 Pure-Superior platform in the Creole field, a mile and a half from the city of Cameron, was the first truly freestanding structure that produced oil in the Gulf. The developments of the 1930s, combined with the doubling of base domestic oil prices upon the lifting of price controls at the end of World War II, generated interest in the adjacent offshore domain and financed a new wave of exploration and drilling by the established firms. Kerr-McGee's Ship Shoal Block 32 platform, installed in 1947 in 18 feet of water, 10.5 miles from the Louisiana shore, is recognized as the first offshore platform "out of sight of land."

Drilling and development were suspended in the early 1950s, as the coastal states and federal government litigated ownership of offshore submerged lands.

Supreme Court decisions in the early 1950s, however, awarding the federal government rights beyond the 3-mile boundary (10.4 miles in the case of Texas and Florida), allowed for the resumption of drilling. Oil companies such as Shell Oil, Gulf Oil, Humble Oil (Exxon), and the California Company (Chevron) took the lead in pushing development into deeper waters.

The seeds of the larger Gulf Coast offshore industry were planted during this period with the emergence and growth of geophysical contractors (i.e., Geophysical Services Incorporated, Western Geophysical); engineering and construction firms (Brown & Root, J. Ray McDermott); supply and transport firms (Tidewater, Petroleum Helicopters); diving companies (Taylor Diving); naval architects (Friede-Goldman); onshore support centers (Morgan City and Lafayette, La.); labor camps (Venice, La.); and shipyards (Houston and Beaumont, Tex.; Pascagoula, Miss.). The drilling companies, such as ODECO, Zapata, Global Marine, and the Offshore Company, captured imaginations with the invention of a variety of submersible and jack-up rigs. Most activity was concentrated in offshore Louisiana, which was more oil-prone than other parts of the Gulf, but offshore Texas also became the scene of major natural gas developments.

The 1960s through the 1970s was a fertile period for innovation in offshore technology. Shell Oil's launching of the first semisubmersible drilling vessel, the *Bluewater 1*, and installation of the first subsea well greatly extended exploration into deeper waters. Gulf Coast diving companies continually set new depth records in assisting platform and pipeline installation. Digital computing revolutionized the gathering and interpretation of seismic data, making exploration more cost effective. Three major hurricanes (Hilda, Betsy, and Camille) in the 1960s helped bring about a convergence of improved ideas and practices on platform design and construction. Three major platform disasters and spills in 1970–71 led to improvements in facilities engineering, environmental protection, and safety. Since the early 1970s, major accidents and spills have been quite rare, although the thousands of miles of canals dredged and laid with oil pipelines in the swamps and marshes of south Louisiana have contributed significantly to coastal erosion.

By the late 1970s, the industry had moved production from fixed platforms into 1,000-plus feet of water in the Gulf of Mexico. The collapse in oil prices in the mid-1980s, however, decimated the offshore industry in the Gulf, especially the drilling, service, and supply companies that assumed a great deal of the infrastructure and economic risk of offshore operations. In the 1980s and 1990s, continued technological innovation and a new federal "area-wide" leasing system, which leased much larger offshore acreage than previously, revived the offshore industry in the Gulf, leading to spectacular "deepwater" (1,500 feet and deeper) developments involving massive tension-leg platforms, floating spars, and subsea wellheads. By 2002 at least 40 different operators had drilled deepwater wells in the Gulf, and the industry had discovered 192 fields.

Thirty-eight of these fields contained more than 100 million barrels of oil equivalent. Hurricane Katrina in August 2005 crippled much of the offshore oil industry, with 17 rigs damaged, 1 rig drifting away from its bearings, and 6 rigs of indeterminate status by late 2006.

TYLER PRIEST
*University of Houston*

Clyde W. Burleson, *Deep Challenge! The True Epic Story of Our Quest for Energy beneath the Sea* (1999); Robert Gramling, *Oil on the Edge: Offshore Development, Conflict, Gridlock* (1996); Joseph A. Pratt, Tyler Priest, and Christopher Castaneda, *Offshore Pioneers: Brown & Root and the History of Offshore Oil and Gas* (1997); Tyler Priest, in *Nature, Raw Materials, and Political Economy*, ed. Paul S. Ciccantell and David Smith (2005), *The Offshore Imperative: Shell Oil's Search for Petroleum in the Postwar United States* (2007).

## Oil Pollution

Oil production in the South has been an integral part of the economic well-being of the region, but the fiscal rewards have often come at the expense of the environment. Early petroleum producers sacrificed the environment by letting crude, brine, and other oil-related wastes flow uncontrolled into the surroundings in the quest to get as much oil out of the ground as fast as possible. Before the advent of effective regulation regarding pollution, the only thing that kept producers from completely abusing the land was the potential of a lawsuit. However, sophistication in the industry grew so much that some producers eventually considered

pollution inefficient. Oil was and is a valuable commodity that is expensive to get out of the ground and into a usable form. The ability to produce a product economically using every possible drop of hydrocarbon became important for the industry. In the long run, however, it took regulation to ensure that the oil pollution remained in check.

Scholars have called the dawn of the 20th century, when prospectors discovered the large oil fields in east Texas, "the gusher era." If a driller hit upon a deposit of oil under significant pressure, then the oil would gush sometimes hundreds of feet into the air, spilling crude all over the surrounding region. In the early years of petroleum production, technology did not exist to control this free flow of oil, and developers tried in vain to make earthen retention ponds to hold the valuable crude. Prospectors considered it uneconomical to build storage facilities before they were positive they had oil. The crude itself was toxic to flora and fauna, and it often polluted adjacent waterways; but the motivation for impounding oil was purely economic.

In the early 19th and 20th centuries drillers let a gusher run open for an hour or more to clear out the well even after technology existed to control the phenomenon. They believed that it was good well management and potentially better public relations despite the end result of wasted product. The concept of pollution did not really enter the minds of most drillers. At Spindletop near Beaumont, Tex., promoters literally turned a valve and let oil flow under pressure to give the illusion of a gusher to potential investors, and the overflowing crude ran into the nearby areas. Equally fascinating was that the fields around Beaumont were so large that promoters could constantly give the illusion of a gusher. The fields of east Texas unsurprisingly, with all of the pools of crude and oil-field sludge, experienced many fires that choked the sky with smoke and compromised the surrounding communities.

Another pollution problem associated with the oil industry, particularly before World War I, was the saltwater, or brine, that drilling generated in tremendous amounts. The longer a well remained in production, the greater the amounts of brine that surfaced with the oil. At first, operators let the saltwater run into local waterways or stored it in earthen pits. In wet east Texas, rain quickly caused the pits to overflow and spill into area streams. It soon became apparent that the brine from oil fields damaged local farmers' crops and compromised area aquifers. Area residents often sued successfully for damages caused from the contamination.

Poorly plugged wells also contributed to the brine and crude pollution problems because they allowed oil and saltwater to seep into local aquifers. This in turn damaged the drinking and irrigation supply for entire communities. It was especially damaging in Texas because much of the state depended on aquifers for its water supply, and residents constantly sought redress. Southern oil fields did not implement controls to halt brine seeping into aquifers until after World War I.

The size of the oil fields in the South made the pollution problems much worse. Large oil fields meant larger pollution problems, and the Kilgore, Tex., strike of 1930 was one of the largest fields in the world. Local waterways could not dilute the incredible amounts of brine. Operators in the Kilgore field sometimes produced only one barrel of oil for every 10 of brine. Lawsuits surrounding the massive discovery were rampant, and in an attempt to control the growing expense from fines and damages, oil producers formed the East Texas Anti-Pollution Committee. They charged themselves with finding ways to keep brine and other oil pollutants out of Texas waterways. The group had limited success. There were almost 15,000 wells on the field, far too many to keep tabs on in the 1930s for pollution purposes. Also, producers only sought to control pollution to save money. Many operators simply chose to follow the standard procedure and hope nobody noticed.

Eventually, oil-field technology enabled producers to deal with their brine pollution effectively, and managers learned to conserve increasing amounts of precious crude. Beginning in 1942, operators began injecting wastewater back into the oil reservoir. Not only did this solve much of the problem with brine waste, but it made the oil fields more productive. However, problems still can occur through poorly sealed wells and poor oil-field management.

How much did local, state, and federal officials consider pollution problems related to oil? Texas officials were concerned with crude oil pollution in the coastal areas since at least the early

1900s. Many believed that the oil spilled during unloading and loading of crude was to blame. The problem was so bad that area fisherman believed that the crude damaged their oyster beds and fisheries. Petroleum wastes compromised the viability of other formerly lucrative industries, including fishing, lumber, and tourism, during the first half of the 20th century. Regulators in the 1920s found that Port Arthur, Tex., had the worst polluted coastal water in the country. The Houston Ship Channel received equal attention because the city fathers sacrificed the waterway to industry.

By the 1920s, pollution from the petroleum industry concerned the federal government. The Texas Gulf Coast had such a proliferation of possible polluted sites that investigators focused a study on the region. The investigation found that one of the largest causes of oil pollution came from oil tankers. Empty tankers carried water in their ballasts to make their vessels more stable on the ocean. However, once they got near refining regions, they had to clear their ballasts of water to make room for oil. In the process, they dumped any leftover oil into the water with their bilge, and as a result, oil saturated ports and beaches of the South's oil-producing regions. These pollution problems in part helped Congress pass the Oil Pollution Act of 1924. Part of this act forbade tankers from discharging their ballasts within a certain number of miles from shore. However, the law was difficult to enforce, and ships did not have any good technology to separate water from oil. Even as late

as 1971, oil pollution from tanker ballasts contributed 22 percent of the total spilled in U.S. waters. Spent lubricants were the only source higher at 45 percent.

Pipelines represented another source of oil pollution that continues to affect the southern United States. Crude pipelines carried a tremendous amount of oil at various pressures, and almost all leaked at some point. Leaking oil from pipelines saturated the ground, flowed into waterways, and seeped into aquifers. This is not to say that the industry wanted to waste oil. Pipelines became corroded despite operators' best efforts to prevent leaks. Oil companies attempted to stop most leaks in pipelines because losing oil was uneconomical, but at a certain point the technology to monitor pipelines and halt corrosion became cost prohibitive. The costs and benefits of controlling pollution always pervaded the thoughts of oil companies. It became a question of economic efficiency versus engineering efficiency.

Pollution from offshore oil production in the Gulf of Mexico became a real danger to the Gulf Coast states, particularly Texas and Louisiana. The early wells in shallow Galveston Bay in the late 1930s resulted in protests from various groups, including regulators for the state of Texas, over possible pollution. Some of their fears proved justified as major accidents that occurred in the 1940s caused environmental damage. The industry attempted to limit the dangers of offshore pollution, but accidents still happened, including a major blowout off the coast of Louisiana in 1957. The most telling disaster in the history of the Gulf of Mexico, although not directly on the southern U.S. coast, occurred at the IXTOC platform near Mexico in July 1979. The blowout spilled 35 million barrels before operators gained control of the well. Like the Santa Barbara blowout of the 1960s off California, the IXTOC catastrophe dramatized the potential danger of an environmental disaster on the southern United States.

A growing concern attributed to the petroleum industry is waste from refining and the manufacture of petrochemicals. Texas refined 80 percent of the U.S. gasoline by the 1940s and produced 40 percent of the nation's supply of chemicals by the 1970s. The refining process contributed to pollution through various vapors, acid sludge, oily water, pipeline leaks, caustics, and other chemicals. Each of these pollutants posed a threat to the environment. In the 1920s, refineries could daily generate up to 30 tons of acid sludge waste per day that operators generally dumped or buried onsite. Refineries contributed to air pollution through venting, burning, and the general loss of hydrocarbon vapors. The air pollution represented a danger to the personal health of workers and the communities throughout the southern refining region. The chemical corridor in Louisiana along the Mississippi River represented one of the most polluted regions in the country because of a dramatic expansion of chemical manufacturers through the 1970s. The entire environment, including the river, represented a danger to human health.

Many consider pollution from the oil industry as the price of progress. However, petroleum engineers traditionally have viewed pollution in any form from their facilities as inefficient. Often oil producers sought on their own to control pollution because less waste meant more product could go to market. In the early years, contamination was so rampant because the price of oil was too low to justify spending money on pollution control. As refining and production became more sophisticated, operators began to find markets for some by-products. However, large amounts of petroleum wastes have had an impact on the environment in the South despite operators' best intentions.

The federal government finally began to implement pollution control laws in the 1970s. Prior to this, petroleum companies attempted to regulate themselves because they feared environmental legislation would force them to operate on the government's terms. In the 1970s the petrochemical-friendly state of Texas even began to fine refineries for pollution. In reality, the fines did not draw the attention of the oil companies. Instead, the bad publicity surrounding the "polluter" label was often enough to make the industry correct its excesses.

Oil pollution is a complex issue because there are many concerns associated with the petroleum industry. One of the primary employers in the South is the oil business, and attacks on the industry, however justified, affect many jobs. The other reality is that as long as hydrocarbons are used to power the country, pollution will be a reality in some form.

JOSEPH STROMBERG
*University of Houston*

Hugh S. Gorman, *Redefining Efficiency: Pollution Concerns, Regulatory Mechanisms, and Technological Change in the U.S. Petroleum Industry* (2001); Gerald Markowitz and David Rosner, *Deceit and Denial: The Deadly Politics of Industrial Pollution* (2002); Martin V. Melosi, *Coping with Abundance: Energy and Environment in Industrial America* (1985); Diana Davids Olien and Roger M. Olien, *Oil in Texas: The Gusher Age, 1895–1945* (2002); Joseph A. Pratt, *The Growth of a Refining Region* (1980).

## Okefenokee Swamp

The Okefenokee Swamp, located mostly in extreme southeastern Georgia with a small part in northeastern Florida, is comprised of 438,000 acres. It is not really a swamp in the classic sense of a stagnant mire because it gives rise to the St. Marys River, which flows to the Atlantic Ocean, and the Suwannee River, which meanders to the Gulf of Mexico. In scientific terms, it is more like a swamp-marsh complex.

"Okefenokee" is said to mean "land of the trembling earth." The swamp was once part of an ancient ocean floor, and thick deposits of peat 15 feet deep throughout the swamp make some areas unstable when walked on. These peat deposits also help maintain the Okefenokee because they provide excellent fuel for wildfire, which is an integral part of the Okefenokee ecosystem.

This vast mosaic of open water, islands, and forested wetlands provides a wonderfully diverse habitat for animals, birds, reptiles, amphibians, fishes, and hundreds of plants and insects. This natural mosaic ranges from the obligatory American alligators and black bears to endangered sandhill cranes and red-cockaded woodpeckers to water-diving birds like anhingas, and from majestic cypresses draped with Spanish moss to marshy areas called "prairies" to floating islands called "houses" to sandy islands with pines and palms.

Human influence has been documented as far back as 2000 B.C. Several pre-Columbian cultures existed at one time or another in the swamp. Yet by the mid-1700s, the area was largely uninhabited and remained only sparsely settled well into the 20th century. Local residents were known as "swampers," and they lived in such isolation that speech was said to be more Elizabethan than modern English in the 1900s. They developed their own culture well adapted to living in the Okefenokee. Some remaining cultural traditions of these swampers are storytelling, shape-note singing, and hollering.

The outside world took note of the swamp from time to time with schemes to drain the area or dredge canals through it to connect the Atlantic with the Gulf. The Okefenokee has been a locale for several B movies and is the home of the famous cartoon character Pogo.

Most of the Okefenokee became federal property through the conservation efforts of the Hebard Lumber Company, which logged cypress there from 1909 to 1929. In 1937 some 396,000 acres were set aside as the Okefenokee National Wildlife Refuge. Additional protection was afforded the swamp in 1974 through the designation of most of the refuge as a National Wilderness Area. Private ownership conservation of the Okefenokee is coordinated by the Greater Okefenokee Landowners Association.

ROBERT L. IZLAR
*Warnell School of Forest Resources
University of Georgia*

A. D. Cohen, D. J. Casagrande, M. J. Andrejko, and G. R. Best, eds., *The Okefenokee Swamp: Its Natural History, Geology, and Geochemistry* (1984); Richard Conniff, *National Geographic* (April 1992); Francis Harper and Delma E. Presley, *Okefinokee Album* (1981); Robert L. Hurst, *This Magic Wilderness: Part I and Part II* (1982); Megan Kate Nelson, *Trembling Earth: A Cultural History of the Okefenokee Swamp* (2005); C. T. Trowell and R. L. Izlar, *Journal of Forest History* (October 1984).

## Opossum ("Possum")

More than 70 species can be found in the opossum family, which ranges from South America northward to Canada, but the Virginia opossum (*Didelphis virginiana*) once resided only in the Southeast and is still identified closely with the region's culture. It is the only marsupial (a mammal that carries its newborn young in an abdominal pouch for weeks) found north of Mexico and the largest of the opossum family. It weighs from 4 to 15 pounds and is from 25 to 40 inches long. Captain John Smith, leader of the early Virginia settlement, described the female opossum in 1608: "An opossum hath a head like a Swine, and a taile like a Rat, and is of the bigness of a Cat. Under her belly she hath a bagge wherein she lodgeth, carrieth, and sucketh her young."

In the South opossums are brown and black. The head, face, and throat are whitish, and the dark ears have pinkish tips. They have short legs, an opposable thumblike toe on their back feet, and sharp claws on their forelegs. The opossum's tail is long (9 to 13 inches) and unadorned. Good tree climbers and mostly active at night, opossums are omnivorous, consuming insects, frogs, birds, eggs, snakes, earthworms, and small animals; they also eat grains, seeds, and fruits such as apples and persimmons. They are scavengers, eating anything and everything, including carrion. They live mostly in wooded areas but are frequently seen in suburbs and have even been found in urban areas. Garbage dumps attract them, and farmers have charged them with invading chicken yards. Many are killed by automobiles, as the small creatures are attracted to other animals dead on the side of the road. When threatened, an opossum will roll over and play dead. It gives a convincing performance, as it goes semirigid, mouth open and drooling, tongue extended, and eyes open but glazed. Scientists have discovered that this is an actual catatonic state brought on by fear. The phrase "playing possum" has come, nonetheless, to mean feigning sleep or death.

The opossum is generally not considered the most intelligent of animals (25 small white beans would fit in the brain cavity of an adult male opossum's skull; 150 would be needed for the brain cavity of a raccoon of the same size). Its life expectancy is short, but it has shown what can be described as a Faulknerian sense of endurance, surviving since the age of dinosaurs. It has evolved numerous survival mechanisms. Feigning death is a device against

*Oppossom, Male & Female,*
*with their Young.*

Opossum, male and female, with their young (uncredited engraving in A. B. Strong, ed. and comp., *Illustrated Natural History of the Three Kingdoms* [1849])

danger. It spends most of its time lolling about in isolated, lazy seclusion in trees or in underground burrows, avoiding occasions for direct conflict with predators. It has a well-developed sense of smell that is useful for foraging, and its 50 small teeth—more than any other mammal in North America—provide protection. It is extremely fertile, with females in the South bringing forth two to three litters of 8 to 18 young ones in a year, with around 7 normally surviving the early phase of life in the pouch. The opossum has changed little since prehistoric times and now thrives in spite of evolving conditions.

The opossum has long figured prominently in human culture in the South. Stories of this critter's activities were told by Native Americans and blacks. The Choctaws' "Why the Possum Grins" was one such tale, and a Cherokee legend explains that the opossum's tail is naked because he burned it in a fire while trying to make his white tail black. A southern black version of this story has a ghost skinning all the hair off his tail when Possum, along with Fox and Rabbit, tried to steal corn from a graveyard. The Mississippi Delta has a story of the opossum that was killed and put in to cook, but he ate all the sweet potatoes and gravy in the roasting pan and jumped out and escaped when the oven door was opened. Pottery effigies of the opossum from as far back as prehistoric times have been found in south Georgia burial sites, and poor southern blacks and whites have hunted the opossum for its fur and flesh. Roy Blount Jr., after tasting the animal, wrote that "possum was sort of like dark

meat of chicken, only stronger-tasting and looser on the bone, and stringy, like pork." It has also been described as somewhat greasy.

The opossum has been a prominent contemporary southerner. The Pogo comic strip featured the animal. Wausau, Fla., annually holds a Possum Festival in August, and a possum cult appeared in the South in the 1970s. The Possum Growers and Breeders Association of America, Incorporated, sponsored a national meeting in 1971 in Clanton, Ala., and from that beginning the group expanded to include 40,000 members who receive bumper stickers saying "Eat More Possum." The group sponsored an annual gathering, including a Miss Possum pageant for female humans and an opossum judging contest, awarding the most worthy candidate of the latter the designation of "Beauregard." Frank Basil Clark, who managed the Clanton Drive-In Theatre and lived in a mobile home he called the Big C Possum Ranch, was the guiding spirit behind the movement, and at one point he had plans to breed "superpossums" of giant size to provide protein for the world's hungry. Roy Blount Jr. wrote an article on possums for *Sports Illustrated* (1 March 1976) and then featured the possum cult prominently in his *Crackers* (1980). *Possum Opossum* was an award-winning film by Greg Killmaster chronicling, with tongue firmly in cheek, the possum cult's activities. The Opossum Society of the United States and the National Opossum Society work to educate Americans on the appeal of this gentle creature.

Simon is a continuing possum character in Virginia writer Rita Mae Brown's
Mrs. Murphy mystery series.

CHARLES REAGAN WILSON
*University of Mississippi*

Carl G. Hartman, *Possums* (1952); Wayne
King, *New York Times* (16 March 1975);
Stanley Klein, *Encyclopedia of North Ameri-
can Wildlife* (1983).

## Outer Banks

The Outer Banks are low, extremely
narrow islands running from near Nor-
folk, Va., south for 175 miles to Cape
Hatteras, N.C., and ending near Cape
Lookout. They are separated from the
mainland by the shallow Pamlico and
Albemarle sounds. In 1524 Giovanni da
Verrazano landed on the Outer Banks
and thought he was off the coast of
China. The real history of the islands
began, though, in 1584 when Sir Walter
Raleigh chose Roanoke Island, which
was between the Outer Banks and the
North Carolina coast, as the site for the
first attempted English colony in North
America. A fort was built but the colony
remained unstable, and its inhabitants
had mysteriously disappeared by the
time a supply ship arrived in 1590. The
"Lost Colony" is the subject of Paul
Green's outdoor dramatic presentation,
which has been seen by more than
3 million people and is staged each
summer in Manteo, N.C., and the Fort
Raleigh National Historic Site now includes a reconstruction of the early fort.

Captain Edward Teach—the infamous Blackbeard—was the most
famous of a number of pirates who
used the sounds and bays behind the
Outer Banks as a hiding place in the

1700s. Most of the island inhabitants
have been less exotic, though, mainly
farmers, stockmen, fishermen, boat-
men, marines, and pilots. Because of
the relatively consistent winds in the
area, Orville and Wilbur Wright picked
a 100-foot-high hill near Kitty Hawk,
N.C., as the locale for their first successful airplane flight in 1905. The Wright
Brothers National Memorial was set up
in 1927 and has become a center for a
growing tourist industry on the islands.
The Cape Hatteras National Seashore
Recreation Area, established in 1937 as a
public beach and campsite, provides access to the natural wonders of the Outer
Banks.

The Outer Banks are an environmental treasure. Beach grass and sedges
grow there, but sea oats are the most
typical grass, growing in clumps and
serving as an effective sand binder.
Wax myrtle and yaupons (or Sea Island
holly) are widespread, and one can
find American holly, laurel oaks, and
loblolly pines in the woods. Live oaks
have been especially important to these
islands. Near the shore of a sound, the
wind makes them small and twisted,
but several hundred yards away, they
grow straight and tall and are hung with
Spanish moss.

The Sea Island National Wildlife
Refuge has almost 6,000 acres of beach,
dunes, and marshes. Nearly 26,000
acres in the waters of Pamlico Sound are
off-limits to hunters. Estimates are that
265 species of birds visit or live at the
refuge. One sees gulls and sandpipers,
but migratory waterfowl are the most
frequently sighted birds, with snow and
Canadian geese common in the late fall.

Brown pelicans can be seen in the summer, and peregrine falcons and other species live there year-round.

At Cape Hatteras the cold waters from the north meet the warm currents from the Gulf Stream, making for turbulent navigation. The cape contains four lighthouses, including the tallest lighthouse in the United States—a 208-foot-high, black-and-white monument. The area's changing currents and dense fogs have resulted in more than 500 ships foundering near the cape, earning it the reputation of the "Graveyard of the Atlantic." The first lighthouse there was built in 1803, and the present landmark dates from 1870.

CHARLES REAGAN WILSON
*University of Mississippi*

Karen Bachman, *Insiders' Guide to North Carolina's Outer Banks* (2006); Rodney Barfield, *Seasoned by Salt: A Historical Album of the Outer Banks* (1995); Anthony Barley, *The Outer Banks* (1999); Dirk Frankenberg, *The Nature of the Outer Banks: Environmental Processes, Field Sites, and Development Issues* (1995); Charlton Ogburn, *The Winter Beach* (1971); David Stick, *An Outer Banks Reader* (1998); Walt Wolfram and Ben Ward, *American Voices: How Dialects Differ from Coast to Coast* (2006).

## Ozarks

The Ozarks are a mid-American upland region noted for its physical beauty and often associated with stereotypical images of hillbillies and poverty-induced backwardness, on one hand, and rugged, frontierlike individualism, on the other.

Spanning an area of about 40,000 square miles (roughly the size of Ohio),
the Ozarks cover most of the southern half of Missouri and northwestern and north-central Arkansas, as well as much smaller portions of northeastern Oklahoma and southeastern Kansas. Geographers divide the region into four major subdivisions—the Boston Mountains, the St. Francois Mountains, the Springfield Plain, and the Salem Plateau—along with a number of smaller subdivisions. Rivers mark the boundaries of the Ozarks on three sides: the Missouri on the north, the Mississippi and the Black on the east, and the Arkansas on the south. On its western edge the Ozark region tends to fade imperceptibly into the Great Plains. In spite of the frequent references to mountains in the Ozarks, the region is not technically mountainous but, rather, a severely eroded plateau. The highest elevations, found in the Boston Mountains of northwestern Arkansas, exceed 2,500 feet above sea level.

Physically, the Ozarks are noted for an abundance of water resources and karst features and for steep and rugged terrain, although large swaths of the region contain rolling hills of minimal relief. The region bears striking geologic and geomorphic similarities to Appalachia and the Cumberland Plateau. These similarities, combined with the commonalities of the upland South folk cultures found in each region, have led some scholars to describe the Ozarks as a smaller version of Appalachia.

The Ozark region has long been characterized as a rural area peopled by isolated inhabitants. Although this is a relatively modern characterization, archaeologists have unearthed evidence that suggests a tradition of Ozark isolation and sparse population, a tradition with ancient roots that owes much to the region's geography. It appears that the prehistoric residents of the area participated only in a peripheral manner in the developments of the Mississippi Valley. By the time of European settlement along the Mississippi in the 17th century, the Ozarks were the realm of the Osage, though the Ozark fringes provided homes and territories to other tribes such as the Illinois, Caddo, and Quapaw.

The earliest white settlements in the Ozarks date from the early 18th century, when French and French Canadian settlers established Ste. Genevieve and other outposts along the northeastern fringe. These French settlements would exercise little long-term effect on Ozark history, however, as the region was overrun by American settlers who began arriving in the 1790s and flooded the area after the War of 1812. The vast majority of these settlers came to the Ozarks from the Upper South states of Tennessee, Kentucky, North Carolina, and Virginia and in the process transported the society and culture of the upland South, and largely Appalachia, to this trans-Mississippi highland. Although slavery existed in the region, the Ozarks' isolation and ruggedness prevented the development of plantation-style agriculture. One result was a much smaller slave population than in most areas of the South, which, combined with sporadic race-related violence and subsequent black flight around the turn of the 20th century, translated into a modern Ozark region that is home to very few blacks. Because the Ozarks straddle the Arkansas-Missouri border, the region was particularly and tragically affected by the bushwhacker-jayhawker conflicts caused by divided loyalties during the Civil War era.

In the late 19th and early 20th centuries, railroads and timber companies penetrated the Ozark interior, providing new market opportunities for farmers but stripping the region of its grand virgin forests of pine and hardwoods. Mining for lead, iron, zinc, manganese, and other minerals also became a profitable concern in some Ozark areas. Nevertheless, the vast majority of Ozarkers continued to scratch out livings on hillside and creek bottom farms, where general, semisubsistence activities such as dairying, livestock raising, and corn growing were supplemented by cotton raising, fruit raising, or truck farming. By the middle of the 20th century, poultry farming and livestock raising had become the most common agricultural activities in the region.

The Ozark region—or at least most of it—has undergone tremendous changes in the past half-century. Outmigration sparked by agricultural transformation and poverty took tens of thousands of Ozarkers out of the area in the quarter-century beginning with World War II, and beginning in the 1960s tens of thousands of retirees, back-to-the-landers, and more recently Hispanic workers rushed into the hills to replace them. And in many Ozark areas, tourism has replaced farming, timbering, or low-wage manufacturing as the economic linchpin. Nevertheless, in many ways the image of the Ozarks remains unchanged: a backward, or bucolic, land of innocent hillbillies, or rustic frontier people. And, in fact, the Ozark region continues to rank as one of the nation's most rural places. Beyond the metropolitan areas (at least by U.S. Census Bureau standards) of the Fayetteville-Springdale-Bentonville area in northwestern Arkansas and Springfield, Mo., the region's largest city, the Ozarks remain the domain of the small town and rural community. Environmental advantages, both physical and social, largely drive the Ozark tourism industry and fuel the modern fascination with the region.

BROOKS BLEVINS
*Lyon College*

Brooks Blevins, *Hill Folks: A History of Arkansas Ozarkers and Their Image* (2002); W. K. McNeil, *Ozark Country* (1995); Milton D. Rafferty, *The Ozarks: Land and Life* (2001); Vance Randolph, *The Ozarks: An American Survival of Primitive Society* (1931); Carol O. Sauer, *The Geography of the Ozark Highland of Missouri* (1971).

## Padre Island National Seashore

Padre Island is a natural barrier island, 113 miles in length, located off the Gulf Coast of Texas between Port Aransas at Corpus Christi and Port Isabel outside Brownsville. It is the longest undeveloped barrier island in the world. Five islands lie outside the Laguna Madre, a shallow, saline body of water buffering the coast. North to south, these include Galveston Island, Matagorda Peninsula, Matagorda Island, St. Joseph Island, Mustang Island, and Padre Island. The Laguna Madre is the only saltwater rookery in the continental United States

and is the breeding ground for the white pelican.

The island dunes, often rising to great heights, support a fragile ecosystem of native vegetation including sea oats, beach croton, beach morning glory, sea purslane, beach evening primrose, ragweed, seaside purge, partridge pea, and grasses. It is also home to a variety of palms, salt cedars, athols, mesquite, ebonies, royal poncianas, papayas, oleanders, natal plums, bougainvillas, and lantanas. Shell banks extending 20 miles down the island are found nowhere else along the Texas coast.

This rugged landscape was formed roughly 3,000 years ago, and humans have inhabited the island for nearly the same length of time. Bands of native Karankawas and Coahuiltecans were followed by explorers from around the globe, many of whom left behind legends and artifacts that to this day pique treasure hunters. The missing ship of Hernan Cortez's famous fleet, John Singer's $80,000 lost beneath the island sands, and the detritus of shipwrecks and unchartered crossings that litter the beaches add to the legendary mystique that attracts so many tourists.

During the early 1800s the Spanish crown was anxious to occupy all the lands still vacant along the Rio Grande. In approximately 1829 two new coastal grants were made. What is now Padre Island was granted to Padre Nicolas Balli and his nephew, Juan Jose Balli II. The Treaty of Guadalupe Hidalgo was signed by Mexico and the United States in 1848. Among other lands, the United States acquired a large part of Padre

Island. Railroads and the automobile helped build enthusiasm for the South's tropical coast. Development and recreational schemes similar to those along other national seaboards created further interest.

In 1927 the Don Patricio Causeway was built along the Laguna Madre by Colonel Sam Robertson. It was little more than two troughs set apart to accommodate a Model T. In 1936 the Padre Island Park Association was formed in commemoration of the Texas centennial. A bill was introduced by W. E. Pope of Corpus Christi to the Texas legislature to acquire Padre Island for a state park. In 1950 a causeway was constructed from Corpus Christi to the north end of the Island. Further plans were developed by Cameron officials for the southern corner including three parks. The first park opened in 1954.

National interest in preserving the nation's wilderness areas and expanding the park system helped bolster congressional action in 1958 for a national park on Padre Island. In 1934 the National Park Service initiated a study of 20 areas along the Atlantic, Gulf, Pacific, and Great Lakes shorelines for preservation. Concern for the nation's coastlands resurfaced during the post–World War II period as overwhelming numbers of tourists crowded the nation's parks and seashores. In 1955 the U.S. Park Service published *The Vanishing Shoreline*, documenting the loss of untrammeled shorelines because of real estate and commercial development. That year the Department of the Interior rated Padre Island a top priority for public acquisition. In 1958 Texas senator Ralph W.

Yarborough drafted a bill to establish a national park on Padre Island. At that time Texas had only one national park, Big Bend, in west Texas. The bill recommended converting three seashore areas, Cape Cod, Padre Island, and the Oregon Dunes, into national parks. It languished as state officials struggled with contentious mineral rights and development issues. On 13 September 1962 the John F. Kennedy administration supported bill S 4, setting aside 80 miles of the island for the national parks. This legislation was the first in a series of congressional actions that set the stage for the remarkable environmental and wilderness record of the Kennedy and Lyndon B. Johnson administrations. Senator Yarborough's efforts in natural resource protection included oversight of the Guadalupe Mountains National Park legislation, the Golden Eagle Protection law, the 1966 and 1969 Endangered Species Acts, and the Water Quality Improvement Act.

Bird Island Basin is one of many tourist attractions. Padre Island is located on a central flyway between North and South America, making it a landmark in seasonal migrations from Canada to Mexico, the Caribbean, and South America. It is protected by the American Bird Conservancy, which has identified 326 species. Padre Island is also the sight of a binational project to return Kemp's ridley turtle to the Texas coast. The project was begun in 1978; in 2005 the Gulf Office of the Sea Turtle Restoration Project reported that 51 nests were found along the Texas coast, including Galveston, Matagorda Peninsula, Matagorda Island, Mustang Island,

North Padre Island, Padre Island National Seashore, and Boca Chica Beach.

VICTORIA M. GARCIA
*Houston, Texas*

J. L. Baughman, *Houston Chronicle* (16 October 1955); "Congress Due to Expand National Park System," *Congressional Quarterly, Inc.* (16 June 1961); Patrick Cox, *Ralph W. Yarborough: The People's Senator* (2001); "Major Expansion of National Park System in 1961–62," *Congressional Quarterly, Inc.* (14 December 1962); "Padre Island National Seashore," *Congressional Quarterly, Inc.* (21 September 1962); Bob St. John, *South Padre: The Island and Its People* (1991); Florence Johnson Scott, *Historical Heritage of the Lower Rio Grande* (1965); Vernon Smylie, *Vernon Smylie's Lands of Tomorrow, Report No. 1: Padre Island Texas* (1960); Steve Ueckert, *Houston Chronicle Texas Magazine* (1 November 1981).

## Palm Trees

"Florida is the land of Palms," wrote horticulturist Henry Nehrling. "Avenues of Palms in our cities! Forests of Palms beside our streams and lakes! Thickets of Palms in our woods! Groves of Coconut Palms on the East Coast! Majestic Royal Palms in the south Everglades!" His enthusiasm was unbounded but appropriate because the palm has been one of the preeminent cultural-environmental symbols of the semi-tropical South, from the promotional advertising of Henry Flagler luring tourists south to the contemporary lyrics of Jimmy Buffet songs and the visual images of television's *Miami Vice*.

The main physical feature of the palm is the cylindrical trunk, which supports a leaf-crown. Its drooping leaves can be 100 feet off the ground.

The leaves are either plumelike (pinnate) or fan shaped (palmate). The South's native palmettos belong to the second group, whereas the royal, coconut, and date palms have plumelike leaves. About 14 species of palms are native to Florida, and 2 or 3 can be found as far north as North Carolina. The palmetto is the official tree of South Carolina, where it is used to make distinctive Sea Islands baskets. Many imported tropical palms do well in south Florida, and subtropical varieties thrive along the beaches of the Gulf Coast down into the south Texas valley.

The cabbage palmetto (*Sabal palmetto*) is the most common palm in Florida and the one that grows most frequently in other areas of the South. It is often found with hundreds of plants growing close together. The early settlers named this tree the cabbage palmetto because of its heart, which they consumed like cabbage.

The coconut palm and the royal palm are conspicuously displayed, popular palms in Florida. One horticulturist called them "the exclamation points in the poetry of tropical landscape." The royal palm grows straight as a column, while the coconut will bend gracefully. The coconut palm grows in nearly all tropical coast regions of the world but is never found growing naturally inland. The winter resort of Palm Beach gained its name from the stands of coconut trees growing there. When settlement in south Florida increased in the early 20th century, people planted inexpensive coconut palms in droves, further reinforcing the area's association with the plant. The royal palms look majestic in their hammocks, which are seen to best effect in the southern Everglades. Of the five species of its genus, one—the *Oreodoxa regia*—is native to south Florida. It is confined naturally to Biscayne Bay, the Keys, and several hammocks of south Florida. Royal Palm State Park (formerly Paradise Key) is in Dade County, with many trees there at least 100 feet tall.

Date palms also thrive in Florida, south Texas, and along the Gulf Coast. The genus *Phoenix* is Asian and African in origin. The date palms have pinnate leaves, which may be either soft and glossy or, in other species, hard. Many of these were introduced into the Southwest in the early 20th century. Other of the many palms found in Florida include the blue palmetto (*Rhapidophyllum hystrix*), the bamboo palm (*Rhapis flabelliformis*), and the silver palm (*Thrinax floridana*).

CHARLES REAGAN WILSON
*University of Mississippi*

Wilber H. Duncan and Marion B. Duncan, *Trees of the Southeastern United States* (1988); Henry Nehrling, in *The Plant World in Florida*, ed. Alfred and Elizabeth Kay (1933); Robert Lee Riffle and Paul Craft, *An Encyclopedia of Cultivated Palms* (2003).

## Persimmon

*Raccoon up the 'simmon tree,*
*Possum on the ground.*
*Raccoon shake them 'simmons down,*
*Possums pass 'em round.*
—*African American poem (c. 1870),*
*author unknown*

Common persimmon (*Diospyros virginiana*) is one of the most unique trees found in the southern forest. Compared with its peers, it exerts no real dominion such as great size, rapid growth rate, or even form. Instead, the common persimmon finds its niche in southern culture and history through exaggerated features that made it indispensable to those who happened to live within its natural range.

This member of the ebony family is also called simmon or possumwood and commonly grows in both hardwood and pine forests throughout the South, usually under the canopy of taller trees on moist, well-drained, sandy soils. With black, squared-cut bark that is almost alligator plated, the common persimmon is one of the easiest trees in the forest to recognize.

Persimmon fruit is by far the tree's better-known attribute. Actually a berry, the mature, blackish-purple, juicy pulp is a very popular food with wildlife such as raccoons, opossums, skunks, and whitetail deer. Savvy hunters learned early that, during the fall and winter season, where there were persimmons, there would usually be game.

Evidence also points to its value among early Native Americans. They are said to have used persimmon fruit to concoct a thin gruel, cornbread, and pudding; they even combined it with honey locust pods to brew an alcoholic drink. Native Americans are also credited with introducing persimmons as a delectable food to early explorers and settlers. In 1557 Hernando de Soto tasted this "delicious little plum" and witnessed Native Americans eating bread made from dried persimmon fruit.

First-time consumers of a green persimmon berry, though, quickly learned of its astringent taste, owing to the presence of tannin. The resulting "wrongsideoutards" puckered mouth ensured that mistake was never repeated. At Jamestown, early settlers described the ripe persimmon berry as "very sweet and pleasant to the taste." But Captain John Smith gave a more complete description when he said, "If not ripe it will drawe a mans mouth awrie with much torment; but when ripe, it is as delicious as Apricock."

Through necessity, both Native Americans and the original settlers used their ingenuity to discover and create other uses for the common persimmon. Various recipes included using persimmons to make syrup, vinegar, brandy, pudding, pie, cake, salads, and jellies. During the Civil War and into Reconstruction, southerners would resort to boiling persimmon seeds as a coffee substitute. Medicinal values were also important as the inner bark and unripe fruit were used to treat fevers, mouth sores, diarrhea, and hemorrhages.

During the 20th century the common persimmon's value as a commercial tree began to take off. In 1896 the Scots discovered that persimmon wood was a superior material in making golf club heads. Because of its small, light, yet durable wood, persimmon wood reigned supreme in this capacity until the advent of metal club heads. This same wood quality also made it an important material for shuttle blocks, bobbins, plane stocks, shoe lasts, billiard cues, flooring, and veneer. These and other commercial values brought top dollar to farmers and landowners fortunate to own good quality persimmon trees.

W. NEIL LETSON
*Montgomery, Alabama*

G. H. Collingwood and Warren D. Brush, *Knowing Your Trees* (1984); U.S. Department of Agriculture, *Silvics of North America*, vol. 2, *Hardwoods* (1990); Harlan H. York, *100 Forest Trees of Alabama* (1996).

## Red River Expedition

When the Louisiana Territory was acquired by the United States in 1803, no true scientific surveys had been done in the West, and many geographical details were unclear. Thus President Thomas Jefferson conceived of and put into the field two major exploring expeditions to examine the territory. That of Meriwether Lewis and William Clark into the northern territory was the most successful and is the best known. The second, intended to survey similarly the geography and natural history of the southern regions of the territory, only partially accomplished that task, because of Spanish opposition. On the expedition, however, was a young University of Pennsylvania naturalist named Peter Custis, the first American naturalist in the West. His reports are a principal source in determining the "virgin" conditions of the Red River Valley and parts of Louisiana, Arkansas, and Texas.

The plan for the exploration, formulated by Jefferson early in 1804, called for an ascent of the Red River "to the tops of the mountains" and a descent of the Arkansas. Although the plan was at last attempted in 1806, the 50-man expedition was terminated by a Spanish army after four months, at a location 615 miles above the mouth of the Red River. The early termination (near today's Oklahoma border) prevented expedition leader/geographer Thomas Freeman from making many new geographical discoveries. His field courses were drawn into a definitive map of the lower Red River Valley by Nicholas King and appeared on Anthony Nau's 1807 map of the West based on American exploration. The map represents outstanding topographical features, game and trading paths, and Indian villages and sacred places.

The work done by naturalist Custis was of greater significance. He was the last-minute choice in a search that featured an offer of the position to the world-famous William Bartram and included applications by C. S. Rafinesque and Alexander Wilson. Custis's training under Benjamin Smith Barton was sound; but he was inexperienced, and his small reference library was inadequate. He closely followed the directions of Jefferson and expedition supervisor William Dunbar. The result was a wide-ranging survey: he collected minerals and botanical specimens, kept a meteorological chart, and compiled natural history data on 80 birds and animals and nearly 190 plants. He offered eight new scientific names, three of which are currently recognized.

Jefferson's southern exploration failed in its larger objectives, but the data accumulated was important to environmental study. The explorers portrayed an organic environment in a state of change, a valley that European plants were already invading and whose waters were yearly modified by the growth of the immense logjam called the Great Raft. The prairies they saw and the relative absence of undergrowth in the towering virgin forest were, they believed, the result of Indian-set fires. Above all, they were most impressed with the beauty and richness of the river valley wilderness: "The Valley of the Red River is one of the richest and most beautiful imaginable," Freeman wrote in his journal, and Custis added that "were the Rafts removed . . . this country would become the Paradise of America . . . in point of beauty, fertility, and salubrity there is not its equal in America, nay in the world."

DANIEL L. FLORES
*Texas Tech University*

Daniel L. Flores, ed., *The Freeman and Custis Account of the Red River: The Chronicle of Jefferson's Southwestern Exploration* (1983); Donald Jackson, *Thomas Jefferson and the Stony Mountains: Exploring the West from Monticello* (1981); Conrad Morton, *Journal of the Arnold Arboretum* (1967).

## Rio Grande

The Rio Grande runs the course of the Mexican-American border from the state of Colorado down through New Mexico and across Texas to the Gulf of Mexico. It is part of an epic as varied as the people who settled its legendary lands and waters. Flowing through every type of ecosystem in North America, the mighty river shares a place in the history of the desert Southwest with two others, the Western Colorado and the Tijuana. These rivers are bound by a complicated legal and political framework established on the settlement agreements of Spain, Mexico, the southwestern border states, and the U.S. government. These relationships include the cultural history of the indigenous peoples that populated these areas.

The Rio Grande marks a westernmost boundary for most definitions of the American South and creates a unique environmental context in comparison with other parts of the South.

These three river basins include more than 430,000 square miles of rich, irrigable land. Almost 1,900 miles in length, the Rio Grande is the second-longest river in the United States. The Rio Grande and Colorado rivers played prominent roles in the voracious battle for water following the rapid expansion and settlement of the southwestern desert. The construction of Hoover Dam and the All American Canal irrevocably altered human relationships to the land. Periodic droughts, floods, and irregular rainfall aggravated international claims to the waters desperately needed for crops, herds, transportation, and industry. Mexican, Indian, and American interests vigorously competed for the Rio Grande, often trumping its waters in similar negotiations for equitable distribution of the Colorado River.

The Rio Grande is typically referred to by upper, middle, and lower regions, each with a remarkable history and topography. The Upper Rio Grande Basin extends from its home in the Colorado Mountains down to Fort

Quitman in Texas. In the early days of settlement, the rocky lands of the Upper Rio Grande were marginal for human habitation. Early Spanish settlers at the close of the 16th century combined Islamic customs with those of the Pueblo Indians in the region to create an irrigation pattern of acequias. This water system helped support a vast forest of cottonwoods, alders, willows, and grasses. These forests in turn became havens for elk, deer, antelope, and other wildlife. A sustainable agropastoral culture was created by the mestizo community well-suited for the environment.

Located midway between California's mediterranean shores and Florida's tropical gardens and groves, the rich, alluvial lower Rio Grande basin was often compared to the Nile River delta. It is approximately 800 miles in length, extending from El Paso in far west Texas to the Gulf of Mexico. After the Civil War the area prospered as shippers and goods passed through Port Isabel. The railroad, automobile, and enhanced agricultural technologies helped change people's perceptions of the valley. Inspired by the transformations occurring in California and Florida, early turn-of-the-century entrepreneurs and developers recognized the valley's midpoint market potential for fruits, citrus groves, winter crops, and natural resources. The valley's proximity to the Mexican border reinforced its recreational value. Postwar prosperity enhanced the public image of the valley, inspiring such monikers as the Magic Valley, the Golden Valley, and the Glamor Valley.

Mexico, the United States, and

Canada signed the North American Free Trade Agreement in 1993, combining economic and environmental objectives under the rubric of "sustainable development." Biodiversity is a critical factor in the mobilization for sustainable development. Since the 1920s nearly 95 percent of the valley's native habitat has been cleared for agricultural and urban development. On 2 October 1968 Congress approved Public Law 90-542, the Wild and Scenic Rivers Act, with Section 5(a)(20) designating segments of the Rio Grande in New Mexico and Texas for inclusion in the national system. In 1980 Congress designated lands extending from Falcon Dam to the Gulf of Mexico for inclusion in the Lower Rio Grande Valley National Wildlife Refuge. When complete, it will contain 107,500 acres encompassing 11 different biotic communities, giving sanctuary to 115 species of wildlife and some of the rarest species of birds, animals, and plants in North America. Located on the convergence of two major flyways, the Mississippi and Central flyways, the refuge receives hundreds of species of neotropical birds migrating across Canada and the United States to winter in Mexico and Central and South America. Efforts to create a Lower Rio Grande Valley Wildlife Corridor highlight the region's astounding diversity. Of 170 countries worldwide, only 12 are home to nearly 70 percent of the planet's biodiversity. It is estimated that nearly 10 percent of all living species can be found in Mexico.

VICTORIA M. GARCIA
*Houston, Texas*

Daniel Faber, ed., *The Struggle for Ecological Democracy: Environmental Movements in the United States* (1998); Lawrence A. Herzog, *Shared Space: Rethinking the U.S. Mexico Border Environment* (2000); Richard Gear Hobbs, *Glamor Valley: Down Texas on the Rio Grande* (1943); Norris Hundley Jr., *Dividing the Waters: A Century of Controversy between the United States and Mexico* (1966); Pat Kelley, *River of Lost Dreams: Navigation on the Rio Grande* (1986); Mike Leggett, *Rio Grande: The People and Politics of One of America's Greatest Rivers* (1994); Florence Johnson Scott, *Historical Heritage of the Lower Rio Grande* (1965).

## Sassafras

*In the spring of the year when the blood*
    *is thick, there is no so fine as a*
    *sassafras stick.*
—*Ozark ballad*

In the South, anyone who learns the woods learns the sassafras (*Sassafras albidum*) tree. It is easily identified by distinctive leaf shapes, fall foliage that is a flaming scarlet, orange, and yellow, and aromatic oils that when crushed smell like root beer right out of the bottle. Southerners also learn of the sassafras's aggressive tendency to invade disturbed areas or abandoned fields. Many southern farmers have stood in either total amazement or utter despair to see last year's effort to clean out a fencerow now covered with a fresh growth of sassafras sprouts.

Native Americans in what is now Florida first introduced sassafras to early Spanish explorers during the 1500s. The Spaniards found that these Native Americans used the plant for many purposes, including beverages, medicines, and flavoring. Other explorers and colonists were quick to pick up on this native plant, and before long sassafras would become one of the New World's first commercial exports. Sir Walter Raleigh took sassafras material to England from Virginia and caused such a consumer demand that it led to what is commonly called the "Great Sassafras Hunts of 1602 and 1603." During this time, great numbers of ships were sent to the colonies to bring back sassafras. Europeans believed this miracle plant could be converted to a tonic that when consumed would make a person youthful and healthier. This and a number of other uses helped establish the sassafras tree's place in the New World and the South.

Pioneers learned that the tree's properties made it an all-purpose plant. Because of the sassafras tree's natural decay resistance, the wood was popular for ship construction, fence posts, gates, chicken roosts, bedsteads, and railroad ties. Some in the South used sassafras oil to repel bedbugs, lice, and fleas.

Sassafras use in the South was influenced by ethnic and local cultures. Along the Gulf Coast, particularly near New Orleans, African slaves and Creoles used dried leaves from young branches, known as filé, to thicken and flavor their soups and sauces of vegetables, meat, and fish. In Virginia and several other southern states, some folk learned to ferment a beer using sassafras, water, and molasses or sugar. This drink was viewed as healthy and enjoyable during the summertime.

The popularity and usefulness of the sassafras would last well into the 20th century. But in 1960 the Food and Drug Administration made it official that the major chemical in sassafras oil (safrole) causes cancer in laboratory animals and banned its use as an additive. The FDA officially banned the sale of sassafras roots, oil, and tea in 1976. Only filé made from safrole-free leaves remains on the market. Today safrole-free root bark extract is used in perfumery, as a flavoring for candy and beverages, and to make an aromatic tea.

W. NEIL LETSON
*Montgomery, Alabama*

Thomas Nelson Page, *In Ole Virginia* (1895); Francis Peyre Porcher, *Resources of Southern Fields and Forests, Medical, Economical, and Agricultural* (1863); U.S. Department of Agriculture, *Silvics of North America*, vol. 2, *Hardwoods* (1990).

## Shenandoah Valley

Located in northern Virginia, the Shenandoah Valley is approximately 6,500 square miles in area, 180 miles long, and 10 to 24 miles wide. It is drained by the Shenandoah River, which has played an important role in the valley's development as a rich agricultural area.

The Shenandoah Valley was settled in the early 1700s by Germans, Dutch, Scotch-Irish, and English. The valley was an important route for the westward pioneer movement in the early 19th century. Its population at the time of the Civil War was predominantly white and rural.

The valley was the site of an extraordinary Civil War battle in 1862. The residents' loyalties were divided between the Union and the Confederacy, and the area was strategically important to both sides. In an effort to divert Union general George B. McClellan's attack on the Confederate capital of Richmond, Confederate General Thomas J. "Stonewall" Jackson launched the successful "valley campaign" against the Union armies designated to join McClellan's. With an inferior number of troops, Jackson brilliantly used his interior lines of communication, rapid movement of his infantry "foot cavalry," and tactics of strategic diversion to repel the Union forces.

Another successful defense of the valley came at the battle of New Market in 1864 under the command of General John C. Breckinridge. The battle, in which young cadets from the Virginia Military Institute fought, inspires one of the nation's largest Civil War reenactments at the site each May. The Union had its revenge for the losses, however, when General Philip Sheridan's army laid waste the region, wrecking railroad lines, burning factories, and destroying farms and supplies.

After Reconstruction the valley's economy was primarily agricultural, although many small manufacturing plants were established in the late 1800s. Resort spas and summer homes flourished after 1890, and the area became a popular tourist attraction. Today, the valley's rolling plains, stone farmhouses, quaint colonial inns, and small-town southern lifestyle intrigue visitors from throughout the nation. Each May the valley is the site of festivals and historic commemorations such as the Shenandoah Apple Blossom Festival in Winchester, Va. The Museum of American Frontier Culture in Staunton, Va., features 17th-, 18th-, and 19th-century farm buildings from England, northern Ireland, Germany, and Appalachia. An excellent museum dedicated to General of the Army, Secretary of State, Secretary of Defense, and Nobel Peace Prize Laureate George Catlett Marshall is in Lexington near Virginia Military Institute. Lexington is also home to Washington and Lee College.

The Shenandoah National Park, established in 1935, encompasses more than 195,000 acres with tree-covered mountains, trails, streams, waterfalls, and trout-filled pools. The Skyline Drive north-south highway extends for 105 miles through the park and offers an opportunity to view the scenic valley as well as the Blue Ridge Mountains, Massanutten Mountain, and the Allegheny Mountains.

Some Shenandoah Valley residents are concerned that the rural, small-town aspect of their region is disappearing. In 1985 the Adolph Coors Company constructed a $70-million packaging and distribution center and announced plans for a brewery in the area. The valley's underground limestone aquifers would have provided an excellent water source for the plant. Controversy surrounded the announcement of Coors's coming, and critics cited moral objections to alcoholic beverages and possible environmental problems. The brewery was not built. As early as the 1960s, concern over new developments spawned historic preservation societies in the area. These groups have been successful in restoring and improving more than 100 buildings and residences.

KAREN M. MCDEARMAN
*University of Mississippi*

ROBERT L. IZLAR
*Warnell School of Forest Resources*
*University of Georgia*

William Couper, *History of the Shenandoah Valley* (1952); Julie Davis, *The Shenandoah* (1945); Gary D. Ford, *Southern Living* (May 1986); Warren Hofstra, *The Planting of New Virginia: Settlement and Landscape in the Shenandoah Valley* (2004); James I. "Bud" Robertson, *Civil War Sites in Virginia: A Tour Guide* (1982); Scott Hamilton Suter, *Shenandoah Valley Folklife* (1999).

## Spanish Moss

Spanish moss is a soft, silver-gray, tropical herb (*Tillandsia usneoides*) with slender leaves and stems that grow on the branches of trees, often oak or other hardwoods, in the low woodlands and swamp forests of the southern Coastal Plain from Virginia to Texas. It is an epiphyte, using tree limbs for mechanical support but drawing its nutrients from the air. Epiphytes never injure the host plant as do parasites. The long pendant strands may reach a length of 10 to 20 feet and sway with the slightest movement of the humid coastal air.

It is not a true moss but a member of the pineapple family, *Bromeliaceae*. The small, solitary, yellowish-green flowers and the brown, cylindrical, three-parted seed capsules that mark these as true flowering plants and not a moss are seldom noticed. However, a number of other species of epiphytic bromeliads, such as the quill-leaf (*Tillandsia fasciculata*) of peninsular Florida, have very colorful flower spikes. Spanish moss was a major fiber plant of the American Indians and was used to make skirts for Indian women. The French in south Louisiana once used it as a decoration at Christmas, and early settlers in South Carolina mixed moss with mud to make a caulk for their cabin walls. Later it had limited commercial use as a packing and bedding material, with more than 10,000 tons of cured Spanish moss ginned, for example, in 1939. Its primary cultural role has been as a botanical trademark for the lowland South.

Journalist James Kilpatrick sees Spanish moss as a metaphor for the South, "an indigenous, an indestructible part of the Southern character; it blurs, conceals, softens, wraps the hard limbs of hard times in a fringed shawl." It is particularly associated with Gothic imagery of the Deep South, suggesting romantic, mysterious, and sometimes menacing events. Spanish moss shelters chiggers, rat snakes, and bats. Sensitive to the air around it, Spanish moss is now used as a gauge to determine the level of air pollution in points of the South.

C. RITCHIE BELL
*North Carolina Botanical Gardens*
*University of North Carolina at*
*Chapel Hill*

CHARLES REAGAN WILSON
*University of Mississippi*

Todd Ballantine, *Tideland Treasures* (1993); Fred B. Kniffen and Malcolm L. Comeaux, *Melanges*, vol. 12 (1979); D. J. Mabberley,

Spanish moss swaying in front of an old plantation home, south Louisiana, 1930s
(Marion Post Walcott, Library of Congress [LC-USF-34-54302-D], Washington, D.C.)

*The Plant-Book: A Portable Dictionary of the Higher Plants* (1987).

## Tellico Dam

Constructed between 1967 and 1979 on the Little Tennessee River in Loudon County, Tenn., Tellico Dam was advertised as a creator of jobs for a disadvantaged area in the state. It became instead the focus of a battle between environmentalists, dam opponents, and the Tennessee Valley Authority (TVA) and later represented a shift in public attitudes toward dam construction and was evidence to some that by the 1970s perhaps the TVA had outlived its usefulness.

Construction of the dam began in 1967 and, after several interruptions, was completed in 1979. In response to local opposition to the dam, the TVA promised residents, especially those facing displacement, that the completed project would attract hundreds of millions of dollars in investment and create thousands of jobs for the area, as well as spawn a new city by the lake, Timberlake (with Boeing as a linchpin commercial resident). The TVA predicted the construction of skyscrapers, an influx of businesses, and an increase in economic prosperity. As a result of the TVA's projections for economic growth, many residents agreed with only mild resistance to leave their property.

It appeared that nothing could stop construction of the dam until the 1973 discovery of a new species of fish in the area to be flooded, a three-inch perch called the snail darter. After the U.S. Department of the Interior listed the fish as an endangered species, environmentalists filed a lawsuit to stop construction of the dam and reservoir under the provisions of the 1973 Endangered Species Act. To add a bizarre twist to the issue, U.S. Supreme Court Justice William O. Douglas protested the dam's construction alongside environmental and American Indian groups, the latter of whom opposed the dam on the grounds that its completion would flood and destroy historical Cherokee villages, including Tanasi. By 1978 the U.S. Supreme Court ruled in the opposition's favor in *TVA v. Hill* (1978), halting construction on the project. Not until several Tennessee congressmen, including U.S. Senator Howard Baker and U.S. Representative John Duncan, craftily attached an amendment to a piece of energy legislation was the project exempted from all federal laws.

Tellico Dam was completed in 1979, and a year later more than 17,000 acres of land were flooded, including several old Cherokee villages, the original location of the Civil War–era outpost Fort Loudon, and the habitat of the snail darter. Little of the economic boon promised by the TVA occurred.

GORDON E. HARVEY
*University of Louisiana at Monroe*

R. Dana Ono, James D. Williams, and Anne Wagner, *Vanishing Fishes of North America* (1983); William Bruce Wheeler and Michael J. McDonald, *TVA and the Tellico Dam, 1936–1979: A Bureaucratic Crisis in Post-Industrial America* (1986).

## Tennessee-Tombigbee Waterway

The idea for a waterway connecting the Tennessee River and Tombigbee River is quite old. The first mention of such a connector dates to the late 1700s as the French explorer Montcalm searched for a way to speed the transport of goods to the Gulf Coast. Similar calls came throughout the 1800s as residents of eastern Tennessee and Alabama called for a way to shorten the distance between their areas and the ports of Mobile and New Orleans.

The government studied the feasibility of such a project in the 1870s and early 1900s, and both studies concluded that to cut such a channel would require between 43 and 65 locks and a four- to six-foot channel. Congress demurred on both occasions citing the tremendous cost of undertaking the project.

Not until the New Deal–era development of the Tennessee River region by the Tennessee Valley Authority did the project gain a new life, and by 1946 Congress approved of the project. Fierce opposition by nonsouthern congressional delegations and by the railroad industry prevented the appropriation of funds for the waterway until the late 1960s. The project was championed by powerful congressmen from Alabama and Mississippi, including Mobile congressman Frank Boykin and Mississippi's U.S. Senator John Stennis.

Although given funding by Presidents Lyndon Johnson and Richard Nixon, construction of the waterway did not begin until 1972. In 1977 President Jimmy Carter considered cutting the project, along with scores of other similar projects across the nation, but a huge outcry of support for the waterway forced him to reconsider.

Like many large waterway and land construction projects conducted in the post-1945 era, the Tennessee-Tombigbee Waterway was attacked by competing industries and by environmental and conservation groups. Two lawsuits, arguing that the Army Corps of Engineers had ignored several environmental protection laws and had created a general environmental disaster, almost derailed the project. After several years of litigation, the courts ruled in the government's favor. But the long-term result was that the environmental opposition to the project forced the Army Corps of Engineers to eventually adopt less-damaging dredging and construction methods.

Once it was completed in 1984 the Tenn-Tom, as it came to be called, became the largest water resource project in the nation's history, as well as the nation's largest earth-moving project, removing the equivalent of 100,000 dump trucks of earth. With a 175-foot-deep channel, 10 locks that address the 341-foot elevation change from one end to the other, and more than 230 miles in length, the Tenn-Tom connected the Tennessee River to the Tombigbee River, which drained into Mobile Bay and the Gulf of Mexico. It cost almost $2 billion to construct and took 12 years.

GORDON E. HARVEY
*University of Louisiana at Monroe*

David S. Brose, *Yesterday's River: The Archaeology of 10,000 Years along the Tennessee-Tombigbee Waterway* (1991); Carolyn B. Patterson, *National Geographic* (March 1986); William H. Stewart, *The*

*Tennessee-Tombigbee Waterway: A Case Study in the Politics of Water Transportation* (1971); Jeffrey K. Stine, *Mixing the Waters: Environment, Politics, and the Building of the Tennessee-Tombigbee Waterway* (1993).

## Warren County, N.C.

Environmental activists credit protests in Warren County, N.C., with beginning the national environmental justice movement. The protest has also been seen as a continuation of earlier African American struggles, particularly the civil rights movement of the 1950s and 1960s. One scholar has called Warren County "the largest civil rights demonstration since the 1960s."

In 1979 two men involved in hazardous waste disposal dumped 30,000 gallons of PCB fluids illegally in North Carolina, partially in response to tightened Environmental Protection Agency regulations of the substance. Although PCB is among the most toxic substances known, the EPA waited four years to begin cleanup of the scattered drums. North Carolina decided to build its own landfill to deal with the waste and selected Warren County as one of the potential sites. Predominantly lower class and black, Warren County also had been targeted for other waste facilities. Separate plans called for "the completion of an industrial package consisting of Soul City (production), the treatment plant (waste processing), and landfills (waste storage)." Residents of the area quickly organized to protest. In October 1982 a large number of people physically attempted to stop waste trucks from entering the landfill site. Police arrested more than 500 people, including several prominent figures such as Congressman Walter E. Fauntroy; Joseph Lowery, president of the Southern Christian Leadership Conference; and Rev. Benjamin Chavis (now Muhammad) of the United Church of Christ Commission on Racial Justice. Despite this activity, the residents failed to stop the construction of the landfill. The scope, activity of national civil rights organizations, and number of people involved generated significant national exposure for the issues of environmental justice. Soon after, academics and scholars began research and case studies to provide further evidence linking poor and minority neighborhoods across the country with a higher level of environmental hazards.

ELIZABETH BLUM
*Troy University*

Robert D. Bullard, ed., *Confronting Environmental Racism: Voices from the Grassroots* (1993); Ken Geiser and Gerry Waneck, in *Unequal Protection: Environmental Justice and Communities of Color*, ed. Robert D. Bullard (1994).

## Wilson Dam

Wilson Dam is a 4,800-foot-long, 137-foot-high concrete gravity dam stretching across the Tennessee River at Muscles Shoals in northern Alabama. Designed and built by engineer Hugh Cooper under the authority of the U.S. Army Corps of Engineers, work on Wilson Dam started in 1918 and was completed by 1925.

Authorized by the 1916 National Defense Act, Wilson Dam (originally called Muscle Shoals Dam and later renamed in honor of President Woodrow Wilson) was intended to ensure a reliable supply of nitrates for the U.S. explosives industry. Electric power is an essential component of the Haber process for "fixing" nitrogen from the atmosphere, and hydroelectricity generated at Wilson Dam was to be used to power large nitrate plants built nearby. Previously, U.S industry had relied on nitrates imported from mines in Chile, but as World War I loomed, Congress deemed it imprudent to rely on a foreign source for a vital defense material.

World War I ended in November 1918, long before completion of construction, and in the early 1920s the future use of Wilson Dam became an issue of national political concern. Beginning in 1921 industrialist Henry Ford made a series of well-publicized offers to pay about $5 million for control of the dam, hydroelectric power plant, and nitrate facilities on a 100-year lease; the value of the lease was estimated by some to exceed $1 billion. Despite support from many representatives, Ford's offer failed to win congressional approval, and he withdrew it in late 1924.

The struggle over Wilson Dam soon pitted "Public Power" advocates such as Senator George Norris of Nebraska (who wanted the federal government to generate electric power at the dam for public consumption) against champions of "Private Power" (who opposed government involvement in the electric power industry) who sought to have the dam turned over to the Alabama Power Company or some other "investor-owned" utility. In addition, the private fertilizer industry (which used nitrates) also sought control over the system.

From the mid-1920s through 1932 the long-term fate of Wilson Dam remained uncertain as both Presidents Calvin Coolidge and Herbert Hoover opposed the proliferation of "Public Power."

Soon after President Franklin Roosevelt's inauguration, the political tide changed, and in May 1933 the federally sponsored Tennessee Valley Authority (TVA) was authorized to assume control of Wilson Dam and distribute its electricity to consumers and businesses through systems outside the control of private power companies. The TVA subsequently built other dams and power plants to serve the region, but Wilson Dam lay at the heart of the new agency and was essential to its authorization and early expansion.

Wilson Dam, with a generating capacity of 400,000 kilowatts, remains an important component of the TVA system; equipped with navigation locks at the north end of the structure, the dam also facilitates barge traffic along the Tennessee River.

D. C. JACKSON
*Lafayette College*

Donald Davidson, *The Tennessee*, vol. 2, *The New River: Civil War to TVA* (1948, 1991); Preston J. Hubbard, *Origins of the TVA: The Muscle Shoals Controversy* (1963).

# INDEX OF CONTRIBUTORS

# INDEX

Page numbers in boldface refer to articles.

Cape Fear, N.C., 193
Cape Girardeau, Mo., 130, 239
Cape Hatteras, N.C., 259
Cape Lookout National Seashore, **203–4**
Carnegie, Lucy, 209
Carnegie, Thomas, 209
Carolina parakeet, 37, 48–49, 66
Carrier, Willis Haviland, 175
Carson, Rachel, 121
Carter, Jimmy, 232, 249, 274
Cash, Johnny, 73
Cash, Wilbur J., 39
Cason, Clarence, 1, 39
Catawba, 84
Catesby, Mark, 36, 63, 106–7, 113, 241
Catfish, 25, 84, **204–6**
Cedar Key, Fla., 243
Central Lowlands, 5
Chapel Hill, N.C., 115
Chapman, David, 110
Charleston, S.C., 6, 9, 15, 18, 79, 80, 96, 102, 103, 108, 113, 129, 130, 147, 149, 191
Charlotte, N.C., 18, 82
*Charlotte Observer*, 82
Chateaubriand, François-René de, 108
Chattahoochee River, 244
Chavis, Benjamin, Jr., 61, **242–43**, 276
Cherokees, 84, 85, 116, 134, 160, 199, 200, 222, 258, 274
Chesapeake Bay, 7, 122, 139, 171, **206–8**
Chicago, Ill., 171
Chickasaws, 83, 134
Chihuahuan Desert, 194, 223
Chinaberry trees, 161
Chisos Mountains, 194
Choctaws, 27, 83, 258
Civilian Conservation Corps, 111
Civil Rights Act of 1964, 112
Civil War, 9, 14–15, 71, 118, 196, 213, 226, 246, 270–71
Clams, 139
Clanton, Ala., 258
Clark, Frank Basil, 258
Clark, William, 266
Clarke-McNary Act, 67, 76

Clayton, John, 105, 113
Clean Air Act, 69
Clean Water Act, 127, 167
Cleveland, Grover, 66
Climate and weather, 1–3, 7, **39–43**, 96, 99, 102, 103, 177
Clinch River, 45
Clinton, William J., 62, 216, 242
Coahuiltecans, 262
Coal, 54–55, 104, 181–84
Coastal marshes, **43–45**
Coastal Plain, 3, 4, 5, 6, 74, 103, 105, 142, 235
Cobb, James, 16
Coe, Ernest F., 111
Coffee County, Ala., 86
Coleridge, Samuel Taylor, 108, 193
Collinson, Peter, 107
*Colonial Search for a Southern Eden* (Wright), 1
Colorado, 267
Colorado River, 268
Columbia, S.C., 15, 46
Columbus, Ga., 46, 148
Comanches, 225
Conchs, 217
Conservation: and wildlife, 12; and endangered species, 48, 49; of natural resources, 62, 65, 67–69, 234; laws and, 63–64
*Conservation Irrigation in Humid Areas*, 125
Conservation Reserve Program, 78
Convent, La., 202
Coolidge, Calvin, 165, 277
Cooper, Hugh, 276
Cope, Channing, 231
Copland, Aaron, 185
Cornell Laboratory of Ornithology, 230
Corpus Christi, Tex., 262, 263
Cory, Charles Barney, 218
Cotton, 2, 13, 65, 94, 209
Cowdery, Albert E., 12
Cowley, Malcolm, 42
Crabs, 139–40

Mullet, 97
Muscle Shoals, Ala., 155, 162, 163, 164, 165, 276
Mussels, 34, 138–39, 140–41

Naipaul, V. S., 173
Nashville, Tenn., 7, 9, 132, 138, 144, 145, 245, 246
Natchez, Miss., 130, 135, 145, 239, 245, 246
Natchez Indians, 83
Natchez Trace, 134, **245–46**
Natchez Trace Parkway, 246
National Association for the Advancement of Colored People, 245
National Environmental Policy Act, 69, 78, 166, 167
National Park Service, 110, 188, 197, 209, 213, 214, 225, 228, 234, 246, 263
Native Americans, 8, 10, 62, 74, 143–44, 193, 199–200, 208–9, 211, 225, 227; and animals, 26–27, 180; and plants, 116–17, 234, 265–66, 269, 272; trails of, 134, 245; and shellfish, 138; agriculture of, 142
Natural disasters, 18–19, **98–102**
Natural gas, 56–57, 104, 182, 184, 249, 250
*Natural History of Carolina, Florida, and the Bahama Islands* (Catesby), 36, 106, 113
Naturalists, **104–9**, 113–14, 190
Natural resources, 7, 17, 54–58, 62, 65, 67–69, **102–4**, 109, 120, 121, 185, 221
Nature Conservancy, 197, 198
Nau, Anthony, 267
Navigation, 17, 130–31, 133, 162, 240
Neeham, James, 199
Nehrling, Henry, 264
New Bern, N.C., 1
New Deal, 47, 68, 111, 124, 153, 166, 202, 223
New Madrid, Mo., 101
New Mexico, 223, 267, 269
New Orleans, La., 9, 18, 60, 68, 70, 90, 91, 96, 129, 130, 132, 139, 171, 180, 181, 188, 230, 239, 245, 270, 274; and Hurricane Katrina, 19, 40, 101; pollution in, 122, 202; steamboats in, 148, 149

New River, 165
*New Voyage to Carolina, A* (Lawson), 106
New York, 180
*New York Times*, 176
*Niles Weekly Register*, 147
*90° in the Shade* (Cason), 1, 39
Nixon, Richard, 168, 274
Norfolk, Va., 18, 208, 259
Norris, George, 68, 154, 163–65, 276
Norris Dam, 45
North American Free Trade Agreement, 269
North Carolina, 3, 5, 37, 38, 46, 66, 203, 212, 223; natural resources of, 7; agriculture in, 13, 14; hunting laws of, 22; climate of, 41; endangered species in, 51, 204; Indians in, 84; land use in, 94, 95; naturalists in, 105–6, 107–8; parks in, 110, 111; plant uses in, 117; pollution in, 121, 122, 133, 275; swampland of, 125, 127, 172; rivers in, 128, 129; roads in, 136; soil of, 143; azaleas in, 191; mountains of, 200, 201, 221; palm trees in, 264
North Carolina, University of (Chapel Hill), 248
North Carolina State College School of Design, 82
*Notes on the State of Virginia* (Jefferson), 108
Nuclear pollution, **246–48**
Nutria, 35

Oak Ridge, Tenn., 246, 247
Oaks, 159
Ocean Springs, Miss., 180, 181
Ocoee Dam No. 1, 46
Ocoee River, 46
Odum, Eugene P., 171, **248–49**
Odum, Howard Thomas, 171, 249
Odum, Howard W., 160
Offshore oil industry, 56, **249–51**
Ohio, 144
Oil, 55–56, 68, 104, 121, 182, 184, **249–51**; and pollution, **251–54**
Oil Pollution Act of 1924, 253